In the Aftermath of Genocide

Armenians and Jews in Twentieth-Century France

Maud S. Mandel

Duke University Press   Durham and London 2003

© 2003 Duke University Press
All rights reserved
Printed in the United States of America on acid-free paper ∞
Typeset in Quadraat by Tseng Information Systems, Inc.
Library of Congress Cataloging-in Publication Data appear
on the last printed page of this book.

To Ruth and Barrett Mandel
For listening

Contents

Acknowledgments

I am greatly appreciative of the help and encouragement I have received as this project has developed.

I have been fortunate to study with a variety of imaginative and thoughtful teachers. Advice from Geoff Eley, Zvi Gitelman, and Ronald Suny helped shape this project's direction from the outset. In hours of talking and brainstorming, Laura Downs provided me with numerous suggestions and much inspiration. Her creativity and intuition contributed significantly to my thinking. Particular gratitude goes to Todd Endelman, whose advice throughout the research period and careful reading of several drafts focused my writing and challenged my assumptions. Working with such an accomplished historian and teacher provided me with new perspectives on my own research and a solid direction for subsequent efforts. His friendship and support have provided ongoing inspiration over many years.

Various research institutions were graciously opened to me in France, England, and the United States. I am grateful to the archivists and librarians who aided me with their knowledge and expertise. In this regard, special recognition must go to Raymond H. Kévorkian at the Bibliothèque Nubar, who not only patiently provided his time but also permitted me exceptional access to the materials I sought. This project has benefited from fellowships granted by the Mellon Foundation and the Memorial Foundation for Jewish Culture. These grants, along with generous support from the University of Michigan, provided time for its research and writing.

At Brown University, where I have spent several enriching years since completing my graduate education, I have encountered colleagues who have served both as mentors and friends. Particularly helpful have been Omer Bartov, Shaye Cohen, Carolyn Dean, Wendell Deitrich, Mary Gluck, David Jacobson, Saul Olyan, and Ruti Adler. A special thanks to Lynn Davidman and Calvin Goldscheider for reading drafts, providing much-needed guidance and friendship, and helping me make a graceful transition from the world of student to that of professor. Numerous students have also inspired me with their curiosity, intelligence, creativity, and enthusiasm for learning. Thanks in particular to Rachel Nadelman, who directed some of that enthusiasm to this project and voluntarily gave time for research aid.

No acknowledgment would be complete without noting the special environment of the University of Michigan, where this work was initially conceived. There, a cohort of perceptive and imaginative students provided an intellectually inspiring environment in which to work. A small group of these students participated in an ongoing writing seminar, including Rafe Blaufarb, Jennifer Jenkins, Hugh Lane, Kathy Pence, Warren Rosenblum, Greg Shaya, Theresa Sanislo, and Paul Werth. Their helpful comments and the lively discussions of their own work provided an inspiring atmosphere in which to continue my own efforts.

A special thanks also to Elsa Barkley Brown, Vicki Caron, and Nancy Green, whose careful reading of one or more chapters helped me rethink some of the central questions this work addresses. In addition, Nadia Malinovich's insights as well as her own work on an earlier period of French Jewish history provided important food for thought for the ongoing revisions.

A handful of friends not only read chapter drafts and listened to presentations of work in progress but provided immeasurable support in other equally important ways. Over daily pots of tea, Ara Sarafian taught me what it means to be a historian. Long conversations in Paris with Greg Brown about research and life kept my mind active and engaged. Long Sunday walks with Cécile Vidal provided reassurance when it was most needed. Her honesty and loving care, then as now, have been invaluable. In daily writing sessions in the "idea room," David Freund inspired me with his wit, intelligence, and committed friendship; he reminded me that laughing makes the brain function better. Don LaCoss's eyes showed me the world through more colorful lenses; his challenges pushed me to take risks and to dream. I have long ago lost count of the numerous ways that Robin Judd held my hand through this process. Her friendship has been an endless source of support and her thorough and helpful readings of drafts did much to improve this text.

In conclusion, a debt of gratitude to my two greatest influences in scholarship and life, Ruth and Barrett Mandel. Their unconditional love and exemplary guidance have not only sustained me and provided me with the intellectual and life skills that I needed to write this book but offered a shining example in parenting, which I hope I am now emulating with my own son, Lev. The latter's presence in my life, far from being a distraction to this project, provided a much-valued perspective and levity to all aspects of life. Likewise, Steve Simon's strength and creativity and his remarkable belief in me offer more inspiration than he will ever know. Without his sacrifices and support, this work would never have come into being.

Note on Transliteration

The transliterations of Western Armenian used in the endnotes of this text are based on the Library of Congress system of transliteration. However, in the narrative, names of organizations, people, and periodicals are generally presented in those forms that have become standard in Western writing even when not fully conforming to the Library of Congress system.

In the Aftermath of Genocide

Introduction

I imagine that if there were such a thing as a collective Jew, he might well ask himself . . . am I the same today as the Jew of thirty-five years ago? Yes, it is indeed me; it is indeed us. But there are deep clefts, despite appearances: everything has changed and yet nothing has. — Saul Friedlander, *When Memory Comes*

Over the course of the twentieth century, the crime of genocide — the attempt to eliminate an ethnic, national, or religious minority — has grown in scope and frequency. Such attacks have, in the current parlance, allowed nation-states to "construct" themselves — if in the most radical way — around ideals of one nation, one state, forcing out those who would cast national identity into question. Universally condemned, these violent massacres nevertheless have often obtained their objectives, providing some states with a definitive means to establish the nation's citizenry, identifying a particular set of persons as its own while marking others as aliens.[1]

Although scholars have paid attention to the role of genocide in shaping the nature and composition of existing societies, few have investigated its long-term impact on those cast as national outsiders.[2] And yet those dubbed aliens by genocidal regimes have faced more than violent uprootings from their homes and communities; they have also confronted ideological onslaughts that cast doubt on their place in an international civil society constituted primarily along national lines. The growth of the modern nation-state, and its consolidation in Europe following World War I, defined the rights and obligations of those living in its midst, certified their citizenship, and provided for their welfare. Implicit in this relationship between citizen and state was the understanding that those not of the nation were "outsiders" to it. International treaties regularized the status of immigrants from one nation to another; those stripped of any citizenship or national allegiance often have found themselves outside this international web.[3]

This study focuses on how survivors of genocide have responded to being cast so definitively from the nation-state structure. In what ways—if at all—have the religious, ethnic, and national affiliations among escapees shifted to reflect the recent violent past? Have such attacks challenged previously held notions of faith, communal solidarity, and national identity? How have survivors assessed the feasibility of living as national minorities or diaspora populations after an attack on their status as such? How have they come to terms with "transnational" identities in a world seemingly determined to define itself according to national lines?

To address these broad questions, I turn to a comparative study of the victims of two twentieth-century genocides: Armenians fleeing the Young Turks during World War I and Jews rebuilding after the Holocaust. In both cases, the victims had been transformed into national pariahs in states determined to eliminate all traces of their existence.[4] Such violent upheavals had a profound impact on those who escaped. Wherever they settled, whether in the lands in which they had previously been persecuted or elsewhere, survivors had to face significant challenges. Foremost among these was their material reestablishment after years of disruption; indeed, rebuilding homes, families, and communities became a priority for those who had escaped. Also important, however, were broader questions about the nature of community affiliation and minority status after years of being persecuted for that status.

Particularly interesting in this regard were survivor communities in France, the focus of this investigation. Home to the largest Armenian and Jewish survivor populations in western Europe, France nevertheless had a mixed record over the course of the twentieth century with regard to its ethnic, national, and religious minorities. Long committed to a politics of integration, which sought to incorporate ethnic and religious minorities quickly and seamlessly into the polity, French policies shifted direction radically during the Vichy years, as officials isolated foreign minorities, particularly Jews, from their "French" neighbors. This shifting political terrain on the question of national minorities, which once again became "integrationist" in the decades immediately following Vichy, shaped the context in which local Armenian and Jewish communities came to terms with their respective pasts.

For French Jews these shifts were particularly disruptive. Under German occupation and Vichy collaborationist rule, Jews faced a wide range of discriminatory legislation restricting their movements, property ownership, and civil liberties. Furthermore, as the Nazi attack on European Jewry evolved, the Vichy government collaborated in the deportation of approximately seventy-six thousand Jews.[5] And yet, although deportations drastically reduced the size and diversity of the community, two-thirds of the population survived (approximately 250,000), as did much of the prewar institutional framework.[6] Moreover, with the freeing of Paris in August 1944 under de Gaulle's liberation forces, Jews began quickly regaining the rights of which they had been stripped. As one Jewish author described the moment, "For the first time in four years, that day we were finally like other people . . . we could call out our names, cry out who we were on the telephone, in the streets, in the stores, and in the restaurants. . . . We had returned to our true identity, to society, to France."[7]

Yet, could French Jews return so simply to their prewar position in French society? Vichy legislation had rejected a more than century-long tradition of viewing religion as a personal matter regulated by the state but conducted outside the public domain. By introducing religious affiliation as a factor in determining legal status and using this new status as a way to institute state-sanctioned oppression, officials had transformed the relationship between the state and its Jewish minority. Hence, although the duration of the Vichy regime was relatively short, its effects were felt by every Jew in France, as former citizens became aliens in the land of their birth, as newly declared Jewish citizens—those who had migrated to France in the two decades preceding World War II—found themselves unceremoniously stripped of their newly acquired legal rights, and as Jewish refugees and new immigrants faced the ever-increasing threat of internment.[8]

This study considers the impact of these four years on French Jewry *after* de Gaulle's armies had restored democracy and transformed their status back to that of the prewar years. Once again free to live as they chose, how did the local Jewish population respond to their immediate past? After such an attack on their fundamental rights as citizens and as human beings, could they really reestablish their prewar position in their society? Or did notions of community, nationality, and ethnic identity change as a result of the years of persecution?

These questions are addressed by comparing France's post–World War II Jewish population to Armenians who settled in France after the genocide of World War I. Like the Holocaust, the Armenian genocide was an attempt to alter the nature and composition of the existing society. By deporting and murdering populations that had been in place for centuries and by confiscating Armenian property and desecrating places of worship, the Young Turks virtually eliminated all traces of these ancient communities from eastern Anatolia. Those Armenians who were not killed were forced to renounce all connection with their ethnic and religious heritage.[9] Although some survivors escaped the violent onslaught, they did so only by going into exile, leaving their ancestral lands and seeking refuge in the diaspora.

Approximately sixty-five thousand of these survivors ultimately made their way to France, where the post–World War I economy necessitated dependence on immigrant labor. For them, disjuncture and ruptures with the past were far more dramatic than for most of France's post–World War II Jewish population.[10] Not only had the migration to France transformed the primarily rural, agriculturally based peasant population into an urban, working-class ethnic minority, but it had also forced them off their ancestral lands and left them to seek refuge abroad.[11] For many, finding a final settlement point took nearly a decade; for some, it took even longer. Arriving as stateless refugees without passports or visas and with no obvious country of origin, their position in French society was precarious, particularly in the early 1920s, when the government had not yet worked out coherent policies for dealing with stateless minorities. With no protection through immigration treaties and no international rights, the first Armenian arrivals in France were utterly dependent on the government's benevolence and their own meager resources. The combination of their precarious position in the polity and their own search for stability set the scene for their integration into French society.

For these Armenian refugees, then, questions of religious, ethnic, and national allegiance were forged out of their own past of statelessness, genocide, and exile, a story that differs considerably from that of the post–World War II French Jewish population. Armenians never were persecuted on French soil; French Jews, on the other hand, had been victims of native aggression during World War II. Also, changes in French receptivity to immigrants, as well as changing political, social, and economic conditions, affected those populations differently. It should be clear, however, that to make this comparison, the conditions facing the two populations need not have been identical. Although emigration and settlement patterns differed for both, as did modes of integration and communal construction, both addressed remarkably similar dilemmas as they faced the challenges of rebuilding their disrupted communities in the French context.

Four such parallels stand out particularly clearly. First, and most obviously, both Armenians and Jews had been victims of state-sponsored attempts at total eradication. The Nazis' destruction of European Jewry is often held to be the paradigmatic case of genocide in our time, and comparative studies of such massacres have identified the Armenian genocide as most similar to the Holocaust.[12] Such studies have focused particularly on the motives, killing methods, and extent of destruction achieved by the perpetrators. Yet few have extended this methodology to the aftermath of genocide by comparing the responses of the victims themselves.[13] However, the striking parallels linking the Armenian and Jewish cases extend into the reconstructive periods as well. Most important, in both cases, these onslaughts forced survivors to address pressing immediate concerns, such as how best to use communal resources in light of the massive destruction, as well as more existential questions, such as how to assess the viability of living as an ethnoreligious minority within a larger nation-state after having been persecuted for that status.

In addition, the state in which they were living was more than a "host nation" to these two populations. France provided the context in which they rebuilt their homes and communities, a context with little tolerance for ethnic distinctiveness and with a strong state-centered, assimilationist model of governance that shaped the incorporation of all ethnic and religious minorities into the state.[14] Armenian and Jewish genocide survivors were no exception, and the French tradition of intense cultural conformity shaped how they came to terms with their pasts. This context and its impact on survivor communities thus form the second important subject of inquiry for this book.

A third and fourth parallel arise from these first two. Both Jews and Armenians are members of ancient diaspora populations. In both cases, this diaspora network shifted, both empirically and discursively, as a result of the genocides, forcing survivors to reconsider previous notions of communal responsibility, national identity, and transnational solidarity. Such shifts took place, moreover, in a European context itself beset with questions of nationalism and dilemmas over national identity. Furthermore, Armenians and Jews both faced the establishment of independent homelands quickly following the wartime destruction. In both cases, the newly created nation-states and the immediate threats to them forced survivors to question their own relationship to the fledgling states in light of their position in French society.

These four parallels, then—genocide, position in the polity, diaspora, and homeland—provide the central thematic concerns of this study. If, however, such a thematic separation proves conceptually helpful, it should not conceal the great overlap among them. Memories of genocide, for example, shaped how survivors thought about their status as members of diaspora populations, and living in diaspora affected how they conceived of the formation of independent national homelands. Moreover, by focusing on these areas, I do not mean to suggest that all French Jews or Armenians shared a single interpretation or point of view about them. To the contrary, conflict and disagreement characterized survivors' discussions and activities regarding all four of these issues. In addition, the way they played themselves out in each population differed according to chronological moment (whether pre– or post–World War II) and position in the French state (whether refugee, immigrant, or citizen). Yet, in both cases, these issues remained definitive in shaping Armenian and Jewish postgenocide communities, as survivors reconsidered, and at times recast, articulations of nationalistic sentiment, communal responsibility, and ethnic solidarity.

In broader terms, then, the comparison of Armenian and Jewish postgenocide populations in France raises some important questions as to the value of comparative analysis as a whole. In the introduction to a compilation of essays comparing Jewish societies, Todd Endelman notes that "historians of the Jews and their religion have been a conservative lot . . . reluctant if not averse to introducing a comparative dimension to their writing." And yet, Endelman argues, because of its lack of territorial focus, Jewish history "offers unique, almost laboratory-like opportunities for examining how communities with similar but not identical backgrounds and traditions adapt to different environments." Comparing Jewish communities across time and/or space or comparing Jews with non-Jews in the same place or in different national contexts "transcends the borders of Jewish historiography" both by revealing what is "individual, specific and unique as much as what is more general." [15]

By comparing Armenian and Jewish survivor communities in France, this study seeks to do just that: to explore the specificities of the narratives under consideration while still highlighting the wider concerns that transcend the boundaries of either minority population. As such, it builds on the methodological terrain mapped out by recent historians interested in studying structural similarities in different national or chronological contexts. Whereas, as has been recently argued, "historians . . . have been more reticent than other social scientists to move from the particular to the general," a new generation of comparativists have begun to break down these barriers. [16] Particularly influential to my own thinking has been Laura Lee Downs's *Manufacturing Inequality*, which explores the gender division in French and British metalworking industries from 1914 to 1939 and which argues that gender-based job discrimination was a phenomenon that transcended national boundaries. The comparative method allowed her to "suggest how national culture and differences in state structures defined distinctive routes to what were, in many important respects, rather similar outcomes." [17]

Adopting a similar analytic approach, Nancy Green uses the comparative method to trace immigrant labor in the garment industries of France and the United States. She, however, goes one step further than Downs. In addition to examining two national contexts, she makes her analysis doubly comparative by examining different immigrant groups within one industry. This approach allows her to emphasize change over time and space while also demonstrating how "each period reinvents certain perceptions of progress and newness." [18] Green's "post-structural structural" approach thus demonstrates the power of economic structures in transcending chronological and spatial categories while allowing for the histories of specific interests to emerge.

Both Downs and Green thus use the comparative method to determine what is individual and specific while also focusing on what is structural, and both rely on traditional social historical methods to think through larger sociological questions. Likewise, the diachronic nature of the present study offers just such an approach, focusing on genocide survivors as a means to trace both the particular history of each population in question as well as the striking structural similarities that link these two French ethnoreligious minorities. My hope is that such a perspective will raise new questions concerning how genocide shaped communal life in its immediate aftermath and how national and ethnic identities converged in twentieth-century France.

Genocide: Memory, Experience, and Identity

Memories of genocide have defined, in large part, how Armenians and Jews have constructed contemporary understandings of communal affiliation and group solidarity. It took nearly fifty years, however, for Armenian communities to rally around the genocide as a public symbol of their communal life. Likewise, as recent scholarship has demonstrated, several decades passed before the memory of the Holocaust became a central pillar of identification for contemporary Jewry.[19] This "silence" of the immediate post-Holocaust years has been analyzed from a number of different perspectives. Some scholars have considered the difficulty that both survivors and historians have faced when attempting to represent memories of genocide.[20] As Doris Bensimon has described French Jews in the decade immediately following the war, "The overwhelming majority preferred silence. . . . Indeed, in France, three or four decades had to pass before memory could disentangle itself from forgetting [de l'oubli]." [21] Others, less interested in the "silence" of survivors, have examined the reluctance of governments or the general public to recognize or take responsibility for the events of World War II.[22] These works share a common interest in the visible manifestations of memory, such as commemorations, memorials, memoirs, and historical monographs. The former focus on difficulties in representing memory, the latter on shifting interpretations and political manipulations of those memories. Still others, examining the "silences" in the decades immediately following World War II, suggest that the first generation of survivors was able neither to face nor to comprehend the extent of the tragedy. Fleeing painful memories, they silenced discussion of the genocide and omitted systematic commemoration from communal agendas. As Bruno Bettelheim wrote in an essay on the Holocaust's effect on children, "It seems that it requires a distance of twenty years or more, to understand how much a particular tragedy suffered in childhood can transform your whole sense of life."[23]

To focus on survivor silence and the lack of public memorials as a sign that those who escaped could not face their recent past, however, is to misinterpret the impact of the recent upheaval on survivors. Some may indeed have been so traumatized that they opted to remain silent; others "were willing, indeed anxious, to talk of their experiences but made a deliberate choice not to do so, except among themselves," due to a correct perception that "listeners" were not particularly anxious to hear their stories.[24] Moreover, even if public manifestations of communal memory were few and far between, individual Armenians and Jews manifested a different kind of public response to the experiences through which they lived, one that was reflected in the communities they created.

For Armenians, communal memorialization of the recent losses was never totally absent.[25] Not surprisingly, however, such commemorations were not the central concern for a population of refugees seeking to reestablish stable home lives, rebuild a steady family economy, learn the local language, and find lost relatives. As noted above, the migrations to France had transformed the occupational makeup of the population, removing survivors from their peasant-based, agricultural communities and transforming them into a factory-based, urban proletariat. The disruption of patriarchal, familial, and economic norms shaped how the first waves of Armenians established themselves and their communities in France. Most, busy with the task of building a life in a new country, expressed communal identification *not* through commemorations of the recent massacres, but through various other channels, including church life, diaspora political parties, youth groups, and compatriot organizations. It is in these arenas, therefore, where the community's cultural values were both reflected and promoted and where there were plenty of voices to fill in the postwar "silences," that we can trace responses to the genocide. Whether intent on building roots in France or turning their attentions to their "homeland" in the Caucasus, survivors grappled with their recent past as they integrated into their new home.

Unlike the uprooted Armenian refugees, post-Holocaust French Jewry was not forced to build a communal structure from the ground up. Nevertheless, World War II had proven disruptive and traumatic to every Jew in France, whether born there or of immigrant extraction.[26] Many were forced to give up homes and sell businesses as they fled the Occupied Zone. Those unable to flee sometimes paid with their lives, and even those who escaped often lost family and friends to deportations. Others, seeking refuge in Vichy-governed areas of the country, were reduced to second-class status, stripped of the basic human rights to which they had become accustomed.

The war's conclusion brought an end to such discriminatory legislation, but it could not erase memories of the four preceding years. Legal battles over lost homes and property continued well into the 1950s. A constant flow of refugees reminded escapees of the destruction of the war and the pressing needs of Jews throughout Europe and the Middle East. Simultaneously, diaspora organizations, such as the American Joint Distribution Committee, funded the construction of schools, youth centers, and other arenas of Jewish life, transforming the communal landscape over the subsequent twenty years. Thus, from the moment the Holocaust ended, French Jews were faced with its repercussions both personally and institutionally.

Interestingly, the few historians and sociologists who have commented on these years have argued that the Holocaust initially devastated what remained of French Jewish life. As one observer commented, the profound disarray that faced French Jews made "most aspire to erase all difference definitively and to give way to the anonymity of secular society."[27] Similarly, William Safran argues that the reethnicization of French Jewry that occurred during the 1970s and 1980s was "hampered" in the postwar decades because "the Jewish community had been too decimated, impoverished and demoralized to rebuild its institutions quickly."[28] Safran is right to point out the remarkable resurgence in public manifestations of French Jewish ethnic identification in the last decades of the twentieth century, but his characterization of the postwar decades is too stark.

Like Safran, most scholars of French Jewry have focused their attention on contemporary developments, including the arrival of three hundred thousand North African Jewish immigrants, the impact of the Six-Day War, the rising tide of anti-Jewish sentiment throughout the 1970s and 1980s, and the articulation of a particularistic and vocal Jewish politics. Although it is perhaps unfair to criticize these scholars for not fully analyzing the immediate postwar years, as their own areas of interest were directed toward contemporary questions, it is still worth noting that those who addressed the 1945–68 period—and most simply ignore these years—oversimplify the picture. By leaping from the devastation of World War II to the drama of the late 1960s, these scholars simply assumed that the Holocaust brought Jewish communal life to a halt, frightening survivors away from any identification with their religious/ethnic heritage. Furthermore, by treating the prewar, Vichy, and postwar periods as distinct from one another, historical accounts have divided French Jewish history around the Holocaust. Although such an approach highlights the changes that faced French Jewry as a result of the Nazi invasion, it ignores the continuities linking these periods. Thus, postwar Jewish life remains a separate chapter in the history of French Judaism and one that has been covered only minimally in the scholarly literature.[29]

Recent scholarship has begun to rectify the problem. Particularly important is David Weinberg's assertion that far from destroying Jewish communal affiliation, the Holocaust enticed certain of those with assimilationist tendencies to reconsider their Jewish heritage. In his words, "Jewish identity in post-war France was a complex weave of internal tensions born of contradictory memories of deportations and the contributions made by Jews to the Resistance effort. The result was an embryonic new consciousness, which combined the hesitancy and self-effacement of the *français israélite* with a growing pride in the dual heritage of Frenchman and Jew."[30]

This study seeks to explore Weinberg's assertion of a "new consciousness" in greater depth. As such, it challenges earlier assumptions that the Holocaust devastated surviving French Jewish life. It is here where the comparison to the Armenian case proves particularly instructive. For the latter, the genocide was even more disruptive than for most of the Jewish survivors, for its dislocations proved more permanent, causing fundamental transformations in the nature of communal life. Nevertheless, it would be a mischaracterization to describe the postgenocide Armenian communities in France as "decimated" or "demoralized." To the contrary, in these years we find a notable vibrancy taking root. Likewise, French Jewish populations, while also facing great challenges, proved more than capable of beginning the process of rebuilding their communities, and most did not flee their ethnoreligious affiliations in the aftermath of the Holocaust. As one particularly well-known survivor remarked in response to questions of how he readjusted to normal life, "The truth is, it was not that difficult—less difficult than adjusting to death."[31] The ease of this "adjustment" for the communities in question can, in part, be explained by the political and cultural milieu in which they found themselves. It is to this milieu, therefore, that I now turn.

Position within the Polity: Minorities and the French State

Both Armenian and Jewish populations faced a similar paradox after their respective genocides. The persecutions of World War I and II seemed to prove that modern nation-states, even those committed to democracy, could never really tolerate ethnic minorities in their midst.[32] And yet, both Jewish survivor communities rebuilding after Vichy and Armenian survivor communities building anew in France remained just that: minorities within a larger nation-state. Their position within the French state, however, differed from one another. Indeed, although a small community of approximately 4,000 Armenians was already in France prior to World War I, most of France's 65,000 Armenians migrated there following World War I as uprooted, stateless refugees seeking shelter from persecution abroad. In contrast, the 250,000 Jews who made up France's post–World War II Jewish population had generally survived World War II on French soil (although an additional 35,000 Jews migrated to France between 1944 and 1949).[33] It would be too simplistic, however, to reduce the comparison between them to one between citizen and refugee. Indeed, of the approximately 300,000 Jews who lived in France in 1939, nearly 150,000 had migrated there since 1919. Approximately 44,000 other immigrant Jews had preceded them between 1881 and 1914.[34] Thus, if the two populations under study maintained different relationships to France—Armenians as refugees from a foreign oppressor and Jews as victims of a previous French regime—both were influenced by national minority policies, particularly those directed at foreign immigrants. Moreover, and perhaps even more interesting, whereas a certain portion of the Jewish population was of immigrant extraction, a significant percentage traced roots in France back several generations. This study, then, situates the reconfiguration of Armenian and Jewish communities in the context of these different relationships to the French polity and asks: What was the impact of citizenship or lack thereof on communal understandings of the recent past, and how did French minority policies influence this process?

Recent historiography has demonstrated the importance of state-centered, assimilationist models of government in France's civic self-definition, shaping the incorporation of ethnic and religious minorities into the state.[35] This process particularly began gathering steam at the end of the nineteenth century thanks to the ever-growing power and importance of the centralized state, which worked to transmit aristocratic and bourgeois elite cultural norms in Paris over regional languages and practices throughout the country. This national culture was supported and reinforced through schooling, military training, and new organs of information. While regional distinctiveness and local cultures resisted such homogenizing goals, and while ethnic, economic, and religious particularisms continued to assert broader conceptualizations of French national identity, state policies continued to promote a universalistic conception of French citizenship that downplayed minority affiliations.[36]

France's Jewish population, like its regional minorities, was shaped by such integrationist trends. The Revolution had brought full civil and legal rights to local Jewish populations, in exchange for which it was expected that they would meet all the obligations of citizenship and move away from the self-governing enclaves that had characterized communal life prior to this period.[37] Napoleon went even further in confirming the relationship between Judaism and Jews' political status. In 1806, he convened the Assembly of Jewish Notables in Paris, a meeting of seventy-four lay and religious leaders, to attain a public pledge that the religious strictures of Judaism were not in conflict with French law and to guarantee that Jewish allegiances rested first and foremost with the state, not with their own religious-ethnic community. In addition, he organized the consistorial system to centralize rabbinical authority in the state's hands. The Consistoire was to act as the administrative body of French Jewry, overseeing all religious activities, supervising the work of the rabbis, and officially representing Jews to the state. By organizing Jewish life in a centralized and hierarchical manner and by linking it directly to the state, Napoleon sought to bind the internal decisions of the organized Jewish community to France's national interests while removing its power as a rallying point for ethnic identity.[38]

Although historians disagree as to the success of such an assimilatory project on Jewish communities in postrevolutionary France, most agree that over the course of the nineteenth century, Jews slowly began adopting national cultural norms, shedding Yiddish for French and abandoning traditional apparel and practices. Social change did not occur overnight, particularly in the more traditional communities of Alsace, and even the most acculturated were able to cultivate a Franco-Jewish identity that recognized the coexistence of Jewish particularism within the universalism of their French citizenship; yet France's Jewish population, like linguistic and regional minorities throughout the country, was not immune to the pressures of acculturation.[39]

State-centered and assimilationist idioms of nationhood became increasingly important in the early twentieth century, when the acquisition of colonies and widespread labor shortages brought large minority populations to France.[40] As early as the 1880s, government officials began expanding definitions of citizenship in the hopes of incorporating the growing foreign population. Afraid that newcomers were avoiding the increasingly universal obligation of military conscription and concerned that solidarity among ethnic minorities posed a challenge to state centralization, government officials extended the principle of *jus soli* to immigrant populations. With citizenship based on territorial ascriptions rather than solely on the basis of descent, foreigners were thus incorporated all the more rapidly into the national apparatus. Those favoring an expansive citizenship law argued that the legal transformation "would be accompanied by a social transformation: immigrants could be redefined legally as Frenchmen because they would be transformed socially into Frenchmen through the assimilatory workings of compulsory schooling and universal military service."[41]

Such incorporative measures seemed even more important in the early twentieth century, as the nature of the foreign population began to shift. Whereas the immigrants of the late nineteenth century generally migrated from surrounding countries, such as Belgium and Italy, those who arrived during and after World War I were more likely to have come from eastern Europe, Indochina, and North Africa. The distinctive ethnic and cultural characteristics of these new arrivals challenged the government's central role in determining cultural norms.[42] As immigration bureaucracies grew and policies became more coherent, authorities began to institute procedures meant not only to incorporate immigrant labor but also to integrate immigrants rapidly into French culture and society. Such policies remained at the heart of national immigration law until the 1970s.[43] Indeed, although the Vichy regime represented a rupture in French minority policies with its stress on ethnic hierarchies, "the legal framework that would determine immigrants' relationship with the French political system until the mid-1970s was largely in place" by the outbreak of the war.[44] As one French official noted in 1945, following the collapse of Vichy, "It is in France's interest . . . to facilitate the rapid and complete integration of foreign elements who prove worthy and on whom we are obliged to rely due to our demographic insufficiencies."[45] Aware of the need for foreign labor, officials once again formulated policies that were aimed at the full integration of distinctive ethnic minorities.

As we have seen, Armenian and Jewish genocide survivors in France were not all immigrants. Nevertheless, such integrationist policies shaped their relationship to their surrounding society in several important ways. For Armenian refugees, grateful to find a haven after years of flight and massacre, France symbolized stability and safety. Nevertheless, as *apatrides* (stateless refugees), they lacked the basic protections of most immigrant populations, and having arrived some years before the articulation of coherent refugee policies, they occupied a precarious place in the polity. This stigma of being stateless shaped how the new population responded to their adopted home, encouraging most to "lie low" and avoid any activity that would undermine their chances of being allowed to remain in France. For authorities charged with establishing refugee policies in the post–World War I era, the Armenians' statelessness posed interesting dilemmas. For some, co-opting the loyalties of this new and potentially malleable population remained a central concern. Others, however, distrusted this population with no identifiable allegiances. Refugee policies reflected this ambivalence as officials sought both to integrate and police the newcomers. Although sympathy for the uprooted population is evident in certain circles of society, government policies were more concerned with transforming them into loyal citizens of the state than with any humanitarian concern over their recent past.

France's long tradition of political and cultural integration also influenced how authorities addressed the problems posed by Jewish reintegration after World War II. Both a desire to move past Vichy as quickly as possible and a renewed commitment to republican law made government officials hesitant to call attention to Jewish losses. Although the principle of equal rights for all French citizens—and the nullity of all German and French legislation to the contrary— was instituted immediately after republican order was restored in August 1944, the provisional government proved ineffective in creating adequate compensatory legislation for those Jews who had suffered under Vichy's antisemitic laws. With no room for particularism in government policies, Jews were treated simply as equivalent victims of the war.

From a policy perspective, then, France's long tradition of political integration shaped how the government responded to Armenian and Jewish survivors after their respective genocides. In making such a case, however, I am not seeking to make a direct link between French governmental policies toward Armenian refugees in the 1920s and the post–World War II provisional government's response to reintegrating Jewish survivors. In other words, in each case, officials made choices based on the political realities of the day, choices that were informed by the particular relationship of the group in question to the French state. What I am arguing, however, is that a long tradition of policies geared toward ensuring cultural conformity among ethnic minorities influenced how both populations integrated into French society, shaping how survivors came to terms with their pasts.

And yet, as we will see, even while influenced by the surrounding integrationist culture, both populations were also able to cultivate identities that recognized their own particularism.[46] Indeed, neither the appeals of France's universalistic society nor the genocidal persecution led survivors to abandon links to their ethnoreligious heritage. As a comparative study indicates, then, although the French context provided survivors with a framework to understand and come to terms with their recent past, it did not prevent their memories from coalescing into sites of ethnic solidarity.

Thus, relationship to the polity was one of the determining factors in shaping Armenian and Jewish postgenocide populations; equally significant was the shifting relationship to their brethren abroad. Indeed, in both cases, the genocides of World War I and II raised new questions of diaspora solidarity and national allegiance. As noted, both Armenians and Jews are members of ancient diaspora populations. Indeed, traditionally, the very concept of diaspora was rooted in the history of Jewish exile from Jerusalem, a banishment that was viewed as a punishment for straying from God's way. Over time, "the concept of 'diaspora' became suffused with the suffering that accompanies many sorts of exile," particularly that of dispersed Greeks and Armenians.

In recent years, however, the meaning of "diaspora" has broadened, becoming integrated into historical discussions on the nature of difference and expanding to encompass a larger semantic domain, including such words as *immigrant, refugee,* and *expatriate.*[47] Thanks to the increasing globalization of political and economic structures and communication networks, previous constraints on the extent to which individuals might participate in more than one society have diminished. Such shifts have had a profound impact on how scholars have conceptualized minority identities. Thus, whereas those who worked on immigrant communities once focused primarily on "distinctions between the here and the there, the center and the periphery, black and white. . . . [s]uch analyses are being supplemented by a whole set of new, unbounded concepts . . . [including] multiplicity, border crossing, disjunction and ethnoscapes, cultural hybridization, porousness, webs, and transnational communities."[48]

Such conceptual tools, though generally useful in describing contemporary migration waves to advanced industrial nations, are more limited in showing how diaspora identification shifted for Armenians and Jews in the years following their respective genocides.[49] Not yet beneficiaries of the postmodern moment that has celebrated overlapping and hybrid identities, these escapees had been singled out for persecution in part *because* of their multinational identity, which marked them as cultural outsiders to the nations in which they lived.[50] In the aftermath of the genocidal violence, therefore, survivors were faced with new questions regarding where they belonged. Moreover, such questions were inextricably linked to survivors' relationship with the "homeland."

As several recent studies have stressed, the idea of an original homeland — either real or a "mythic place of desire" — is essential to the process of shaping cohesive and conscious diaspora communities as well as to the formation of coherent diaspora nationalist movements.[51] In the two cases under study, the mythical homelands, centered around Jerusalem for Jews and Mt. Ararat for Armenians, remained a constituent part of the diaspora condition until the modern era. What is particularly interesting for both, however, is that following the wartime destruction, the question of a national homeland was brought out of the realm of myth or prayer with the formation of legally constituted, identifiable national states.

The birth of the State of Israel and the Republic of Armenia provided survivors with options that previously had seemed feasible only to a small minority of activist idealists. A national state could bring their diaspora status to an end and could provide security to those who had been persecuted for that status. And yet, few chose to leave France for their new "homeland," most opting to remain where they were while still taking an active interest in diaspora nationalist movements. Thus, they faced a paradox. On the one hand, they remained the "paradigmatic Other of the nation-state," maintaining allegiances that defied the nation-state structure; on the other, they actively sought to integrate into the French state.[52]

Comparing the impact of genocide on Armenian and Jewish survivor communities in France thus sheds light on the power of the national idiom to influence minority culture. Indeed, one can argue that the very consolidation of the nation-state system in twentieth-century Europe made the "transnational" or "denationalized" status of these genocide survivors untenable. Unable to exist comfortably outside of this system, survivors took part in newly energized nationalist movements, which sought to provide a "space" for them—however disconnected from their own settlement plans—in the international arena. Thus, whereas some have argued that contemporary diaspora groups are "emblems of transnationalism" because their existence questions the notion of borders at the heart of the definition of the nation, I would argue that Armenian and Jewish survivors in France were actively seeking to end such questions.[53] This may seem counterintuitive. By participating in nationalistic movements that transcended the borders of the country in which they lived, they were certainly encompassing the diaspora/homeland divide that seems to interest so many contemporary theorists. It is my argument, however, that these now thriving nationalist discourses served not as a celebration of transnationalism, but as proof of the power of the national idiom.

As the above discussion suggests, a comparison between the Armenian and Jewish survivor communities in France makes it clear that, although in both cases genocide disrupted and, at times, destroyed surviving communal life, it did not necessarily force survivors to make a clean break with the past, with past ways of thinking and understanding themselves and their place in the nation. Even Armenian genocide survivors, who faced more disruption than the French Jews under study, did not immediately abandon former understandings of communal organization, nor did they prove incapable of constructing viable communities in their new context. In comparison, it seems hardly surprising that strong continuities link the French Jewish community of the post–World War II era to those of the preceding decades. Indeed, it becomes immediately clear that despite the far-reaching destruction caused by the Holocaust, its occurrence did not delineate a dramatic conclusion to a period born with the civil emancipation of the Jews in 1789, as some scholars have suggested. One historian, whose fine study of inter-war French Jewish history has essentially defined the field for future scholars, nevertheless concludes her book by arguing that the great social, political, and ideological changes that had enlivened French Jewry in the 1920s and 1930s were "cut short by the Holocaust," and that they "withered" after being "denied the test of time."[54] Similarly, as noted earlier, scholars of postwar French Jewry have assumed that it took the arrival of three hundred thousand North African Jews in the late 1950s to reinvigorate a community decimated during World War II. I certainly do not contest the Holocaust's centrality in shaping modern Jewish history, but I do argue that using a central and eastern European model for explaining postwar Jewish life in France is problematic. The Holocaust was tragic, devastating—but it was an important chapter in the unfolding narrative of French Jewish history, not its end.

In broader terms, then, In the Aftermath of Genocide seeks to break down the isolation that tends to bracket the history of genocide from the wider histories of its victim groups. By looking at the years that followed as years of continuity as well as years of change, I seek not to de-emphasize the criminality of these events nor to downplay their devastation, but to consider what structures, perceptions, and institutions were able to withstand such a brutal attack and to explain the historical roots of such resilience. My hope is that such an investigation will offer new avenues of analysis for those interested in the history of genocide as well as those interested in the history of Jews, Armenians, and modern France.

1 Orphans of the Nation: Armenian Refugees in France

Writing in the late 1930s, Aram Turabian, an Ottoman-born Armenian who migrated to France in the 1890s and fought as an officer in the French army, thanked local authorities for opening the nation's doors to Armenian refugees in the aftermath of World War I. Assuring his readers that in their gratitude Armenians would "respect and submit willingly to the laws of this noble country," he asked only "that our French friends do not confuse us with all the other foreigners. *Our situation is special*, we have neither consulate nor ambassador to defend us, we do not even have a national homeland . . . where we could seek refuge if necessary; all our trust is placed in French Justice and we respectfully request that the competent authorities of this country take our grievances into serious consideration."[1]

Although Turabian viewed the Armenian plight as "special," the situation he described in fact clearly illustrated the problem that most refugees posed to post–World War I European governments intent on consolidating along national lines. The war had led to the disintegration of the large multiethnic Romanov, Hapsburg, and Ottoman Empires. The small national states that replaced them and the violent conflict that accompanied their births produced large populations of stateless refugees. Having been stripped of citizenship and national allegiance, these new refugees posed particular problems for the international community. Unlike earlier generations of political exiles who had sought refuge in central and western Europe, these newcomers arrived in unprecedented numbers, straining the international community's abilities to care for them. In 1926, for example, approximately 9.5 million refugees were said to be wandering Europe. Moreover, twentieth-century European refugees often remained in exile for extraordinary lengths of time without being able to "regularize" their status, at times even passing this refugee status on to a second generation. Perhaps most important, however, the exiles of the post–World War I era and after were a unique addition to the European landscape because of the particular nature of their homelessness, "which removed them so dramatically and so uniquely from civil society." The consolidation of the modern nation-state in the war's aftermath increasingly solidified the relationship between the citizen and the state. Presuming that citizens followed through on all national obligations, the state provided for their basic protection and welfare. International treaties provided some protection to those who migrated from one nation to another, but refugees, by virtue of having lost their citizenship, were not beneficiaries of such arrangements; they found themselves "deprived of legal protection, mutual support, the access to employment, and the measure of freedom of movement which happier mortals take as a matter of course."[2] Although diplomats in Paris attempted to make some provisions for refugees in postwar peace treaties and the League of Nations created a High Commission for Refugees, "these efforts were like using bedroom sheets to block a hurricane."[3]

Rendered stateless by the Ottoman genocidal attack against them, Armenian refugees who made their way to France were thus part of a larger problem facing European nations in the aftermath of World War I. If Armenians like Turabian saw their postgenocide plight as exceptional, French authorities were blind to the distinction. On a per capita basis, France ranked highest among western European nations to open its doors to World War I refugees.[4] Eager to rebuild its war-devastated economy, the French government recruited foreign labor of all kinds. Immigration numbers had been steadily increasing since the midnineteenth century, especially from countries such as Belgium, Italy, and Poland, and liberal immigration policies accompanying the labor shortages of World War I transformed France into the leading "immigrant nation" in Europe. Newcomers from central and eastern Europe fleeing the First World War's political and economic upheaval as well as those from former French colonies not only increased the number of foreigners in France but changed the makeup of the population as well.[5] Then, after 1924, when the United States began tightening its own immigration policies, the numbers coming to France increased further. By 1931 a full 11 percent of France's workforce was made up of foreigners, and for all but three years in the 1920s, between 150,000 and 200,000 foreigners arrived annually.[6]

For government officials interested in increasing the labor pool, distinctions between immigrants and refugees were irrelevant. As a result, when large numbers of Russian émigrés began to flee the Russian Revolution and the Bolshevik regime, France admitted nearly 120,000, basically opening the door to any who were willing to work as industrial or day laborers.[7] In the early 1920s approximately 65,000 Armenians (nearly 30 percent of all Armenian refugees in Europe and the Near East), driven from their homes first by the Young Turks in the genocide of 1915 and then by Kemal Ataturk's forces a few years later, sought shelter in France.[8] These new populations, however, presented the French government with complex socioadministrative problems for which they had no ready solutions.[9] Whereas most foreign immigrants settling in France at this time maintained an obvious national-political (and thus administrative) link to their country of origin, the apatride, or stateless person, fell "under no particular state's jurisdiction."[10] These "orphans of the nation," as one sympathetic journalist referred to them, had no passports or visas to facilitate their movements, no consulates to represent them, nor any treaties to protect them. Nor could they return to the lands from which they had come.[11]

As a result, the apatrides threw into question previous understandings of immigrant participation in the polity, defying previous immigration categorizations and befuddling administrators seeking to integrate them into the country's broader economic structure. As we will see, for French officials Russian apatrides posed less of a conundrum than Armenians because the League of Nations' High Commission for Refugees created an internationally recognized juridical category for them in 1922; it took until 1924, however, for this privilege to be extended to Armenians. Thus, in the initial years of their settlement in France, Armenians, lacking all international documentation, "often were unable to establish of what country they were citizens — who they *were* in a juridical sense."[12] For French authorities working within a national paradigm, Armenians — stripped of any national status by the World War I genocide — proved a challenge.

Although this lack of an internationally recognized "identity" was solved in 1924, the Armenians' anomalous position in the state had important consequences. In particular, some officials, wary of the vague loyalties of this ancient diaspora population with no identifiable national allegiance, actively sought to enact policies that would encourage their transformation into citizens. As such, Armenian integration into French society is part of a larger story. Indeed, if, as recent historiographical discussions have suggested, France's state-centered and assimilationist model of civic self-definition and governance shaped the incorporation of ethnic and religious minorities into the state, the eventual incorporation of Armenian genocide survivors followed a similar pattern, providing us with a clear example of conscious and directed attempts to extinguish foreign distinctiveness through the implementation of state policy.[13] As this trend suggests, French authorities, even those aware of the genocidal attack against Ottoman Armenians, saw no reason to implement policies to preserve "Armenianness." If anything, local authorities distrusted the refugees' "transnational" identity and sought to remove any sign of ethnic distinctiveness as rapidly as possible.

It is important to note, however, that such integrationist approaches to incorporating the foreign "other" were not uniformly implemented by French officials, particularly in the 1930s, when new waves of mostly Jewish and Spanish refugees began testing the boundaries of France's tradition of political asylum. The growing antagonism directed at these most recent arrivals was not particularly aimed at those who had come in the 1920s. If anything, public sentiment was sympathetic to these first waves of apatrides and even positively distinguished them from the refugees fleeing fascism in the 1930s. Nevertheless, the new anti-refugee atmosphere of the 1930s reminded Armenians of the precariousness of their stateless status. Wary and insecure amid the growing hostility, the new refugees felt compelled, as Turabian would in 1938, to justify their inclusion into their surrounding society. Thus for them, having been rendered stateless meant more than being uprooted from the land that had once been theirs; it also shaped how they integrated into their new society.

Exile and Dispersion: The Development of an Armenian Refugee Problem

To understand the relationship between Armenian refugees and the French state, one must first consider the role of Western governments in the Armenian exile and dispersion during and after the genocide. The Armenian refugee problem arose *both* as a result of the brutal massacres of World War I *and* from the geopolitical settlements of the postwar years. One of numerous second-class Christian minorities in the multinational and multireligious Ottoman Empire, the Armenians had consistently been subjected to official discrimination throughout the centuries of living under Ottoman rule.[14] Nevertheless, they were able to live in relative peace and even prospered as the Empire grew. In the eighteenth and nineteenth centuries, however, as the Empire began to collapse under growing economic and administrative problems, intolerance and exploitation of the non-Muslim minorities began to increase. In response, Armenian communal leaders petitioned the sultan for protection from increasing taxation, administrative corruption, and sporadic violence. When promised reforms proved inadequate, Armenians began turning westward in the hopes that European powers to whom the Ottoman Empire was indebted would be able to enforce reforms to benefit local Christian minorities. Indeed, beginning with the Treaty of San Stefano following the Russo-Turkish war of 1877–78 and rearticulated in the Treaty of Berlin, the Ottoman sultanate did agree to enact reforms for Armenian peasants and artisans living in the Empire's eastern provinces. Widespread massacres in 1894–99, however, as well as those at Adana in 1909, indicated that the government had no intention of carrying out such reforms, and the Armenian plight worsened. In response, Armenian intellectuals continued to turn to western European powers, now legally bound through the treaty to ensure that the sultan carried out the much-needed reforms. Despite the promises, however, such aid was never forthcoming.[15]

The success of the Young Turk revolution in 1908 initially gave Armenians renewed hope that their situation would improve, as the new leadership initially seemed interested in working to resolve the problem of minority relations in the Ottoman Empire. Within a few years, however, under the strain of increasing economic and political problems, the liberal and egalitarian government was transformed into one of extreme chauvinism determined to bring an end to the Armenian Question. In 1915, the Young Turks used the cover of war to initiate a genocide against the Empire's Armenian population, first by accusing local Armenian populations of aiding the Russian army's advance, then by eliminating the intellectual elite in Constantinople, and finally by deporting and slaughtering entire Armenian communities from the eastern provinces. Of those who managed to escape, many moved to the Russian Caucasus; others made their way to the Lebanese and Syrian provinces of the Ottoman Empire. Although Western relief workers attempted to help survivors, by the end of World War I, starvation and disease were prevalent throughout the refugee populations wherever they were located.[16]

Like Armenians from the Ottoman Empire, those living in the Caucasus under Russian dominion also experienced great upheaval during World War I. Both the refugees who settled there as well as the natives of the region were caught up in the Russian Revolution of 1917, and independence for the small Armenian Republic was thrust on its reluctant leadership shortly thereafter. After the new Soviet government signed the Brest-Litovsk Treaty in March 1918, ending Russian involvement in the war and, in exchange, handing over large areas of Transcaucasia to Turkey, Armenia—and Transcaucasia more generally—became vulnerable to Ottoman advances. After a minor attempt to coordinate a Transcaucasian federation, Georgia negotiated its own treaty with Germany and declared independence; the Azerbaijani Tartars rapidly followed suit. Armenian leaders had little choice but to declare independence for the tiny region of eastern Armenia that had not been conquered by the Turks.[17]

The end of the war brought some optimism to Armenian leaders attempting to build a state and solve the refugee problem. With the defeat and collapse of the Ottoman Empire and the Allied victory, Armenian leaders hoped that Western powers would meet their previous obligations, protect Armenians from further harm, and even support their struggle for national independence. Indeed, every Allied power was initially pledged to support a separate autonomous or independent existence for the Armenians in their historic lands.[18] In addition, the small republic in the Caucasus gradually expanded as the Turkish army withdrew from the area. In this atmosphere, many war refugees began returning to their ancestral lands. French forces, in particular, repatriated tens of thousands of Armenian refugees from Syria, Lebanon, and Egypt to the southeastern region of the former Ottoman Empire known as Cilicia, now under French control, and Armenians in Transcaucasia also began returning to the lands they had fled.

Armenian optimism, however, quickly dissipated. To be sure, throughout 1919 and 1920, the Western powers remained publicly committed to establishing a united Armenian state, which would combine the Russian and Turkish Armenian provinces under the mandatory leadership of the United States. If, however, all the Allies theoretically supported the idea of a free Armenia, none would commit sufficient financial resources to repatriate hundreds of thousands of refugees to the new state or to defend it properly. The United States, under its own domestic pressure and isolationism, ultimately refused the mandate, and Great Britain and France, despite the entreaties of Armenian delegates to the Paris Peace Conference, turned their energies to the Ottoman Empire's former Arab provinces, which were of far greater strategic value to them and where they fought over territorial control. Indeed, rivalries among the Allies in the Near East caused long delays in drafting a peace settlement. In addition, the formation of a Turkish nationalist movement under the leadership of Mustafa Kemal aimed at preserving the territorial integrity of the region began to gain momentum at the end of 1919. The occupation of the Cilician region of the former Ottoman Empire, for example, into which tens of thousands of Armenian refugees had streamed, proved unacceptable to Kemal and his nationalist forces, and throughout 1919 and 1920, he began attacking French-controlled areas. The isolated and weakly defended French forces often fled, providing little cover for Armenian repatriates who were, once again, deported or massacred by Turkish nationalist forces.

When the Treaty of Sèvres was finally signed and imposed on the Ottoman Empire in August 1920, nearly two years after the war's end, it recognized certain Armenian concerns. Most important, the Turkish government officially recognized the free and independent Armenian Republic and renounced rights to important regions of eastern Anatolia that would be included in the new state. The concessions of the treaty, however, were worthless without Allied enforcement, and it soon became clear that no government was willing to accept that responsibility. Shortly thereafter, when Mustafa Kemal ordered his army to advance into the heart of the independent Armenian Republic, the Allied powers took no action to protect the fledgling state, thus forcing local leaders to turn to the Red Army for aid. By the beginning of 1921, hopes for a free, autonomous Armenia had been dashed as Soviet forces occupied the small republic. Kemal also turned against the small areas of western Cilicia that the Treaty of Sèvres had left under French mandate. In response, the French signed an independent accord with Kemal that allowed them to maintain their mandate in Syria as long as they pulled out of Cilicia. Panic seized the local Armenian populations, and when the French evacuated, most Armenians went with them. By January 1922, the final French contingent had left the region, and most of the sixty thousand Armenians — many who had been repatriated since the war under promises of French protection — had fled and were once again seeking homes as refugees.[19] In 1922, when Turkish forces attacked Greek troops and burned the city of Smyrna, Armenians were, with the exception of Istanbul, forever eliminated from Turkey.

In their attempts to normalize relations with Mustafa Kemal, the Allies continued to retreat on Armenian matters, finally signing the Treaty of Lausanne in 1923. Among other things, this treaty brought an end to the Armenian Question by ensuring that the Armenians from the eastern provinces of the Ottoman Empire would no longer be able to return to their ancestral homelands. As one scholar noted, "The absolute Turkish triumph was reflected in the fact that in the final versions of the Lausanne treaties neither the word *Armenia* nor the word *Armenian* was to be found. It was as if an Armenian Question or the Armenian people themselves had never existed."[20] Stranded and without recourse, Armenian refugees made their way to whatever countries would admit them. Although most fled to the eastern Mediterranean — Lebanon, Syria, Iraq, and Greece — these countries were incapable of economically absorbing all of them. Others sought homes in Soviet Armenia. Still others made their way westward. Indeed, by 1925, more Armenians were living in scattered communities throughout the world than were living in Soviet Armenia.

Of all European countries, France accepted the greatest number of these refugees. A certain sense of responsibility concerning the Armenians' plight after French forces had evacuated under Kemal's attack may have encouraged officials to keep an open-door policy toward them, although open-labor policies were undoubtedly the more decisive factor. Certainly, local political rhetoric often cast Armenian refugees as the true victims of the war. As national orphans, pushed off their own land, massacred without mercy by one of France's World War I rivals, the Turks, Armenians were pitied for all they had suffered. In some cases, political commentators, journalists, and politicians argued that France, well-known for its humanitarian tradition, should provide shelter for these new refugees. Indeed, those who were aware of the Armenian plight were often quite sympathetic to the trials they had undergone. As early as the 1880s, after Sultan Abdul-Hamid unleashed the first wave of massacres against his Armenian subjects, certain well-known French writers and propagandists began agitating on their behalf. From 1895 to 1923, such French Armenophiles, as they were called, held demonstrations, wrote books, published journals, and petitioned their government to aid the Ottoman Armenians. Whereas the majority of French officials took no interest in Armenian concerns, this small but active group of pro-Armenian activists in Paris agitated for French intervention in the Ottoman Empire.[21]

With the outbreak of World War I, the pro-Armenian movement established a propaganda organization to continue bringing Armenian concerns to the larger public. This organization, known as the Société France-Arménie, was founded in 1916 as one section of the Amitiés Franco-Etrangères. Numbering prominent French officials among its members, this organization's self-proclaimed goal was neither political nor philanthropic.[22] Rather, members vowed simply to build sympathy for the Armenians among the French population. Aware that most French citizens knew absolutely nothing about Armenians and that those who did viewed them merely in caricaturistic terms either as martyrs of Ottoman bloodshed or aggressors against Turks (some French newspapers initially reported that Armenian revolutionaries had brought the massacres upon themselves by provoking the government with their nationalism), French Armenophiles worked to counter this image.

Organizing a demonstration on 9 April 1916 in the Sorbonne amphitheater, the Société vowed to educate the French public about Armenia, "its historic role, the important part it has played for civilization." Speakers included Paul Deschanel, the president of the Chamber of Deputies, Paul Painlevé, the minister of public education, and Anatole France. Approximately fifteen hundred people attended to hear these speakers as well as to "condemn the enormous crime committed by the Turks and Germans in Armenia and to pay homage to the heroism of the Armenian people."[23] Likewise, the Society sponsored other efforts to bring news of the Turkish atrocities to the wider public. One member, for example, wrote a pamphlet to teach schoolchildren about the Armenian people.[24]

After the war ended, the Société France-Arménie transformed itself into a new organization, the Association Franco-Arménienne. Unlike its predecessor, the new organization had expressly political goals, which included establishing

permanent contacts with the Armenian delegation to the peace conference, sending aid to the Armenian population in Turkey, and spreading information about
Turkish atrocities. Believing that France had a moral responsibility to aid Armenians, the members argued that their country should endorse Armenian claims
for the establishment of an independent homeland and should play an active role
in caring for the displaced refugees. In addition, the Association sent a delegation
to the minister of foreign affairs in November 1918 requesting that Armenians
be recognized as wartime belligerents; by being counted among those who had
been the war's primary actors and victims, Armenian leaders hoped to be given
the right to participate in postwar peace negotiations. Association members also
pushed French authorities to establish an autonomous Armenian region in Cilicia
and insisted that the government take action against postwar massacres in the
Caucasus.[25]

The Association's activities were only marginally successful, and though its
members often gained audiences with government officials they sought to convince, the results were never very satisfactory. Pronouncements of moral outrage
could not withstand the pressure of France's larger political, economic, and strategic interests in the former Ottoman Empire.[26] Nevertheless, the Association
was active into the early 1920s, keeping news of the Armenian plight before the
French public. In 1922 alone, the Association Franco-Arménienne presented a
petition to Poincaré concerning the status of Armenians in the Ottoman Empire,
attended meetings on the evacuation of Cilicia, held conferences on the Armenian Question, organized a banquet to discuss the political situation of Armenians abroad, worked in the provinces to spread information outside of Paris, and
collected photographic evidence of the deportations and massacres.[27]

Although it is hard to determine the effect of such pro-Armenian efforts on
French society at large, some intellectuals were undoubtedly moved by stories of
the Armenian plight. Thus, when the refugees began migrating to France, they
were met with some sympathy. As one film reviewer put it after attending a viewing of the Armenian film *Andranik*, "In modern history, there is no people who has
suffered as much as the Armenian people." Some journalists called on France to
aid the refugees as they settled in their new homes. After comparing Marseille's
rich Armenian colony of seventeenth-century merchants with the poor postwar
refugees, one journalist wrote, "It does not matter; the heart of Provence is open
even more to misfortune than to success. If she has in the old days taken advantage of a few rich merchants, today she welcomes the poor exiles with tender-
ness."[28]

Without exception, those journalists who showed pity for the Armenian refugees reminded their readers that France was obliged to aid them for humanitarian reasons. Helping Armenians was the least France could do, it was argued, after having failed to protect them in Cilicia after World War I. Such humanitarian concern undoubtedly fueled the government's decision in 1920 to provide 100,000 francs to a Franco-Armenian committee working to aid refugees in Greece and the Caucasus. Similarly, in Syria and Lebanon, where nearly a hundred thousand Armenians settled and which were under French mandate, the government established orphanages, schools, and vocational training for the professional reeducation of refugee populations and contributed 3 million francs to aid in their settlement.[29]

Far more important than humanitarian concerns in encouraging open-door policies toward the refugees, however, was the enormous national labor shortage. By the end of the war, 1.3 million French men were killed or missing and another 1.1 million had been severely wounded.[30] Immigrants, it was believed, could fill the labor gap created by these losses. Throughout the 1920s, contractors and industrialists toured Greece, Lebanon, and Syria in search of refugee laborers. Through the offices of the Haut-Commissariat français in Lebanon and intermediary Armenian recruiters, the practice of delivering work contracts to refugees became widespread. These contracts were valid for one year and directed those interested to mining and textile centers throughout France. Between 1922 and 1931, when the international economic crisis hit France, a significant number of Armenians came to France to take advantage of the open-door policy; some went immediately to the industrial centers, others headed for Paris, and a significant minority remained in the port of entrance, Marseille.[31]

The open immigration policies that had encouraged so many Armenians to come, however, soon proved ineffective in addressing the particular problems of their settlement. Indeed, although the refugees were encouraged to come as part of the wider immigrant labor force, it was soon clear that Armenians were not economic immigrants and that previous policies were inadequate for dealing with the new stateless refugees of the post–World War I era.

Refugee, Apatride, or Immigrant: Armenian Refugees in French Legislation

The problem of statelessness did not arise for the first time at the end of World War I. Indeed, the constitution of 24 June 1793 proclaimed that the French state would provide refuge to foreigners who had been exiled from their own country. Theoretically, the Republic was open to all; in practice, foreigners posed a problem for the new state seeking to define who was "of" the nation and who was not. That said, the problem of statelessness per se emerged fairly infrequently throughout the first third of the century, when the number of political refugees counted in the hundreds. Even when that number jumped into the thousands as a result of the revolutionary fervor that swept Europe between 1830 and 1848, most officials did not view these newcomers as a permanent problem. Having instituted a variety of policies to both welcome and monitor the refugees, authorities simply assumed that most would return to their country of origin as soon as it was politically possible; others would blend into French society. For them, the "refugee problem" was thus a temporary and containable phenomenon.[32]

Such views began to change, however, at the end of the nineteenth century, as homogenizing institutions such as the popular press, the educational system, and the military began to solidify what until then had been relatively fluid notions of national identity. As conceptions of "Frenchness" solidified, so too did conceptions of the "foreigner," a shift that was quickly reflected in policies toward the latter. Backing away from the laissez-faire policies of previous decades, the Third Republic leadership began taking an ever growing interest in monitoring the relationship between citizens and immigrants. Naturalization policies are a case in point. Committed to instituting universal and equal military service throughout the country, the Third Republic's governing elite soon realized that nonnationals, who were exempt from serving in the army, had a competitive advantage over French citizens in the labor market. As a result, they began broadening nationalization policies based on the principle of jus soli; citizenship would now be granted to immigrants on the basis of territorial ascription rather than descent.

Paradoxically, however, if such integrationist policies allowed authorities to broaden notions of French citizenship, they also allowed for the establishment of greater juridical distinctions between natives and foreigners. Thus, those who were not naturalized faced an ever growing administrative system designed to identify and control their movements. First by requiring all foreigners to register their residence in France and then by requiring foreign workers to obtain a license at their local town hall or police station (proving their identity with a birth certificate or an identity document validated by a consulate), officials began attempting to control a process that had been much more haphazard in the early decades of the nineteenth century. Subsequently, border dwellers or "nomads" were required to adopt a fixed identity by carrying a booklet that attested to their civil status and provided their physical description, fingerprints, and photograph.[33]

Politics around immigrant issues intensified dramatically during and after World War I, when increasing numbers of ever more diverse and non-Western immigrants sought work or shelter in France. The suspension of the standard practices of democratic life during wartime paved the way for the adoption of greater policing mechanisms of such foreign populations, and soon all immigrants above the age of fifteen were required to carry identification cards. In a relatively short time, officials also outlined regulations to control borders, to issue passports, and to set public health standards. Yet, despite all this regulation to monitor foreign residents, France remained dependent on immigrant labor, meaning that it was in the state's interest to encourage their migration. As a result, the state established two foreign worker recruitment services in 1919, one in the Agricultural Ministry and one in the Ministry of Labor. Moreover, in July 1920, an interministerial commission on immigration was established to coordinate the activities of these two ministries as well as to prepare and regulate a series of treaties and conventions regarding immigration.[34] The treaties, made with all the countries of emigration, guaranteed the rights of foreign workers when in France and ensured the same rights for French workers abroad. One commentator of the day noted, "The state that had, until then, remained unconcerned or opposed to intervening in migratory movements at once became recruiter, importer, inspector, and employment agent for the foreign labor force."[35]

From the first, the stateless Russian and Armenian refugees seeking shelter in France in the 1920s did not fit into this highly bureaucratized system. By the 1930s their status had improved considerably due to a number of international conferences; then, in the first years following World War I, when "having a nationality was as important for an individual as having a nose in the middle of his face," they faced numerous problems.[36] Most important, the newcomers had no passports or visas nor any documents attesting to their civil status.[37] These identity papers were crucial to the French system of registering and monitoring the activities of noncitizens. When the system functioned correctly, an immigrant worker would arrive with a work contract already in hand. The contract ensured transportation from the border to the place of employment. There, after registering with the police (within forty-eight hours of arriving), the immigrant would receive an identity card that specified occupation and civil status. The card, which had to be renewed every two or three years, gave the foreign worker the right to reside in a given region. Although valid anywhere in France, the slightest change in address or occupation required an entirely new document. Without it, no employer could legally hire the laborer, nor could the migrant obtain any state social services.[38]

The system did not always work as well as intended. One immigration specialist lamented in his 1932 study, "All this control, however theoretically well organized, is unfortunately far from being effective as a result of the great number of cards there are to distribute, the notorious inefficiencies of the administrative services, as well as the difficulty in adjusting such services that are by definition rigid to populations that are particularly mobile." Commenting on the many foreigners who entered France illegally each year, he singled out "the 27,000 Greeks and Armenians entering between 1921 and 1926, only 1,100 [of whom] have been registered [controlés]."[39] As such a comment suggests, the apparatus put in place for welcoming immigrant laborers was not immediately able to adapt itself to the particular problems that these early waves of apatrides posed. With no special governmental office of refugee affairs to which they could turn for answers and few policies adopted to address their stateless position, the stateless refugees who migrated to France in the first half of the 1920s found themselves sunk in an administrative hole.[40]

Time and again, immigration regulations proved to be inadequate for the first waves of incoming Armenians. Many had already obtained work contracts before migrating, relying on the aid of labor recruiters throughout the Middle East; others fell through the cracks.[41] For example, those who arrived with travel documents issued by a French consulate but without a work contract were directed immediately to Marseille's Office of Foreign Labor. In theory, the travel documents required refugees to accept any farm or industrial labor that the office had to offer, and many did so. Others, however, were unable to find work in Marseille. Seeking jobs elsewhere, these Armenians left for other towns in southern France, where they discovered that their right to work was invalid; their travel documents that named Marseille as their final destination could not be used elsewhere. Officials in these towns immediately sent them back to Marseille, where unemployment levels were higher and work opportunities more limited.[42]

In truth, the apatrides' lack of international documentation was not solely a French problem. In 1922, the League of Nations' High Commissioner for Refugees, the Norwegian explorer, scientist, and diplomat Fridtjof Nansen, called an intergovernmental conference to consider the problem of Russian refugees attempting to move across borders without passports or visas. Nansen had been named head of the League's High Commission in 1921 with some reluctance on the part of the member states, who viewed caring for refugees as a fairly low priority, particularly because they continued to understand the problem as temporary in nature. Although uprooted populations had been wandering throughout eastern and southeastern Europe since the beginning of World War I, their care had been left primarily to private charitable organizations such as the Red Cross. Russian refugees, however, caught the Allied nations' attention in a different way. At first hoping that fleeing Russians would return to their homes to continue the fight against the Soviet government, Western powers supported these refugees for political as much as humanitarian reasons. When it became clear that the anti-Bolshevik struggle was hopeless, the League turned to Nansen to help the uprooted population, eight hundred thousand of whom were living scattered throughout Europe, primarily in Constantinople and Poland, in desperate conditions and clamoring to enter other European countries. At the 1922 Geneva meeting, sixteen countries agreed to issue travel documents to facilitate their movement. Then, in May 1924, thirty-eight states agreed to grant the same right to Armenian refugees.

The new document, called a Nansen passport, was not a passport in the conventional sense. Rather, it served as an identity certificate that could be used as a travel document. Issued for one year, after which it could be renewed once, it gave the holder the right to return to the country that had issued it (after 1926). Although it did not guarantee the refugee's equal treatment in regard to labor permits, social security, or taxation, it did provide a certain measure of international protection. One commentator noted, "The refugee who is de facto stateless and has neither protection nor representation from his state is provided with both by the High Commissioner for Refugees."[43]

France was one of the original countries to recognize and issue the Nansen passport, but prior to 1924 none of the Armenian apatrides had any legal travel documentation.[44] This did not, however, stop them from coming. Some made their way to France in the years immediately following World War I and the Russian Revolution; the largest waves did not arrive until after the Greco-Turkish war and the burning of Smyrna (where many genocide survivors had settled) in 1922. As these boatloads of refugees began arriving, they brought unique problems. Most important, no foreign government was sponsoring and financing their settlement. The French army donated several military camps in Marseille (previously used for German war prisoners) as temporary housing for the refugees and repatriates who arrived in September and October 1922, but it was expected that the consulates of the states from which these refugees had come would fund their settlement. Thus, in September 1922, the Ministry of the Interior provided 100,000 francs for the lodging of French repatriates. As for foreigners, it was up to the prefect in Marseille to arrange the costs of lodging and repatriation with the concerned consulates.[45]

Armenian refugees lacked a state to care for their needs. The independent Armenian state had collapsed in 1920, and the Soviet Republic did not have the resources to care for those refugees abroad.[46] In addition, Turkey refused all responsibility for the refugees.[47] Despite this, French officials treated the refugees as if they were immigrants. Indeed, although the Armenian Republic collapsed in 1920, because of the uncertainty over the long-term fate of the region French bureaucrats did not mark that fact on official documentation for several years. Thus, it was only in 1925 that the Ministry of the Interior finally informed various prefectures that "since the signing of the Treaty of Lausanne [1923], the provinces that once made up Armenia are now divided between Soviet Russia and Turkey. There is thus no Armenian state, and as such, no Armenian nationality." Until then, however, many French officials operated as if these apatrides actually *did* have a national base.[48]

When the first Armenian refugees arrived, they were immediately put in the care of the consul of the Armenian Republic in Marseille and the president of the Comité de secours aux réfugiés arméniens, Tigran S. Mirzayantz. He took charge of this small group by transferring them from the refugee camps to the Hotel du Levant. By November 1922, however, when four hundred Armenians arrived in Marseille on the ship *Tourville*, Mirzayantz's resources were quickly overwhelmed. The French military was forced to intervene, establishing two refugee camps on the outskirts of Marseille, Camp Mirabeau and Camp Oddo, the latter of which remained a home for Armenian refugees for several years.[49]

The establishment of Camp Oddo and the hands-on/hands-off approach of the authorities illustrates the problems the apatrides posed for French bureaucrats. On the one hand, the government's active intervention on behalf of the apatrides was a necessary result of their stateless position.[50] Without a foreign government to protect them, the French administration was forced to intercede. Thus, the government turned over the camps to Armenian organizations and even provided 80,000 francs to aid their settlement, insisting that they were doing all they could "to respond in the most favorable manner possible to the requests of individual Armenians in France."[51] And yet, they did not want to become overly involved with Armenian settlement. Reluctant to absorb the full cost of settling these refugees, officials depended on Armenians to care for their own. Although the military provided camps, it was up to the refugees and their compatriot unions to run and maintain them, including all the costs of lodging, bedding, mail service, hygiene, discipline, and medical services.[52]

The example of medical care well illustrates the degree to which Armenian apatrides were expected to care for themselves. As noted earlier, the interministerial immigration commission forged agreements with most foreign governments to protect their nationals abroad. These international treaties assured the immigrant equal taxation, equal pay for equal work, and equal access to social services. No such agreements protected the apatrides, making them particularly vulnerable in areas where other immigrants remained protected. Access to medical care was one such area.[53] In the late 1920s, the French Armenian population was particularly susceptible to contagious diseases such as tuberculosis.[54] The standard French response to the disease was to house those afflicted in a sanitarium, but the government refused to subsidize the same care for foreigners. Fortunately, most of those infected with the disease could return to their own country, where they were eligible for medical care or at least could rely on their consulate for financial or medical assistance; Armenians could not. Tuberculosis posed such a threat to the local Armenian population that Dr. Eugène Prat-Flottes wrote a pamphlet encouraging Armenian benefactors around the world to raise money for a private sanitarium in France. "From the most distant corners of Europe," he wrote, "the sick Armenian will be admitted in a sanitarium where he will be at home and in which he will be certain to find air, sun, and hygiene as well as the most modern and dedicated care." In his pamphlet, Prat-Flottes implicitly argued that because French aid was not forthcoming, Armenians would have to depend on their own generosity and sense of group solidarity.[55] Without the protection of standard international treaties, Armenians fell between the cracks of French bureaucratic regulations. Thus, while liberal immigration policies brought large numbers of refugees to France, the immigration bureaucracy was unprepared for the particular problems they raised.

What many officials did not realize, however, was how poorly prepared Armenian organizations were for the task of caring for thousands of refugees. At first, the incoming refugees were cared for by the Comité de secours aux réfugiés arméniens, which raised money for its task from Armenians already settled in France and from those new refugees who found work quickly. As early as September 1923, however, the Comité de secours's resources were extremely taxed, and local officials worried that additional arrivals would lead to its insolvency. The situation became difficult so quickly that the president of the Délégation de la république arménienne wrote to the League of Nations asking for help.[56]

Despite their lack of resources, Armenian officials were forced to house many boatloads of Armenians in Camp Oddo. By October 1923 the camp was full to capacity with twelve hundred refugees. Nevertheless, no provision was made to house newcomers elsewhere. Although the commandant de la base de Marseille requested that measures be taken to direct the refugees at their disembarkation to some place other than Camp Oddo, no action was taken to ease the situation at the camp. By 1924 it housed over two thousand refugees, with several hundred sleeping without shelter in front of the barracks. Local leaders voiced complaints over the hygiene and poverty of the new refugees. Siméon Flaissières, the mayor of Marseille, for example, worried that "this number, already troubling, will continue to grow . . . from day to day, and . . . is intolerable for the hygiene of our town." In a letter published in Le Petit Provençal, he requested that the government refuse entrance to these "immigrants" and that they "repatriate without delay these lamentable human herds who pose such a grave public danger to the whole country."[57]

Marseille's prefect, who shared the views of these local officials, informed the national government of the problems that Armenian settlement posed to his city. In numerous appeals to the Ministry of the Interior, he requested that further arrivals be curtailed and that the government intervene more actively in refugee settlement. In response, the Ministry finally gave permission for some of the newcomers to move to Paris. Likewise, the Foreign Affairs Office told its consulates in Constantinople, Salonica, and Athens to limit future Armenian migration and particularly to admit only those refugees who would accept employment immediately upon arriving. Nevertheless, the prefect complained that he was not getting enough support from the national government: "In spite of all my repeated requests for subsidies to aid Armenian refugees, never was any credit put at my disposition either by the Foreign Affairs Ministry or by the Sanitation Ministry." Only private charity organizations and the Armenians themselves, he continued, "through pure self-sacrifice . . . and without any official aid," had carried out the task of settlement.[58]

Ironically, however, it was not a desire to solve such settlement problems that finally induced French authorities to shut Camp Oddo. Rather, having successfully relied on Armenian sources to fund and maintain the establishment of the refugee camp, authorities began to fear that a "véritable colonie" of Armenians had taken shape in the camp and surrounding area. As one French official remarked, "The Armenians have installed themselves freely in the camp without being subject to any control and under the direction of their compatriots have constituted a veritable colony with its own stores for provisions and its own schools." By late 1924, officials feared that the colony would endanger French assimilationist policies and national security, and soon the Commission interministérielle permanente de l'immigration determined that the camp should be evacuated.[59]

The details of the evacuation, which stretched over several years, are addressed more fully in chapter 5. It seems that the Armenians living in the camp had no interest in leaving—a fact that officials were reluctant to address. What is important here, however, is to note the contradictions in policy toward them. By the mid-1920s, fears about the establishment of an autonomous Armenian colony caused officials to evacuate Camp Oddo. Noting that the nature of the camp had changed, the labor minister warned that "it has become a veritable administration in the hands of certain Armenians."[60] Yet it was French authorities who had initially insisted that Armenians rely on themselves. New fears of Armenians' "unassimilability," however, quickly encouraged authorities to contradict their initial policies. Such fears were bolstered by the local press, which at times hinted that rather than integrating into French society the Armenians would take it over. The eminent journalist Ludovic Nadeau, for example, though not unsympathetic to the Armenian plight, warned readers that over time, "these men who played as children at Camp Oddo will be municipal officials or even deputies from Marseille; they will control the major newspapers and will rigorously work those few native Frenchmen who may still remain."[61]

Although Camp Oddo was a source of particular concern for French officials, their worries over Armenian social cohesion spread to all areas where the refugees had concentrated. A local Valence official, for example, complained that the Armenians' preference for living clustered together was preventing them from integrating into the wider population. Armenians, he claimed, were the only foreign group displaying a tendency to live outside the population and to preserve their original customs: "They are grouped, indeed, piled up, in the same spaces," he noted, and "certain women are even still wearing their national garb." Commenting on how slowly Armenians were assimilating to French customs, he implied that they remained too preoccupied with their own ancestral traditions. Interestingly, however, though quick to point out hygiene problems and poverty among the Armenian population, he also praised them for their work ethic, describing them as industrious, submissive, and fairly clever.[62] As will become clear, Armenians often escaped the harshest criticisms that were later directed at Jewish refugees, particularly in the 1930s, when those fleeing Nazi Germany began pouring into France. Nevertheless, praise for their industriousness did not alleviate concerns over their ability to integrate into the wider society. As another official commented, "It is certain that for the most part Armenians are less assimilated than the Russians; many speak French poorly and their physical attributes are certainly less European than those of the Russians."[63]

Hardly a major journalistic concern of the day, Armenians—distinguishable by language, customs, and culture as well as for their trials during World War I—did surface occasionally in the French press. Inevitably such discussions commented on the Armenians' preference for living close to one another. Rather than assuming that poverty drove the refugees into close quarters, an article in *Paris-Midi*, for example, attributed their tendency to house twelve in a three-room apartment to their "essentially sociable nature" and likened them to a primitive tribe.

Similarly, an article in *Paris-Soir* noted that Armenians in the Parisian suburbs had established a "veritable foreign enclave on French soil." By living "unsociably withdrawn into itself," continued the article, this "enclave" had "formed a perfectly homogeneous community" that held only "the strictest, most necessary and minimal dealings with official bodies. . . . rarely does one find among a group of individuals a collective instinct that is so extreme."[64]

Concerns that Armenians would not integrate into the wider society if they remained clustered together began pushing policymakers in new directions. Indeed, the financial concerns and bureaucratic inefficiencies that had encouraged Armenians to rely on their own initiative during the first two or three years of their settlement began to give way to the more pressing interest of turning the newcomers into loyal and productive citizens. As Rogers Brubaker has demonstrated, twentieth-century French immigration policies were geared specifically to turning immigrants into Frenchmen.[65] Such aggressively assimilationist policies, though not directed toward the Armenian apatrides specifically, were expected to operate in the same manner for all foreign minorities. As the 1920s progressed, however, local authorities became increasingly concerned with helping that integration along. In fact, for some, the refugees' statelessness, which signified their lack of citizenship anywhere and the impossibility of returning to their country of origin, worked well with assimilationist ideologies; the apatride's fate was tied to his or her inclusion in the heart of the welcoming society.[66] As a result, officials began adopting policies to encourage Armenian workers to move away from their fellow refugees. When Camp Oddo was closed, for example, authorities provided employment incentives for residents to leave Marseille.

Interestingly, however, a renewed commitment to integrationist policies did not always bring an end to contradictory refugee policies. Indeed, from the granting of the Nansen passport to Armenian refugees in 1924 until the early 1930s, two conflicting strategies seemed to shape French policies for Armenians and for stateless refugees more generally. On the one hand, the granting of the passport seemed to signal policies of inclusion and a greater willingness to recognize these refugees' distinct situation. Likewise, the government's participation in various international endeavors to regulate the position of refugees signaled a growing willingness among French officials to take the specific nature of the apatride's plight into consideration.[67] These endeavors included two intergovernmental conferences in 1926 and 1928 that discussed expanding travel rights for those holding Nansen passports, guaranteeing their right of residence, and encouraging the recognition of their legal status in such areas as the protection of acquired and matrimonial rights. To prepare for the 1926 conference, for example, the government finally made a serious attempt to count its Armenian and Russian populations and to establish some system for regulating them.[68] As a result of this conference, the Ministry of the Interior issued official definitions for both populations, in which Armenians were defined as "all individuals of Armenian origin, formerly subjects of the Ottoman Empire, who do not enjoy or will no longer enjoy the protection of the Turkish government and who have not acquired some other nationality." Those in a similar situation who came from the Soviet side of the border were considered Russian refugees.[69] Special offices were also established and legally recognized to facilitate the issuing of Nansen passports and to administer the affairs of each of these refugee groups, such as granting identity cards, permits, and the like.[70]

Yet, although the French government seemed prepared to recognize the distinctive position of these initial apatrides, contradictory policies toward them did not immediately disappear. Such contradictions emerged particularly clearly around the issue of expulsion, where the government continued to apply standard mechanisms for settling and policing foreigners with the status of apatride. Here too, the contradictions were not a specifically French problem. Most European nations resisted international attempts to restrict their rights to expel any foreigner, stateless or not. In the French case, however, expulsions of refugees proved a particularly vexing problem because of the large numbers involved.[71] With a large foreign population of both immigrants and refugees, the state turned frequently to expulsion as a means to monitor and police their activities.

In the eyes of the state, all foreign residents were expected "to conform to the principles of law and order and to respect French authorities and institutions scrupulously." The government would provide liberty, security, and the right to work freely, in exchange for which foreigners were obliged to avoid "disrupting the general peace by taking part in provocative demonstrations or by transporting the political struggles and conflicts of their country onto our territory." In the eyes of French officials, refugees and apatrides were no different from other immigrants in terms of how they should behave: "To political refugees, [we offer] the asylum that our country has always been honored to give to victims of oppressive regimes provided that they observe our laws, do not disrupt public life, and do not compromise our interests."[72]

If the immigrant refused to follow these rules, the state reserved the right to expel him or her.[73] In the interwar years, French officials were particularly nervous about revolutionary activities. Thus, any immigrant accused of anarchist or communist activity could be expelled. Because the only existing Armenian national entity was based inside the Soviet Union, the refugees were assumed to have strong pro-Soviet sympathies and as a result were watched closely by the police. In 1925, for example, four Armenian students were arrested and expelled for having founded a communist propaganda organization whose goal was "to promote communist ideas among Armenian workers in France." In justifying the expulsions, government officials noted the importance of "ridding French territory of undesirable elements suspected of spreading propaganda or of offending common law [droit commun]."[74] In this case, the four suspects were well-known communists in whose homes the police found incriminating propaganda.

Many immigrants, however, were expelled for lesser crimes. Indeed, once having served time in prison for any reason, a foreigner could be expelled. Thus, vagabondage, minor theft, or disruption of the peace could—and often did— lead to expulsion.[75] In one case, for example, an Armenian woman was arrested for fighting with her Armenian neighbor and subsequently expelled. Similarly, in November 1926, Minas Keusseian, a laborer living in France since 1924, was arrested for vagabondage and subsequently imprisoned and ordered to be expelled. Others were sent on their way for as small a misdemeanor as having migrated to France under a false name or even for reasons they themselves did not understand.[76]

In most cases, however, the apatride caused unexpected problems for a government committed to using expulsion as a central means of policing its foreign minorities. Generally, the authorities carried out expulsions by transporting the criminals in question to the border of their country of origin and handing them over to the border police there.[77] Immigrants who did not come from a surrounding state were transported to a bordering country, and officials there, theoretically at least, would give the immigrant safe passage to his or her country.[78] The apatride, however, had nowhere to go. Stateless and without resources, many apatrides pleaded for clemency. In cases where the government denied such appeals, the apatrides often went into hiding. In 1926, for example, Youghaper Kotchoglonian, a mother of two who had been living in a refugee camp for over three years, was caught stealing coal. Although she had no previous record and served six months in prison for her crime, the Ministry of the Interior ignored numerous pleas on her behalf and ordered her expulsion. Appeals and rejections of such appeals went back and forth for many years, but Kotchoglonian was unable to normalize her situation. Rather than leave the country as ordered, she left the refugee camp and went to live illegally with one of her sons in Paris. Although French authorities never gave her clemency, they also never pursued the case, allowing her to remain indefinitely. Similarly, authorities searched for Keusseian for three weeks but ultimately gave up.[79]

In such cases, the apatride often remained in France, living in hiding without official working papers or access to social services. According to the law, any foreigner who refused to leave or who returned from an expulsion without authorization could be imprisoned for one to six months, after which he or she would be reexpelled. One newspaper article commented in response to such cases: "These guests that we have welcomed and lodged presently find themselves in a situation with no escape. Indeed, if they commit the slightest misdemeanor—even by accident—they are automatically expelled. But hardly have they put a foot on the soil of a neighboring country when the authorities of that country, after having left [the refugees] to rot in prison for some time just on principle, drive them back to France. There, as they are found in violation of the order that had [originally] expelled them, they are reconvicted, expelled, and so it goes until they have been driven to despair or suicide."[80]

Indeed, in certain cases, expelled apatrides resorted to drastic measures. In 1929, the Armenian paper Le Foyer reported that Antranik Krikorian drowned himself because of an expulsion order. Despite such reports, however, the numbers of expelled Armenians never rose higher than several hundred.[81] French officials relied more heavily on expulsion as a means to police foreigners as the 1920s progressed, yet the number of Armenians expelled still remained small. From February 1925 until December 1929, approximately 34,300 foreigners were ordered to leave French territory. Of these, approximately 370 (or just over 1 percent) were Armenian.[82] The figure is small, but the size should not discount the impact of expulsions on the individuals themselves and on their surrounding community. Having already survived numerous deportations and state-sponsored exiles, the Armenian refugees regarded the possibility of expulsion with great trepidation. As one newspaper editorialized, "Expulsion measures toward Russian and Armenian refugees are so tragic that those who are struck by one are lost forever."[83] Anxious to build stable lives in their new homes, refugees viewed expulsions, no matter how few and far between, as a reminder of their precarious position in the state.

From the perspective of the state, however, expulsion policies for the apatrides, although almost impossible to enforce, remained the main punishment for transgressors of the law. Indeed, even after the French government began officially recognizing the special status of such foreigners in the aforementioned international conventions—the second of which included a recommendation that no expulsion should be ordered in the case of Russian and Armenian refugees—members of both populations were still occasionally expelled. In 1930, for example, an official at the Ministry of the Interior assured the prefect in Marseille that the League of Nations' propositions were "only recommendations" and that Armenian refugees could still be expelled after a careful examination of the case against them.[84]

Thus, throughout the 1920s, as incoming refugees raised new questions for national immigration officials seeking to settle the large foreign presence in their midst, the French government shifted between policies that recognized their distinctiveness and those that lumped them together with all other foreign migrants; between those that viewed their statelessness as a quality that would facilitate their integration and those that viewed their statelessness as a particularly dangerous threat. Such contradictory policies continued to dictate the state's response to incoming refugees in the crisis-ridden 1930s, as rising numbers of asylum seekers fled crises in Spain, Germany, and further east. Interestingly, however, while attitudes toward later waves of refugees—particularly Jews—fluctuated widely in the 1930s between those who favored more open-door policies and hard-liners who sought to protect France from foreign influence, policies toward earlier waves of apatrides stabilized considerably.[85] Indeed, by the end of the decade, those holding Nansen passports benefited from unabashedly assimilationist policies that sought to bind this initial wave of refugees all the more closely to their adopted land.

The Enemy from Within: Refugees in 1930s France

The 1930s was a traumatic decade for France. On a national level, a crippling economic crisis in the early part of the decade turned into the longest and deepest economic crisis in national history. In 1932, for example, production fell 27 percent and over a quarter of a million people were unemployed. This economic decline was coupled with internal political instability as ministries fell in rapid succession and as Nazism took root in neighboring Germany. In this tense atmosphere, France's large foreign population soon began bearing the brunt of national fears. Although some of these foreign workers left as the economic crisis developed, any decrease was offset by the arrival of new eastern and central European refugees, many of whom were Jewish. These new refugees were often viewed as a threat to national interests. Most obviously, they seemed to threaten the already unstable national labor market. In addition, rising xenophobic sentiment suggested that the newcomers would endanger French culture, already weakened by millions of immigrants. Moreover, the refugees were seen as a political threat, as, most often, they were fleeing countries that France hoped not to antagonize. In response to these fears, a virulent xenophobia began to develop, which linked

France's international weakness, its economic decline, and its political disorder to the involvement of foreigners, particularly Jews, in French society.[86]

Refugee policies reflected these concerns. Fluctuating throughout the 1930s, such policies indicated officials' desire to reduce the numbers of incoming refugees while still bolstering the country economically and militarily. Thus, while still receiving more refugees than any other European country, the government's immigration bureaucracy began working to keep numbers down, particularly during the antirefugee crackdowns in 1934–35, when officials turned back some refugees, refused entry to others, and expelled those who entered illegally. Under the socialist-led Popular Front that came to power in 1936, the situation eased somewhat, leading to the overturning of some of the harshest antirefugee policies of the previous years. The collapse of the Popular Front in 1938, however, brought a new refugee crisis. As increasing numbers of Jews and Spaniards sought asylum, government officials, wedded to a policy of appeasement, grew to believe that "the refugees, together with their alleged communist allies, were seeking to drag France into war against Hitler merely to satisfy their personal lust for revenge."[87]

In this environment, an increasingly vocal distrust of the apatride took shape. "It must be feared," warned the head of national security in 1938, "that some number among those foreigners claiming to have lost the diplomatic protection of the consulate of their country of origin [are] agents of foreign powers." Similarly, the Minister of the Interior reminded the various prefectures that because of the country's liberal refugee policies, foreigners from various countries would flock to France pretending to be apatrides or political refugees. In light of such threats, he stressed that every attempt should be made to find another nation willing to take those expelled from France.[88] Thus, as the nation moved toward war, the allegiances of any individual not linked with some recognized state became increasingly suspect, and fear of foreigners, particularly those with questionable loyalties, grew all the stronger.

Interestingly, however, if distrust of refugees' political loyalties was voiced repeatedly in official circles, governmental policies demonstrated an ever-growing willingness to actively incorporate into the polity those holding Nansen passports.[89] As early as 1933, as officials began narrowing the eligibility criteria for refugee status, they made exceptions for stateless persons who had already been granted the Nansen passport.[90] Expulsion policies provide another case in point: Russian and Armenian apatrides continued to face the threat of expulsion throughout the 1930s, and the numbers of those suffering such a punishment even grew considerably in the antirefugee atmosphere of late 1934, when the government sought to reduce the entire foreign population. By 1935 the new Minister of the Interior, Joseph Paganon, began to realize the hopeless situation in which most refugees found themselves. Unable to return to their country of origin, many languished in prison, either unable to regularize their position or to attain visas to any other destination. As a result, Paganon issued two circulars that exempted apatrides and refugees from arbitrary expulsions, insisting that only his office could pronounce an expulsion of an apatride and only in extremely serious criminal cases or when the accused had acted against national security or the interests of the state. Thus, at the very moment when foreign populations of all kinds, particularly Jewish refugees from eastern Europe, whom the Sûreté Nationale refused to recognize as stateless, saw their expulsion numbers increase for the most minor offenses, Armenians, Russians, and other formally recognized apatrides found themselves protected.

Even more important, however, was the government's decision in early 1936 to ratify the League of Nations' Convention of October 28, 1933 regarding Nansen refugees. The rights protected by this convention—including far-reaching social benefits, the right to attend French educational institutions, the provision of international travel documentation, and an agreement not to apply expulsion orders to refugees who were authorized to reside legally in the country (barring any action on their part against national security or the public order)—gave Nansen refugees a legal status almost equal to that of French citizens. Moreover, in 1937, desire to increase military recruitments led to new provisions designed to incorporate Nansen refugees into the French military. While other refugee groups—particularly Jews from Germany who had already been settled in France for several decades—also benefited from more inclusive policies that recognized their difficult situation, Jewish refugees continued to face conflicting and contradictory policies throughout the remainder of the decade. Those holding Nansen passports, in contrast, continued to benefit from the more inclusive policies that, from 1936 forward, sought to integrate them into the French polity militarily, economically, and educationally.[91]

Such policy shifts should not suggest that Armenians entirely escaped the anti-immigrant attitudes so prevalent during the period. Many lost their job during the depression as foreign workers were let go to protect the native-born. Indeed, for many French, Armenians were an indistinguishable addition to the mix of peoples they blamed for overcrowded cities, job competition, and the general degeneration of French culture.[92] Others saw them as part of the larger refugee problem. In such cases, antiapatride sentiment became entangled with rising antisemitism, as commentators conflated Jews and Armenians. In an article labeling Armenians "dirtier and less adaptable than others," for example, the right-wing journalist Lucien Rebatet compared Armenians with Jews: "[They share] the same aptitudes, the same absence of an attachment to any territory (all left without any thought of returning), the same promiscuity in the ghettos, where they seem crushed, where the same pogroms decimated them, and from where they suddenly emerged just as cliquish and as congested as they had been previously. The Armenian is, with the Jew, the same type of foreigner [métèque-type]. The only differences are: [the Armenian] is more deceitful; he does not have the feverish vitality of the Semite. Further, having recently come to the West, he is not yet concerned with politics." Blaming the Armenians for their own massacres, Rebatet accused them of being dirty beggars who polluted the streets of Paris.[93]

More interesting, however, were the cases where commentators made special exceptions for Armenians. Indeed, as apatrides became increasingly suspect, some advocates for the Armenians stressed how their stateless nature made them a particularly *welcome* addition to the French polity. In 1930, prior to the new wave of antirefugee sentiment, there were already examples of such rhetoric. A three-part article on Armenians in Marseille, for example, described the local population in the following terms: " 'All men have two fatherlands: their own and France.' The fifteen thousand Armenians who live in Marseille find that this aphorism is no longer true for them. They only have one fatherland, they say, France. Their own has ceased to exist for them." The series concluded by arguing that France should not regret having granted asylum "to this hereditarily unhappy people. This heredity can fade away and open for the Armenians, future French citizens, an era of happiness and prosperity."[94]

Such a defense of France's Armenian population may not seem particularly out of place in 1930, when the most virulent xenophobia had yet to take root. More interesting, however, are those defenses that came in the middle of the decade as unemployment and economic upheaval caused an increasing hostility toward foreign populations. A 1936 article in Le Petit Journal, for example, insisted that giving refuge to Armenians had been a correct and worthy decision. The Armenians, noted the article, "work quietly, without our having to take care of them. . . . far from giving way to despair, which would certainly be understandable when we know the sum of the misfortunes that have fallen upon them, [the Armenians of France] work and hope. In 1936, these are great virtues." Similarly, Camille Mauclaire, the well-known anti-immigrant art critic, defended Armenians to the French public: "It is with chagrin and indignation that I recently saw an Armenian colony in Valence—maintaining itself, just as perfectly as the Spanish Reds maintain themselves dishonestly—referred to as 'unemployed foreigners.' Unemployed? Perhaps out of necessity. But 'foreigners'? They are protégés, and only this name suits them. We should never confuse them with other suspect individuals, undesirables who invade us and who with the sinister manipulations of the communists can become auxiliaries of social upheaval. Among the Armenian refugees in France, we will find in times of danger only loyal soldiers. And it is urgent to grant them a special status, for they are ours."[95]

Mauclair's defense of Valence's Armenian population is particularly interesting given his general disgust with foreigners and particularly Jews. As a contributor to the populist paper L'Ami du peuple, Mauclair regularly denounced the foreign influences eating away at French culture. "One really does not have to be xenophobic," he wrote in an attack on German Jewish art dealers and critics in Paris, "to feel concern at the growing number of métèques who, brandishing a naturalization certificate whose ink is scarcely dry, install themselves in France to judge our artists without an intimate sense of our race."[96] Armenians, however, were not really foreigners. Rather, Mauclair argued, they were in a special category and should be treated as such. In their case statelessness was an asset, because they would prove a dependable and loyal addition to the polity.

Such views are particularly striking on the eve of World War II, when Jewish refugees were often distrusted precisely because of what was perceived as their cross-national affiliations. Whereas Armenian refugees were viewed as stateless, Jewish refugees, particularly those from Germany, were distrusted as alien spies. Thus, French xenophobia was not monolithic. By the mid-1930s, Jews occupied a particular place both symbolically and materially in the surrounding society. Although most of the anti-Jewish campaigns were directed at the foreign-born, they often spread to include all Jews, French-born or not. Thus, campaigns against Jews were not merely expressions of general xenophobia.[97] One scholar has argued that by the late 1930s Jews and refugees had become synonymous (both sharing an entirely negative connotation) in the public imagination, yet it is clear that Armenian refugees who had arrived prior to the major antirefugee wave were, at times, able to escape such antagonism.[98]

Certainly the xenophobia of the 1930s and the racial distinctions that eventually "justified" legal sanctions against Jews polluted the environment for other immigrant groups as well. Once war broke out, the policing of nonnatives increased tenfold as local prefectures watched noncitizens closely for the smallest signs of "disloyalty." If immigrants participated in any anti-French propaganda, associated with the wrong types of people, traveled too often, or "did not observe the neutrality imposed on all foreigners," they could be legally interned or deported.[99]

Antiforeigner sentiment flourished even more after France's collapse in May and June 1940, when three-fifths of the country came under German occupation. As part of the armistice agreement, a new regime run by Marshal Pétain and temporarily located in the resort town of Vichy administered the unoccupied regions of the country. This new government's program—authoritarian, traditionalist, and pious in form—adopted an officially neutral position in regard to the war between Germany and the Allies. Its policies capitalized on the anti-Jewish and anti-immigrant sentiment of the 1930s, allowing for the active persecution of both over the next four years.[100] Thus, after the Pétainist government had fully established itself, articles condemning the impact of immigrants on French society appeared ever more frequently in the national press. In this environment it is not surprising that Armenians also came under attack. In October 1942 for example, Le Matin, a prominent daily newspaper, accused Armenians of actively participating in the black market along with Jews, Turks, and "bad Frenchmen." Similarly, in August 1943, a diatribe against immigrants published in Echo des étudiants argued that government immigration policies should prevent newcomers and their descendants from living in dense collectivities; otherwise, "turbulent and sometimes irredentist minorities" could work against France's interests and in favor of their compatriots elsewhere. Cases where collective living had negatively influenced the population could be documented, the author continued, by looking at the example of Armenians: "Isolated, they are hard-working, capable artisans who do not exploit their clients, although they are after a profit. In contrast, concentrated in colonies of many hundreds or thousands . . . they stand out with their swindling and for their serious engagement in the black market."[101] In this and other articles, Armenians were portrayed as a perfect example of the foreign threat. Whether Armenian, Polish, or Jewish, the nonnative population posed a menace to the surrounding society.

In this atmosphere, the work of race scientists and immigration theorists began moving further into the mainstream. Immigrants were soon being viewed not simply as a drain on the national economy but as a threat to the French nation and "race." In 1942, for example, an article entitled "Race et nation," published in the journal Illustration, argued that interwar integrationist policies had failed and that large unassimilable foreign groups were seeking to dominate and transform French society. These millions of immigrants had been gallicized only superficially, argued the author, and were "incapable of feeling and thinking as those of the French race." Refugees were particularly corrupting, having been chased from their own homes because of their distasteful ideas, religious practices, or racial makeup. Having come to France as antagonists and fanatics, they had swelled the ranks of social and revolutionary movements and provided an army of disruptive forces all too willing to participate in strikes or street demonstrations. Warning of the moral and physical contamination of "our race" by those of inferior makeup, signs of which were already evident in literature and the arts, the author suggested that immigrant populations be sent by small groups into the interior of the country, mixed in with the native-born, and kept as far as possible from their own kind.[102]

Interestingly, however, despite criticism of refugees and worry over racial contamination, race scientists and immigration theorists tended to downplay Armenian racial distinctiveness. In the initial debates over blood purity in the late 1920s, just as French scientists and anthropologists began focusing attention on the question of racial types, Nicholas Kossovitch, one of the most prominent anthropologists of blood groups in France (himself a native Serb who moved to Paris after World War I and obtained a position at the Pasteur Institute), published a study of Armenian refugees in Paris. By examining 380 Parisian Armenian refugees from Turkey, Persia, and the Caucasus, he attempted to determine if blood groups could be related to other anthropometrical characteristics. His study provided basic information on the physical characteristics of the "Armenian race," such as height, skin color, head size, and eye color, although from this information he concluded that Armenians did not constitute one homogeneous race.[103] Nevertheless, he categorized them in a biochemical index that his teacher, Ludwik Hirszfeld, had created for categorizing and ranking the different blood groups. In the 1930s, as immigration theorists began seeking a more "rational" basis for selecting and controlling the influx of foreigners into France, they relied on Kossovitch's work, with its biochemical index as proof that certain types of blood would lower France's racial index.

It is significant for our understanding of the Armenian position in France in this period, however, to note that for two of the most important race and immigration theorists, René Martial and Georges Montandon, Armenians ranked much higher when compared to other non-French minorities. Martial, whose respected position as a specialist in public health provided him with a wide audience for his work, taught a course on immigration at the Institut d'hygiène of the École de médecine and wrote numerous books and articles in which he stressed the central role race should play in the selection process for new immigrants. Most interesting is the hard-line attitude that Martial adopted toward France's apatride population. Like other immigration theorists of the day, Martial questioned refugees' loyalty and ability to assimilate and called for their immediate expulsion. Interestingly however, he made a special exception for Armenians. After some prominent Armenians took issue with Martial's antiapatride position, he explained that he never meant to collapse Armenians into the category of apatride: "The Armenians have a homeland [patrie] — of which we all know the venerable antiquity — and are ardent patriots. Yet it seems that the League of Nations categorized them with those who have no state. The diplomats know nothing of the question of races; this is regrettable but this is not the case with me, and I would never confuse the Armenians with the man who does not have, or no longer has, or never had, or does not even want to have a homeland [i.e., the Jews]."[104]

Like Martial, Georges Montandon, a professor of ethnology at the École d'Anthropologie de Paris, also believed that Armenian racial stock put them in a higher category than other groups. Montandon's work, in May 1943, won him the editorship of the journal La Question juive, the official journal of the Commissariat général aux questions juives, the agency established by the Vichy government to coordinate all anti-Jewish programs in France. In this position as well as through his directorship of the Institut d'études des questions juives (IEQJ), Montandon made it clear that he was no fan of racial mixing. Indeed, he believed that the ethnoracial makeup of France's foreign population was central to national interests, particularly when considering questions of intermarriage. He did not, however, believe in categorically rejecting all non-Europeans as non-Aryans. In particular, he focused on the Armenians, whose "Aryan" language, Christian heritage, and low level of "negrification" required a more complex assessment. Although not ready to label them all Aryans, Montandon encouraged the adoption of German racial hierarchies that assessed Armenians on a case-by-case basis.[105] For him, as for Martial, Armenians' Christianity as well as their Indo-European language placed some of them in a higher racial category.

This conflation of religion and culture with scientific discourses of biological properties characterized most of the discussions of late nineteenth- and early twentieth-century race scientists.[106] Similarly, economic status and political inclinations were often used to prove the racial superiority of one group over another. In a summer 1942 article, the newspaper Appel, for example, attacked Jews who had "baptized themselves Armenian" so as to reenter auction houses (Hôtel des Ventes) from which they had been banished. However, after receiving numerous letters complaining that the article treated France's Armenian population unfairly, Appel's editors published a formal apology: "We never meant to attack the Armenians, whose age-old friendship as well as their heroism under our flag is well known to us." The paper then reminded its readers of the Armenians' love for French culture and of the thousands who had mobilized for the short-lived war against Germany, two thousand of whom remained in captivity. As further evidence of the positive Armenian contributions to French society, *Appel* indicated that Marshal Pétain had accorded them his personal protection.[107]

It is curious to a contemporary eye just how easily Armenians escaped the harsh criticisms to which Jews were subjected during the same period. Indeed, while antiforeign sentiment among the wider French population—unlikely to distinguish between one immigrant and another—certainly influenced how Armenians experienced the 1930s and early 1940s, we cannot dismiss the fact that the most influential racial theorists of the day, as well as the head of state, Marshal Pétain, sought to exclude Armenians from the general antiforeign bias they otherwise promoted. This is particularly curious given that, superficially at least, Armenians were the segment of the foreign population that *most* resembled Jews. As stateless refugees, they had no homeland to which to return, despite Martial's arguments to the contrary. Moreover, the "homeland" they did claim was located in the Soviet Union, hardly an ally to the German-friendly Vichy regime after 1941. Like Jewish immigrants, Armenians had congregated in cities and in artisanal trades, often rejecting attempts to move them away from their compatriots or into agricultural professions. Most ironically, they stood out physically, many exhibiting characteristics that had been ascribed to Jews by the prominent racial thinkers of the day.[108]

Why, then, were Armenians exempted from the criticisms leveled at Jews? Did their Christianity make them less offensive to their French hosts? This is certainly possible, although the traditional Armenian religious rite, practiced in an ancient dialect and rich with customs that Western Christianity viewed as superstitious, would certainly have proven as foreign to the French as the traditional rites of the Jewish immigrants. Moreover, as has been well documented, the antisemitic sentiment of the World War II era was considerably more complex than simply a rejection of Judaism. Is it possible that two decades of the argument put forth by Armenians themselves—that they were the most loyal of minorities, a trope they adopted to defend themselves against attacks of those fearful of their statelessness—had influenced French political and intellectual leaders? Such an explanation rings hollow when we remember the much longer tradition among acculturated French Jews of pledging loyalty to their native land.[109] Perhaps, then, Armenians were viewed less antagonistically by virtue of their statelessness— their lack of a national affiliation making them seem less threatening than later refugees, who often had lost diplomatic protection but were not necessarily stateless. Such an explanation is compelling, because there is no doubt that German Jews, many of whom still had passports, at times seemed to French national security officials to pose a military threat. And yet, many eastern European Jews who came to France during the 1930s had also been rendered stateless, yet, if anything, faced harsher refugee policies than their German coreligionists.

The Armenian exemption from racial stereotyping can be explained by considering the nature of racism in Western societies itself. Beginning in the mid-nineteenth century, Jews became Europe's enemy from within. Having accepted the liberal promise that they could participate fully in their surrounding societies if they adopted the rules that defined those societies, Western Jews fought for and then took full advantage of the emancipation awarded them throughout the nineteenth century. The more they tried to integrate, however, the more they encountered hostility and rejection. In France, such hostility was evident in the Dreyfus Affair at the turn of the century and even more violently throughout the 1930s and during the Vichy regime. In his analysis of Jewish self-hatred, Sander Gilman has defined this relationship of western European Jews to the states in which they lived as one in which the "Other" negotiates a place within a society. "On the one hand," writes Gilman, "is the liberal fantasy that anyone is welcome to share in the power of the reference group if he abides by the rules that define that group. . . . On the other hand is the hidden qualification of the internalized reference group, the conservative curse: The more you are like me, the more I know the true value of my power, which you wish to share, and the more I am aware that you are but a shoddy counterfeit, an outsider."[110]

According to this model, a clear difference arises between the Jewish and Armenian populations in France. Whereas there had been a significant Jewish presence in France for well over a century, Armenians were truly outsiders. Or, to put it another way, Jews were France's internal outsider, the "other" against which society defined itself, whereas Armenians were clearly not part of the host society but an oppressed minority group from another society (in which they had been the internal "other") who deserved sympathy and aid. Although immigrant Jews were new arrivals in much the way Armenians were, perceptions of them were influenced by a longer tradition of French antisemitism that shaped discourses against all Jews, whether of native or immigrant origin. Indeed, what is particularly interesting about the antisemitism of the 1930s and 1940s was its tendency to blur the lines between native and immigrant Jew, hence marking the anti-Jewish rhetoric as distinct from other xenophobic movements of the day.[111]

Yet if hindsight shows that Armenians had little to fear from the xenophobia of the 1930s, life "on the ground" was undoubtedly quite different. Facing little threat from policymakers, Armenian refugees were nevertheless surrounded by an antiforeign, antirefugee rhetoric. Such rhetoric was particularly disconcerting because of Armenians' recent past of deportation and genocide, during which they had been viewed as pariahs in their own society. Thus, whatever the real threat, Armenians in France viewed the rising tide of xenophobia with great alarm. For them, antirefugee sentiment was an indictment of their position in society; hence, they believed they occupied a tenuous place in their adopted home. Throughout the first decades of their life in France, they thus came to understand their position as that of uprooted, stateless wanderers, and this understanding shaped how they integrated into the wider society.

The genocidal attack against Armenians during World War I was an attack on their juridical existence. By stripping survivors of residency rights, the Young Turks removed their victims not only from their regions of birth but from the international community, constituted increasingly around national lines. In migrating to France survivors sought, among other things, to regularize their anomalous status. Initially, however, French authorities proved unable to distinguish them from the mass of foreigners arriving during the same years. Indeed, policies toward them were rarely, if ever, based on humanitarian concerns over their recent past. Rather, such policies were shaped by two contradictory impulses: the first sought to integrate a population whose loyalties were potentially malleable; the second sought to police a group whose allegiances were unidentifiable. Over time, however, it was the former approach that prevailed, as international agreements provided Nansen passport holders with a juridically recognizable position and as French officials continued to pursue strategies designed to transform immigrant minorities into French nationals. Indeed, even in the 1930s, when hard-liners began backing exclusionist policies designed to marginalize the most recent immigrant and refugee populations to France, Nansen refugees were increasingly integrated into the state's welfare, military, and economic structures.

A similar stress on integration is evident in the post–World War II policies toward Jewish Holocaust survivors. Although the two populations had different relationships to the French state, Armenians as refugees from a foreign oppressor and Jews as victims of a previous French regime, both had been stripped of their juridical rights and cast outside the nation-state system. Although French authorities certainly did not have Armenians in mind as they created policies for the reintegration of Jewish survivors after World War II, once again France's long tradition of political and cultural integration influenced how authorities addressed the problems posed by Jewish reintegration. In both cases, such models profoundly influenced how survivors came to terms with their minority status in the aftermath of their respective genocides.

2 The Strange Silence: France, French Jews, and
the Return to Republican Order

Although World War II proved traumatizing for the stateless Armenian refugees who had arrived in France in the previous decade and a half, the years of German and Vichy rule proved far more devastating for local Jewish populations. As has been well documented, during World War II the Vichy government actively collaborated with the Nazi occupiers to implement its own program of anti-Jewish legislation—a set of policies that ultimately led to the deportation and murder of a quarter of the French Jewish population. Thus, unlike Armenians who arrived in France stripped of their civil and juridical status by a foreign power, Jews in France, by and large, reconstructed their communities on the land in which they had been persecuted.

There were dramatic differences in the genocide histories under consideration, yet there were also remarkable similarities to the situations both minority populations faced in France in the decades following their respective genocides. Indeed, despite the gap of over twenty years and the dramatic shift in political regimes over the period, those Jews who survived World War II in France, like the Armenians who had come previously, found themselves face-to-face with a well-entrenched political tradition of cultural integration that survived the Vichy era and returned strengthened after the upheaval of the previous years. Thus, the country's long tradition of political and cultural integration, which so influenced how authorities addressed Armenian integration after World War I, also shaped how officials addressed the problems posed by Jewish reintegration after World War II. Indeed, if any lesson seemed to emerge from the years that the Vichy regime singled out and persecuted local Jewish populations, it was that earlier models of state-sponsored integration were the *only* viable means through which the state should interact with its ethnic and religious minorities. As chapter 3 documents, such assimilationist models of incorporating ethnic and religious minorities into the state profoundly influenced how both Armenian and Jewish communities integrated into it, ultimately shaping their resettlement options and ethnic expression.

Reintegrating the Jewish population in the postwar era depended first and foremost on restoring the citizenship and civil liberties of those who had been stripped of them in the early years of the conflict. Indeed, long before liberation, on 12 November 1943, the government in exile agreed to eliminate all racial distinctions as soon as the French Free Forces retook the country. The postliberation government kept this promise, and on 9 August 1944, after General de Gaulle's forces retook Paris from the Germans and brought an end to the Vichy regime, the Jews of France were immediately freed from the four years of state-sponsored discrimination. Once again equal citizens, they were able to participate freely and openly in their society. Further anti-Jewish measures were henceforth illegal: government officials no longer confiscated Jewish homes and businesses and the yellow star no longer distinguished Jews from the rest of the population.

Moreover, as news of the death camps became more well-known, blatant antisemitism and xenophobia were generally suppressed. Hostility still surfaced in regions where housing shortages were particularly acute after former Jewish residents returned to reclaim the homes from which they had been evicted or fled. However, what is most striking about the immediate postwar years is the *absence* of Jews from public discourse. Indeed, "a strange silence" suddenly surrounded the entire Jewish Question.[1] Although occasional newspaper articles documented the horrors of the gas chambers, journalists, social commentators, and even Jews themselves seemed reluctant to isolate their experiences from those of the rest of French society.[2] Government officials in particular, anxious to reestablish republican rule, were hesitant to call attention to Jewish losses during the war. To do so would mean once again singling Jews out as a distinct group in the population, and French officials were seeking to do just the opposite, that is, to erase the category "Jew" that had been erected by Vichy and the German occupiers.

This unwillingness to recognize the particularities of the Jewish experience during World War II interfered with all other efforts to reintegrate French Jews after the conflict. Most significant, authorities were called on to provide Jews with an economic base to ensure their successful return to society. A vital stage in the exclusion of French Jews from national life during World War II had come from laws depriving them of their means of subsistence. By "Aryanizing" the economy, first the Germans and then the Vichy authorities—who wished to prevent the Germans from confiscating Jewish assets and hence taking their wealth out of France—drove Jews from French economic life.[3] Thus, returning civil rights to those from whom they had been stripped could not in and of itself ensure the successful reintegration of France's Jewish population. Government authorities would also have to write legislation that would recognize the specificity of their suffering and restitute them for their losses. These same officials, however, were anxious to return to the previously established relationship between Jewish citizens and the state, a relationship that since the Revolution had conceived of Jews "in terms of the individual, in terms of the private person."[4] This contradiction in governmental goals—on the one hand de-emphasizing Jewish particularity, on the other recognizing their losses—interfered with the conceptualization and implementation of coherent restitution legislation.

Five policy areas affected the reconstruction of Jewish life in postwar France: the restoration of their rights and the suppression of racial distinctions; the return and reintegration of surviving deportees; the establishment of welfare and relief activities; the return of confiscated and stolen property; and the punishment of those functionaries, administrateurs provisoires, and others who profited illegally as they carried out Vichy's anti-Jewish laws. As we have seen, few juridical or practical problems prevented government officials from eliminating discriminatory statutes or returning full civil rights to all French Jews. In all other areas, however, government officials immediately faced controversies that placed returning Jews against other French citizens who also claimed to have suffered greatly during World War II. For example, thousands of Jewish enterprises had been sold to non-Jews during the war, most of whom were disinclined to return their newly acquired property.[5] Government restitution policies had to determine if the contested property belonged to the new buyer, or if the original owner had a legitimate claim given that he or she had not agreed to the sale. And what if the original owner had agreed to the sale as a means to protect his or her property while in hiding? Did he or she have the same rights as the Jewish owner whose property was sold without consent? Similarly, restitution policies had to address cases where the claim by a French Jew would displace another war victim, as in the numerous cases where a French family who had lost its own apartment as a result of a bombing or another war-related disaster had moved into an apartment previously occupied by a Jew.

Even when considering a relatively simple question, such as how long to wait before declaring the property of deported Jews "unclaimed," the provisional government faced controversy. In such cases, officials had to determine whether the Vichy-appointed administrateur provisoire should continue managing the property. During the war, the Vichy administration and the German occupation government had named nearly eight thousand administrateurs provisoires as trustees of Jewish property. Their role was to take control of Jewish enterprises and force their sale to "Aryan" owners. If the sale was impossible or likely to be unsuccessful, the administrateur saw to its liquidation. By 1 May 1944, 42,227 businesses had been placed under such trusteeship.[6] Hence, these eight thousand administrateurs had participated in the implementation of German and Vichy anti-Jewish policies and many had profited as a result. Postwar policies regarding these functionaries had to consider if they were criminals simply by virtue of their compliance with Vichy laws, or if they were the unsung heroes of the war who had protected their "clients" as best they could given German pressure and Vichy anti-Jewish legislation.

These are but a few of the quandaries the provisional government was left to untangle in the years following Vichy's demise. Moreover, reintegrating Jews was not the highest on the government's list of priorities given the chaos that the country faced as it rebuilt from four years of war and occupation. Influenced by conflicting claims and interested in settling matters as quickly as possible, governmental authorities wrote restitution policies that de-emphasized particularities in the population. By considering all who had suffered as "equivalent victims" of the war's upheaval, the new legislation rarely had the needs of despoiled Jews at heart. As will become clear, such policies did not necessarily result from a latent antisemitism still hovering in governmental circles after the war. True, anti-Jewish sentiment had not entirely disappeared from society at large. Moreover, certain Vichy officials still held administrative positions in the postwar government and in some cases attempted to interfere with Jewish reintegration. In most instances, however, officials were sympathetic to the plight of Jewish citizens.[7] Nor can the formation of restitution policies be attributed to pandering to right-wing pressure groups, as one scholar has suggested, an analysis that overemphasizes the size and impact of such groups.[8] Rather, as in the case of Armenian genocide survivors whose specific plight remained invisible to policy shapers intent on integrating the large foreign and refugee populations as rapidly as possible, a long tradition of political integration shaped the provisional government's relationship to France's postwar Jewish minority.[9] In this case, a firm commitment to restoring republican order and prewar stability as well as a desire to distance the postwar regime from the Vichy past encouraged officials to back away from any legislative initiatives that singled out particular groups in the population. Maintaining legal distinctions, even for compensatory purposes, seemed incompatible with the basic principles of republican justice. De Gaulle and his followers, actively seeking to distance themselves from the recent past, thus adopted a rhetoric that stressed French unity above all else.[10] Focusing on the particularity of Jewish suffering could only detract from this goal. If, however, eliminating racial categories and discrimination was a laudatory aim, the effects were often counterproductive. By refusing to acknowledge the categories established under German and Vichy rule, the provisional government continued to disadvantage returning Jews.

The Postwar Climate

Although German forces occupied eastern France until the end of 1944, the liberation of Paris brought an end to German rule and Vichy collaboration. In the euphoria of victory, French citizens moved rapidly to wipe out the vestiges of the previous five years. Individuals seeking personal or political revenge against Vichyites and collaborators instituted an unofficial *épuration* (purging) of those associated with the Vichy government. Soon after, special courts were established for the sole purpose of carrying out the purges, and within a short time most of the Vichy-era political elite had been removed from positions of power.[11] Similarly interested in erasing the Vichy legacy, de Gaulle and his advisors sought to establish a new government that returned the country to prewar stability. The interregnum government that established itself with the liberation of Paris was thus neither insurrectional nor revolutionary. Rather, it sought to centralize power and to allow for a legal and peaceful reconstruction of the republican state.

Efforts to centralize authority had begun as early as September 1941 in London, Algiers, and within France itself on the assumption that once liberated, a ruling power would be needed to assume direction of the state quickly and peacefully. The Comité français de libération national thus became the Gouvernement provisoire de la République française on 2 June 1944. The new body quickly worked to consolidate its authority by sending commissaires de la République to take over from de facto authorities working to liberate individual regions of the country. According to Jean-Pierre Rioux, these governmental representatives were above all "to safeguard a national consensus which was no longer simply that of the Resistance itself; the Jacobin conception of the State they incarnated was to be a vital counter to the fragmentation of the country. Thus at every level of the hierarchy were appointed men committed to the reconstruction of the machinery of the State in its pre-war forms." Anxious to protect their position in the postwar government, various political parties and resistance groups, including the Communist Party, either fell in behind this effort and behind de Gaulle or were slowly excluded from exercising any influence. Rioux continues: "With its reintroduction of political parties into national life, the emphasis on the continuity of the State and the submission to military goals and government authority, a strong atmosphere of 'Union sacrée' pervades this carefully ordered interregnum."[12]

Over several months, de Gaulle and his appointed officials attempted to address the problems facing France, including the reestablishment of law and order, the formation of a sound and legitimate government, the rebuilding of a devastated economy, and the repatriation of French citizens who had fled or been deported during the conflict. France had emerged from the occupation economically devastated. In the fall of 1944, over a million families had no home. Transportation was at a standstill, as most roads and railways had been destroyed. Energy supplies such as oil and coal were depleted. Industrial production had fallen to 40 percent of the 1938 level. Food was scarce, a black market flourished, and unemployment raged.[13] Immense problems such as these could not be solved quickly. The provisional government could not even begin to tackle some of them until the war had reached a conclusion and the deportees and political prisoners had returned home. Over a year after D-Day, therefore, France still lacked coal, adequate transportation, shelter, and material supplies.[14]

Despite such widespread upheaval, the government immediately took steps to regain control of French society, which included the reintegration of the Jewish population. The ordinance of 9 August 1944 reestablishing republican law expressly nullified all racist measures and discriminatory laws. In principle, this decree provided the legislative basis for dispossessed Jews to recover their possessions and property, and certain policies were immediately enacted. In September 1944, for example, most Jewish bank accounts that the Germans had blocked in 1941 were returned to their rightful owners, providing that there were no third parties involved whose role had to be adjudicated.[15] Similarly, as news of the death camps became more well-known, the blatant xenophobia and antisemitic propaganda that had characterized the previous several years all but disappeared.

Nevertheless, five years of anti-Jewish propaganda had taken its toll. Although there were few public antisemitic attacks in the years immediately following the war, some anti-Jewish hostility still surfaced. This hostility was often rooted in social tensions related to postwar shortages, particularly in the housing market. In the two years following liberation, both Jews and non-Jews faced housing shortages and a depressed economy. Such shortages had induced non-Jewish war victims—those who had lost homes in bombings as well as repatriated prisoners and deportees—to begin to occupy abandoned Jewish apartments.[16]

Having themselves lost family members, property, and homes, these new occupants felt justified in demanding rights to their new apartments. One, for example, pleaded with the government for permission to keep the property she had obtained from a missing Jewish family: "[I have] two cases worthy of interest in my family—a sister, mother of three children of whom the eldest has been a prisoner since 1940 and who has been seriously wounded by the war and a brother who was in a concentration camp for nearly five months and who came out sick, possibly for the rest of his life. [He] has received no financial support [nor has] my sister who upon returning from her exodus found nothing in her home."[17] Such war victims felt their sufferings entitled them to keep their new possessions.

As Jews began returning to their homes and attempted to reclaim their property, anti-Jewish sentiment flared, particularly in regions where the war had been exceptionally devastating, such as Alsace-Lorraine. In Strasbourg, for example, where bombings, administrative confusion, and war pillaging had left nine thousand French families without homes, the prefect complained that the sudden, massive return of three thousand foreign-born Jews was causing widespread resentment among the native population. Most of these Jews had come to Strasbourg just prior to the war and had fled when the Germans conquered the territory. After liberation, they returned to a chilly reception. Though sympathetic to their plight, the prefect considered their presence a burden on the city's French citizens, Jewish and non-Jewish alike: "I try to reconcile all these diverse antagonisms, but I have to pay attention to the discontent that has already taken hold in all parts of the population on this subject of the return of the foreign Jews."[18] Clearly, here, old prejudices against foreign-born Jews remained firmly in place.

This kind of hostility was not limited to Strasbourg. In Paris in April 1945, disputes over housing shortages led five hundred demonstrators to march through the streets crying "Death to the Jews" and "France for the French."[19] Nina Gourfinkel, a Russian Jewish writer who had lived in France since the Russian Revolution, observed of the postwar years that German propaganda had not made the French antisemitic; rather, they had become so in the days after liberation. "The Jews began returning," she wrote. "They were reclaiming their homes, their stores, and even, what impudence, their accounts. Then the provisional owners felt a bitter regret: 'Why didn't they all perish in the ovens!' "[20]

Supporting the efforts of such anti-Jewish agitators was a new network of organizations formed to defend those who had rented or purchased Jewish property during the war. Claiming to be free of antisemitic motivations, these organizations sought only to protect their members' rights against "all Jewish claims of redress."[21] Their pamphlets, however, were often enmeshed with distinctively anti-Jewish subtexts. The Association nationale intercorporative du commerce, de l'industrie et de l'artisanat, for example, argued that all purchases of Jewish property were juridically and economically legitimate. Juridically, these assets had been sold according to a law promulgated by the authority recognized as the de facto French government; the current government was bound to protect the sales even if power had shifted hands. From an economic perspective, the Association argued, those who bought Jewish property protected French interests. By buying property that the Germans threatened to liquidate, the purchasers "preserved a precious inheritance [*patrimoine*] for the national economy." Moreover, by paying taxes on earnings from these businesses and by keeping them in French hands, the buyers prevented the inevitable perturbation that would have been caused had so many Jewish businesses, so important in every area of commerce and industry, fallen into enemy hands. Such actions, the Association contended, prevented widespread postwar unemployment and bolstered the national economy.

The seemingly "objective" nature of this defense was actually peppered with anti-Jewish rhetoric. Not content with simply defending the purchases from a juridical and economic perspective, the Association also asserted that French businessmen were more honest than their Jewish counterparts. The new owners, they insisted, had "filled the state coffers with significant back-taxes not paid by the *Israélites* for many years." Moreover, Jewish businessmen shirked other financial responsibilities: "It is indispensable to eliminate those businessmen who do not respect employer association dues and who pay neither social security nor family allowances." [22] Such anti-Jewish overtones contributed to a postwar discourse that was not particularly racial in nature but that nevertheless distinguished between *juif* and *français*.

Even those citizens who were not overtly antisemitic often made distinctions between their own plight and that of their Jewish compatriots. One non-Jew, for example, whose apartment the Germans had emptied complained to postwar officials that he had been "robbed for no reason" and that he and his family could not return to Paris to an empty apartment. The implication was that Jews had been justifiably robbed or at least that those citizens who had been punished for "no reason" should receive restitution first. In another case in which a company had been "Aryanized" despite the fact that none of its associates was Jewish, the partners complained, "We emphatically insist that we were victims of an act that was absolutely illegal; not even Vichy laws authorized the French administration to take such measures against us without the least proof. These measures, already arbitrary with respect to Jewish businesses, were all the more unjustifiable vis-à-vis a venture that was exclusively Christian, or, to use the racist word, 'Aryan.' "[23] The author of this letter clearly sympathized with those Jews dispossessed by the racial laws of the Vichy years, but he also makes a distinction between those "legally" and those "illegally" persecuted. The World War II environment had thus affected even those who had never actively adopted antisemitic attitudes. By recognizing Vichy as a legally legitimate government, organizations and even "ordinary citizens" pointed to its policies as a basis for supporting their own restitution claims.[24] However unjustly Jews had been treated, other "truly French" citizens had prior claim to access postwar resources because their losses could not be justified *even* by Vichy's standards.

It is not surprising that some of these discriminatory categorizations spilled over into the postwar years. Although the épuration in theory purged the government, the bureaucracy remained largely intact, allowing some Vichy officials to retain their positions. As elsewhere in post-Nazi Europe, the new government "punished the makers and shapers rather than the executors of policy except where underlings had sinned by excess of zeal for the occupying power."[25] In most cases, therefore, civil servants were able to retain their positions, and even in cases where a high civil servant or minister was removed from his post, his vacancy was generally filled from within the already established administrative ranks. Indeed, most of the *grands corps de l'état* were characterized by a surprising continuity from 1939 to 1946, and even those whose activities most strongly enforced state policy, such as the judiciary, diplomatic corps, and prefectural corps, displayed a basic stability.

Certainly the prefectural corps came the closest to undergoing a full purge. Immediately after liberation new prefects took over in all eighty-seven mainland departments, only twenty of whom came from the old corps. Nevertheless, by 1947 many of these newcomers had returned to their former jobs, and those who had come up through the old prefectural corps and who had held junior posts under Vichy held half of the new prefectural positions.[26] Such administrative continuity occasionally caused problems for Jews attempting to reintegrate into French society. For example, Michel F., a Polish-born Jew who had fled to Spain when the Germans occupied the southern zone, complained that he could not obtain a visa to reenter the country because of the police commissioner in Marseille. During the war, the official (who was working for the Toulouse police department at the time) had twice asked F. to inform on fellow Jews. F. had refused, and as a result his visa applications were rejected after the war.[27]

Other returning Jews complained about continuity in the judicial system. Although the judges of Vichy's extralegal courts had been sentenced during the épuration, most of those in the state's ordinary courts survived the worst purges despite having applied Vichy's law for four years. Such continuity created certain legal quandaries. In one instance, a judge who had himself been the purchaser of a Jewish business sat on Limoges's commercial court. For victims, his presence was paradoxical at best, fraudulent at worst.[28]

However, although certain Vichy officials escaped épuration and continued to work in the postwar administration, occasionally using their positions to interfere with Jewish reintegration, such antisemitism was not officially sanctioned by governmental policies, nor was it supported by the majority of the administration. In F.'s case, for example, the president of the county council of the Haute Garonne intervened, arguing that F. deserved pity because he was an *israélite*. Less than a month later, F. and his wife were awarded visas.[29] Indeed, what is striking about the immediate postwar years is that despite occasional anti-Jewish demonstrations and a certain hostility toward those attempting to regain lost property, Jews were eerily absent from public discourse. As a 1945 article for the Jewish Telegraphic Agency commented, "Observers here note a general reluctance in official circles not only to do anything to remove the disabilities against the Jews, but even to discuss them. The attitude seems to be one of desire to smother the whole issue under a blanket of silence, perhaps on the principle that the situation will not exist if it is not acknowledged."[30]

As the article asserted, governmental attempts to ignore a specifically "Jewish" plight were intentional. Indeed, authorities were anxious to remove *all* signs that Jews had ever been considered a legally distinct category of the population. A striking example of this occurred in December 1946, when the Ministry of the Interior instructed departmental prefects to destroy all wartime dossiers and records in which the category "Jew" had been used as a basis for discrimination. Such documents had no place in the French administration, for republican law had been reestablished.[31] Such an order did not arise out of any conscious attempt to destroy the history of Jewish persecution. Indeed, the Ministry of the Interior repeatedly proved itself sympathetic to Jewish concerns and maintained close contacts with prominent members of the French Jewish community.[32] Rather, in this order we see efforts to eliminate discriminatory categories from official documentation and to move toward a prewar conception of the place of minorities in French society. But four years of systematic discrimination could not be erased by simply destroying its paper trail. In a rapid reversal, a month later the Ministry requested that previous orders be ignored so as not to "inconvenience the interested parties themselves." In the new circular, prefectures were requested to keep all documents relating to investigations and arrests "of those persons considered Jews" when those documents would be advantageous to the victims. Nevertheless, the circular noted that in the near future the complete destruction of these archives should be expected.[33]

The Ministry of the Interior was not the only government department to make efforts to eliminate the racial categories established under German occupation and to avoid calling attention to Jews. General de Gaulle, who stood at the head of the provisional government and who set the tone for France's relationship to its Vichy past, was particularly interested in stressing French unity after World War II and in establishing Vichy as an aberration.[34] One component of establishing this "founding myth" of the post-Vichy era was to downplay the suffering of any one group of the population. All French citizens had suffered and society as a whole had to move forward together. Such a perspective inevitably influenced matters of legislation, and that, coupled with the drive to return to republican law and order, dictated that in most policy areas Jews qua Jews were notably absent.[35] Nowhere is this more clear than in government-organized relief activities that generally treated Jews and non-Jews as equivalent victims.

Relief Activities

The enormous economic and political problems facing the provisional government—repatriating refugees, deportees, and political prisoners; creating social welfare programs for those most affected by the war; writing restitution policies for those who had lost their homes and belongings—overextended its abilities to provide comprehensive aid to any one needy group in the population. Jewish war victims found government-sponsored relief efforts particularly inadequate. As citizens, aliens, former soldiers, or returning deportees, they qualified for government aid, but as Jews they qualified for nothing. Many thus had to turn to communal agencies for financial support. The American Joint Distribution Committee (AJDC), an American Jewish relief organization, reported in fall 1944, "There are huge gaps in the assistance program, particularly for needy Jews. Every effort has been made to close those gaps, and to persuade the French government to assume responsibility for basic assistance which we feel is a governmental obligation, but not only have they failed to assist many thousands of Jewish displaced persons, but we have had to maintain many thousands of French nationals as well."[36]

Government programs for returning deportees were indicative of this problem because the provisional government felt no desire to call attention to the specific nature of Jewish deportations. Particularly influenced by the Communist Party—whose strength in the immediate postwar period was unprecedented and which for political reasons focused on those deportees who had suffered for their patriotic acts of resistance rather than those who had been deported for their "racial status" — government officials opted to emphasize the role of French Resistance and heroism during the war rather than the suffering of one specific minority.[37] Given that the number of returning Jewish deportees was infinitesimal when compared to the larger population of war prisoners and French deportees, it was easy for officials and the population at large to overlook the specificity of their plight. Thus, while 37,025 of the original 63,085 French men and women who had been deported returned (59 percent), only 2,500 of the at least 75,721 Jews who had been deported returned (3 percent).[38] This handful of returning Jews received the same aid as other deportees even if the extent of their losses was greater.[39] Thus, all returning deportees, regardless of religion or political affiliation, and provided that they had lived in France prior to deportation, were given a one-time grant of 5,000 francs (later raised to 8,000) as well as a ration book for food, clothing and shoes, free transportation, free medical care for nine months, access to small business loans, a work permit, and other support.[40] Such services were often adequate for returning deportees who had a familial support network to which they could turn. For many Jews, however, such a network was lost with the rest of their homes, jobs, and property.[41]

Nonnaturalized, foreign-born Jews who had lived in France prior to World War II faced a more dire situation, as they were often ineligible for certain relief programs. For example, in the last few months of 1944 the government awarded a military allowance to those French nationals whose family head had been mobilized or deported. Foreigners could benefit from this allowance if they had fought in the French army. Because many foreign-born Jews had been deported on racial grounds and not because they were military personnel, they were ineligible for the military allowance. Similarly, all French families who had been obliged to leave their home as a result of the war or occupation were guaranteed financial aid. Foreigners, however, were granted this allowance only if the authorities had *ordered* them to abandon their home prior to their departure. Because many had fled to avoid Nazi persecutions and hence before receiving "official" orders to do so, they were not compensated for their losses.[42]

Moreover those who *did* qualify for state aid did not always receive the promised sums. As one AJDC official complained, "The policies are for rather broad coverage by category although the amounts given are inadequate. However, in actual practice the agencies just simply fail to give assistance to all who qualify, the reason usually given being lack of funds. I don't think this situation will soon be remedied because of the general confusion in the government and also because the virus of antisemitism has had a real effect here as in all occupied countries."[43]

Despite this official's willingness to attribute government actions to anti-semitism, evidence suggests otherwise.[44] In light of the great demands on the government from all sectors of the population, Jewish losses were relatively insignificant. Relief programs may have proved inadequate for foreign-born Jews and returning deportees, but many surviving French Jews did not fall into either of these two categories.[45] And although many had suffered great losses during the war, they were rarely indigent. When considering the most pressing priorities for the postwar years, the government thus turned elsewhere. Moreover, and perhaps even more important, a commitment to the restoration of republican government and to the removal of all legal distinctions among categories of the population encouraged the formulation of policies that blended Jewish war victims into other, broader categories of the population. Such policies may, in fact, have been based on a "pro-Jewish" sentiment, one that hoped to reintegrate Jews rapidly into French society. Nevertheless, the great reluctance to recognize the specific nature of Jewish losses ultimately slowed this process, particularly in the area of property restitution.

Restitutions

In February 1997, Prime Minister Alain Juppé appointed Jean Mattéoli, a former Resistance worker, deportee, and chairman of the Economic and Social Council, to examine the history of Jewish property confiscation and its return during and after the German military occupation and Vichy regime. A glance at the reports of this commission suggest the complexities facing any researcher interested in the question of postwar restitution. Several years of work and dozens of researchers have only recently produced a complete account of how the various restitution laws were implemented and who benefited from the legislation.[46] The following abbreviated discussion thus cannot begin to cover the scope and complexity of restitution as it was carried out from 1944 forward. Rather, I offer an overview of the restitution legislation and some cases of its implementation as an example of the difficulties that arose as the provisional government came to terms with the legacy it had inherited. As in the case of postwar relief activities, we will see how the return of republicanism and calls for French unity influenced the writing and implementation of laws designed to restitute Jewish losses.

As noted earlier, French liberation forces committed themselves to ending all racial distinctions and to reestablishing republican law even before Paris was liberated. In so doing, they created the legislative basis for dispossessed Jews to recover their possessions and property. The principle was formally tested for the first time as early as July 1944 in the Tunisian courts, when a local Jew claimed that he had been compelled to sell his property because of the Vichy administration's anti-Jewish laws in North Africa. The court's vindication of his claim was welcomed as an important legal precedent. Within a month, however, the commissioner for the liberated areas of France cautioned against easy optimism concerning the restitution of Jewish property. Prophesying that profound irritation and anti-Jewish feeling would be engendered when new purchasers were required to return Jewish property, particularly if their purchases had been legal according to law of the day, his comments reflected what would become the government's cautious approach to property restoration.[47]

Indeed, if from the outset the government displayed its intention to restitute despoiled Jewish property as quickly and entirely as was feasible, officials also realized that simply declaring Vichy's antisemitic statutes null and void would not be enough to erase the consequences of the previous several years. Rather, new legislation would have to be written that took the years of property transfer into consideration. Creating such laws was a long and difficult process, requiring close study of the problems at hand and careful legislative responses. In the meantime, many sectors of the French population—including Jews who had been despoiled during the war, those who had purchased Jewish property at reduced prices, and administrators of Jewish estates—anxiously awaited the settlement of the restitution question. Inevitably it was impossible to satisfy all the conflicting interests and needs of such a diverse set of individuals. Indeed, many officials believed that the rapid creation of simple restitution laws was ill-advised and would lead to "inextricable chaos."[48] As the commissioner of liberated France had predicted in August, influential pressure groups made up of the purchasers of Jewish properties argued that restituting Jewish property would lead to grave societal problems. The Association nationale intercorporative du commerce, de l'industrie et de l'artisanat, for example, claimed that by supporting such restitutions, the government would be favoring one part of the population over another. As the Association explained:

> One can only disapprove of the inhuman persecutions that certain Jews suffered (unfortunately many French resistance fighters suffered them as well) but can one distinguish between the Israélite whose business or industry was sold and the homeless businessman who also often had to mourn the mutilation or death of his family members and who also lost everything: business, merchandise, stock, and furniture? They are both war victims, only in a different way. . . . Because of the hostilities and the four years of German

occupation, France unfortunately lost a part of her wealth. The Israélites lost some of their property and at least that was bought and paid for. The war victims, however, lost everything. The Israélites must, thus, be considered the same as war victims and reparated like them. If we even consider the possibility of returning businesses to the Israélites, it will be impossible to do so equitably.[49]

According to the Association's members, although Jews had suffered, their losses were no less severe than those of other citizens, and by favoring the former, French leaders risked alienating the latter. Similarly, anonymous pamphlets circulated in the streets asking French Jews to have pity on those who had inhabited their homes and purchased their businesses and who had themselves lost so much during the war. "It is easy," noted one, "when you have lived in England or in hiding for the last four years to say, 'one ought to have done this or that.'" Those who had remained in France, however, did the best they could and should be considered victims as well. There can be no "privileged victims," the pamphlet declared: "Accept what is irreparable as other children of France have accepted the damages caused by the war."[50]

Pressure groups such as those that distributed the above propaganda began organizing as early as the end of 1943 to ensure their interests in the event of a German defeat, and although the provisional government disbanded several after liberation, they immediately reorganized under new names. Of course, not every purchaser of Jewish property belonged to one of these pressure groups or accepted their often barely disguised anti-Jewish biases. Indeed, restoring Jewish property might have been easier had it all fallen into clearly collaborationist, antisemitic hands. Unfortunately for the dispossessed Jews, however, restoring their property often meant creating new conflicts among almost every segment of the population, conflicts that government officials hoped to avoid. Therefore, although the National Assembly appointed a commission on 11 October 1944 to draw up equitable restitution regulations, the first two such laws published in early November seemed incomplete and unsatisfactory to many of those who were primarily affected.[51]

In some regions, local officials did not wait for national policies before taking radical and rapid steps to aid their Jewish residents. The period immediately following liberation was one of transition, during which representatives of the provisional government and other Resistance factions vied for power throughout the country. Before centralized power had been completely restored, local officials, usually made up of members of various Resistance movements, exercised a certain autonomy over local affairs.[52] Thus, in some regions sympathetic officials quickly moved to return Jewish property. In Languedoc-Roussillon, for example, the commissioner of the republic established a delegation to protect Jewish rights as early as September 1944. Similarly, in the department of Hérault, the prefect relieved the administrateurs provisoires of their duties and named new trustees to oversee Jewish property provisionally while waiting for the publication of national restitution laws.[53] These new managers were generally more sympathetic to their "clients" than the original administrators had been.[54] Naming these functionaries did not, however, solve the problems of the dispossessed. One complained, "Now . . . we find ourselves once again under the guardianship of a provisional administrator while those who purchased our property retain complete freedom."[55] Elsewhere, attempts to implement more radical steps failed. In Lyons, for example, Professor E. F. Térroine, a physiologist of the University of Strasbourg who had himself been imprisoned during the occupation, was put in charge of liquidating the local Commissariat-Général aux questions juives. He immediately froze all funds of the former administrateurs provisoires but was soon removed from office under their storm of protest.[56] Even in those regions where local administrators were anxious to aid dispossessed Jews, therefore, missing legal texts tied their hands.

On 14 November 1944, the provisional government finally produced the first restitution law "nullifying all seizures carried out by the enemy or under his control." The special nature of Jewish plundering, though taken into account in certain aspects of subsequent legislation, was not mentioned in this initial ordinance, which was instead directed at the implementation of broad legal principles. In its introduction, the law explained what had already become clear: "The despoilment measures adopted or imposed by the enemy were so considerable . . . that they pose problems that cannot be resolved by a single legislative text which can be passed immediately." In this initial text, the provisional government addressed only the least complicated cases. The scope of the law, therefore, was limited to laying out the procedures for the return of property that had not been liquidated or sold. Other possessions, declared the 14 November ordinance, would be addressed in forthcoming legislation.[57] In addition, the decree introduced a complicated judicial procedure with which to claim this unliquidated property. Rather than entrusting return of Jewish property to an administrative commission (as, indeed, the liquidation had been carried out), such returns were placed within the jurisdiction of the courts, a step that paved the way for arbitrary rulings due to the lack of clarity in the formulation of the initial ordinance.[58]

Although the goal of dividing restitution legislation into several stages was designed to allow those affected to regain at least part of their property in the shortest time possible, few people were happy with the government's decision to treat the restitutions in a series of ordinances. Some argued that this method was less favorable to Jewish war victims than the traditional laws of the French legal code. Moreover, the slowness with which these texts were being prepared forced many of those whose property had been seized to wait in destitution for months.[59] In the department of Hérault, the delegate working to safeguard Jewish interests reported that although the new ordinance allowed their office to close certain cases quickly, "in other cases the difficulties continue and even worsen."[60]

The limitations characterizing the 14 November restitution legislation were also present in a second ordinance published the same day concerning tenant rights. This ordinance declared that tenants could legally reclaim their former apartment or place of business if they had been forced to leave as a result of the war. Like the restitution law, the proclamation on tenant rights was not particularly directed at Jewish war victims. Nevertheless, on its surface, this law allowed dispossessed Jews to petition a civil court to reinstate them as tenants even when the new tenant had occupied the apartment in good faith. Because of the severe housing crisis, however, the provisional government provided several exceptions, exempting from eviction war victims, evacuees, and refugees as well as widows, spouses, children, and parents of mobilized soldiers, war prisoners, and deportees. As a result, many Jews were unable to claim their home.[61] Indeed, according to the socialist newspaper *Populaire*, 10,000 out of 25,000 occupants of Jewish homes were able to keep their apartments.[62]

The delays and contradictions in the two November laws made resettlement difficult for those Jews whose lives had been greatly disrupted by the war. Although some qualified for aid available to all French citizens, such as grants for the resettlement of deportees or military allowances, the needs of many others far surpassed the limitations imposed by the provisional government's restitution attempts.[63] One lawyer favoring more rapid restitutions noted, "It seems to me that there is reason to end the current situation as quickly as possible; five months after liberation, people whose commercial activities were under jurisdiction for years have urgent need for the blocked sums in order to rebuild their lives."[64]

The provisional government did not legislate more comprehensive restitution policies until 21 April 1945.[65] This new law attempted to redress some of the more delicate problems raised during the restitution process, including the annulment of official measures confiscating property and, more important, the restitution of property that had been liquidated or sold. Given the intricacies with which it was involved, this ordinance was the longest and most complex of all the restitution laws. With its passing, those whose property had been sold without their consent were finally authorized to reclaim what they had lost. Moreover, the law protected the rights of former owners who had died or disappeared during the war, ensuring that new purchasers could not benefit from the original owner's disappearance.[66] Those who could prove that the sale of their property had taken place under the threat of violence or to avoid imminent forced sale were also protected under the April ordinance. If, however, the purchase had taken place at a fair market price, the dispossessed owner was now in the position of proving that he or she had sold the property under threat of violence. If the former owner was unable to prove coercion, he or she was legally obliged to compensate the new buyer's expenses in increasing the value of the business, and the buyer was able to retain any proceeds generated from the time of the sale. Thus, the law sought to address the rights of those who had purchased plundered assets in good faith. While not allowing them to keep what did not belong to them, it addressed the question of what compensation they should receive.[67]

In its attempt to protect the dispossessed, new buyers, and those who had disappeared during the course of the war, the April restitution ordinance was widely heralded for its benevolence and comprehensiveness.[68] But even this law did not fully solve the problems of the dispossessed. To cite but one example: Article 16 promised that legislation on the reimbursement of appropriated bank accounts would soon be written, but several months later individuals were still complaining about the lack of adequate legislation.[69] Moreover, the new legislation did not protect victims of Vichy in all circumstances. In several cases, individuals complained about having to pay property transfer taxes when reclaiming property that they had sold to non-Jewish friends for protection during the war. In May 1942, for example, shortly before their deportation, the K. family bought a house in Varennes. Due to Vichy's anti-Jewish legislation, they asked family friends to buy it in their name. Following the war, Robert K., son of the original purchasers, attempted to reclaim the property, but to do so, he was told that he would have to pay property transfer taxes. In response to his protests, authorities remained inflexible. The law "only applies to despoiled victims and not to acquisitions made with their money in order to escape Nazi legislation." In a similar case, the despoiled party was told that no such ordinance would be written. When repurchasing, the original owner would have to pay the same property transfer taxes as any citizen.[70]

The government also encountered problems enforcing the 21 April ordinance. The law required purchasers of Jewish property to declare themselves to government authorities. In Alsace-Lorraine, however, where 40,000 wartime files attested to such property transfers, only 2,000 individuals initially came forward.[71] As such examples indicate, restitution ordinances, no matter how comprehensive, did not fully address all concerns.

Two more ordinances rounded out the overall program for the restitution of looted property. An order of 9 June 1945 automatically canceled property transfers and transactions conducted by the enemy. Here, however, the order only applied to property belonging to French individuals or legal bodies and thus did not cover property owned by foreigners. Although this law was seen as part of the body of restitution legislation, its primary aim was to attack the legality of acquisitions of French economic interests by the enemy. The government chose to view such purchases as looting rather than as legal purchases. In this instance, however, the victim was not only the original owner but the French state, hence the exclusion of foreigners' property located in France. Clearly, then, the overall purpose of this legislation went well beyond that of restituting looted Jewish property—and indeed excluded the property of foreign Jews. Rather, in this instance the government sought to use restitution legislation to protect the national economy, even if not fully protecting all individuals in the process. A last ordinance of 16 June 1948 declared that the government would accept liability for the repayment of deductions from the proceeds of property disposal or from other assets belonging to the victims of the theft.

These four ordinances, although later followed by numerous amendments and laws regarding their implementation, remained the most significant legislative record of restitutions. Indeed, none of the subsequent laws influenced the broad outlines of the original government orders.[72]

In addition to writing legislation to address the restitution of stolen property, government officials were faced with creating an administration to implement the process—another vexing task, as numerous organs of state had either been informed of the looting as it had taken place or had actually participated in the systematic pillaging. Governmental agencies, such as the Caisse des Dépôts et Consignations, the prefecture of police, and the national museums, had been involved in some aspect of the looting and now had to reverse their activities of the previous years. The agency most involved in the pillaging of Jewish property, however, was the Commissariat-Général aux questions juives (CGQJ). This agency, established in spring 1941 by the Vichy government, had coordinated all anti-Jewish programs. Its functions were to propose legislation concerning Jews, to coordinate the various governmental agencies to this end, and to initiate police measures against Jews. Its primary responsibility, however, was the management and liquidation of Jewish enterprises. As such, its employees appointed and supervised the agents involved in this task and kept methodical records of all their activities. It was to this organization, therefore, that the postwar government turned when commencing restitution procedures.[73]

Immediately after liberation, government agents shut down all administrative activities at the Commissariat-Général. Moreover, liberation forces acted quickly to safeguard these records by placing the building under surveillance and forbidding all personnel from entering.[74] Until restitution legislation had been written, however, little could be done with these materials.[75] Finally, in January 1945, the Ministry of Finance established a Restitution Office based on the CGQJ's archives, the Service des restitutions des biens des victimes des lois et mesures de spoliation, under the direction of Professor Térroine, who, as we have already seen, was active in Lyons's restitution activities in September 1944.[76] While other agencies were established to help with restitution, including the Commission de récupération artistique (in the Ministry of Fine Arts) and the Office des biens et intérêts privés (OBIP), a department in the Ministry of Foreign Affairs that dealt with assets removed from France by the Germans, it was the Service des restitutions that was in charge of returning property that had remained in France and, hence, found itself administering property exchanges among French citizens.

Térroine and his staff were committed to reversing the injustices of wartime discrimination. Their ability to help victims was often constrained, however, by the limitations of the legislation under which they were working, legislation that was slow in coming and often not comprehensive in scope. Those working in restitution services, therefore, were often besieged with requests that they could not fulfill. Similarly, although restitution services faced an enormous task, they were not given the staff to complete the job efficiently. While the CGQJ carried out its tasks in three years with the aid of 10,444 agents, Térroine's office had 192 agents who were expected to complete their task much more rapidly.[77]

Despite these limitations, the Office of Restitutions sought to establish itself throughout the country. This meant coordinating the activities of the local independent restitution offices under one central Parisian administration. To do so, Térroine actively recruited those individuals who had worked at the local level into his own regional offices. Over 1945 and 1946, he established nine such offices in Limoges, Lyon, Marseille, Nice, Toulouse, Bordeaux, Dijon, Nancy, and Rouen.[78] The size and scope of each branch differed according to the Jewish population of the region and the degree of pillaging that had occurred there. Whereas the office in Limoges had 568 dossiers from the former CGQJ, the one in Nice had approximately 3,000. Each one, however, was responsible for applying national restitution legislation at the local level, keeping the central office informed about all restitution activities, classifying files, searching for and sequestering property abandoned by deported Jews, giving advice to victims of racial laws, compiling files on the administrateurs provisoires, and, when possible, facilitating amicable settlements.[79]

Exploring one of the major activities of these restitution offices in depth— that of the return of stolen property abandoned by the German army during its rapid retreat—demonstrates the problems that Térroine's well-meaning administrative task force faced.[80] During the final month of the war, the German army, which had appropriated and transported a good deal of furniture and other property out of France for distribution to bombed-out German citizens, abandoned large stockpiles of everything from priceless rugs and grand pianos to used clothing and old silverware. Because this property was stolen by the Germans and not the Vichy government, its return proved less controversial than the return of property purchased by other French citizens.[81] Nevertheless, even this seemingly simple task proved extremely difficult to carry out in a systematic and rapid fashion. Indeed, the property stood unclaimed until April 1945, when the provisional government finally legislated its return to its rightful owners. As with the other postwar restitution policies, these laws were not specifically directed at French Jews. Other citizens had been pillaged, and so the laws included anyone whose property had been confiscated during the German occupation. In practical terms, however, Jewish homes and businesses had been most affected by the German occupation, and hence an examination of this legislation and its implementation further illustrates the complexities of postwar restitution policies for French Jewish citizens.

The ordinance returning stolen property dictated that all confiscated books, furniture, clothing, linen, china, and so on should be divided into two categories: identifiable and nonidentifiable. The latter category—which included all linen, clothing, underwear, curtains, drapes, blankets, bedspreads, toys, leather, and leather scraps—was donated to Entr'aide française and to other charity organizations to distribute to returning deportees. Identifiable objects were put on display for those who claimed to have been pillaged to view and repossess.[82]

Implementing these restitution procedures did not, however, function efficiently. Although the law was promulgated in April, most regional restitution activities did not begin operating for several months, and even then many victims were unable to reclaim their property quickly.[83] Assuming that those who had been pillaged just prior to liberation had a greater chance of finding their property than those whose belongings had been stolen several years earlier, officials gave the first authorizations to visit the furniture depots to the former. Nevertheless, even they often had to wait months. One woman whose apartment was emptied in June 1944 complained that she had requested authorization to visit the depots three times with no success. Others had to wait for over a year before receiving permission.[84]

The 11 April ordinance also did not take into account the differences among various regions of the country. The decree stipulated that claimants had two years from the date of liberation to make their claims, but the Germans had abandoned certain regions of the country before others. The department of Moselle, for example, was not liberated until six months after the rest of France. Although this region had been characterized by some of the worst pillaging in the country, dispossessed residents were often unable to file a claim for their property within the two years stipulated by law. About 350,000 of Moselle's inhabitants had either been deported or sent to the interior of the country. As a result of the late liberation date and a severe housing crisis, repatriation was slower, and those who had been dispossessed had less time to identify their furniture, request restitution, and pursue claims. Indeed, by January 1947, 40,000 of those expelled had still to be reintegrated.[85] By not taking such regional differences into account, the 11 April ordinance could not satisfy the needs of those most affected by the pillaging.

The restitution officers also faced problems unlinked to faulty or tardy legislation. Occasionally clients would identify a possession in the furniture depots, but when they returned to claim it, it would be gone. Preventing individuals from claiming furniture that was not their own was virtually impossible. On 8 June 1945, the Restitution Office broadcast a warning over the radio reminding listeners that such behavior was criminal and would be prosecuted.[86] In most cases, however, they had few reliable methods for proving ownership. Because few war victims had receipts of purchase, restitution officers depended on signed and notarized inventories detailing prewar belongings. Unfortunately, such procedures also posed problems. Many despoiled Jews had fled their homes early in the conflict and had stayed away for a number of years. For them, completing comprehensive inventories proved daunting, and their lists often lacked relevant and important details. Problems would arise when individuals, after visiting the depots of stolen furniture, would claim a piece not listed on the original inventory. One Polish Jewish family explained the inconsistency by arguing that their poor knowledge of French caused oversights in the original inventory. Another man insisted that his son had very hastily compiled an inventory for him when passing through Paris with the army: "Having myself only returned to Paris at the end of April 1945," he wrote, "I could not control the statement that was sent to you. It was inevitable under such circumstances and after an exile of several years that omissions would be present in the enumeration of missing objects." Another woman remarked that her own inventory was incomplete because her sons were still at the front and were unable to help her: "I had, thus, to rely entirely on my memory. But I am seventy-five years old and have suffered a stroke, and the six years of war with its accompanying worries for freedom, for the lives of my own family threatened doubly as Jews, as well as [for] my own unstable life as a wandering Jew . . . have made me forget a good deal."[87]

Many war victims regarded as unfair policies restricting them to their original inventory. Yet how else could restitution officers determine which claimants were taking advantage of the relatively open system? Often visibly uncomfortable when demanding further precision on inventory lists, the restitution officials claimed to be doing their best "to safeguard the right of the rightful owners."[88] Their efforts were often fruitless, however, such as in the case of ten people claiming the same piece of furniture as their own. In such contested cases, the clients were invited to take their claim to the courts. These legal fights could turn ugly, some lasting a number of years.[89]

For Jewish returnees attempting to put their lives in order, the incomplete legislation and the bureaucratic slowdowns caused great difficulties. For example, G., who had fled Paris in June 1940, returned in 1944 to discover that she and her husband had lost their apartment, furniture, and jobs. Unable to repossess her home, she attempted to regain some of her property by adhering to the various restitution regulations. After a ten-month delay, the couple were finally allowed to view the furniture displayed in the depots, where they found little that was theirs. Finally, after turning to l'Entr'aide française for aid (where G. claimed she was received in a shameful manner and insulted by the employees), she began to lose all hope. "After an entire life of work, to find oneself without money, without anything," she wrote, "to have so much to reconstruct, it's almost not worth having survived." Citing her family's great sacrifices, including seven in the army, nineteen deported, and twenty-three dead, she called on the government to honor its obligations: "One year after liberation, there are still families without anything and without restitutions of money, linen, or furniture. These are French families who did as expected both in 1870 and in 1940. . . . These are the families who are insulted by various services when they go to request aid. . . . These are the families prevented from claiming the little they can find."[90]

Such appeals did not fall on deaf ears. Indeed, Térroine himself was all too conscious of the plight of those he represented, and he worked actively to fight further injustices.[91] To his great dismay, however, his own actions were constrained under the incomplete restitution legislation. As he wrote to one discontented client, "I do not need to tell you how aware I am of your difficult situation, which, unfortunately, is that of a great number of your co-religionists. You know that I do my best to try to bandage all the wounds, but they are so numerous that our actions are not always effective. I realize that the responses you receive from all agencies—that you must wait—are frustrating, but we are all subject to the laws and we cannot institute any policies nor give any advice as long as we do not have precise texts to guide us."[92] Without more comprehensive legislation, even Térroine, a sympathetic and active advocate, could do little to facilitate a more complete restitution process.

Even when clearly frustrated by his inability to do more, however, Térroine was also convinced of the importance of his office. When he resigned in the spring of 1946 to work for the Ministry of Education, he pleaded that the office be kept open. Both he and his successor, André Braun, believed such work should continue until all businesses and real estate had been returned to the legitimate owners and that new laws should be written to address the gaps in existing legislation.[93] Nevertheless, Braun faced severe budget cutbacks almost immediately and was expected to cut his staff in half in September 1946. Most regional restitution offices were shut down by 1947.[94]

Despite the bureaucratic and legislative difficulties, those working for the restitution offices tried valiantly to protect the rights of those who had been most hurt by the war. They sent circulars to all victims asking if they had recovered their property or if they had initiated proceedings to do so. They published notices in local papers asking victims to come forward and instructing them in how to research their particular claim. They actively sought out property that had gone unclaimed by working closely with local police prefectures and courts. They chased down those who had overseen the liquidation of Jewish property, demanding that they submit their accounts.[95] Clients were not always happy with the service, and it did take several years to satisfy many requests for aid, yet some were able to regain some property without significant problems. Still, there were those who felt abandoned by the new system. A year after liberation one woman tellingly complained, "I do not understand why nothing can be done for me. I have no furniture. My father, who fought in the war of 1914, has been deported and I still have no news of him. I am taking care of my mother. My husband died in June 1940 fighting the war, and I have a daughter who is five and a half years old. My brothers, former prisoners of war, have just returned. My furniture was taken at the last minute and I have great hopes that I can reclaim it, but I already made a request over a year ago and I wonder if anyone is even aware of it."[96] To clients such as these, the massive restitution proceedings instituted in the postwar years seemed inefficient and unhelpful.

Procedures to regain homes, businesses, and property provided the main means through which French Jews could redress material losses, but they were not the only available option. In some cases, dispossessed Jews could demand reparations from the administrators who had managed their property. The laws regulating this process were, however, equally complex and contradictory. By sympathizing with Jewish victims without unequivocally condemning all those who had profited at their expense, the government was unable to compensate all victims for their losses.

Administrateurs Provisoires

Although some well-known antisemitic officials, such as Xavier Vallat, were tried after the war, the state's position toward those functionaries who implemented anti-Jewish measures was frustrating for those who desired rapid and severe rulings. As we have seen, the purges removed Vichy's most visible policy shapers while ignoring "ordinary" civil servants and professionals. Nowhere were such policies more evident than in the postwar treatment of the administrateurs provisoires. These "trustees" had carried out the seizure and Aryanization of Jewish property. Through such legalized confiscation, argued some, thousands of "ordinary" French citizens had helped systematically dispossess Jewish citizens while simultaneously legitimizing Vichy's antisemitic regime. Nevertheless, the postwar government remained reluctant to condemn them. While many returning Jews clamored for justice against those who had sold and liquidated their properties, the former administrateurs defended their tenure, as did others who had worked under Vichy, on the grounds that they had acted legally in the service of the state. Some argued that they had actually protected Jews as best they could from even harsher German persecution.

In the months following liberation, the provisional government sought to sort through these contradictory visions of the administrateurs' tenure and to write legislation that protected those Jews who had been persecuted and those administrateurs who had carried out their tasks while strictly adhering to the laws of the state. Protecting both, however, proved difficult. Not hesitant to prosecute those who had illegally taken advantage of their position, officials remained sympathetic to those who had simply followed the letter of the law as it was written under Vichy. Thus, even when sensitive to Jewish losses, the government proved reluctant to promote further divisions in the population, opting instead to bring an end to further conflicts by placing most administrateurs out of the law's reach.

In September 1940 Vichy laws created the position of administrateur provisoire, a trustee whose task it was to manage the property and businesses of all those legally incompetent to own or run such enterprises. Although explicit mention of Jewish enterprises was not detailed until July 1941, the creation of the CGQJ in March of that year provided a structure through which the administrateurs would ultimately carry out their task of liquidating Jewish businesses or selling them to "Aryan" owners. The proceeds of these transactions were turned over to a specially created account, most of which was used to pay the German "fine" on the Jewish community. The administrateurs themselves—some of whom were named by local prefects, others by German authorities, and others by a Service de contrôle des administrateurs provisoires created in December 1940—were provided with a broad mandate to take over the operations of Jewish enterprises, which generally included granting themselves healthy "administrative fees" for their work, dismissing the Jewish employees, and frequently raising wages of the non-Jewish employees so as to win their confidence and undermine their loyalty to their previous employer.[97]

At the time of France's liberation, 50,000 to 55,000 Aryanization proceedings had been instituted, but not all had been concluded. Although in many cases the property had been sold or liquidated, particularly where the business had little ongoing value, in other cases the provisional administrator was still managing the property with which he had been entrusted.[98] The liberation of France brought the status of such administrators into question, and certain regional liberation forces moved quickly to freeze their bank accounts and to return nonliquidated property to the original owners.[99] For these officials, allowing Vichy functionaries to maintain control over Jewish property seemed contrary to the very essence of the liberation movement. Similarly, many returning French Jews saw the administrateurs provisoires as guilty of participating in Vichy's antisemitic regime and of collaborating with the Germans. To them, rapid punishment was the only conceivable option. One angry returnee insisted, "If we do not ask for personal reimbursement from all the administrateurs, what can we say to the good French citizens who refused to accept this very lucrative job?" Without strong punishments, he warned, future generations would believe that they could appropriate the money of others without fear. Similarly, J. angrily argued that the administrators should be forced to reimburse three times what the owners had lost, "otherwise we must fear that in case of a future invasion of France in fifteen or twenty years, sons will follow the example of their fathers and collaborate." Despite the virulence of J.'s denunciation, however, his administrateur did not believe that he had broken any laws or hurt J. in any way. Instead, he defended his tenure, claiming he had protected J. from full liquidation despite orders to the contrary.[100] As this example illustrates, the administrateurs and their "clients" often had contrasting understandings of their relationship, and both believed they had the moral and legal right to demand satisfaction from national officials once the war had ended.

Government leaders, however, were initially unprepared to sort through the competing claims. Although the Minister of Justice declared in August 1944 that "placing [an enterprise] under an administrateur provisoire usually led the enterprise to ruin," and that even Vichy officials had been distressed by "the innumerable and incredible abuses carried on . . . by a good many administrateurs provisoires of Jewish property," the postwar government remained reluctant to condemn all such functionaries of criminal behavior.[101] To do so would be to implicate those administrateurs who had done exactly what J.'s administrateur *claimed* to have done, that is, to protect those whose property and businesses were in their care. And such cases did exist. In one example, the administrateur provisoire not only protected Zélick J.'s fur business from liquidation but also accepted his three-year-old daughter into his home after his wife had been deported. In another case, the administrateur left Felix B. "completely free." "Knowing perfectly well that the sale of my business in 1941 . . . was fictive," B. noted, "[he] gave us advice, never putting a foot in our business." This same administrateur even helped B. avoid paying 9,000 francs demanded by the government. Still another returning Jew reported that because of his administrator's helpful attitude, he was able to keep his restaurant.[102]

Many other administrateurs simply did their job, neither aiding nor persecuting those they supervised. One never met the owner of the business he managed; in this case, the administrateur turned over the store's books and keys to the owner's wife after she returned from an eighteen-month absence. Because the business had never been sold, the owner was able to take possession immediately upon his return. Another claimed that although his administrateur provisoire was an antisemite, he had not acted criminally. Throughout his tenure he "behaved perfectly correctly and even quite amicably." [103]

Basing their claims on such cases, the administrateurs provisoires worked rapidly and effectively in the months following liberation to foster their image as innocent bureaucrats doing their best in a bad situation. Having organized the Association des administrateurs provisoires de France well before the war ended as an advocacy group to protect their interests, the administrateurs maintained that they had acted in good faith by following the laws of the state in which they lived: "We have neither to defend ourselves nor to bear the brunt of attacks," noted their September 1944 circular. "We are administrateurs who took charge of abandoned and unclaimed property so that the Germans would not themselves take over its management and auction it." Fundamental to their defense was that they had committed no crimes: "We have managed this property according to the law and under governmental supervision." Having scrupulously followed French law was justification enough for their actions.[104]

Despite reassuring their members that they required no defense, the directors of the Association clearly felt insecure with their postwar position. The initiatives of September 1944, during which certain local officials moved to freeze the accounts of administrateurs provisoires in their region, left the trustees feeling nervous about their position in French society. In addition, occasional newspaper articles accused them of collaborating with the German occupiers. Given the anti-collaborationist sentiment fueling the épuration, such public attacks made the administrateurs provisoires uneasy. Thus, like much of the French Jewish population, the administrateurs hoped that the chaos surrounding Jewish property would be quickly resolved, along with their own legal and financial status, and in the months while restitution legislation was under consideration, they actively lobbied on their own behalf. Seemingly surprised by the rancor with which their former "clients" criticized them, they insisted on the completion of legal texts that would regulate their relationship with those whose accounts they had administered. Forever defending their position, the administrateurs insisted that returning Jews should thank rather than insult them.[105]

Defenders of the administrateurs provisoires came from other quarters as well. Albert Neuville, honorary director of the Bank of France, defended their work in glowing terms, implying that they were the unsung heroes of the war years. By resisting orders for the complete liquidation of Jewish property and by struggling to preserve assets in their care, these administrateurs, Neuville insisted, often found themselves in dangerous opposition to the German administration. Moreover, their work was costly. In many cases, he argued, the administrateurs had worked against their own interests, deliberately reducing their own possibilities of remuneration, whereas their "clients" had returned to find their affairs intact or in good shape, some worth more than before.[106]

Not all government officials accepted such exaggerated claims. Still, pressure from the administrateurs and their advocates certainly had a decisive impact. In a short time, officials began to look leniently on the administrateur provisoire, viewing him primarily as a government functionary whose role was administrative rather than political. This shift had far-reaching implications for the creation and implementation of policies concerning their status in postwar France. If the administrateur provisoire held an administrative position, then the new government had no incentive to dismiss him no matter which regime had originally appointed him. Certainly, in cases where a Jewish business owner had come to an amicable agreement with his or her administrateur, the latter's tenure ended rapidly. However, in more complex cases where Jewish owners could not immediately return to their former activities or take over their businesses, the original administrateur seemed the best qualified to maintain and preserve the business, protecting its personnel from being deprived of jobs and salaries.[107]

Moreover, if administrateurs provisoires were simply apolitical bureaucrats, the legality of their tenure would have to be adjudicated on a case-by-case basis. No single law could condemn their role in the liquidation of Jewish property because to do so would mean judging those who had never taken advantage of their position and, more important, would reemphasize divisions in the postwar population. Thus, when finally written, the ordinances that addressed the administrateurs provisoires' tenure generally went far in legitimizing their acts. While the 14 November ordinance ruled that all sequesters, administrateurs provisoires, managers, or liquidators of property would have to render accounts of their management or liquidation within two months of receiving a request to do so, it also recognized their legitimate rights by promising to create laws regulating the fees they could charge for their management and expertise. Thus, the 14 November ordinance recognized the administrateurs provisoires as state functionaries whose administrative role had no relationship to the political nature of the regime under which they had served. Then, as promised, a second ordinance on 2 February 1945 guaranteed the administrateurs' fiscal rights by establishing a procedure for the retribution of losses they might have incurred.[108]

It should be noted that these ordinances did not protect all administrateurs. "No fees can be kept," proclaimed the 14 November ordinance, "when the goods were not administered with due diligence [*en bon père de famille.*]" Though vague, this stipulation provided means to prosecute those who had broken Vichy laws, cheated the state of legal revenue, or behaved in a criminal fashion.[109] As such, the provisional government accepted Vichy's legislative precedent that had declared in July 1941 that all administrateurs provisoires would be prosecuted if they did not administer their accounts diligently. According to the initial law, the administrateur was a salaried agent, liable before judicial tribunals, and subject to the rules of common law. Yet, according to legal historian Richard Weisberg, the "bon père" statutory standard was not enforced under Vichy and the courts stood aside, permitting the legalized looting of Jewish property.[110]

By accepting Vichy's legal precedent—even if attempting to enforce it more fully—the provisional government protected the administrateurs provisoires and legitimated their activities. The legality of the "administration" had been recognized; the administrateurs could retain their profits and be indemnified for their losses.[111] As Neuville remarked when analyzing this legislation, "There is no doubt, no discussion possible: the administrateurs provisoires who conducted [their business] as good upstanding citizens have the right to remuneration. That is the will of the law."[112] Furthermore, nothing in either ordinance permitted the prosecution of those who carried out their duties in a poor or negligent manner. Accordingly, Jews whose property had been sold at undervalued prices and whose merchandise had been dispersed had little legal recourse.[113]

Unlike under Vichy rule, however, the postwar government did not allow all administrateurs provisoires to escape justice. In cases where the "trustee" attempted to avoid restituting required sums, the courts intervened, as they did in cases where the administrateur had overstepped legal duties by stealing from or persecuting those in his trusteeship. Hence, in one example, where an administrateur not only stole his "client's" furniture but also denounced her parents to the authorities—leading to their arrest and deportation to Germany—the courts prosecuted.[114] Determining guilt or innocence in such cases was rarely this straightforward, however, as very often contrasting viewpoints and fuzzy evidence blurred guilt.

To address such cases, the Justice Ministry created the Service de contrôle des administrateurs provisoires et liquidateurs de biens israélites in February 1945 as an advisory body to the courts. Created neither to prosecute nor defend former administrateurs, this department's goal was merely to inspect the records of the property's management after a complaint had been filed and to inform the courts of the specifics of the case. Such records, housed in the Office of Restitutions in the archives of the ex-CGQJ, provided the history of the Aryanization, how it was implemented, and who if anyone was guilty of committing illegal acts.[115] As a result, this verification department worked closely with the Restitution Office, and as the latter spread throughout the country, so did the Contrôle générale des administrateurs provisoires de biens israélites.[116]

Despite the important task with which it was assigned, the verification department, like Térroine's office, was never given the resources to do its job well. Initially staffed with only a head comptroller and an adjunct, the department was quickly overrun with requests for information. In March 1945, the government responded to the overflow by instructing the Finance Ministry to supply the verification department with necessary agents. In response, a paltry four new employees joined the office. Although the comptroller requested more hands in April, his pleas went unheeded despite the debilitating effect the lack of personnel was having on his department's services. By November 1945, the department was receiving approximately 450 requests per month and had dealt with 1,300 complaints or litigations. Still stressing the impossibility of treating these numerous cases with care if continually refused the required personnel, the comptroller again begged for more help. Once again the requested aid never came. As a result, though promised 77 agents in March 1945, the verification department had only 28 by 1946. With new cutbacks in 1947, the number dropped to 17.[117]

Despite these problems, by February 1948 the verification department had received 9,530 written and verbal requests and had settled 2,916 complaints or civil suits. In each of these cases, the comptroller researched the history of the Aryanization process and summarized the events for the courts. The goal of these reports was to present all the relevant details affecting the case. Rarely did the comptroller take a position on the innocence or guilt of the administrateur provisoire. Rather, he would present the "facts" to the court and leave interpretation to the judges. Nevertheless, the comptroller was occasionally moved to draw certain conclusions from the evidence he reviewed. In one case, for example, he concluded, "Having not found in the dossier the essential elements proving embezzlement or misappropriation of funds, it seems . . . that the complaint lodged by L. against M. and Mme. C. is unjustified."[118]

This example should not suggest that the comptroller always took the side of the administrateur. In one case, he accused the administrateur of forgery, falsifying written documents, causing mental and material injury, and intending to harm. Whether defending or indicting the administrateur, however, the comptroller always built his case on the records of the CGQJ. But relying on these archives to determine the administrateur's guilt or innocence was not without problems. Although the CGQJ's archives were systematic and well-organized, they did not, for obvious reasons, always indicate clearly if an administrateur provisoire had behaved criminally. Establishing guilt or innocence was thus a complicated matter. In one case, for example, the plaintiff accused his administrateur of having ordered his sister's arrest and deportation to Drancy, a fate from which she never returned. When examining the CGQJ's records, the comptroller determined that, indeed, the administrateur provisoire had denounced the plaintiff's sister but was unwilling to say that her arrest had resulted from the denunciation: "It does not seem established that [her] arrest was the direct consequence of [his] denunciation because while the report [of the denunciation] is dated 19 November 1941, [she] was not arrested until July 1942." As evidenced here, the comptroller examined the complaints literally. If he could not prove that the administrateur's actions led directly to the deportation, then the complaint was unfounded. Nevertheless, the comptroller judged the administrateur's actions as falling under laws condemning antinational activities.[119]

Other difficulties also interfered with the work of the Contrôle générale des administrateurs provisoires des biens israélites. Most notably, the gaps in national restitution legislation, which so hindered the Office of Restitutions, equally frustrated those working for the Justice Ministry. In some cases, no relevant restitution laws could answer the questions of those submitting claims; then, the comptroller had to make his own determination of how to settle a case. Occasionally, however, he did not know how best to proceed, such as in one case, where the administrateur provisoire, having been deported himself, was unable to provide the documentation of his administration legally required by the 14 November ordinance. The comptroller forwarded the case to Térroine, unsure how to safeguard the interests of the relevant parties.[120]

A decree of 11 August 1947 stipulated that civil suits or judicial complaints filed after 31 December 1947 would no longer be submitted to the verification department. The office was given ten months to complete its work. This decision seemed arbitrary to its employees because in their minds restitutions were far from complete. By 1947, however, government officials no longer felt any urgency to complete restitution activities. Although the war had ended only two short years before, as the Fourth Republic took shape and government policies began to focus on the future rather than the past, in some ways it was already ancient history.[121]

In the year after liberation, government officials struggled with how best to tackle the controversies related to the restitution of property and the persecution of those who had implemented anti-Jewish legislation. Once French Jews were no longer legally viewed as a distinct subject minority, government officials were hesitant to create special laws protecting them. However, for them to be rapidly and fully reintegrated into the surrounding society, the government could not avoid addressing their plight. Eventually, officials instituted compromise policies that simultaneously restituted and de-emphasized Jewish losses. A commitment to republican government that since the Revolution had de-emphasized all cultural pluralism in the public sphere (and that had encouraged government officials to misunderstand the Armenian plight following World War I) led them to treat Jews as one among many of Vichy's numerous victims.

Ultimately, the delays and gaps in these policies slowed but did not prevent French Jews from regaining economic stability. Granted, many spent the first year after the war in dire conditions. As one writer complained, "More than a half year after their liberation, France's disillusioned Jews are still awaiting enactment of measures that will permit them to reconstruct the economic bases of their existence and rebuild lives shattered by four years of relentless persecution."[122] A year later, Jewish publications were still complaining about gaps in the restitution legislation.[123] And yet, the provisional government did make active efforts to restore stolen property to its rightful owners. Property that had not been liquidated or sold was returned. New buyers were legally required to report their purchases; if they did not, they were subject to severe fines. The previous owners' rights were protected both through out-of-court settlements and through summary procedures in civil and commercial courts. Moreover, previous owners could sue those who had managed their property for poor work or excessive fees. In many cases, survivors could receive compensation for property that had been stolen or destroyed during the occupation. As a result of such policies, about two-thirds of all stolen assets were claimed and returned after the war.[124]

Nevertheless, postwar welfare and restitution policies had a lasting impact on French Jews in two ways. First, when restitution policies proved inadequate, the surviving Jewish population was forced to rely on its own initiatives. Because their lack of resources made them ill-equipped to create a widespread welfare support network, they turned to diaspora organizations such as the American Joint Distribution Committee for help. Compensating for government inadequacies, the AJDC created welfare institutions, centers for returning refugees, and employment agencies for those Jews unable to construct viable living conditions on government subsidies. By relying on private organizations to provide the assistance they could not, French officials may have encouraged the very movement they were trying to avoid, namely, the creation of a "Jewish" infrastructure, which, though not fighting integration, would still highlight and encourage Jewish difference.[125] Thus, in an indirect way, restitution policies directly influenced the nature of Jewish expression in the postwar era as well as the way resettlement played itself out. The next three chapters document the intricacies of that process.

Second, the postwar welfare and restitution policies, though well-meaning in the sense that they sought to reintegrate Jews into French society, also downplayed the specific nature of their losses during the war and in so doing contributed to silencing discussion of the Holocaust. As Henri Rousso, Annette Wieviorka, and others have documented, it took nearly twenty years for that history to begin resurfacing in France, as filmmakers, historians, and journalists began to review the Vichy legacy and suggest greater culpability for wartime atrocities than had previously been recognized. Postwar welfare and restitution policies were not written in an effort to silence discussion about the mistreatment of Jews during the war years; still, they served to bolster a trend that had already begun to take root, which de-emphasized the suffering of particular minorities in an effort to point to French solidarity and heroism in a time of war.

The genocidal attacks of the first two world wars raised new questions about the ability of modern nation-states to integrate ethnic and religious minorities. Victims of a spreading ethnic nationalism, both Armenians and Jews were singled out as " 'alien' to the historic culture-community" in which they had previously lived.[1] Yet, paradoxically, in the aftermath of the persecutions, both populations found themselves constituting minority communities once again. This chapter thus asks how the recent past of ostracization, harassment, and expulsion influenced survivors' integration into the French state. How was their minority status understood in light of having been persecuted for just such a status? And how did the French context influence these understandings?

As a comparison of the two populations shows, the first priority for both, not surprisingly, was to rebuild themselves materially. Financial and demographic losses coupled with large-scale communal upheaval disrupted and temporarily devastated both populations, albeit in different ways. In both cases, therefore, the drive to reestablish stable financial, familial, and institutional structures shaped how each population responded to the challenges of integrating or reintegrating into state and society.

Perhaps even more important in shaping their integration, however, was the larger national context in which they found themselves. As the previous two chapters have demonstrated, French authorities in both the 1920s and 1940s pursued assimilationist models of incorporating ethnic and religious minorities into the state. Armenians and Jews, despite maintaining extremely different relationships with that state, thus faced similar policies with regard to their incorporation within it. Such policies ultimately encouraged survivors to believe integration was possible and even desirable, a particularly noteworthy development in the case of French Jews, who seemingly had the most to distrust when confronting national authorities. As a result, neither incoming Armenian populations nor the longer-established Jewish communities responded to the systematic attacks against them by questioning the possibility of living as national minorities in a larger nation-state. Indeed, if to some these genocides posed a challenge to the feasibility of living in diaspora, most survivors did not draw similar conclusions, seeking instead to secure their position in France.

Material Consequences and the Pace of Recovery

Rebuilding Armenian Lives

As noted earlier, Armenian migration to France took place primarily in the 1920s, several years after the genocide occurred. Having spent nearly a decade wandering throughout Russia and the eastern Mediterranean, most of these first arrivals anxiously sought an end to the state of flux caused by the massacres and deportations of World War I. Thus, for most, the earliest priorities were shaped by the drive to put food on the table, put a permanent roof over their heads, and put in place a basic institutional framework.

The initial settlement of Armenian refugee communities suggests the degree to which the drive for stability shaped their first years in the country. Bound by the one-year work contracts that had provided them with the legal papers to gain entry, many refugees were directed to the industrial regions of France. After stopping in Marseille, they moved to mining centers in Lorette, Gardanne, and Saint Chamond; textile centers in Ardèche and Isère; or ironworking regions in Saint-Etienne (although the most educated often went directly to Paris). Having lost a job or having met the obligations of their initial labor contracts, however, many of the refugees ultimately joined their family or sought a spouse in Paris, Lyon, or Marseille, where the biggest concentrations of Armenians gathered.[2] Such family reunification often meant negotiating the complex French immigration bureaucracy, which was more interested in integrating laborers into the French economy than creating cohesive Armenian communities in the largest French cities. Thus, when one young Armenian woman requested to go to Paris to join her family, officials in Marseille told her she would first have to fulfill the obligations of her travel permit, which had directed her to Strasbourg.[3]

Such barriers to internal migration, however, did not prevent Armenians from eventually joining their family and friends in the largest cities. There they generally grouped together in ways characteristic of most immigrant populations. In Marseille, for example, they congregated in the place d'Aix and on the rues Victor-Hugo and Dominicaine, as well as in Camp Oddo; in Lyon, they settled on the perimeters of the seventh and third arrondissements; in Paris they migrated to the rue Belleville and the rue Mouffetard.[4] Such collective living arrangements provided a sense of security in their new environment. As one refugee, Jean Der Sarkissian, described his youth in Valence in the early 1930s, "I lived in Paradise. A paradise of Armenians, rue Bouffier, a small artery of Valence on which the Genocide survivors lived."[5]

Although Der Sarkissian painted an idyllic vision of his childhood, for most new arrivals, the first few years were less than ideal. Finding a permanent place of settlement was no small relief after many months of wandering, but not all Armenian refugees fell rapidly into stable working conditions. For example, Edouard Khédérian, a professional diamond cutter in Constantinople, did manage to find a job in a Parisian diamond workshop. However, the salary of 1 franc an hour proved insufficient for procuring enough to eat. To supplement, he began helping out in an Armenian restaurant where he could eat for free.[6] Similarly, Takvor Philipossian, a fifty-one-year-old lawyer who had fled with his family from Smyrna, tried to make ends meet by teaching French to incoming immigrants at the Foyer français. With the small sum he earned, however, he was unable to pay the 375 franc fee necessary to renew his family's identity papers.[7] For many others, finding employment in their new environment required a shift away from their traditional occupations. Indeed, the needs of the French labor market transformed what had been a largely artisanal and agricultural population in the Ottoman Empire into a population of unskilled laborers, miners, and textile workers.[8]

A glance at the professional breakdown of the population in Camp Oddo demonstrates just how poorly this new population fit the needs of the French labor market. As we saw in chapter 1, the French government established Camp Oddo in the early 1920s as a temporary home for a few hundred refugees. For initial arrivals, this camp, and others like it, operated as intended, with families remaining days or weeks until they could be moved to their permanent place of settlement. In this capacity, approximately six thousand new refugees passed through Oddo's gates en route to jobs in the growing industrial sectors of the national economy. The Armenian population, however, was made up not only of young, strong, unskilled laborers but also of the very old, the infirm, and children. Indeed, the Armenian population mirrored the patterns of other refugee groups with its considerably larger number of women and children. Of the 2,505 in the camp in December 1923, for example, 857 were men and 894 were women; in addition, there were 754 children.[9] Furthermore, the Armenian population had been largely rural before being uprooted from the Ottoman Empire. Hence, of the 817 who made up Camp Oddo's working population in November 1923, 460 were agricultural workers or farmers; the rest were small craftsmen such as blacksmiths, woodworkers, tailors, and shoemakers, while others worked as butchers or bakers. Only 100 of the group worked as day laborers, mostly on the docks. These men had difficulty obtaining permanent employment in the Marseille region, preventing them from establishing their families in more stable living conditions. Furthermore, many refused work that would take them too far from the region as they feared an even greater isolation from other Armenians.[10] As a result, within three months in 1923 the camp population rose from several hundred to nearly three thousand, many of whom had few resources and no plans to move elsewhere.[11]

Thus, those in Camp Oddo, like other Armenians in France, migrated to their new country with skills that did not address the most pressing needs of the national labor market; however, the work-related similarities end there. Indeed, although a high percentage of the camp's permanent residents were unemployed and without prospects, pushing some to beg or to steal, most Armenians — nearly 90 percent of the first generation — had found work as unskilled laborers by 1930.[12] By way of comparison we can look briefly at the Armenian population in Courbevoie, a northwest suburb of Paris well-known for its textiles and foundries. Over the mid-1920s, this town attracted a tiny Armenian population of approximately eighty, most of whom congregated together in two buildings on the rue de Bezone and worked in local automobile factories. Here, as throughout other industrial and agricultural sectors that hired Armenian laborers, the initial work contract offered a measure of security for the new refugees, providing them with an income and often with lodging, medical care, and even food.[13] They often worked long hours for low pay and were, at times, subject to anti-immigrant hostility from their French colaborers; nevertheless, they were able to provide for themselves and their families. Indeed, although, as we will see, some Armenians eventually moved from industry to more familiar artisanal professions, the early 1920s were shaped first and foremost by a drive to find employment and financial stability, pushing many into large French factories where they stayed for a decade or longer.

Also shaping the refugees' initial years in France was a desire to reproduce the family they had lost. Indeed, many of those who had survived the genocide and migrated abroad were young orphans who had lost all their immediate relatives to the slaughter. After finding a permanent settlement place, these young men and women quickly began to marry and have children. Birthrates were thus high, even among those whose resources were reduced, and raising these young children became a preoccupation for a generation that had lost so much.[14]

In addition to creating stable financial and familial structures, the new refugees also turned immediately to providing for their basic spiritual and educational needs. Here too, an examination of Camp Oddo is instructive. Initially, conditions in the camp—as for Armenians everywhere in France—were extremely difficult. Aside from the major financial deprivations that accompanied unemployment, refugees also lacked medical care and other essential services. As one French author described the camp's living conditions, "Decidedly, this is the lowest level of living, the only lower being under the bridges." Another claimed that Oddo's population was living like animals. Indeed, conditions became so unbearable that a group of refugees chose to live on some vacant land along an ill-smelling stream near the rue des Aygalades rather than in the camp's crowded barracks.[15] Over time, however, and in response to the various problems, the local Armenian population began to care for its own. Indeed, it is instructive to look at Camp Oddo as a microcosm of Armenian activities more generally in the initial months following their arrival in France, for even here, where conditions were at their worst, the newcomers were able to establish a functioning community.

From the beginning, those in the camp were given the responsibility of caring for their own administration. Having established the Comité des secours aux réfugiés arméniens de Marseille, local Armenians ran the camp and raised money for the new refugees. Employed residents paid the committee 50 centimes a day, providing funds for the barracks, heating, and electricity.[16] Inside the camp, the Comité de secours selected representatives to keep order and to enforce basic discipline. This internal administration quickly became permanent under the watchful but noninterfering eye of the local police. Indeed, in keeping with the assimilationist logic discussed in the previous chapters, the police viewed both the director of the camp, Takvor Hatchikian, and its director of public health and mail delivery, Mosès Deirmendjian, as acceptable liaisons between the refugees and the national government because both had fought under the French during World War I and because the former was a French citizen and the latter was in the process of naturalization.[17]

Inside the camp, residents were assigned the task of maintaining hygiene, medical, and mail services. Thus, although a French doctor visited the camp two times a week to distribute medicine, an Armenian nurse lived in the camp and provided daily first aid to residents. Similarly, education of the camp's several hundred children was provided in its own school by three French teachers, paid for by the government, and three Armenian teachers, paid for by Oddo's administration. Because many of the students were too old to attend Marseille's schools, the camp's educational system provided essential language training to teenagers who may not have been able to acquire it elsewhere.[18] In addition, despite housing shortages within the camp itself, the residents transformed one barracks into a chapel.

From 1922 to 1926, then, the Armenians in Camp Oddo set up their own village, one that functioned in relation to but independent of the larger city. Although living conditions were far from ideal, it provided its residents with a sense of community in which they were surrounded by familiar language and customs. As such, Camp Oddo served as a retreat from the life of the city where those who held jobs spent their days. Moreover, it provided those who had spent years looking for a permanent place of settlement with a safe environment in which they could rebuild from the upheaval of the preceding decade. Yet, as will become clear, the camp's stability proved temporary. Nevertheless, a focus on camp life suggests that for most incoming Armenian survivors, material concerns such as finding a home, employment, education, and medical care dictated communal priorities for the better part of the 1920s as residents sought to make a place for themselves in their new country. Whether creating new families to replace those they had lost, working to put food on the table, or establishing basic communal institutions, Armenians in the camp as well as throughout Paris, Marseille, and Lyon were preoccupied with establishing the basic structures to support their life in France. Not surprisingly, for Jewish survivors of World War II, such concerns were also paramount.

Rebuilding Jewish Lives

Like their brethren throughout Europe, Jews in France suffered severely as a result of the Holocaust.[19] Not only was a quarter of the prewar population deported and killed, but communal life was also severely damaged, as synagogues, schools, and cultural organizations throughout the country were systematically closed and dismantled. As one returnee to Strasbourg reported in October 1945, "The synagogue has been destroyed. None of our rabbis has returned—either due to deportations or to death—everything must be rebuilt from top to bottom." In Paris alone, seventeen of the city's consistorial rabbis were deported, leaving only six to rebuild religious life.[20] As one surviving rabbi described the community's state of affairs, "We find ourselves in the aftermath of the Liberation in the presence of a destroyed community. Our rabbis are prisoners, deported, or have been shot. Our institutions have vanished in the torment."[21]

Foreign-born Jews who had immigrated to France during the interwar years were hit the hardest. Although antisemitic policies were directed at all Jews, French xenophobia ensured that those policies were most fiercely enforced against recent arrivals.[22] As a result, immigrant Jews lost property, places of worship, and communal centers and were deported in larger numbers than native French Jews. Indeed, entire congregations disappeared from the Parisian map as they were systematically arrested and deported.[23]

In the aftermath, however, both foreign-born and native-born faced similar struggles. To cite two examples, Camille C., an Iranian Jewish immigrant, lost her husband and home and was left alone to raise eight young children. Paul B. was a French citizen and an upper-middle-class businessman; nevertheless, his home and two major commercial enterprises were sold without his consent. In addition, his brother, brother-in-law, sister-in-law, and niece were deported.[24] Although his postwar resources were greater than Camille C.'s, both faced great challenges, and both were left to replace their material losses while coming to terms with those that were irreplaceable.

Following World War II, then, rich and poor, immigrant and native faced comparable dilemmas. Reestablishing themselves, however, did not necessarily occur at the same pace. Several months after liberation, when some had already taken significant steps toward reclaiming jobs, homes, and property, others "were still using false addresses and fictitious names" and "were just beginning to come out of hiding in remote rural areas."[25] As this quotation suggests, those lucky enough to have suffered only minimal material losses or who had suffered few displacements faced fewer problems picking up where they had left off. Such was the case for those native Jews who had preserved some wealth or who were well-connected to postwar government officials. Perhaps the majority, however, spent the immediate aftermath searching for lost relatives, recommencing interrupted careers, and fighting legal battles over homes and property. Edouard B., for example, a Jewish lawyer from Strasbourg, reported to friends in 1945, "Outside of professional work for my clients, I am still preoccupied with my own affairs, searching for dispersed furniture, rental questions, and above all the one hundred administrative formalities in place everywhere but particularly here." Although he ultimately played an active role in rebuilding his local Jewish community, before turning to communal concerns, B. first had to concentrate on his own great losses. Like him, many French Jews spent the mid-1940s preoccupied with the material concerns of daily living. "The first needs," noted one AJDC report of this period, "were basic human needs for food, clothing, shelter and medical aid," followed quickly by the quest for gainful employment.[26]

One of the first steps in the search for these basic necessities entailed a decision to relocate. Of the approximately two hundred thousand Jews who had remained on French territory throughout the war, many had been displaced from their homes. While Paris remained an important demographic center for the population, many others moved to Lyon, Grenoble, and Montpellier as well as to a variety of small rural towns. Moreover, ten to fifteen thousand had been held as prisoners of war since 1940, and several thousand others had fled the country for Switzerland, London, and Algeria. Immediately following the liberation of Paris, surviving Jews began flocking to the nation's capital in search of family members, homes, and employment.[27]

For most, finding work was the first priority, as it could provide the means to reestablish all other aspects of life. And yet, obtaining employment could prove particularly vexing. Even those ready and willing to work often lacked the necessary capital to regain their former business or purchase the materials and supplies required to fund new ventures. One war victim, for example, having regained possession of his clothing store, found only a depleted stock of outmoded styles. Having no resources, he was forced to close the store.[28] Others like him who had been dispossessed by anti-Jewish legislation faced tremendous difficulties in the first few months following liberation.

Four overlapping categories from within the Jewish population proved particularly vulnerable, "[remaining] seriously maladjusted, dependent and in need of long-time assistance or institutional care."[29] First were the old and infirm, such as Berthe R., a seventy-eight-year-old war widow, or Jules D., a crippled soldier whose entire fortune was seized under anti-Jewish legislation. Second were immigrant Jews who had migrated to France from central and eastern European countries during the 1930s. When World War II hit, many had only recently fled their own country. Having just begun the process of integrating into French society, they were suddenly forced to uproot themselves yet again. In the aftermath, they found themselves, as one put it, "once again in a situation of difficult flux without family, money, work, furniture, and with my health very affected by so much unhappiness." Establishing homes and finding employment when they lacked both experience and connections often proved difficult.[30]

Third were those Jews, native and immigrant alike, who had survived deportation. Returning to France "morally destitute," many had lost not only every member of their family but also their communal support network. Jewish relief agencies sought to house them temporarily with other Jewish families, but lack of housing meant that in many cases these former deportees were forced to remain in refugee centers. René P. and his wife, for example, returned from seven months of imprisonment and torture to find themselves residing in a refugee center with few hopes of finding surviving family or property. In other cases, deportees required convalescent care and intensive retraining after years of unemployment.[31]

Fourth were new Jewish migrants to France, a significant percentage of whom were Holocaust survivors themselves. Unable to return to their own country in light of new antisemitic violence that had broken out in eastern Europe in the months following World War II, many so-called displaced persons sought shelter in central and western Europe. A large percentage remained residents of concentration camps (now transformed into refugee camps) in Germany as international authorities sought solutions for their settlement; others made their way to whatever country would take them in.[32] For France, these newcomers provided a necessary labor force to bolster the floundering postliberation economy, and as a result immigration policies remained relatively open in the years following the war. This fact, coupled with a steady flow of illegal immigration, ensured that Jews from all over eastern and central Europe as well as those from Algeria, Tunisia, Morocco, and Egypt made their way to Paris and other urban centers.[33] Slightly less visible than their eastern European brethren, these latter populations became numerically significant only in the late 1950s. As early as 1949, however, Jewish officials were reporting on the large numbers arriving in Paris and Marseille. The sum of all these migration waves meant that by 1949, thirty-seven thousand new Jewish immigrants had arrived in France.[34]

These refugees often arrived destitute and in desperate need of medical, occupational, and financial aid. One Jewish social worker described the North African arrivals as "sometimes simply naked and hav[ing] numerous families with small children." Despite their tremendous needs, however, the newcomers could expect little aid from the already established French Jewish population, which was seeking desperately to regain its own footing. Robert Gamzon, the head of the Éclaireurs israélites de France and a leading member of the Jewish Resistance, commented in 1946: "The wandering Jews from Eastern Europe are coming in every day for aid but we have become so poor ourselves, we have no houses, no furniture, no jobs. Our whole country is in ruins, and often, too often, all we can give is an understanding smile, a handshake, moral help."[35]

As noted in the previous chapter, in the months immediately following the liberation of Paris, the French government was not prepared to handle the numerous political, social, and economic problems facing its population, and particularly not that of surviving Jews. Local Jewish welfare agencies thus did their best to fill in the gap. Lacking adequate resources themselves and often dependent for funds on diaspora organizations, particularly the American Joint Distribution Committee, numerous agencies made a valiant effort to provide financial grants, medical treatment, and legal assistance to a diverse population of new immigrants, returning deportees, children, and senior citizens. Particularly significant were the actions of the Fédération des sociétés juives de France (FSJF), an umbrella organization originally formed in 1913 to coordinate the activities of immigrant Jewish groups, particularly those sympathetic to Zionism and hostile to communism.[36] Under the wartime persecutions the Fédération had transformed itself into a "multi-faceted social agency," instituting a wide range of welfare projects such as child and senior citizen care, aid for immigrants and returning deportees, and medical and financial relief, all of which continued in the war's aftermath.[37]

The diverse activities of the FSJF were seconded by other Jewish institutions. The Union des Juifs pour la résistance et l'entr'aide (UJRE), a communist organization that had been active in the Resistance, helped Jews with restitution claims, aided them in their fight for apartments, built children's homes, and tried to influence the government to work on behalf of Jewish interests.[38] Likewise, various organizations provided care for Jewish children and orphans, including the Éclaireurs israélites de France, a Zionist youth movement; the Oeuvre de protection des enfants juifs (OPEJ), a Zionist child care agency that had grown out of the Resistance; and, mainly, the Oeuvre de secours aux enfants (OSE), an international child care organization that worked actively in France prior to, during, and after the war.[39]

Relying both on the aid of these local and diaspora Jewish agencies and on their own efforts and energy, the Jewish population in France spent the first months and years after liberation "pounding the pavement," seeking apartments, belongings, jobs, and lost family members. The struggle for housing was among the most pressing problems they faced. The delays in the creation of restitution laws meant that those whose apartments had been occupied were often forced to remain in the provinces or abroad.[40] After November 1944, when the provisional government issued laws to allow dispossessed Jews to reclaim their homes, many still had to wait for lengthy court proceedings while the current occupants contested their eviction. Such cases were particularly difficult in war-torn regions like Alsace and Lorraine, where returning refugees and the native population vied for the few remaining apartments that had not been bombed by the Germans or occupied by military and civil administrations.[41] Legal cases, though often successful for those who sought redress, stretched well into 1946. Even those settled out of court often required months of negotiations.[42] Moreover, many such "amiable exchanges" ended up in court if simply to recognize legally that which had been agreed upon in principle by the two concerned parties. Despite simply representing legal recognition of a friendly exchange, they took time and money to settle.[43] Moreover, the struggle to reclaim or locate housing, even when successful, did not complete the resettlement process. Edward A., for example, finally won the right to reclaim his apartment; unfortunately, once there, he had nothing to put in it. Hence, even when a war victim received an apartment relatively quickly, the struggle to regain lost possessions often stretched on.[44] During the first few years after liberation, then, survivors turned inward, directing their energies to reassembling their property, rebuilding their professional lives, ensuring their economic stability, and in many cases, building new families.[45] Not surprisingly, they, like the Armenians discussed above, sought first and foremost to regain a sense of personal and communal stability. This search for the foundations of a stable life had profound implications on how both populations integrated into the French state in the aftermath of their respective genocides.

Integrating into the Polity

Version Originale vs. *Version Doublée:* Armenians and the French State
For the thousands of Armenians fleeing deportation, violence, and dislocation, France seemed a particularly welcome haven. Indeed, unlike local Jewish survivors who had suffered at French hands, Armenian refugees saw France as a clean break from the recent past of massacre, flight, and poverty. Grateful for the stability France afforded after all the years of upheaval, many voiced real love of their new home. Memoirs such as that of the well-known Armenian filmmaker Henri Verneuil depict the joy the refugees felt as their boat pulled into Marseille's docks, finally ending months and sometimes years of flight. Other authors recount the awe and happiness that newcomers felt upon arriving in Paris: "They had been taught to love and venerate this country," writes Marig Ohanian, "where the words 'Liberty, Equality, Fraternity' represented all that they had never known."[46]

But although, for many, France seemed to provide a new beginning, this relationship was tinged with insecurity. In his memoir and subsequent film of his childhood, Verneuil captures how first-generation Armenian refugees mediated between that from which they had come and their new society. "In a constant state of vigilance to insure that the habits of the past [*plis d'origine*] did not offend their new environment," he writes, the refugees, like a film, moved at all times between the original version (*version originale*) and the dubbed version (*version doublée*), mediating their own customs, culture, and fashion of seeing things into the language and customs of their new setting.[47] Although Verneuil's metaphor could describe how most immigrants interact with new surroundings, it is particularly insightful when characterizing the plight of Armenian refugees in the 1920s and 1930s. As stateless refugees and genocide survivors, these apatrides could not return to their land of origin. Having been uprooted and permanently cut off from the past, they were left only with what lay before them — in this case, France. Fearing further disruption and realizing how entirely dependent they were on French benevolence, the local Armenian population remained constantly aware of its precarious position. This awareness, coupled with the intense search for stability described above, shaped how Armenian refugees integrated into their new state.

Particularly nervous was the generation of Armenians who had come to France in the decades preceding World War I. Given the importance of Paris for World War I diplomacy, numerous Armenian representatives had flocked there hoping to influence foreign powers on behalf of their causes. One scholar has noted: "It was in Paris that Armenia's fate was decided, where the church and Armenians rushed their representatives. During the war, it was to Paris that Armenian volunteers . . . flocked en route to the Caucasus or for the Eastern front."[48] These men joined an already well-integrated population of prosperous businessmen and intellectuals, many of whom were active participants in the city's highest social and cultural circles.[49]

This small community of approximately four thousand thus witnessed the genocide from afar. Although actively involved in Armenian affairs — particularly with mediating the Armenian Question in diplomatic circles and establishing an autonomous homeland for Armenian refugees under Western mandate — they suffered few daily consequences either from the genocide or from the subsequent refugee problem.[50] For them, the refugee crisis was a political problem that had to be managed, preferably by establishing an autonomous Armenian region in the borderlands between the Ottoman and Russian Empires. As one well-known French Armenian writer noted in 1916, "The Armenian majority will be quickly reestablished in an autonomous Armenia by the return of a large number of the numerous émigrés who are scattered throughout Europe, Egypt, America, and in the diverse non-Armenian regions of Turkey."[51] Thus, while actively involved in providing for the thousands of uprooted refugees, local political leaders and wealthy philanthropists in Paris tended to view the post–World War I upheaval as temporary. The refugees' dispersion and displacement would end as soon as Armenian national aspirations were realized.

In 1922, however, local understandings of the refugee problem began shifting radically as thousands of Armenians began migrating to France. No longer an abstract or distant category, the newcomers arrived with real problems and needs, often turning to the settled population for aid. Furthermore, the signing of the Treaty of Lausanne in 1923 brought a new permanence to the refugees' fate. Local philanthropists rose to this new challenge, establishing facilities to which the newcomers could turn for material support. One such organization was the Office National Arménienne, a multifaceted employment and settlement agency established in Marseille in 1922 by Aram Turabian, an Armenian who had settled in that city in the late 1890s. Understanding that his newly arriving compatriots had suffered great hardship in recent years, he worked tirelessly to ease their integration into their adopted country, interceding with government officials on their behalf and helping them find work in local industry. If sympathetic to their plight, however, he also worried that they could quickly wear out their welcome. Those lucky enough to find refuge in France, he explained, "must never lose sight of the fact that we are guests." As such, Armenians had to continually prove their worth to their hosts by working hard, respecting the laws of the land, keeping a low profile, and avoiding any involvement in French internal affairs. "The Frenchman is a good child, a good comrade," he wrote, "but he does not like being taken for a sucker [prendre pour une poire]; if due to the tactfulness of his race he does not tell you bluntly how he thinks of you, he has an opinion just the same."[52]

Turabian's advice to his fellow Armenians is particularly interesting given that it came several years before the most virulent anti-immigrant sentiment surfaced in France. Never enthusiastic about the foreign influx, the public displayed considerably less aversion to non-French workers prior to the economic depression of the mid-1930s.[53] Moreover, as we have already seen, even when the population turned aggressively against foreign workers, Armenian refugees often escaped some of the harshest criticisms. Certainly there were those who came under attack, such as those concentrated in Camp Oddo or singled out occasionally by labor organizations protesting their hiring at low wages.[54] Such responses were rare, however, and most were able to blend into the wider foreign labor market without calling much attention to themselves.

Why, then, was Turabian so concerned with influencing his compatriots' comportment? If Armenians faced little threat, why was it necessary to instruct them on how to behave? Turabian's concern, like that of the established Armenian leadership more generally, can be seen as a reflection of a shifting understanding of the urgency and permanence of the refugee problem as well as a growing awareness of their dependence on French benevolence. Once it was clear that the status of the refugees would not be addressed adequately in any of the postwar peace treaties and following new waves of massacres in Turkey, the Armenian leadership began looking for other alternatives to the refugee problem. With no national base of their own, however, and with most international doors remaining closed to the refugees, Armenian leaders had little leverage. Indeed, as dreams of a national homeland faded, France's willingness to take in two hundred thousand Armenians (including those in Syria and Lebanon) seemed ever more significant. As Turabian argued, "Among our war allies, France is the only country (other than Greece) that has given us hospitality on its territory, and it is perhaps the only Great Power [puissance] that resents the injustice committed towards the Armenian people."[55] Concerned that if the newcomers alienated the government they could be deprived of the right to settle, Armenian communal leaders from across the political and social landscape thus began urging their compatriots to blend into their new home.

This new awareness manifested itself in constant public praise for the "generous hospitality" France had provided to Armenians. Indeed, all public communal events became opportunities to express gratitude to France and to encourage loyalty to its culture and institutions.[56] More important, however, were the attempts of various Armenian benevolent institutions, like Turabian's, to influence refugee behavior. For example, while the benefactors of the charitable organization the Société de bienfaisance des Arméniens de Paris, were committed to aiding indigent refugees, they worried that too many unemployed workers were arriving in Paris.[57] Relying on French charity, however, was out of the question because they feared that in so doing Armenians would be perceived as a financial drain. To encourage self-reliance, the Comité des jeunes filles, an auxiliary organization of the Société de bienfaisance, awarded a 2,000 franc prize annually to five young Armenian women. The prerequisite for winning was that the woman, having arrived without resources, had supported her family "through diligent hard work without turning to a third party" and thereby "given proof of the best virtues of our race." Thus, although the Société de bienfaisance was a charitable organization, its award celebrated those who cared for themselves and their family, kept a low profile, and did not rely on institutional support. According to those providing communal charity, then, self-reliance and a strong work ethic were the traits that most deserved recognition and should serve as a model for others.[58]

The most vocal efforts to shape refugee behavior were made by the half-French, half-Armenian paper Le Foyer. The bilingual paper, which went into production in 1928 under the direction of editor H. D. Nersessian-Massis, continually stressed the harmonious and mutually beneficial relations between the Armenians and the French dating back to the Crusades.[59] Similarly, it praised Armenians as the "the most conscientious and devoted agents" of the "dissemination of French [rayonnement français] in the Orient."[60] For Nersessian, celebrating these former ties was more than a rhetorical ploy to ingratiate Armenians with government officials. Rather, he believed that the past links between these two nations had serious implications for newly arriving refugees. For them, he insisted, France was more than a second homeland: "Armenians who came to France because we did not have a home elsewhere, because we were exiles, émigrés, refugees, wanderers seeking a land, a home, we have proclaimed: Here is our new homeland."[61]

Numerous of Le Foyer's articles stressed the contributions that Armenians would and did make to French society, as if trying to convince a skeptical reader that the refugees deserved a special place in the average citizen's heart. The defensive nature of these articles reflects the notable insecurity emerging among the Armenian community's established leadership. For example, one article argued that Armenians would not be a continual source of trouble like other foreigners because their immigration was confined to a limited number; no newcomers would augment the sixty thousand already there and, hence, they could pose no danger to the national labor force. Moreover, the high birthrate among Armenians posed no threat: "Their children, born in France, are no longer refugees; most often they are registered as French [citizens] and, as a result, will be assimilated." The article also stressed practical contributions that Armenians could make to the national economy: having no homeland to which to return and no loyalties anywhere else in the world, they would keep their wealth inside the country. Furthermore, they would bring in new industries through their involvement in the silk trade and their links in commerce and industry with other Armenians throughout the Near East. In sum, the refugees were a stable addition to the national landscape who, having arrived without resources, had rapidly sought "to create a home, a house, a nest." The results "constituted obvious proof of the Armenian people's inherent virtues: dedicated labor, family spirit, love of the home, frugality, sobriety, and saving."[62]

If the French half of Le Foyer stressed the refugees' assets to an imaginary non-Armenian reader, the Armenian half—directed at the new refugees—stressed rules of behavior that would transform them into citizens worthy of respect. One article, for example, noted, "Every Armenian living in France will find that in this country he is obliged to live according to precise rules and laws." Neglecting this legal code would bring swift punishment. Nervous of expulsion laws that could instantly turn the newly settled workers into refugees again, the article provided instructions for how the newcomers should behave. Moreover, the first Armenian-language editorial, "Our Goal," reminded readers that France was the only country to open its doors to the refugees after waves of terrible massacres and thus deserved their loyalty. To inculcate the appropriate pro-French sentiment among its readers, the editor also included a section on the country's geography and history so that they would "better know and appreciate this admirable country that is henceforth our home."[63]

Like Le Foyer, other Armenian publications attempted to influence the refugees' comportment and to teach them about the country in which they found themselves so as to make them feel more attached to their new setting. One Armenian-language guide in Marseille, for example, provided newcomers with a pictorial and textual history of their new city. In a slightly different vein, the Parisian Armenian satiric journal Gavroche published a tongue-in-cheek article called "The Ten Commandments According to Armenian Refugees Wherever They May Be," which demonstrated the importance of blending in while simultaneously pointing to the impossibility of the task. "Remember that you are not in your father's house," instructed the first "commandment," "but that you are only a guest wherever you are. Thus, do not forget that a guest makes no fuss in the house to which he has been invited; he stays calm, eats what is put before him, and conforms agreeably to all of their manners and customs." The second reminded Armenians to be kind and polite to their hosts, staying far removed from their business and trying to remain in their good graces. Furthermore, the third continued, "Do not annoy the master of the house and his family with your own personal quarrels and discussions. You have no right to disturb the decent people who opened their home and their arms to you and do not leave them saying: 'What disagreeable people. It is not surprising that they could not be accommodated in their own home!' " The other "commandments" continued along similar lines, insisting that a good guest fulfills his duties, conforms to the rules of the house, speaks the language of the host, and never presumes to act as he would in his own home: "The master of the house may walk in slippers . . . but you are not permitted to take off your shoes." The evident irony in this list of instructions suggests that its authors were aware of how well it would resonate with a public conscious of such admonitions about their behavior. Indeed, if not yet entirely clear in the nine other "commandments," the tenth summarized them all: "Be polite, act with tact, keep the laws, do not argue, do not speak in a loud voice, do not bring your quarrels with you to your new country, and . . . do not put on the airs of the master of the house where you are only a guest."[64] In short, do nothing to call attention to your existence.

Thus, in numerous examples there is evidence of efforts to control the behavior of newly arriving refugees. In this respect, the established Armenian leadership responded to their incoming compatriots much like native French

Jews responded to eastern European Jewish refugees in the same era, using their philanthropic institutions "as agents of assimilation" in an attempt to remake the culturally, linguistically, and ethnically distinct refugees "in their own image."[65] However, whereas the French Jewish leadership was motivated by fears of developing antisemitism, Armenian representatives were primarily concerned that if the newcomers alienated the national government, they could be deprived of the right to settle in France. Moreover, if, as has been well argued, many immigrant Jews proved hostile to these attempts to influence their behavior, incoming Armenian refugees clearly shared the insecurities of their leadership. Although *Gavroche*'s ten commandments clearly adopted the integrationist rhetoric as a tool of parody, other refugee publications often pleaded with the newcomers to adopt "respectable" behavior and to remain as inconspicuous as possible, particularly in public spaces. One newspaper, for example, reported with dismay that the benches in the garden surrounding Marseille's train station had been removed because they had become meeting places for Armenian women and children whose veils and "colorful untidy rags . . . presented a very unpleasant view for the traveler's eye." Such careless behavior, the article continued, was typical of the Armenian presence in all public areas where they refused to wear suitable clothing or to accommodate themselves to the local population; this negligence was discrediting the Armenian name. To address the problem, the article asked local compatriot associations to teach their members rules of hygiene and proper conduct in public arenas such as the street, market, and stores.[66]

Unsurprisingly, such organizations did take shape. In Marseille in 1925, the Union arménienne des amis du progrès was established to educate Armenian youth and young adults morally and intellectually and to familiarize them with Western civilization. A secondary goal consisted of providing aid to indigent members, but the Union was focused primarily on fostering a knowledge of literature and art through its adult education classes and its library.[67] Similarly, other compatriot organizations stressed the importance of learning French and adopting basic cultural standards.

The newcomers thus remained quite conscious of how they appeared to their neighbors, particularly in the public sphere, where some feared that any disruption could lead to new difficulties. In Valence, for example, one communal representative publicly congratulated the police for arresting three Armenian burglars. According to him, the arrests had created an inaccurate impression of the local refugee population, which was hardworking and dedicated to making an honest living. "Concerned with safeguarding the honor of a civilized people of whom we are only the debris . . . and indignant over the misdeeds committed by certain dishonest people," he remarked, "I am obliged to make a public appeal to the conscience of our French friends and to ask them not to attribute to a whole nation the abominable acts of the few whom we detest just as much and whom we are happy to see fall into the hands of Justice."[68] Clearly, no loyalty to other Armenians transcended the need to keep up appearances for the surrounding population.

Verneuil speaks directly to this desire to "pass unnoticed" in his description of his discomfort with his apatride status. "To benefit from this title of 'Mr. Nobody,'" he writes, "I was required immediately to substitute a new fashion of speaking for my own."[69] Referring here to the necessity of learning French in order to "disappear," Verneuil suggests that some of the new refugees saw language not only as a useful tool that would allow them to participate in the world around them but as a step on the road to seeming less foreign. Admittedly, Verneuil was a child when he arrived in France and, therefore, much more inclined to adopt surrounding cultural norms as his own. Indeed, for tradesmen interested in selling wares to French buyers and for children attending local schools, French skills were a necessity. Although some Armenian communities established their own schools that attracted a substantial number of children, they often lacked funds to function well.[70] In fact, the refugees generally preferred to send their children to French schools, well aware that without language skills the children would be at a disadvantage in their new society.[71] Rapidly, then, Armenian—like most immigrant languages—became a language of the home and local community, and French became the language for the public sphere, often with children acting as the connection between them.[72] As Verneuil's comment suggests, however, this shedding of foreignness had a particular resonance for these apatrides, whose settlement options remained so constrained.

As the above examples suggest, the recent past of genocide and deportation induced tremendous caution among Armenian refugees in France. For them, this new context provided the safe haven they so craved after years of disruption, and they opted for a path of peaceful integration into their new home. But if to Armenians integration into the French state seemed a way to protect their safety in a postgenocide world, one might well ask how this national context appeared to French Jews in the aftermath of World War II. Unlike Armenians, most Jews were rebuilding their community in the country in which they had been persecuted. It seems inconceivable that for them France could seem an equally welcome haven. Nevertheless, Jews in postwar France, like the Armenians who settled there previously, rarely questioned the state's ability to integrate them. With the restoration of republican government, French Jews fully expected to regain their former status and, like the Armenians preceding them, they relied on their faith in the French state to reestablish stability in their postgenocide world.

Reintegrating after Genocide: Jews in Postwar France
To think about how French Jews constructed their relationship to the state in their post-Vichy society, we must first recall the particular relationship that France had carved out with its Jewish residents in the century and a half following the Revolution. Such an examination will highlight the shock that followed the promulgation of Vichy's first antisemitic laws for those who believed that their position was guaranteed by the rule of law. It will also reveal why French Jews were so eager to reintegrate into the French polity following the Holocaust.

As noted in the introduction, the immediate impact of the 1791 emancipation of France's Jewish population has been a matter of considerable debate. And yet, although historians disagree over the rate and degree of Jewish religious and ethnic transformation once citizenship was granted to them, most agree that the legacy of the legal shift determined the relationship between the Jewish communal leadership and the state throughout the nineteenth and early twentieth centuries. As historian Paula Hyman has observed, "[French Jews] were able to identify with the French political system and express confidence that its rule of law would ensure their continued equality." Simultaneously, however, "they recognized that as the adopted children of France they would have to repeatedly prove their devotion and worthiness as French citizens."[73] As such, Jewish institutions sought to create patriotic citizens, comfortable both with French social norms and a Judaism that was compatible with French citizenship. Although few French Jews understood their citizenship to be a rejection of their Jewish identity, by the end of the nineteenth century most had come to wholeheartedly embrace Enlightenment and republican ideals, believing themselves to be protected and equal members of their society. Indeed, "to one degree or another," as one scholar has put it recently, "all French Jews . . . remained *fous de la République*, or zealots of the Republic."[74]

Such an assessment is not to suggest that Jewish faith in the French state never wavered. In eras of particularly strong hostility toward Jews, most notably during the Dreyfus Affair, some Jews reconsidered their place in their national community and reaffirmed their commitment to Jewish culture and communal ties. Indeed, the cries of "Death to the Jews!" that accompanied the arrest and trial of the French Jewish army captain for treason "marked a critical reference point in the development of [French] Jewish identities."[75] Interestingly, however, even in these periods, few believed their status in their birth land to be in question.

Indeed, Dreyfus's eventual exoneration was proof positive that the Republic was ultimately blind to religious differences among its citizens and that justice would prevail even in the face of intolerance.[76] Moreover, active Jewish participation in French military activities during World War I and a marked decline in antisemitism in the years after the Dreyfus Affair, particularly in the 1920s, reconfirmed the secure position of Jews within the state.[77]

In the 1930s, however, this status came into question once again. Indeed, during the ten years preceding World War II, a rising antisemitism threatened once again to undermine the position of Jews in French society and challenge the long-established relationship they had maintained between their ethnoreligious affiliations and their national loyalties. This surge in antisemitic rhetoric coincided with rising numbers of Jewish refugees flocking to France from Germany and further east. By 1939, between 45,000 and 50,000 new Jews had arrived, joining the ranks of approximately 100,000 other Jewish immigrants from the east who had migrated to France in the previous decades.[78] Worried that the newcomers' "foreignness" would undermine their *own* position in French society in this new atmosphere of economic depression and rising anti-Jewish sentiment, the local Jewish leadership actively worked to encourage the immigrants' acculturation, prevailing on them to adopt French customs and to shed their "Jewish" traits. Indeed, even those Jewish communal leaders most sympathetic to the refugees' plight and dedicated to creating a safe refuge for them in France never stopped admonishing the newcomers to acculturate quickly, arguing that in exchange for such transformations, the French government would provide immigrants with citizenship and defend their equality.[79]

Many of the recent newcomers, however, were unconvinced. Unlike earlier waves of eastern European Jewish immigrants who had already begun the process of adapting to French cultural, social, and political norms, those who came in the 1930s, particularly from eastern Europe, were more wary.[80] In *their* native countries, antisemitism and administrative discrimination had provided Jews with few means of integrating into the larger society. As a result, few trusted that national governments would act benevolently, protecting them from anti-Jewish discrimination. Moreover, they "could not understand the natives' continual allusion to the distinctiveness of the French Jewish experience," and many "remained unimpressed by native arguments about the differences between an 'enlightened' French government and 'backward' eastern European regimes."[81]

When, in October 1940, the Vichy government enacted the Statut des juifs, officially relegating Jews to second-class citizens, those who had migrated to France most recently were in some ways more psychologically prepared, as they already doubted their host society's ability or willingness to protect them. Those whose allegiance to France went back a generation or more, however, were taken by surprise when Vichy imposed its anti-Jewish legislation, no matter how aware they had been of a growing antisemitism in their midst.[82] Indeed, many responded with "pain and anguish," whereas recent arrivals reacted with "nothing like the emotional soul-searching that characterized native Jewry's response."[83]

As the war continued, however, it became increasingly difficult for French Jewish citizens to defend their *patrie*. Vichy's anti-Jewish policies, which at first affected immigrant Jews more than the native-born, soon caught up with even the most devoted French Jewish patriots.[84] Moreover, in the immediate aftermath, various communal authorities could not help but distinguish the particularity of the Jewish fate during World War II, thereby distancing themselves from their French compatriots even in the glorious days of liberation. As Guy de Rothschild noted in 1945, "The tragedy is too great to be fully grasped but it dwarfs in the eyes of France the wonderful, victorious war news." Likewise, the *Bulletin d'information*, a journal of international Jewish news, reported, "Although French and foreign Jews hail [the victory] with immense joy the same as all their compatriots, they have been too branded in their flesh and spirits by the defeat of June '40 and by the ignominious Hitlerian persecution to be able to detach themselves for even a moment from the memory of their dead and their martyrs." Or as one French rabbi later remarked, "On the day of the Liberation of Paris, we did not have the heart to surrender fully to the collective joy."[85]

And yet, if for some France's victory was shrouded with memories of the preceding years, for others the end of the war meant principally the immediate abrogation of all of Vichy's discriminatory statutes, after which Jews in France were once again emancipated. In some sense, whatever conclusions had been reached during the war had now to be reassessed in light of the restoration of full equality. On the one hand, the four years of state-sanctioned discrimination and persecution had proven that Jewish emancipation was reversible and therefore insecure. On the other hand, the restoration of full equality also suggested that the recent past was nothing but an aberration. The active attempts to defeat the Germans, the flowering of a native French Resistance movement, and the postwar prosecution of Vichy officials bolstered this theory and validated the prewar position of the native Jewish leadership. For nearly 150 years republican government had protected Jewish rights, and it would continue to do so as long as fascist dictators were contained.

In the postwar years, advocates of both positions made their case, as survivors reconsidered, or in some cases reconfirmed, their understandings of Jewish national identity in light of their wartime experiences. For example, Samuel René Kapel, a native-born rabbi and a member of the Orthodox Zionist organization Mizrachi, repeatedly stressed that if there was one lesson to be learned from the "bloody events" it was that emancipation had failed to ensure Jewish integration. "It is in our interests and in that of our children to reject assimilation once and for all," he declared. "We will no longer allow ourselves to be deluded by vain promises; the awakening was cruel and our deception profound." Kapel believed that antisemitism had so infected French society that it would take years for it to be purged; his own solution was a Jewish nationalism that would allow Jewish voices to be heard and their culture and traditions to flourish. Indeed, in 1954, after working for ten years to encourage the spread of Zionism, he settled permanently in Israel. For Kapel, therefore, the Holocaust had proven the need for a Jewish homeland; assimilation was a profoundly dangerous choice, not only because it undermined Jewish life but because its adherents had misjudged its success, believing themselves safe in a country that, in fact, proved ready to turn against them without provocation.[86]

Others shared Kapel's strong viewpoint, as is clear by an excerpt from the Zionist paper La Terre retrouvée, which chastised those who still remained committed to prewar assimilationist tendencies:

> Numerous are those among us who believe that the pure and simple return to the prewar status quo will suffice to end [the war] and to make us forget the nightmare through which we have lived; according to them we must simply cross our arms and wait until the complete abrogation of all anti-Jewish measures redresses the wrongs that were done. . . . However, there are those of us who believe that a return to the past, however marvelous [it] can seem amidst the infernal distress in which we currently reside, is not enough, and that it is necessary, on the contrary, to uncover in this past all the germs that could breed the illnesses from which we suffer today in order to eliminate them.[87]

Yet despite such charges, for others, recent events reconfirmed that assimilation was, in fact, the correct response to resolving the Jewish Question once and for all. Jean-Jacques Bernard, for example, a well-known native French Jewish writer, and son of the even better known French dramatist Tristan Bernard, became a public proponent of radical assimilation. Already in the mid-1930s, Bernard was insisting that the solution to the Jewish Question was the integration of the Jews "into the great mass of humanity." Despite being interned in Compiègne from December 1941 to February 1942 as part of a sweep of French intellectuals and daily faced with the increasing anti-Jewish hostility in his society, which eventually led to his own father's incarceration, Bernard's faith in integration never wavered. Rather, the events of World War II reconfirmed his belief that assimilation was the answer to any residual anti-Jewish sentiment in society. As if proving that Judaism was simply an affiliation that could be changed as easily as an old suit, Bernard converted to Catholicism soon after the war. Moreover, in his memoir and several controversial articles, he argued that French Jews had come out of the war with their understandings of citizenship, loyalty to the nation, and love for country intact.[88] "We cannot hold two nations in our hearts," he wrote, and French Jews could and should be loyal only to France. For him and his comrades in the concentration camp, Bernard claimed, there was no racial or national link between themselves and non-French Jews, only a "complete solidarity with our brothers of persecution without distinguishing between origins." Thus, unlike Kapel, Bernard adamantly refused all Jewish national aspirations, criticizing those whose only true desire is "to annex us, to demonstrate to us that the land that is ours is not really our own, to chain us to their vagabond fate." Such individuals, he insisted, should be fought against as aggressively as Hitler.[89]

The publication of Bernard's book and articles in 1944–45 unleashed a storm of controversy. Some accused him of providing fodder for antisemites in his criticisms of fellow Jews. Others insisted that the war years had proven that whatever ideological, religious, and political divisions separated Jews from one another, they shared a common fate. All Jews had been persecuted and must henceforth stand together.[90] Marc Jarblum, a Polish Jew by birth and president of the Fédération des sociétés juives de France, took such a stance, criticizing Bernard for placing his French citizenship ahead of his Jewish heritage. "The facts are in: the Germans arrested many Frenchmen, but because they were socialists, communists, Catholic resistors, and not because they were French. On the other hand, they arrested Jews independent of their opinions or their nationality in France as well as in Belgium, Holland, and other occupied countries." Nevertheless, Jarblum did not urge his readers to revoke their citizenship, nor did he criticize France for its role in persecuting Jews. Rather, like Bernard, he placed the burden of guilt on the Germans and maintained that Jewish efforts in the Resistance and at the front were offered in their "double capacity" as French citizens *and* as Jews.[91]

Intrigued by the controversy and by the "strange silence" surrounding the Jewish persecution and losses in postwar France, Emanuel Mournier, editor of the Catholic journal *Esprit*, devoted the 1 September 1945 issue to the Jewish Question. In the journal, Jean-Jacques Bernard's assimilationist views were pitted against those of Henri Hertz, a poet, novelist, and critic who rejected all such notions. Like Bernard, Hertz was a native-born French Jew who had distinguished himself in journalism and literature. Unlike Bernard, however, he had been drawn—even before World War II—to the nascent Zionist movement, writing much on Jewish problems in the French press and in 1925 becoming the general secretary of France-Palestine, an early Zionist organization. For Hertz, who survived the war while fighting in the Resistance, the Holocaust reconfirmed his belief in a Jewish national identity.[92] In his article in Esprit he advocated a double patriotism, claiming that if there was no identifiable Jewish "race," there was certainly a Jewish people. For him, like Kapel, the war provided clear indication that emancipation had not worked; rather, Jews must be given the "city, metropole, political center that they have lost." However, Hertz did not suggest that French Jews should abandon their birth land for a new national homeland, but rather that such a state would provide them with "a clear and distinct reference of their lineage and of their legitimacy."[93] Thus, even among those most willing to criticize Bernard's stance, there was a clear preference to emphasize dual loyalties. The Vichy legacy did not mean that Jews had to reject their French patriotism; rather, they had to *supplement* this loyalty with a stronger commitment to Jewish nationalism.[94]

What is most striking to the contemporary reader, however, is the degree to which neither Bernard's call for total assimilation nor Hertz's notion of double patriotism resonated for many of those in positions of communal authority—at least initially—despite the upheaval that their community had recently experienced. Certainly Bernard's assimilationist stance and particularly his conversion to Catholicism proved unacceptable to those striving to rebuild Jewish life after the war. Georges Wormser, president of the central administrative body of French Judaism, the Consistoire de Paris, called Bernard's views "repugnant." Willingly condemning all forms of radical assimilation, however, Consistoire officials proved reluctant to publicly endorse those arguing against him, commenting nervously that "the moment did not seem propitious for engaging in politics."[95] Although, as we will see in chapter 4, the Consistoire leadership did eventually come to support a measured Jewish nationalism, in the immediate aftermath of the war they preferred the "strange silence" surrounding the Jewish Question to a public debate on the place of Jews in French society.[96]

Others, such as the editors of the Bulletin du Centre israélite d'information, reflected the measured response of the Consistoire leadership, adopting an actively "centrist" position on the controversy: "It is fitting to note that 'double patriotism' is Mr. Henri Hertz's personal conception . . . [which] corresponds to the tendencies of only a limited faction of Zionists, while on the other hand, Jean-

Jacques Bernard . . . recently converted to Catholicism, which was naturally his right but which does not indicate the position of those Jews in favor of assimilation."[97] Like the Consistoire, the editors of the Bulletin, in reporting on what they believed to be the attitude of most French Jews, adopted a position that continued to view integration into the French state as a possible and desirable goal.

Indeed, to the extent that the controversy surrounding Bernard's publication provides a window into postwar Jewish responses to the Vichy years, it is clear that for many, the losses and upheaval associated with these years *reconfirmed* much of what they had already assumed prior to the war's outbreak. For Bernard himself, confinement in a concentration camp provided strong evidence that his allegiances lay not with other Jews but with fellow French prisoners. His postwar conversion and publications served as public pronouncements of that loyalty, but his views favoring integration took root in the years *preceding* World War II. Similarly, those favoring a more active Jewish nationalism, such as Hertz, Kapel, and Jarblum (as well as many members of the immigrant Jewish community, as we will see in chapter 4), were also working to that end in the 1930s. Meanwhile, those who had previously been concerned with keeping a low profile to maintain what they viewed as the delicate balance between "Frenchness" and "Jewishness," such as the leaders of the Consistoire, remained committed to that goal.

In all of these cases, then, the Holocaust did not provide a *complete* break with previous ways of thinking about national identity. This is even clearer when we consider the responses of those not in communal authority. Although difficult to document, most evidence suggests that the years of Vichy persecution had not visibly shaken most native Jews' faith in the French state and that neither radical assimilation nor radical nationalism resonated with most French Jews. Bernard's conversion to Catholicism was not widely imitated, despite the fears of some communal leaders. Nor did many take Kapel's route by migrating to Israel—a paltry 6,436 deciding to make the move between 1948 and 1966.[98] One Mossad agent commented when describing the small numbers of French Jews interested in uprooting for Palestine, "Nowhere else have I met Jews who have suffered so much without learning anything." To Ben Gurion and other Yishuv leaders, it soon became clear that "unlike survivors of the death camps, French Jews continued to view their country as their homeland."[99]

Further evidence of Jews' faith in the restored Republic is evident in their attempts to reclaim property after the war's end. Confident that the state would return what was rightfully theirs, thousands applied to government-established restitution offices for compensation. Their requests indicate that most had *not* lost faith in France's will or power to protect its citizens, Jews and non-Jews alike. Moreover, their letters illustrate that they understood their citizenship as their historical right. Many claimants indignantly reminded officials of their sacrifices for la patrie and of their roots in France dating back to the Revolution. Maurice P. wrote, for example, that he belonged to a family of old French stock and that his father had been a veteran of the Franco-Prussian war. Another demanded the arrest of one of his French persecutors "in the name of French humanity and for the future and security of the Republic." The claimant strengthened his own rights by citing his participation in both world wars and his son's service in the Resistance.[100] Such assertions of loyalty and historical lineage are not particularly surprising given that the writers in question were seeking to prove the legitimacy of their restitution claims. Nevertheless, it is also clear that these Jewish citizens did not hide from the public spotlight, nor did they assume that the persecution they had suffered would have repercussions for their postwar status in French society. Rather, they insisted on their legal rights to defense and financial reparations on the grounds that their citizenship offered such protection.

True, not all returning Jews proved quite so willing to overlook their persecution at their neighbors' hands. One quipped, "It was bad enough that we had to suffer through the continual persecution of the enemy without also having to suffer through that of the French." [101] For the majority, however, France remained a country of liberty and justice. Although occasionally complaining that the government was not attending to their needs rapidly enough, few French Jews voiced ambivalence, publicly at least, about their country or its leaders. Indeed, the opposite seems to be true; most seemed secure in the knowledge that republican law in general and the provisional government in particular would right Vichy's wrongs. Moreover, despite an awareness of having suffered at French hands, many were quick to excuse the majority of French citizens from any connection with the persecution. Robert Gamzon, for example, stressed that "with the exception of very few, the French people helped us a great deal. I can say without exaggeration that every living Jew in France was saved at one time or another by a non-Jew." [102] Such an assessment was, in fact, based in reality. As Susan Zuccotti has shown, many Jews in France survived the attack against them largely because of the aid of courageous fellow citizens.[103] Nevertheless, the degree to which Jews sought to put the past behind them is striking. Guy de Rothschild, for example, linked the worst of the persecutions to the Nazis. Although claiming that during the war, he had read Vichy's Statut des juifs in "a state of nausea," feeling "excluded, insulted, designated for public vindictiveness, marked with the brand of infamy," he quickly thereafter "never gave it a thought." Firmly convinced that the French had "rejected this wicked plagiarism of the Nazis," he excused his own nation from any wrongdoing.[104]

It is in this response of Rothschild's that we begin to discern an explanation for the willingness of many Jews to reembrace their prewar faith in the French state. As we saw in chapter 2, unlike Jews from Poland and elsewhere in the east who returned to their homes after the war only to find ongoing antisemitic persecution, those from France returned to a notable silence on issues having to do with the Jewish fate during World War II. Indeed, if some antisemitic rhetoric still singled out Jews from others in the population, the *absence* of Jews from public discourse was far more striking. As Sartre noted in his well-known essay on antisemitism, "Now all France rejoices and fraternizes in the streets; social conflict seems temporarily forgotten; the newspapers devote whole columns to stories of prisoners of war and deportees. Do we say anything about the Jews? Do we give a thought to those who died in the gas chambers at Lublin? Not a word. Not a line in the newspapers."[105]

Such silence on questions of Jewish losses were part of a larger phenomenon that Henry Rousso has labeled "the Vichy Syndrome." This national myth de-emphasized French complicity with the Germans by stressing that the Vichy government had been administered by a small group of misguided men, and that the Germans had committed most of the crimes. If a few French citizens had collaborated, the population as a whole had resisted. The Vichy years could thus be regarded as an aberration; the majority of French citizens had done their part by resisting German fascism and saving their nation's honor.[106]

Most Jews in France participated in maintaining this public myth, which prevented them from calling attention to France's role in the persecution of its Jewish residents.[107] Although, as we will see in chapter 4, some Jews of immigrant extraction were more unforgiving of the recent past, the lines dividing immigrant and native were becoming increasingly blurry in the 1940s. Immigrant Jews had indeed suffered a more dramatic fate during the Vichy period, but those who had arrived in France in the 1920s or previously had, in fact, already gone far in integrating into their new society prior to the outbreak of war.[108] Indeed, in the immediate postwar years, naturalization rates were high among those of immigrant extraction despite the persecution they had recently faced.[109] Thus, for all such "French Jews," whether of more recent or more distant lineage, the post–World War II French recommitment to republican norms was enticing. For most, therefore, public silence on the implications of French complicity with anti-Jewish violence during the war was the rule of the day, and returnees pursued a rapid reintegration into their state.

Why Integration?

Although the two cases under study are undeniably different, a comparison between them displays a striking confidence in the French state's ability and desire to integrate minorities into its fold. Given that both Armenians and Jews had been recently persecuted for their status as distinctive minority groups and given that the latter had been persecuted for that status on French soil, this confidence is quite noteworthy. How can it be explained?

As this chapter has argued, the most pressing concern facing both post-genocide Armenian communities and the post-Holocaust Jewish population was the quotidian needs connected with the reestablishment of their lives and communities. At least in the immediate aftermath, such concerns far outweighed larger existential questions about the position of minorities in nation-states. For both, France seemed to provide a safe context in which to pursue this much desired stability. Indeed, in both cases, improving economic conditions rapidly indicated that the deprivations of the previous years would soon be a thing of the past. For most survivors, therefore, it was the present and not the past that seemed the best measure of their relative safety and potential to thrive. And in both cases, there were few indications that the present posed any dangers whatsoever.

Although Armenian refugees spent 1922 and 1923 struggling to establish some kind of economic stability, the new society in which they found themselves nevertheless provided numerous opportunities and freedoms, allowing them to improve their position rapidly. Not only did most find employment quickly on arriving, but within a relatively short time, large numbers of refugees began moving away from factory work to more familiar artisanal trades, such as tailoring and shoemaking. This shift brought a new economic mobility that allowed Armenians, as we will see subsequently, to build private homes on individually purchased land.

And whereas the arrival of the world depression in 1931 signaled a downturn in the economic fortunes of most French citizens, for Armenians these years actually continued to facilitate their economic integration and occupational diversification, as even more were pushed from industry to artisanship and shopkeeping.[110] As factories began to close and unemployment rose, new laws limited to 10 percent the proportion of foreign workers in French factories. Although the

Armenians' status as apatrides often made them the last foreign workforce to be fired, many eventually found themselves unemployed.[111] In response, the poorest among them turned to peddling or set up small grocery and clothing stands. Over time, the number of these stands increased, some transforming into small shops, groceries, and bakeries. Not all Armenians abandoned manual labor for shop-keeping and craftsmanship, but the population did overwhelmingly transform its economic makeup. By as early as 1923 in Marseille, for example, Armenians were already moving toward more familiar trades, and by 1939, literally dozens of Armenian tailors and shoemakers had set up shop.[112]

Moreover, the economic crisis of 1931–32 led to the development of subcon-tracting, particularly among unemployed Armenian women, who, after having been laid off from the factories, began to make and sell scarves, lace, and knit-wear. Over time, some families invested in sewing machines and designated one member, usually the male head of household, to become the intermediary be-tween those working at home and the local clothing merchants of the quarter. In the most profitable cases, after accumulating some capital, the family could open its own store. A similar process took place among shoemakers. True, the conditions in which most of these families lived remained generally deplorable and most were faced with great poverty and poor living conditions, yet a small group was able to make its way into the middle class by the outbreak of World War II. Moreover, in shifting to subcontracting, even those without great means had begun the process of moving away from industrial labor as their primary means of subsistence. This shift in professional makeup was the first step in the process of creating new and more durable roots after years of rootlessness.[113]

Similarly, although the process of recovery for post–World War II Jewish populations was neither smooth nor immediate, particularly in the first year or two following the cessation of fighting, a number of positive indications sug-gested that life would return to normal now that the Germans had been ousted. Indeed, those with connections and means quickly reported an improvement in their condition, sometimes as early as 1946.[114] For most others, however, the pro-cess took longer and many were faced with great poverty. Nevertheless, a variety of economic and political measures suggested that such conditions might remain only temporary.

In some cases, economic stabilization was facilitated through the restitu-tion legislation, which, though not ideal, still functioned to some degree, par-ticularly in the provinces. Thus, although restitution laws prevented many dispos-sessed families from retrieving their former apartments, some were able to use the November 1944 ordinance to their advantage. Others were able to reclaim their businesses and stores without engaging in protracted battles with new owners. Still other dispossessed French Jews began using the legal system to their advantage, sometimes in contested cases that would take several years to settle, but also in "amiable" exchanges that placed the original owner quickly at the head of his former business. Restitution thus proceeded apace, allowing the Toulouse restitution department, for example, to declare in March 1946, "The businesses and furniture that had been sold or maintained under provisional administration until liberation have been returned to their legitimate owners almost in their entirety." There were numerous cases still in dispute, but by the end of 1946, most Jewish property in this region had been returned to its rightful owners.[115] As this case suggests, in some regions of the country, restitution was an effective means of restoring to Jews what had been taken from them and, hence, providing them with a restored sense of "normalcy."

In Paris, restitution moved more slowly, often giving Jewish war victims the impression that they were being ignored or marginalized. Nevertheless, the political conviction to reverse Vichy's discriminatory legislation provided an optimistic indication that the government was committed to restoring Jews into the body politic, and over the course of several years, restitution legislation did work to put this political conviction into practice. Indeed, as the Mattéolli Commission recently concluded in its review of restitution procedures in postwar France, even if such procedures were not put in place as rapidly or efficiently as some would have liked and even if there were gaps, the most essential losses were covered: "Overall, the restored Republic did its duty."[116]

Perhaps more important than property restitution in the stabilization of French Jewish economic life, however, was the potential to find employment. Indeed, by the first few months of 1946 there was a marked improvement in employment levels in all but a few lines of work. Because the war had caused "no direct or sharp break in the continuity of the economic forms and structure" of French Jewish life, many were able to return to their former occupations and trades.[117] Those who needed more help, such as the immigrant Jews discussed above, could turn to various AJDC subventioned organizations such as loan societies and credit cooperatives to provide funds for their professional reestablishment. From 1945 to 1950, for example, the Funds de démarrage économique and the Caisse israélite des prêts, two such loan organizations, aided approximately 23,500 borrowers.[118] In addition, local vocational institutions such as those sponsored through the Organization for Rehabilitation and Training (ORT) retrained those unable to return to their previous professions or trained those youth who had received no education or training of any kind. In France, ORT also provided over two thousand artisan families with the necessary machines and tools to enable them to establish themselves.[119]

In addition, over the course of the next ten years, the French economy expanded, facilitating the process of Jewish financial reestablishment, although in the first four years after the war, the country faced severe economic problems as increasing inflation and labor shortages demoralized the population and undermined governmental attempts to stabilize the economy. Nevertheless, advances in social policy and an active state intervention in production meant that by 1947 "industrial output reached its 1938 level, labour productivity was rising, and the economy appeared to have recovered its suppleness and dynamism." This is not to suggest that for the working public life had returned to what it was prior to World War II. Indeed, for most, work weeks were longer and purchasing power had declined. With the implementation of the Marshall Plan, however, through which the United States offered significant financial support to help restore stability to Europe and to prevent the spread of Soviet influence, new prosperity came to the French economy. As a result, from 1948 to 1952 industrial output rose, trade was revived, and production was modernized.[120]

This economic stimulation provided returning Jews with the opportunity to reestablish their financial well-being. Those engaged in commerce, both wholesale and retail, were able to take advantage of rising consumer needs. As they had before the war, Jews continued to occupy an important place in these areas, particularly in textiles, ready-to-wear clothing, leather goods, jewelry, and handicrafts. In Paris, the Jewish immigrant population—both those who had survived Vichy and incoming refugees—often worked in these fields. In addition, the expanding economy and the end to legal restrictions meant that Jews could return to positions in the civil service and education. Therefore, doctors, lawyers, and teachers were able once again to practice the occupations in which they had been trained. Although no precise figures indicate the exact rate of Jewish economic recovery in France, anecdotal descriptions suggest that within ten years the population's economic situation had radically improved. In 1956, the World Jewish Congress reported that "the material lot of the majority of Jews of France . . . is relatively good and there remain only residual traces of the distress which prevailed immediately after the war." Similarly, the AJDC reported, "Ten years after the liberation of France the Jewish community has recovered economically to the same extent that the rest of France has and is developing more and more the patterns and activities of any normal community."[121]

Thus, for both Armenian and Jewish populations in France, improving economic conditions helped ease their integration (reintegration) into the French state. Though previously persecuted for their status as minorities, evidence suggested that in the current context they would prosper. French integrationist rhetoric and policies helped bolster such views. For Armenians, this is perhaps less surprising, because for them France seemed a sanctuary far removed from the lands in which they had been persecuted. Concerned with securing their position in the state, they never questioned the wisdom of integration and instead pursued it without reservation. Even for Jews, however, a successful economic reintegration, coupled with the removal of all anti-Jewish legislation, a profound silence among those who had previously called for anti-Jewish restrictions, and the persecution of war criminals provided concrete evidence that the four years of Vichy rule had been a violent deviation from a long century and a half of republican commitment to equal Jewish participation in the polity. As Georges Wormser remarked in 1955, "The Jewish community in France enjoys a position of complete equality in national life. . . . to be a Jew is merely one of the many ways of life for a citizen in a country where diversity is an essential feature."[122] Such a comment, coming only ten years after the end of the war, suggests that belief in France's liberal tradition remained strong and that the massive disruptions of the war years had not shaken confidence in the state's commitment to protecting its minorities.

For both groups, then, France's integrationist culture proved sufficiently welcoming to help distance survivors from the fears of the past. To some, the genocidal attack proved the impossibility of maintaining viable and enduring communities outside a national homeland; however, most survivors did not concur. Nevertheless, both populations were quickly faced with questions over just what kind of relationship should be established with just such a national homeland. It is to these questions that we now turn.

One of the striking similarities in the histories of Jewish and Armenian survivor communities is the emergence in both cases of national "homelands" in the years immediately following their respective genocides. These new states posed interesting dilemmas for two minority populations determined to integrate successfully into the state in which they lived. Because these "external national homelands," to use Rogers Brubaker's term, defined their "ethnonational kin in other states as members of one and the same nation," Armenians and Jews around the world were suddenly implicated in the political history of a state in which they did not live. For some members of each population, particularly the ideologues who had been making such nationalist claims for decades, the birth of such states simply legitimized what they had always held to be true. For others, however, the claims of these new states to speak for their "nationals" wherever they lived were disconcerting. For Jewish and Armenian genocide survivors just beginning to rebuild some stability, the birth of the State of Israel and the Republic of Armenia thus raised new questions about national and transnational allegiances.

In France, these questions were particularly pressing because, as we have seen, survivors of both genocides were seeking to establish themselves in a broader integrationist culture that discouraged distinctive minority political affiliations. And yet, the emergence of these "external national homelands" in fact emphasized their minority status by shifting it from an ethnic to a national designation. Indeed, in theory at least, Armenians and Jews could now "demand state recognition of their distinct ethnocultural nationality" and as such assert "certain collective, nationality-based cultural or political rights."[1]

Such political leverage was appealing to some survivors, given their recent past of disenfranchisement and persecution, but most rejected any political designation that suggested they were displaced members of a distant state. That said, they did not reject nationalistic discourse entirely. Indeed, in both cases, emerging nationalistic movements became central to group identification, allowing both to assert their right to existence — crucial in the postgenocide decades — according to internationally recognized norms. For both, then, albeit in rather different ways, negotiating a relationship with Armenia and Israel, respectively, was as much about articulating a distinctive political voice at home as it was about establishing a rapport with the "homeland."

Diaspora and Homeland among French Armenians

The recent past of genocide and deportation naturally induced tremendous caution among Armenian refugees in France, predisposing them to integrate peacefully and rapidly into their host nation; these events had also transformed the nature and character of the larger Armenian diaspora, raising new questions about the potential success of that integration. For centuries prior to the war, small pockets of Armenians gathered in scattered colonies throughout the world; this dispersion steadily increased in the nineteenth century.[2] Thus, small Armenian colonies took root in France, Holland, Italy, and England, which attracted an intellectual and cultural elite seeking political freedom, educational opportunities, and commercial success. Larger and more significant colonies took shape throughout the East. Hence, the Russian Empire, the Middle East, eastern Europe, North Africa, and Afghanistan, as well as India, Indonesia, and the Philippines all housed Armenian colonies of differing sizes and importance.

After World War I, however, the profile of the diaspora changed as a "diaspora of elites became a diaspora of refugees."[3] The ultimate effect of postgenocide migrations was that nearly half the Armenian population established homes in the diaspora, the other half finding shelter in Soviet Armenia. Such significant demographic and geographic shifts had important consequences for those colonies already in place. Familial links from the United States to the newly established Soviet Republic tied the communities closely to one another. One survivor noted of his family scattered in France, Iran, Colombia, and Belgium, "My family is 'international.' "[4] An intensified "transnational" consciousness grew out of this new dispersion, which shaped how this first generation of genocide survivors in France viewed their position at home and abroad.

Thus, at the very moment when Armenian refugees were seeking to ensure their position within the French polity, new questions were emerging as to where and with whom their allegiances lay. For some, maintaining relationships with Armenians elsewhere meant navigating what were at times conflicting loyalties. The focal point around which these various loyalties converged was Soviet Armenia. Most Armenians had enthusiastically supported the small Armenian Republic that had declared independence in the aftermath of World War I; far fewer had been pleased a few years later, when the Red Army asserted its control in the region, transforming the independent republic into a Soviet state. Subsequently, negotiating a relationship with Armenia became even more complicated, with the French government watching its supporters closely as potential spies. As we will see, whereas certain enthusiasts chose to "repatriate" when Stalin provided the opportunity in 1936 and then again in 1947, the majority of French Armenians, although unwilling to renounce all connections to the Soviet Republic, were wary of cultivating strong links with it. Their passive support was often influenced by their desire to prove their allegiance to their host nation. As a result, Armenians in France mediated between their enthusiasm for the *idea* of an Armenian homeland and their ambivalence about the Soviet Armenian state.

In response to these dilemmas, distinct divisions emerged throughout the Armenian diaspora over how best to pursue Armenian national aims. In broad strokes, these divisions coalesced around two poles: those who supported Soviet Armenia as the only viable option for Armenian national aspirations and those who viewed Soviet involvement as the collapse of those national aspirations. Such disputes ricocheted throughout the diaspora, shaping the nature of Armenian political life in highly antagonistic ways and dividing small refugee communities into even smaller factions.

Likewise, for those in France, home not only to the incoming refugee population but also to a vocal political elite, the relationship with Soviet Armenia was complex from the outset. Where was "home" for these transplanted masses? Was it in the ancestral lands from which they had been torn? Was it in the country that had welcomed them? Or was it in Yerevan, the Soviet Armenian capital? Such questions emerged most clearly in Armenian political articulations, as various factions of the population debated their relationship to the Soviet Armenian Republic.

Three diaspora political parties dominated Armenian political life throughout the diaspora. Two of them, the social democrats or the Hnchak Party, founded in Geneva in 1887, and the Armenian Revolutionary Federation, the Dashnaktsutiun, founded in Tiflis in 1890, had already established themselves in Paris in the late nineteenth century, when small numbers of Armenian journalists, writers, and revolutionaries fled antiminority oppression in the Ottoman Empire. Sharing a common desire to raise political consciousness among the masses, to break the Church's monopoly over political decisions, and to interest rural communities in the Armenian Question, these two parties differed from each other and from the Armenegan Party, a third party of the day, in method, timing, and degree of Marxist and/or socialist orientation.[5] Thus, they often opposed each other while working for the same greater causes.

In the postwar era, they were joined by a bourgeois liberal party, the Ramgavar Azadagan Gusagtsutiun, or the Ramgavars, originally founded in Cairo in 1908 as the Sahmanadir Ramgavars and merging in 1921 with other groups to become the Ramgavar Azadagan. Support for this party generally came from the wealthy and established Armenian bourgeoisie, many of whom had roots in France dating back to the previous century or earlier, when a merchant class had been attracted to France's ports. Concentrating in commercial and trade endeavors, this population made a name for itself in the diamond and Oriental carpet businesses and, with the intellectuals and revolutionaries mentioned above, constituted a well-established, if small, Armenian colony prior to the arrival of genocide escapees.[6]

The significance of this well-integrated, politically literate elite — no matter what their party affiliation — became particularly noteworthy in the years leading up to and following World War I due to the importance of Paris as a diplomatic center for discussing cross-European problems. Indeed, a discussion of Armenian political life in France during these years indicates just how central the Parisian Armenian population was to Armenian diaspora politics more generally *before* masses of genocide survivors began migrating to France. As such, it also helps explain why the pro- and anti-Soviet Armenian debates that characterized the entire Armenian diaspora throughout the history of that regime were particularly salient in France in the 1920s and 1930s.

In 1912, as new problems surfaced inside the Ottoman Empire, the Catholicos in Russian Armenia, Kévork V, turned to Boghos Nubar Pasha, wealthy son of the former prime minister of Egypt and himself previously the director of the Egyptian State Railways, to establish an Armenian delegation in Paris. The delegation, it was hoped, would advance the Armenian national cause and encourage European allies to enforce reforms in the Ottoman Empire.[7] Once World War I broke out, the delegation's importance increased, as Nubar worked in conjunction with other Turkish Armenian intellectuals and clergy to free Armenian provinces from Ottoman control and, in 1918, to secure the status of belligerents for Armenians so that they would be allowed to participate in the Paris Peace Conference.

Following the war, the poles of leadership split between those in the newly declared Republic of Armenia in May 1918 and those in France. Paris, however, remained the political center of Armenian life in the diaspora and the voice for western Armenians uprooted from the Ottoman Empire.[8] Representatives from the Republic of Armenia attended the Paris Peace Conference under the leadership of Avetis Aharonian, the celebrated author and chairman of the Armenian National Council, hoping to influence the direction of political events. Their arrival was quickly overshadowed by the work of the long-established Armenian National Delegation.[9] Thus Armenians in Paris, already the center of diaspora political life during World War I, maintained that role well into the early 1920s. Their position was bolstered as civil war in the former Russian Empire forced local leaders in Transcaucasia to focus on problems at home. When the independent republic fell to Bolshevik control in December 1920 (initially, it was an independent Soviet republic and in 1922 was absorbed into the Transcaucasian Soviet Federated Socialist Republic), Paris remained an important political center of Armenian life outside the Soviet state. Indeed, many ousted leaders of the independent republic made their way there.[10]

Thus, by the early 1920s, the Parisian Armenian population had already established itself as one of the most politically charged Armenian populations in the diaspora, despite its tiny size. There, debates raged over the best path for realizing Armenian national aspirations. These debates centered around the three main political parties described above. Although, for reasons that will become clear, most refugees did not affiliate directly with any of these parties, their rhetoric and positions nevertheless had a fundamental impact in shaping the nature of diaspora-homeland relations among the refugee population. Hence it is crucial to explore their activities and positions in greater depth.

Two of the diaspora political parties enthusiastically supported the Soviet Armenian state, although for very different reasons. The Hnchaks, whose influence in the diaspora was the weakest, maintained their Marxist socialism, which led them to support the new regime primarily for ideological reasons. Similarly, the Ramgavar Party, which was made up largely of the wealthy and established French Armenian bourgeoisie, also actively supported Soviet Armenia. Though perhaps not enthusiastic about its political regime, Ramgavars believed the Soviet state could provide Armenia with the protection it needed to survive in the post–World War I world. In contrast, the Dashnak Party, initially the most influential diaspora political party, was both anti-Soviet and anti–Soviet Armenian. Having made up the majority of the government of the independent republic until it fell to the Soviets, Dashnak leaders believed that any outside rule was detrimental to Armenian interests and dedicated themselves to rebuilding a free and independent state.[11] In addition to these parties was the Haistani oknoutian gomidé (HOG), or the Armenian Aid Committee. The French chapter of this international organization was created in 1924 through the efforts of the Soviet Armenian government's representative in Paris, Siméon Piroumian. It was charged with promoting procommunist propaganda, raising funds to support national reconstruction, establishing intellectual and economic links between those in the "homeland" and those abroad, and facilitating their "repatriation."[12]

It is worth noting that political divisions among the Armenian parties did not necessarily divide neatly into "right" and "left." While the conservative party representing the bourgeois classes defended Soviet Armenia, the Dashnaks, whose political ideologies were shaped by socialism, were fiercely opposed to the communist regime.[13] Thus, although political divisions among these groups often fell neatly between those who supported Soviet Armenia and those who did not, the political map of French Armenians was more complex than this dichotomy suggests. On the one hand were those among the wealthy French Parisian elite who did not support the communist regime; yet, because they favored Armenian nationhood, they would not speak out against the Soviet republic and even supported it through their charitable works. Nevertheless, due to their political, social, and economic position in the French state, they actively opposed the HOG and its local activities and even came into conflict with Soviet Armenian officials who attempted to encourage support of communist activities in France.[14] On the other hand were those who supported socialism but actively opposed Armenia's Soviet incorporation. Moreover, participation in French political structures did not predicate repudiation of Soviet Armenia. Hence, one of the first leaders of the HOG's activities was a naturalized French citizen and a World War I veteran.[15] Complicating this picture further were those Armenians allied with the French Communist Party who participated in this Party's *international effort*, which downplayed loyalties to any national movement whatsoever. The Comité intersyndical arménien thus argued that HOG was simply a propagandistic organization that did nothing to help Armenian workers in France. Such overlapping and conflicting loyalties often led to confusing messages from political leaders. The HOG leadership, for example, actively dissuaded its members from joining the *French Communist Party* (although there were members who participated in both), arguing that the refugee population should refrain from participating in their adopted country's internal politics. Simultaneously, however, they advocated a procommunist stance, one that was frowned upon by the French government.[16]

During the interwar years, the various parties fought for influence in communal affairs, and, as elsewhere in the diaspora, each created its own organizational structures, schools, youth movements, newspapers, sporting groups, and women's groups to forward its causes, particularly among the young.[17] Beginning in August 1925, for example, the Dashnaks began publishing *Haratch*, a triweekly newspaper (which became a daily in 1927). Initially driven by its political agenda, *Haratch* declared itself a literary and political journal whose goal was the "national rebuilding of Armenia and the struggle against Soviet domination." The HOG, in contrast, published *Erivan*, which was dedicated to disseminating pro-Soviet propaganda. Although this paper closed in 1930 due to lack of funds, it was followed by several others promoting a similar agenda. Yet another series of papers promoted the Ramgavar's views.[18]

By publishing newspapers, organizing cultural and educational conferences, and providing aid to their compatriots, the parties provided a variety of political *and* social outlets for their members. The Dashnaks were particularly sophisticated in this regard, functioning in the diaspora like a government in exile and using all the buildings and resources of the former independent Armenian Republic to forward their cause.[19] Hence, the Party scheduled seminars to discuss Armenian culture and history and established a women's charitable organization dedicated to providing Armenian language courses to children, visiting the sick and aged, and organizing annual *colonies de vacances*. In addition, the Dashnaks established schools for Armenian children such as the École Khrimian Varjaran, opened in Issy-les-Moulineaux in 1921.[20] Likewise, the HOG operated its own schools throughout various regions of France, seeking to teach Armenian and to foster a connection between Armenian youth and the "motherland." The Ramgavars, in contrast, though not bolstered by as sophisticated a local infrastructure, had great wealth at their disposal thanks to the makeup of their membership, allowing them to promote their views both locally and through their philanthropic endeavors in Soviet Armenia.

Such contrasting political and social structures led, at times, to conflicts among these groups as each struggled to represent the refugees to local authorities. They also fought over emotion-laden symbolic issues, such as which date should mark the official celebration of Armenian independence: 28 May 1918, when the Dashnaks came to power, or 29 November 1920, when Soviet forces entered Armenia? Debates also raged over which flag should represent the Armenian state at political functions. The Dashnaks insisted that the diaspora should adopt the first flag of independent Armenia; their opponents recognized the flag of the Soviet Armenian Republic.[21] Not surprisingly, advocates of each group held their own celebrations/commemorations despite the objections of their opponents. Like clockwork each year at the end of November or early December, several hundred Armenians gathered in Paris, Marseille, and Lyon to celebrate the anniversary of the Soviet Armenian Republic. Replete with speeches by Soviet, Armenian, and French communists and films and concerts, these events allowed those who supported Armenia, whether officially affiliated with the Communist Party or not, to demonstrate their allegiance to the Soviet Republic. In Lyon in November 1925, for example, participants gathered to express their "affection and love" for the government of Soviet Armenia. Moreover, they published propaganda attacking their political rivals. One, entitled *How Was a Free and Independent Armenian Born*, for example, insisted that the Dashnaks had tricked the Armenian people by proclaiming 28 May a day of struggle, sacrifice, triumph, and freedom. Instead, it had been a day of defeat and mourning, as subsequently the Armenian people had been trapped in the "Dashnaks' claws."[22]

Meanwhile, the Dashnaks sponsored their own celebrations of Armenian independence. These events where marked by a strong anticommunist tone while still attempting to unite all Armenians in a single nationalist agenda. In 1926, for example, one former official of the independent republic insisted that independence had not been a victory for the Dashnaks but for the Armenian people as a whole, who, after six centuries of fighting oppressors, had finally been freed. "None of the political parties has the right to claim the honor of having saved Armenia," he proclaimed. "This honor belongs to the Armenian people themselves, to their heroic children who fell while fighting against their enemies." Such a nonpartisan tone, though perhaps rhetorically pleasing, did little to close the gap between Dashnaks and their opponents. Indeed, representatives of the Armenian notables and wealthy businessmen who supported the Soviet Armenian state were notably absent from this very meeting, which was filled instead with workers and the owners of small businesses.[23]

The most visible public conflicts, however, broke out between the Dashnaks and the HOG. In May 1926, to cite one example, Armenian and French communists disrupted a meeting of the Société littéraire arménienne in Lyon at which Aharonian was speaking; the ensuing fight left one participant dead. As Aharonian continued to tour France, anti-Dashnaks distributed tracts demanding that their compatriots refuse to attend his talks: "There is no longer room for adversaries of Soviet Armenia," proclaimed one. "Aharonian is the representative of a committee responsible for the misfortunes that have stricken the Armenian people. He should not be able to speak, the wretch! The working class in Lyon and its surrounding area must protect its reputation and assert its fellow-feeling [*sympathie*] for Soviet Armenia!" Violence did not accompany all political events, but in some cases, such as in Lyon in December 1928, disputes between Armenians of opposing political opinions led to gunfights. Even in cases where no blood was shed, French and Armenian communists often stood outside communal gatherings singing the "International" and shouting "Long live the Soviets!"[24]

Even the Armenian Church, theoretically a central meeting ground for those of different political ideologies, could not avoid becoming enmeshed in the turmoil. In 1930 a violent outbreak during the Church's commemorative ceremony for the 1915 massacres led to its dissolution. Likewise, in Valence, conflict between Dashnaks and their opponents led to the dismissal of a local priest for his allegiance to Soviet authorities.[25] Certainly religious leaders used their position to promote peaceful coexistence among the various factions of Armenian life, to encourage their compatriots to conduct themselves in a dignified manner, and to observe French laws faithfully. This is not to say, however, that they held no political opinions of their own. During one mass, five hundred congregants were told that although the Soviet regime was not ideal, it was not in Armenian interests to oppose it. First Armenian unity had to be reconstituted. "Later there will always be time to explore if the current regime . . . will need modifications or adjustments." Such measured instructions, theoretically promoting unity among the population, actually reinforced the Ramgavar position: Armenians should remain supportive of the Soviet Republic while remaining silent over its relative merits. This position on the part of the religious leadership was not surprising. Because the Armenian Apostolic Church was under the jurisdiction of the Holy See in Echmiadzin, which was located in Soviet Armenia, religious officials had an interest in adopting measured relations with the Soviet Republic. While Dashnak sympathizers were also active in the Church administration, it—like all areas of communal life—could not escape political conflict, leading often, as Haratch noted, to disunion, spite, and enmity among the various segments of the population.[26]

Reviewing the history of violence and enmity among the political parties demonstrates the saliency of homeland politics in Armenian life in the 1920s and 1930s. Indeed, if to a contemporary eye these debates seem oddly intense given how far removed they were from the daily concerns of most refugees or to the playing out of international politics, to political activists of the day they were central to determining the place of Armenians in the postgenocide world. As a result, wherever Armenians lived in large numbers, these debates raged, often determining not only individuals' political viewpoints but also where they socialized, prayed, and lived. Clearly, for those on the front lines of the political parties, physical distance from the "motherland" did not translate into a sense of detachment. For them, the "homeland" was not abstract but played a significant role in shaping their sense of national identity and affiliation.

And yet, in the French context one must be cautious in estimating the significance of party politics. Although the parties were extremely vocal and although they had a profound impact on social interaction, they were also somewhat limited in their reach. Unlike in Lebanon, home to a significant postgenocide Armenian community, where party representatives could actually run for office in the local government, in France Armenian political parties had no power in national affairs. Moreover, some evidence suggests that the parties' visibility did not translate into large memberships. To cite one telling example: in Grenoble in 1933, a brawl between Dashnak and HOG supporters led to the serious injury of five people. This event provoked police officials to worry about political infighting among Armenian refugees and to watch them even more closely for signs of upheaval. They determined, however, that those actively supporting either party were very few. The Grenoble Dashnak chapter numbered fifty-six members and the HOG sixty-four. At the event in question, only thirty people had attended. Similarly in Valence, out of a community of approximately 3,500, the Dashnaks had 45 active members, the HOG 30, the Ramgavars 7, and the Hnchacks only 2.[27]

As these numbers suggest, most Armenians avoided active participation in the parties. Usually only a few hundred people attended rallies or political events, and even the largest never attracted more than two thousand. The HOG, for example, though extremely vocal, had a tiny membership that dropped over time. Its two thousand members in 1928 had decreased to nine hundred by 1932.[28]

It is perhaps not surprising that the majority of the Armenian population avoided activist politics. Even under the best of circumstances, most people are not politically motivated or mobilized. Moreover, as refugees, the population had more pressing daily problems, far removed from the concerns of the political parties. Even more important, however, was the concern among the refugee population that active engagement in political life would hamper their much valued integration. Worried about incurring the government's disapproval, they thus primarily supported those parties that would allow them to express their Armenian nationalism without damaging their position in their new home. The Dashnaktsutiun was most appealing in this regard because of its anticommunist stance and because the Party discouraged any activities that might infringe on French hospitality. Indeed, such rhetoric was an explicit part of the Dashnak effort to attract supporters in France. Avetis Aharonian, for example, argued that whereas the refugees should refrain from supporting the Soviet regime because of their political convictions, they also should do so because their continued welcome in France depended on their abstinence from communist activities. Similarly, in 1926, he reminded an audience of over twelve hundred that France was more hospitable to Armenians than Armenia itself under the current regime. Therefore, it was up to the refugees to respect the country's laws and to conduct themselves without reproach.[29]

Communist sympathizers, in contrast, often sought to disrupt public events. As a result, many blamed the HOG rather than the Dashnaks for the continual disturbances that upset communal life.[30] The HOG sought to reverse the charge and even formed an international subcommittee ostensibly to protest against the Dashnaks' use of violence, but the preference to remain inconspicuous discouraged most members of the Armenian population from supporting any pro-Soviet activism. As noted previously, national officials were inclined to watch those with communist sympathies very closely and had even expelled four Armenian students in 1925 for having promoted such sentiment among Armenian workers.[31] Moreover, in the mid-1930s, the French government shut the HOG down completely.[32] Government officials kept an eye on Dashnak activities as well, but they were far less ready to condemn this group, which "presents no political characteristics hostile to our country" and which "struggles against the current Turkish government and the Communists." Indeed, the anti-Soviet position of the Dashnaks made them a natural ally of the post–World War I French government, itself wary of Soviet Russia.[33]

Attempting to avoid trouble with their hosts, then, kept many Armenian refugees from defending communism, and even those who supported Soviet Armenia did not necessarily take a public stand to defend its regime. In 1925, for example, after police authorities reported that certain Armenian refugees were suspected of communist agitation, the prelate of Armenians in southern France, Mampré Calfayan, begged his congregation to refrain from such activities. As guests of France, he insisted, they had no right to participate in a movement so frowned upon by government officials.[34]

Fear that Armenian refugees might be attracted to communism was not entirely without basis. Certainly, a handful of radicals believed that their recent experiences of exploitation and persecution necessitated an active engagement with communism. Such was the case for Mélinée Manouchian, wife of the famous World War II Armenian communist Resistance fighter, who linked her decision to join HOG to her own suffering during the genocide. She wrote, "I discovered then that misery was not only the fate of the Armenians and that in the countries through which I had traveled, it seemed that the combat was always the same, between those who had exploited and those who worked without having anything."[35] Others were attracted to the French Communist Party, which distributed pamphlets in Armenian trying to incite the refugees to protest against their own national parties and to strike against managerial persecution and unfair policies. Moreover, Fraternité, the Party newspaper linking French and immigrant workers, published an Armenian issue in 1937. These appeals, however, never went far. Indeed, Le Foyer, while repeatedly warning its readers against the "subversive maneuverings" of the Communist Party, noted that, with the exception of a handful of radicals, most Armenians were not attracted to communism or to French political life more generally. Although in some cases the HOG received financial support from those who feared reprisals against their relatives living in Armenia, few others responded to their appeals. General attempts to attract Armenians to worker solidarity movements gained even less ground. In March 1926, for example, French syndicalist workers in a Valence truck repair factory came into conflict with Armenian coworkers over the latter's reluctance to participate in a work stoppage. Preferring to alienate their fellow workers rather than endanger their status in their host nation, Armenian laborers actively avoided struggles for better wages and working conditions. Indeed, in the Valence case, the tension rose to such levels that French and Armenian workers began fighting in front of the factory gates over the latter's refusal to participate in the strike. In most cases, however, Armenian workers simply responded with indifference to communist propaganda, avoiding all situations that would reflect badly upon them.[36]

The reluctance of Armenians to participate in labor struggles was clearly linked to their concerns over angering the French government and endangering their newfound security. In this atmosphere, political involvement was discouraged and many refugee organizations policed their members to that end. Several compatriot unions, for example, refused admission to anyone who had served time in prison or to any communist who had taken part in demonstrations against the government. In addition, they forbade their members from participating in any political movement—communist or other—and even prohibited the discussion of political matters at meetings.[37]

While distancing themselves from party politics, however, these compatriot unions were actually deeply engaged in the refugees' efforts to negotiate the "triadic nexus" among themselves, the state in which they lived, and their ancestral lands.[38] A closer examination of these organizations, which sprang up throughout the refugee community in the 1920s and 1930s, demonstrates the significant relationship that many Armenians maintained with the "homeland," even when downplaying political activism on its behalf.

As noted, the new refugees did not constitute one homogeneous entity. Although a large majority came from the eastern provinces of the Ottoman Empire, others arrived from Russia, Transcaucasia, and Constantinople. Their host society labeled them all Armenian, yet these regional differences were not insignificant to the refugees themselves, many of whom began forming associational networks with others from similar regions. Thus, those who had fled Russia under the Bolsheviks came together in one group and those from Constantinople formed another.[39] Most, however, were survivors from small cities or villages in the Ottoman Empire seeking connections to one another in their new land. Armenians from Arabkir thus formed one group, those from Yerznga another, those from Ghantaroz another, and so on. Even those in Camp Oddo, a homogeneous unit in the eyes of the surrounding population, broke into subgroups.[40]

Similar in form to the landsmanshaftn, which sprang up among the eastern European Jewish immigrant population in France and elsewhere during the interwar years and served as their organizational core, or to local compatriot organizations that united French migrant workers in Paris and other cities, Armenian compatriot unions provided emotional and material assistance to their members, easing their transition to their new home.[41] One association of Armenians from Tchepni (Sivas), for example, founded in the Parisian suburb Issy-les-Moulineaux in 1930, provided financial aid to its members, developed solidarity among those from Tchepni, instituted language courses, and aided the new refugees with their administrative problems. Another group from Sivas helped its members to establish, educate, and care for themselves, located and reunited their dispersed family members, and helped them find work.[42] Likewise, other groups provided aid to orphans, unemployed workers, the elderly, and the infirm.

Most such groups were quite small. The Union of Armenians from Marash (in Marseille), for example, had only sixty voting members, and in Valence more than half the compatriot unions had fewer than twenty. In addition, because these groups were generally composed of day laborers, tailors, shoemakers, other artisans, and small-scale merchants, their budgets and activities were limited. Nevertheless, by providing financial aid to others more unfortunate than themselves, they helped one another integrate into the new country. Thus, five compatriot unions in Marseille, for example, worked together to establish evening courses in Armenian, French, math, history, and geography. In this way, they worked to integrate the newcomers while keeping them connected to that from which they had come.[43]

Indeed, like the landsmanshaftn, which allowed Jews who collectively identified with a particular foreign origin to ease into their new environment, the Armenian compatriot unions also relied on regional ties to facilitate the transition to the new country. By uniting those from a particular region, suburb, quarter, or even street in France according to their place of origin, the unions relied on past ties to create institutional forms in the new setting. The administrative leadership of the union from Tomarza, for example, all came from one small area of Saint-Antoine. In other cases, the entire associational headquarters was based in the president's home, with several members of the administrative board living at the same address.[44] Thus, in addition to providing basic financial assistance to members, the compatriot unions created new links among those dispersed by the genocide, providing them with a substitution for the physical link to the land they had lost.[45]

Furthermore, in some cases, the compatriot unions actually sought to *recreate* this physical link to their lost territory by transforming their associations into "reconstruction" organizations as soon as the membership had become financially established in France. In 1935, for example, members from the Yenihan (Sivas) union changed their organization's by-laws; subsequently, the bulk of their resources was directed to rebuilding their destroyed village rather than to mutual aid. A compatriot union of Armenians from Ak-Chehir followed suit in 1936. These new villages were not to stand where they had once stood, which was a political impossibility, nor, interestingly, were they to be built in France. Rather, they were to be constructed in Soviet Armenia as a home for those refugees who had yet to find a stable living environment. Armenians from Tcharsandjak thus worked first and foremost to provide moral and financial aid to their compatriots in France and to teach them the French language and laws. Their long-term goal, however, was to "rebuild" Tcharsandjak in Soviet Armenia.[46]

Jonathan Boyarin has argued that the landsmanshaftn allowed Polish Jews in Paris to mediate among three conflicting claims to their loyalties: the land from which they came (Poland); the land in which they lived (France); and the land to which they were ideologically committed (Israel/Palestine).[47] Similarly, the Armenian compatriot unions provided an outlet for members to maintain a connection to the regions from which they had been uprooted, to their new patrie, France, and—in many cases—to Soviet Armenia. In this last case, however, the connection was not straightforward, because Soviet Armenia did not enjoy universal support among the refugees. Thus, in some cases, disputes erupted over whether to rebuild the destroyed village in the Soviet Union. When those from Sivri-Hissar voted to begin rebuilding their village, eleven of the thirty-seven members voted against the decision.[48] Nevertheless, the organization turned 75 percent of its resources away from helping refugees in France and toward the reconstruction project. Not surprisingly, however, the association's membership had no intention of moving to the newly founded village. Rather, as in the earliest western and central European Zionist projects, the new city was envisioned for those refugees more unfortunate than themselves who had yet to find a permanent settling place. Some French Armenians did hope to "repatriate," particularly after 1936, when Stalin opened the doors to those from the diaspora, but only a small minority chose to leave. Indeed, only after the Soviet Union fought on the Allied side during World War II and just prior to the cold war did several thousand French Armenians "repatriate." In the 1920s and 1930s, however, they had little desire to go anywhere: uprooting again after finally finding some stability and prosperity was inconceivable. The reconstruction efforts allowed them to connect with a national agenda, therefore, without endangering their newfound security.

Clearly, then, the compatriot unions played a role greater than that of mutual aid. Having lost their own territory, they nevertheless grouped by territory, seeking to make connections with one another and to recreate a sense of familiarity in the unfamiliar setting.[49] Hoping to bring together as many Armenians from the same area as possible, most of the associations sought to transcend all divisions in the population. Therefore, they were generally inclusive, permitting membership to all regardless of sex or age (although sometimes only those over fifteen could join, and women, in some instances, were not allowed to vote). To ensure an open environment some, as we have seen, forbade political debates at meetings, hoping to keep a unified front among their small memberships.[50] But when such differences interfered, the Armenian population simply broke into smaller groupings. Such was clearly the case in Marseille when two compatriot unions from the same village opened within a few months of each other, both based in a similar region of Marseille and both proclaiming similar goals.[51]

As this example again indicates, political divisions, particularly around the issue of allegiance to Soviet Armenia, were often heated. As survivors came to terms with the disruptions of previous years and the inability to protect themselves in the international arena, many hoped instead to create a homeland. But the nature of that homeland, as it evolved, raised concerns among those seeking to integrate into their new diaspora communities. Hence, a political landscape evolved that allowed refugees to participate in their own nationalistic culture while also integrating into their new environment. For those opposed to the Soviet state, the "homeland" was simply an ideal that had still to be obtained and that thus raised no questions of dual loyalties for its supporters. Given these realities, it is not surprising that the overwhelming majority of the refugee population supported the Dashnak cause and its antagonistic relationship to Soviet Armenia. This is not to suggest that the refugees' preference for the Dashnak agenda was entirely utilitarian. Those who had survived the genocide tended to be far more willing than their predecessors to believe in the importance of a free and independent Armenia, and for many the "return" to Armenia remained their declared objective. Indeed, committed Dashnaks refused to obtain French citizenship on the grounds that such a choice would not be compatible with their ultimate aim to return to the homeland.[52] In 1925 the journal *Haratch* described the various diaspora communities as "ports where we have been forced to dock while waiting to be able to return to our homeland. . . . Our compatriots must actively maintain the idea of the homeland, their language and their national conscience."[53] For those comfortably settled in France, however, the drive to "return" was more an "expression of immense nostalgia than a genuine political strategy."[54] For such refugees, the Dashnak platform was the ideal nationalistic vehicle, allowing them to stress the importance of Armenian nationhood in the postgenocide world without invalidating the diaspora experience.

For those who supported Soviet Armenia, the tension between Armenian and French interests was considerably greater. Nevertheless, a significant minority came to terms with the problem by supporting the Soviet regime as the best option for those refugees who had yet to find a safe place to settle. Most of these efforts were centered on the Armenian General Benevolent Union, which, though technically politically neutral, was made up primarily of Ramgavars.[55] Founded by Boghos Nubar Pasha in Cairo in 1906 to provide charity to Armenians throughout the world, the AGBU moved to Paris in 1911. By the 1920s, its board of directors pulled together some of the wealthiest and most well-known members of the international Armenian elite, many of whom donated substantial sums for Armenian orphanages, schools, artisanal workshops, medical dispensaries, and soup kitchens, particularly in the Near East. The bulk of the AGBU's resources, however, were directed at Soviet Armenia. Indeed, in 1928 the organization spent over 2.2 million francs on orphanages, workshops, refuges, dispensaries, and schools, particularly in Syria; still more telling were the sums raised at its twenty-fifth anniversary fundraising drive in April 1931, projected at 10 million francs and earmarked for the construction of refugee homes in the Soviet Republic.[56] By supporting the Soviet state as a site for refugee resettlement in this way, those comfortably settled in France could thus help their compatriots without raising doubts about their own loyalty.

Thus, if on the surface, the political leanings of French Armenians seemed divided into two diametrically opposed camps, they actually shared a significant core assumption. For neither group did a commitment to the notion of "homeland" require physical relocation to that territory. While HOG representatives worked in France and elsewhere to encourage "repatriation," in the 1930s only about two thousand Armenians left France for the USSR.[57] In this regard, the Armenian refugees in France in the 1920s and 1930s very much mirrored the relationship of post-Holocaust French Jews to the founding of the state of Israel. Indeed, for both groups the commitment to a newly invigorated national politics without any commitment to become nationals of the state in question allowed genocide escapees to be politically active on their own behalf, while still allowing for their comfortable integration into the French polity.

Diaspora and Homeland among French Jews

As for Armenians, the founding of an independent "homeland" had a significant impact on Jewish diaspora communities throughout the world. For those in France, many of whom had suffered through the persecutions of both Vichy and the Nazis, the birth of Israel was welcomed with great fanfare. The Jewish press followed with great interest the struggle for Israeli independence as well as the war that ensued. In addition, support for the fledgling state was widespread among those active in communal life. Aware that the displaced persons camps in Germany were filled with Jewish refugees, communal leaders encouraged their government to support the new state. Similarly, Jewish philanthropic organizations contributed a significant portion of their funds to provide Israel with necessary financial support.

And yet, as we have seen, between 1948 and 1985, fewer than twenty-five thousand French-born Jews decided to make Israel their new home. Of those, most went to Israel after the Six-Day War, more than twenty years after World War II had come to an end.[58] Such low emigration numbers remind us that neither the Holocaust nor the birth of the State of Israel had induced most Jews to question the validity of their French citizenship. These statistics mirror the responses of Jews throughout the Western world to Israel's birth, but the French Jewish response is particularly noteworthy. Unlike Jews in the United States or Great Britain, who also welcomed Israel's birth with great fanfare without opting to leave their comfortable diaspora communities, Jews in France had been victims of Vichy persecutions. One might well have expected them to respond to the new state with the explosive excitement that characterized the response of Jews further east. And yet, French Jewish responses were actually much closer to those of their coreligionists further west, where material and political support for the new state rarely translated into an abandonment of the "diaspora condition."[59] Rather, as with Armenians, nationalist discourses evolved that allowed French

Jews to respond to the previous years' upheavals by publicly affirming a distinctive political identity without forcing a reevaluation of their position in the French state.

Engaging in Zionist discourse as a way of affirming a distinctive Jewish identity in the public sphere had already emerged in France during the first decade of the twentieth century among a small group of French Jewish intellectuals.[60] For the most part, however, the organized Zionist movement had few adherents. Indeed, from the birth of political Zionism at the end of the nineteenth century until World War I, the native French Jewish leadership remained quite hostile toward the movement. Long committed to proving their ardor for France, most feared that support for the movement would lead to questions about Jewish national allegiance and accusations of dual loyalty. Although the well-known philanthropist Baron Edmond de Rothschild sponsored Jewish agricultural settlement in Palestine, by and large most French Jews, committed to preserving their position in their own land, felt at best indifferent to and at worst threatened by an ideology that affirmed a Jewish identity that transcended national boundaries.

Nevertheless, the movement developed some roots in France as elsewhere throughout the Jewish world, particularly as an ever worsening Jewish refugee problem in central and eastern Europe forced some to consider the value of a Jewish state for those facing unacceptable conditions in their birthland.[61] With the issuing of the Balfour Declaration in 1917 declaring Britain's support for the establishment of a Jewish homeland in Palestine, and with the arrival of large numbers of eastern European Jewish immigrants in France following World War I, many of whom were sympathetic to Zionism themselves, "increasing numbers of French Jews began to look to Zionism for inspiration." Though never embracing the notion of a Jewish state in which all Jews should live, some Jewish intellectuals and communal leaders were influenced by Zionism's promotion of Jewish pride and its legitimization of an ethnic Jewish identity. Even French Jewish notables, rabbis, and some of the consistorial leadership—those most hesitant to concede any validity to the nationalist movement—became more willing to support Zionist goals if only as a means to help refugees from the East. Thus, although the vast majority of French Jews did not define themselves as "card-carrying" Zionists, by 1939 the movement had significantly influenced notions of Jewish identification: "Whether rejected, embraced, or critically examined, the Zionists' re-framing of Jewishness as an ethnic or national heritage provided a changed conceptual framework through which to understand the place of the Jew and Judaism in the modern world."[62]

During the German occupation, many of these subtle shifts regarding Zionism that had begun in the interwar years took firmer root, and the movement found a new legitimacy. What had once been a divided, institutionally weak movement primarily among immigrant Jews became more unified as various factions began working together to bring relief to families in distress. During the interwar years, the Zionist movement in Paris had been highly sectarian, as secular nationalists, socialists, religious traditionalists, and philanthropists debated in ideological and often utopian terms the nature of a future Jewish state and how best to achieve it.[63] The German occupation, however, transformed the movement into a unified relief effort. After the occupation of Paris, most Zionist leaders fled to the Southern Zone, where they became actively involved in welfare, relief, and Resistance activities. Bolstered by the participation of Jewish youth, they established agricultural communities to teach them farming and helped refugees flee France. Moreover, the emergence of a common enemy and a common goal — overthrowing the German occupants and the Vichy government — allowed those with different political visions, such as communists and Zionists, to work together.

By the end of the war, this unified effort became even more pronounced. Of particular note were the efforts of the Consistoire Centrale and the immigrant Zionist leaders to form a new umbrella organization, the Conseil représentatif israélite de France (CRIF). The goal of this organization was to study political questions, particularly those raised in regard to restitution, to articulate a united public voice against further antisemitism, and to provide a unified front to the government on Jewish issues.[64] Such cooperation between immigrant and native leaders was extremely rare in the pre-occupation years due to an inability to agree on a common communal agenda. Moreover, faith in the state had long prevented native Jews from organizing to safeguard their political rights. Because this council vocally defended Jewish rights and represented all political, religious, and social affiliations, its birth was unprecedented.[65]

Despite its lofty goals, CRIF's ability to effect change was "practically nonexistent."[66] Indeed, the much heralded unity broke down when splits between communists and their opponents prevented the organization from maintaining a single voice with regard to political questions, hence weakening its strength in the eyes of its constituents.[67] Nevertheless, the attempt to organize in this way suggests that the native leadership was becoming increasingly vocal in defending French Jewry on the public political stage. Moreover, and perhaps more important to our current discussion, the new organization took an actively pro-Zionist stance. Its final charter called for the elimination of the British White Paper of 1939, a policy paper that had established quotas on Jewish immigration to Palestine and declared British intentions to transfer political control of the territory to the local Arab majority within ten years. Like other Zionist organizations of the day, CRIF called for the free immigration of Jewish refugees to the region and an official political resolution to the problems of the region, one that recognized Jewish national rights. This one organization, uniting all components of French Jewry around a single charter, thus gave Zionism the official legitimacy it had lacked previously.[68]

This formal institutional recognition of Jewish nationalistic claims reflected a widespread willingness among those representing Jewish life to become more vocal in such activities. Like Jewish organizations throughout the Western world, which at early points in the century had publicly declared their hostility to Zionist goals, French Jewish organizations became actively involved in the Zionist cause.[69] An example of such a shift is clear in the pronouncements of the Alliance israélite universelle de France (AIU). The AIU had been founded in 1860 to educate and aid Jews throughout Muslim lands as well as to encourage their legal emancipation in places where they were still living as second-class subjects. Yet, although the AIU committed itself to bettering the lives of their coreligionists abroad, the organization was equally driven by concerns at home. In their efforts to regenerate and transform poorer and more traditional Jews into "civilized" citizens, AIU leaders sought to prevent these more distinct Jews from reflecting badly on their coreligionists in France. Thus, while certainly committed to a certain kind of transnational Jewish solidarity, the AIU leadership was, in fact, made up of devoted French patriots, anxious to promote the dissemination of French culture in places that were, in their estimation, more "backward."[70] Zionism, with its claims of a Jewish national identity, seemed seditious to these men. Initially extremely hostile to the Zionist agenda, the AIU leadership began moving toward a more measured nationalist stance only in the interwar years, but even then they viewed Palestine as a refuge for eastern European Jews, not as a place of general Jewish settlement.[71]

Once World War II ended, AIU leaders became more vocal in their efforts to create a refuge in Palestine. In a 1947 memorandum on the Palestinian question, René Cassin, the AIU president as well as an important member of de Gaulle's provisional government, called for the abrogation of the White Paper and for the immediate transfer of one hundred thousand Jewish displaced persons to Palestine. In addition, he suggested that a United Nations' trusteeship guarantee Palestine's security and remove it from British control. Ever a diplomat, Cassin did not insist on the immediate formation of a Jewish state, for he believed that a political solution must be found that would satisfy both Jew and Muslim. But "if a general solution agreeable to all countries proves to be truly impossible," he insisted, "then the Alliance would favor all other solutions that would permit a massive immigration and colonization as well as the free development of a Jewish state in Palestine [Foyer national juif]." Neither Cassin nor other Alliance members were prepared to give up their faith in emancipation or their own national connection to France, yet they strongly affirmed the rights of those Jews who longed to construct a new life in Palestine.[72]

It is by turning to the Consistoire de Paris, however, that we can best begin to evaluate the impact of Zionism on post-Holocaust French Jews. Like the AIU, this centralized religious institution, created under Napoleon to serve as the administrative body of French Judaism and to represent French Jews to the state, proved extremely hostile to the emergence of Zionism. Even after the separation of church and state in 1906, when the Consistoire lost this official governmental role, its leaders viewed themselves as self-appointed representatives of the community. In this capacity, they actively opposed the Zionist movement, arguing that as a loyal minority within the state, Jews made up a religious group and not a national entity. Although Zionism made some inroads with Consistoire leaders in the 1930s, supporters and opponents alike were quick to insist that a state for Jewish refugees could have no claim on those Jews who were citizens of other countries.[73] Having long been linked directly to the French state, Consistoire officials were thus its staunchest defenders, believing that a Jewish state was of no consequence to those living in politically open societies such as their own.

Such views were surprisingly unshaken by the Vichy years. Indeed, despite the persecution and violence directed against them, those directing the Consistoire "continued to trust the ultimate goodness of France and its bond with the Jewish religion." Rejecting all racial distinctions, the Consistoire leadership maintained that Jewish communal affiliation remained a voluntary religious affiliation with no bearing on national or racial makeup. Even by the end of the war, when Consistoire officials had comprehended the severity of the crisis and begun to adjust accordingly, they never rejected their faith in the republican tradition.[74]

Thus, in the war's immediate aftermath, Consistoire officials recommitted themselves to familiar goals: on the one hand, guaranteeing the regular and dignified practice of Judaism and the maintenance of a well-managed Jewish community; on the other, demonstrating that Jews deserved their citizenship because of their loyalty and devotion to their patrie.[75] In fulfilling the latter, the Consistoire leadership, like the French government, was not interested in overemphasizing the distinct nature of Jewish suffering during World War II. As Annette Wieviorka has shown, the Consistoire's initial commemorations built for Jewish war victims focused first and foremost on those "martyrs" who had fought in the

French army or in the Resistance, thus de-emphasizing the "Jewishness" of their suffering.[76] Even though the Consistoire Centrale immediately began gathering names for a memorial to French Jewish losses, their interest was in distinguished and wounded soldiers, prisoners, and Resistance fighters.[77] The great majority of Jews who had died in deportation were not included on this list.

Similarly, to families who hoped to rebury their war dead in Jewish cemeteries the Consistoire gave only an ambivalent nod. Concluding that individual families must decide the fate of their own kin, Consistoire officials nevertheless strongly recommended that Jewish soldiers remain interred with others who fought for France: "The interest and honor of Judaism requires that the israélites who were condemned to death and shot stay mingled with the other victims of the capitulation, occupation, collaboration, and treason. If Jewish martyrs are kept shut away in our own cemeteries, the public would forget what contribution we made to the Resistance and to the Liberation."[78]

Clearly, the Consistorial leadership felt no inclination to call attention to Jewish war-time losses, preferring instead to unite their own experiences with those of their non-Jewish French compatriots. In this respect, the Consistoire's stance mirrored its prewar positions that had placed national identity and religious affiliation in different spheres; Jews had fought as French citizens, not as Jews.

Yet even if certain Consistoire attitudes mirrored those of previous decades, a sense that the war had united all French Jews in a common fate caused a shift in previous dismissals of Jewish nationalist claims, particularly after the founding of the State of Israel. As before the war, however, this support was not offered without some qualifications. Thus, a telegram congratulating the chief rabbi of Palestine after the United Nations declared its support for the creation of an autonomous Jewish state was quick to note that the new refuge was specifically for "our brothers still in distress." In no way would the new state impinge on the status of Jews already well-established elsewhere. Adolphe Caen, the vice president of the Consistoire Centrale, reaffirmed this position in a March 1949 speech welcoming representatives from the Israeli army to France. On the one hand, Caen celebrated the heroism and strength of the Israeli forces. On the other, he reminded his visitors that their success in establishing a state was "for all who do not have the good fortune, like us, to have one, for all our fellow Jews — unfortunately still so numerous — who have neither the desire nor the ability to stay in or return to their countries of origin."[79] Moreover, he placed Israeli military accomplishments in the context of military victories wherever Jews may have fought. Thus, although his remarks were meant primarily to celebrate the heroism of the Israeli forces, he also recalled how, since the Revolution, Jews had fought for France, "the first to give us liberty and civil rights." French-born Jews, he maintained, would continue to provide France with "signs of indefectible attachment in all domains," including militarily. In this way, Caen's comments both honored the Israeli army and reaffirmed that those Jews born in France still owed their country a debt of loyalty that would not be superseded by the birth of Israel.

If Caen's remarks reflect a certain continuity to Consistoire positions regarding Jewish national assertions in the prewar era, we also see a subtle shift taking place. Thoroughly insistent that French Jews could be citizens of only one state, Caen nevertheless could not ignore the implications of Israel's birth for Jews throughout the diaspora. Now an Israeli military, identified with a "legitimate" state, was asserting its claim to defend a Jewish state for all Jews. Having been claimed in this way by an "external national homeland," the native French Jewish leadership could no longer simply dismiss Zionist assertions that a national link tied all Jews together, no matter where they called home. Indeed, as the chief rabbi of Paris, Jacob Kaplan, noted in a 1949 speech to Jewish religious, social, and cultural leaders: "The State of Israel is a reality from which henceforth no Jew will be able to disassociate himself, a state that thrusts itself upon us as on all other men." [80] The new state's existence was thus raising profound questions about prewar assumptions that religion was the most significant component of Jewish identification in the modern world. Such questions had already emerged in the 1920s and 1930s as the Zionist movement gathered steam; now Consistoire officials could no longer avoid tackling them head on.

Kaplan, a Parisian-born rabbi who succeeded Isaïe Schwartz as the chief rabbi of France in 1955, had already struggled with these issues while working as an auxiliary to the chief rabbi of France from 1929 to 1939. Like other Jewish communal figures of the interwar years, Kaplan had begun supporting the notion of a Jewish state in Palestine as a place for suffering Jewish refugees. For him, however, the links tying Jews together were primarily religious rather than the secular nationalism stressed by many political Zionists. Thus, even before World War II, he stressed a Torah-centered, religious Zionism, insisting that religion should be the significant bond tying Jews together. As such, he mirrored a growing trend among French Jewish leaders emphasizing the spiritual, religious aspects of Zionist ideology and linking the ethnic and national aspirations of the movement with the need for a religious revival throughout the diaspora. [81]

In many ways, World War II did not challenge Kaplan's fundamental beliefs in this regard. He spent the occupation working as a rabbi in Vichy and Lyon and was ultimately chief rabbi of France from January 1944 until the liberation, although the Gestapo arrested him briefly that August. As one of the few surviving rabbis of the German occupation, Kaplan greeted Israel's birth with enthusiasm. While insisting on the primacy of Jews' links to their countries of birth, Kaplan also believed that Jews in the diaspora were called on to feel more than a passing interest in the new state. In fact, he compared international Jewry's love for Israel to the love an adopted child has for his newly discovered birth mother. On the one hand, the child cannot reject the mother that fed and raised him; on the other, he cannot help but love the mother who gave him life. Moreover, these two loves were not and could not be mutually exclusive; the Jew's love for Israel was like the Canadian's attachment to France or the Irish American's dedication to Ireland. French Jews, he explained, could be loyal to France and Israel simultaneously. Indeed, he added, given the French state's good relations with Israel, "We will be the first to rejoice, knowing that in serving the cause of Israel we are simultaneously serving those of our French nation."[82] Most interesting, however, was Kaplan's defense of those Jews who chose to leave France for Israel. Their motives, he explained, were entirely commendable. Worried that apathy, mixed marriages, and occasional conversions were rapidly diminishing the number of Jews in France, those who fled to Israel sought to protect themselves from the ravages of assimilation. They were not disloyal French fleeing their homeland but those most concerned about the future of their people.

And yet, even while seeming to endorse the adoption of Israeli citizenship by French Jews, Kaplan was quick to insist that Jews were neither a nation nor a race but a religion. "This is the solid, unassailable ground," he insisted, "on which Israeli Jews and those in the diaspora can constantly meet each other." A leading Consistorial religious figure, Kaplan therefore reaffirmed that the strongest bond linking Jews around the world was their religious tradition.[83] In adopting such a position, Kaplan was thus able to welcome the birth of the Jewish state without raising questions about the status of Jews at home. Rejecting Nazi and Vichy determinations of Jewish identity as well as those of the secular founders of the Jewish state, Kaplan promoted a Zionism that was consistent with the intellectual traditions of the Consistoire and that could in no way be interpreted as a threat to the national identification of French Jews with their birthland.

Not surprisingly, no absolute consensus shaped how all French Jews, or even how all Consistoire representatives reacted to the founding of the State of Israel. Some adopted Kaplan's stress on religious links above all else; others encouraged a cautious stance toward the new state; still others insisted that the Consistoire link its own interests directly with those of the new state. And yet, it seems clear that, with the exception of a small handful, most understood the new state to have a claim on them in a way that previous nationalist discourse did not. In May 1948, for example, immediately after Israel's declaration of independence, one Consistoire official requested that all synagogues add a special prayer on its behalf in addition to the traditional prayer for the French Republic. Similarly, he proposed adding prayers for the Haganah and for dead Israeli soldiers. Others went further and requested that a formal ceremony be held in one of the Parisian synagogues honoring the birth of the new state. The administrative council for the Montmartre synagogue, for example, "convinced that the life and honor of world-wide Judaism [was] implicated in the struggle in Palestine," strongly urged the Consistoire israélite de Paris to demonstrate its sympathy as well as its moral and material support for Israel and to "offer its deep admiration and infinite gratitude to the glorious fighters of Israel in the Holy Land."[84]

In contrast stood the views of the Consistoire de Paris's president, Georges Wormser, who still feared that if Jews linked their aspirations too rapidly to the new state their loyalties would be called into question. Professionally, Wormser had maintained a long involvement in French national politics. A graduate of the École Normale and an *agrégé* in letters, he had worked closely with Georges Clemenceau first as his civil staff director in 1919 and then in 1934 as the head of the ministry staff of the postal system. In later years he worked in the Ministry of the Interior. During this period, Wormser was not entirely hostile to Zionism, and while serving as a member of Clemenceau's cabinet in 1917 and early 1918, he played a significant part in France's recognition of a Jewish settlement in Palestine.[85] Nevertheless, in a speech to the directors of the Consistoire de Paris in June 1948, Wormser pleaded that they respond cautiously to Israel's arrival on the international arena. For him the new state posed a real dilemma. Although he believed it important that Jewish refugees uprooted by World War II have their own nation, he felt compelled to remind the Consistoire leadership that French Jews were French first: "Jews and gentiles alike [must] know that we who enjoy all the rights of Frenchmen and in so doing accept all its obligations are determined to remain French above all else." It was essential to him that the Consistoire refrain from recognizing Israel until France had done so. In this way, their loyalties to their own country would remain unquestioned.[86]

Such views, already well in place prior to World War II and seemingly unaffected by Vichy, continued to be voiced long after Israel had been officially recognized. As much as a decade later, another Consistoire official insisted:

A French Jew is above all else French . . . and feels French like a French Catholic, Protestant, Muslim, or free thinker. French Jews love France as much as any other French citizen, feeling equally the joys of their homeland and commiserating with its misfortunes. They know how to live and die for it. . . . And if against all odds war should break out between France and Israel, the duty of French Jews—no matter what it would cost them—would be to fire against the Israelis. . . . For if we feel the greatest admiration and love for Israel, we French Jews would put France, our country, above all others. And if there is a Jew who declares, I am Jewish before French, he should leave.[87]

As such examples indicate, the Consistoire's prewar identity politics, which stressed allegiance to one state and downplayed a national component to Jewish ethnic and religious affiliation, remained part of its ideological makeup after the war as well. Indeed, for some at least, neither the Holocaust nor the birth of the State of Israel was enough to challenge their universalistic notions of citizenship: national allegiance, they suggested, should not be informed by particularistic ethnopolitical concerns.

What is interesting about the postwar period, however, is that even if such views existed, they did not necessarily reflect those of the majority. In response to the heated debate that followed Wormser's speech, which led to his temporary resignation when his colleagues would not accept his position, Consistoire officials ultimately compromised, agreeing to hold a *religious* ceremony that recognized Israel's struggles without pledging political support to the new state. Nevertheless, Wormser's more traditional appeals for caution were rejected on the grounds that it was not, in fact, *prudent* for the Consistoire to ignore Israel's birth and that a show of strength and solidarity was the only wise position. As one official remarked, "In light of the current struggle, we cannot be cowardly and [we must] associate with those who fight for Palestine." Another member noted, "An attitude that is too cautious will put the Consistoire in a poor position vis-à-vis our enemies and our friends."[88] Indeed, even those who did not believe the Consistoire should hold an official celebration of Israeli independence believed that, at the very least, they should organize a religious service commemorating those dying in the war of independence and praying for future peace.

Thus, although not all members agreed on the extent to which they should support the new state, it is clear that many, if not most Consistoire officials accepted at face value that a relationship between French Jews and Israel must now be articulated. As a legitimate actor on the political stage, Israel could not be ignored, if for no other reason than that its officials claimed to be speaking for world Jewry. Indeed, in a world that recognized a Jewish state, rejecting Jewish nationalism seemed "cowardly." No longer a high-minded position among those who felt secure at home, anti-Zionism was now perceived as weak. Moreover, most Consistoire officials believed that public sentiment stood in favor of the new state and feared alienating their Jewish constituency. As one member remarked when suggesting that the Consistoire send two representatives to a meeting sponsored by Secours à l'état d'Israél, "An absence would not be a wise policy vis-à-vis the majority of our fellow Jews."[89]

The belief that Zionism had captured the hearts and minds of French Jews was shared by other communal leaders unaffiliated with the Consistoire. As early as October 1944, Joseph Fisher, director of the French chapter of Keren kayemet le Yisrael (the international fundraising arm of the Zionist movement) prior to the war and founder of the Zionist paper La Terre retrouvée, reported to the Zionist Executive that "the Zionist movement in France has never been as strong as it is now." Indeed, the organized Zionist movement was extremely visible in the postwar years, as militant Jewish nationalists staged vocal rallies denouncing all assimilatory projects and calling for the immediate creation of a Jewish state. For such activists, Consistorial insistence on protecting the place of Jews in French society was below contempt. To them, the Nazi years had only proven once again how vulnerable Jews remained throughout the diaspora. An article in La Terre retrouvée asked in 1945: "Did the so-called civilized countries, belligerents and neutrals, do everything in their power to save our hundreds of thousands from deportation and extermination?" One revisionist Zionist proclaimed at a rally in 1946 that there were only two solutions to the Jewish problem: "a Jewish state . . . or the crematoriums."[90]

Such radical views tended to emerge from the remnants of the eastern European Jewish immigrant population. As noted previously, most of the war's antisemitic persecution had been aggressively directed at those not born in France. Immigrant Jews were uprooted and deported in higher percentages than native Jews, and their survival rates were considerably lower. Some of these immigrants had in fact integrated comfortably into French society prior to World War II; others, and particularly those who arrived in the 1930s, tended to make up a highly politicized group, many of whom firmly believed that the only acceptable response to the Jewish Question was to found a Jewish state. For these committed Zionists, World War II was only further proof of this position.

Moreover, the numbers of such pro-Zionist activists increased after World War II as waves of new refugees, freed from across occupied Europe and en route to Palestine, sought temporary shelter in France. The French government, sympathetic to the plight of Jewish survivors and disgruntled with Britain over the latter's attempt to oust France from any substantial role in the Middle East, took little action against the migrants, allowing border and port officials to turn a blind eye to their movements. Thus, by spring 1946, the illegal migration of Jewish refugees to Palestine was operationally based out of Paris, with twenty thousand departing from Marseille's ports between March 1946 and May 1948. Following the declaration of Israeli statehood that month, the numbers increased dramatically. Local Jewish agencies processed so many of those migrating to Israel from Europe each month that Marseille's ports were "packing them in from all sides." By December 1948, the main organization facilitating this migration process, Hechalutz, maintained twenty holding camps where an average of five thousand people waited for a period of five days to three weeks—and sometimes as much as six months—before embarking for Israel.[91] In addition, various Jewish organizations worked to bring children throughout Europe to France until they could secure safe passage. Rabbinical and yeshiva groups also moved through France on their way to the Promised Land.[92]

Clearly, these migrants held pro-Zionist views; hence, throughout the mid-1940s, France saw numerous rallies held in Yiddish that protested British actions in Palestine and antisemitism in eastern Europe and that called for the immediate transfer of all Jewish refugees from the DP camps to Palestine. Such rallies brought Zionism tremendous visibility in Paris and elsewhere. After British officials ordered the arrest of the Jewish Agency's leaders in Palestine in 1946, for example, rallies were held in Paris, Lyon, and Alsace. Demonstrators demanded the liberation of the leaders, the immediate admission of one hundred thousand Jewish displaced persons into Palestine, and the abrogation of the White Paper. Such demonstrations, though often numerically small, attracted many important figures from French public life. On 4 July 1946, for example, twenty-five hundred people gathered to hear speeches from several former cabinet members, Léon Blum, and David Ben Gurion.[93] Numerous prominent intellectuals, both Jewish and non-Jewish (including Léon Blum) had supported Zionism in the interwar years; now the growing participation of well-known French political figures gave the postwar Zionist movement an increasing legitimacy and visibility.

Postwar support for the new Jewish state was also aided by the fact that although the French government did not officially recognize Israel until more than a year after its creation, public sentiment lay strongly on its side. Well-publicized events like the plight of Jewish refugees onboard the Exodus bolstered French public opinion in favor of a Jewish state. In this famous incident, the British Navy attacked and captured a boatload of refugees after they had attempted to enter Palestine clandestinely in the summer of 1947. Although the boat had sailed from a French port, the French government would not permit the British to defuse the issue by returning the refugees to Marseille. In frustration, the British government forced the boat to sail to Germany, where the passengers were compelled to disembark and then placed under military guard. Both during the Exodus incident and after the declaration of the State of Israel, newspaper articles and government officials declared support for the Jewish state.

In this atmosphere, those who had feared that a Jewish state would place their own allegiances in doubt now had evidence that Jewish and French national interests were not at odds. Even in this supportive environment, however, most French Jews did not become militant Zionists. Indeed, rallies attracted no more than a few thousand people. One Zionist organizer complained, "In the aftermath of the liberation of our territory, the Jews have concerned themselves principally with recuperating their stolen belongings rather than with the Zionist movement." This activist, incensed by German and Vichy persecutions, assumed that French Jews would reject their formerly passive interest in Jewish nationalism and reevaluate their position in their surrounding society. However, while international organizations such as the World Jewish Congress and Keren Hayessod attempted to foster Zionist sentiment throughout the population, few French Jews became activists and even fewer considered leaving their native land. Indeed, David Ben-Gurion, having interacted extensively with French Jewish Resistance fighters, particularly those in the pro-Zionist Jewish Army, initially believed that France provided the most welcoming base on which to build support for Zionist activity in Europe. It soon became clear to him, however, that unlike survivors of the death camps, French Jews continued to view their country as their homeland. Indeed, even those who had fought in the Resistance viewed themselves as full members of French society.[94]

Those hoping for a more visible pro-Zionist response from French Jewry suggested that fear of a resurgence of antisemitism prevented the population from acting. In August 1945, for example, Ben-Gurion explained, "In France, people are not interested in Zionism; they are afraid that antisemitism will grow and deepen."[95] Similarly, in 1946, when Lyon's native Jewish leadership criticized Zionist activists for asking that more Jewish refugees be allowed to migrate to France in light of Britain's closed-door policy to Palestine, observers suggested that fears of provoking a new antisemitic movement were driving them.[96]

If, however, some Jews feared new waves of antisemitism, a reaction that would not have been particularly surprising given the recent past, far more had been touched by the new Zionistic atmosphere than the more militant activists conceded. "Even in the circles most removed from Zionism," noted one government report, "people generally approve of the energetic attitude of Zionists of all tendencies and of Jewish patriots who call for the creation of an independent Jewish state in Palestine."[97] Indeed, it seems that only a minority hesitated to support Zionism out of fear that it might lead to the resurgence of the sentiments that had driven Vichy persecutions.

On the contrary, according to various observers, French Jews, like Jews throughout the world, began exhibiting an unprecedented interest in Jewish nationalism immediately after the war and thereafter. "The devastation caused by the war and the extermination of six million Jews," wrote Guy de Rothschild of his family's transforming views toward Zionism, "radically changed all our former attitudes. The idea of a Jewish homeland acquired an intense emotional appeal; I myself became an ardent Zionist, without however envisaging a change of direction in my personal life or that of my family." Like Rothschild, few expected "a change of direction" in their personal lives because of their new support of a Jewish nationalistic agenda; nevertheless, a growing interest was evident. As early as spring 1945, Chief Rabbi of France Isaïe Schwartz reported to the Ministry of Foreign Affairs that French Jews, having felt abandoned by government authorities during the war, were adopting less reserved attitudes toward Zionism than had been true in the 1920s and 1930s: "Now they have a real and active attraction to this movement."[98]

Once the State of Israel had been established, the AJDC's representative Harry Rosen went even further, calling the concern for Palestine among French Jews "the strongest single cohesive force" in communal life. Similarly, in their report on European Jewry ten years after the war, the World Jewish Congress noted the great popularity of Zionism in French Jewish circles: "In present conditions given the feeble influence of the synagogue, Zionism, with its manifold bureaus, numerous officials, and continuous agitation, is still the most manifest 'address' of Jewish existence in a country like France."[99] Thus, although the WJC considered the Zionist movement to be "feeble" in France, they, like Rosen, were convinced that it played a significant role in the postwar period, even replacing religion as the single most cohesive factor in Jewish life.

Such assessments of Zionism's strength may have been exaggerated, but there is no question that throughout the late 1940s and beyond, interest in Zionism was significant. Fundraising efforts for Israel are indicative of its appeal. By June 1948, Rosen estimated that a variety of pro-Zionist organizations had raised 200 million francs on behalf of the Haganah and other organizations. This number was undoubtedly inflated and based more on his impressions than any empirical data, yet fundraising for Israel grew throughout the 1950s. In 1955, for example, the Aide à Israel, a fund dedicated to raising support for Israel, brought in 190 million francs.[100]

Even more noteworthy than the steady financial support for Israel among French Jews was the fact that following World War II organized opposition to the Zionist movement disappeared. Although occasional lone voices called for a cautious approach to the new state, all organized anti-Zionism had been silenced. This silence stands in sharp contrast to the years before the Holocaust, when native French Jews were much more likely to criticize any project that might call their own loyalties into question and when communal organizations proved cautious toward and often hostile to immigrant Zionist activism. Indeed, for most French Jews, as for most of the Armenians discussed earlier, supporting nationalist priorities was a significant part of their postgenocide politics. And yet, as for Armenians, their commitment to a more vocal Jewish nationalism was not based on migration. Rather, in even greater numbers than before the war, they supported a Jewish state for those who had been stripped of statehood while remaining committed French citizens themselves.

Comparing Nationalisms

When comparing Armenian and Jewish nationalisms in post–World War I and –World War II France, obvious differences emerge. Most glaringly, whereas the independent Armenian state had fallen to Soviet control within a few short years of its declaration, the independent Jewish state that was declared in 1948 retained its autonomy. One result of these differing historical paths was that diaspora-homeland relations were shaped quite differently. For Armenian genocide survivors in France, any relationship with the "homeland" was influenced by the knowledge that their host government was no particular friend of communist Russia. In contrast, French Jews were generally confident that their government shared their interest in and support of the emerging Israeli state. Thus, whereas most French Jews felt comfortable expressing enthusiastic support for Israel, most Armenians cautiously avoided any public declarations on behalf of Soviet Armenia. Moreover, Armenian survivors, newly arrived in France, were far less "rooted" in the country than their Jewish counterparts twenty years later. In contrast, French Jews, despite their recent history of de-emancipation, generally proved secure enough in their post–World War II citizenship to "risk" public pronouncements on behalf of Jewish statehood. Not surprisingly, then, different political and social contexts influenced the range of nationalistic discourses among survivors, shaping expressions of transnational allegiances somewhat differently. Moreover, it is worth noting that different types of source material render different types of conclusions. Hence, the highly political nature of the Armenian sources cited above provides a somewhat different picture from the religious and cultural sources from which the material on French Jews is drawn.

Yet, despite these differences, some interesting similarities emerge. Particularly noteworthy is the impact that statehood had on both of these national minorities. As "external national homelands," both Israel and Soviet Armenia sought to create dynamic relationships with Jews and Armenians across the globe. Both thus adopted "the axiom of shared nationhood across the boundaries of state and citizenship and the idea that this shared nationhood [made] the state responsible, in some sense, not only for its own citizens but also for ethnic co-nationals who live[d] in other states and possess[ed] other citizenships."[101] In concrete terms, this meant that politically active states were now claiming to speak in the international arena for Jews and Armenians everywhere and calling on them to support the new states economically, politically, and even militarily.[102] Moreover, both Israeli and Soviet Armenian officials assumed that Jews and Armenians throughout the diaspora would opt to leave this dispersion behind to settle in their newly established "homelands."

For Armenian and Jewish genocide survivors in France—no matter how different their situations—facing these claims presented a similar set of options, which broke down into roughly three categories. First, some, of course, demonstrated their allegiance to the new states by promoting immediate migration or by packing their own bags. For both populations, however, this option was extremely rare. Indeed, despite having been singled out and persecuted for their status as foreigners in their respective diaspora communities and having been "claimed" by newly formed external national homelands, most Armenians and Jews in France remained committed to staying put. Nationalist discourse, though powerful, was not enticing enough to challenge the even more powerful French integrationist discourse, which promised survivors an opportunity to prosper again in the diaspora.

Second, there were those in both populations who absolutely rejected the nationalizing claims of their respective homeland on the basis that citizenship was not a transnational phenomenon. In some sense, this was the most common response in both populations, whether seeking safe haven in France or victim of French-sponsored persecution, whether drawn ideologically to the new states' regimes or opposed to them. For Armenians, such a stance was shaped, in part, by the Soviet character of the Armenian state, but even most French Jews believed that the new Jewish state had no legal claim to their political allegiance. If they supported Israel it was because of the ethnic or religious connection they felt for Jews living around the world, particularly those seeking shelter in the post-Holocaust era, not because they believed the new state had any say in their legal status in the world. Here too we see the impact of the French context on the two populations in question. Because France itself was not an "ethnocultural nation but a political nation open, in principle, to all," most Armenians and Jews, whether refugees or citizens, believed there was a place for them on French soil. With this belief came the concomitant rejection of the notion that they were displaced citizens of foreign states.[103]

And yet, even while rejecting the nationalizing claims of their external national homelands, Armenians and Jews in France were influenced by them, bringing us to a third response that can be discerned in both populations. Having in both cases recently suffered through several years of isolation and persecution and having narrowly escaped exterminatory policies shaped around their minority status, escapees were not immune to the powerful political presence these new states constituted in the international arena. Thus, if representatives of both populations publicly rejected the notion that any government other than the French had legal claims on their international status, they also were visibly active in nationalist politics, helping to assert their cultural and political presence in France. Indeed, in both cases a distinctive political agenda emerged, even among Armenians whose communal representatives were emphasizing the importance of blending into the surrounding society and culture. As the example of politics suggests, therefore, although survivors of both genocides proved readily willing to integrate (or reintegrate) into the French state, few opted to flee their "dangerous identities" completely. Rather, as the next chapter demonstrates, the assimilationist rhetoric of the state, coupled with concrete proof of economic and social integration, provided survivors with a "safe" place to be Armenian and Jewish.

In considering the impact of the recent genocidal persecutions on Armenian and Jewish escapees, the previous two chapters documented the ways in which fears of the past were overcome by the promise of a secure and prosperous future on French soil. Integrationist policies backed up with evidence of real economic opportunities suggested to members of both populations that the persecutions through which they had recently lived were a thing of the past. Nor did the allure of nationalist politics convince escapees to abandon their minority status or their diaspora condition. The question, therefore, remains: How did survivors understand the nature of their minority status? Or, to put it another way: How did "Armenianness" and "Jewishness" manifest themselves in these postgenocide communities?

Not surprisingly, the answer differs considerably when comparing the two populations. As refugees, first-generation Armenians in France were clearly outsiders in their adopted home. Like all new immigrants, they came with their own linguistic, cultural, religious, political, and economic traditions, few of which fit seamlessly into their new Western setting. Thus, despite the communal rhetoric stressing the importance of blending in, most remained marginal to their host society, rebuilding familiar familial, organizational, and cultural structures that could help them maintain their links to the past. Unable to avoid acculturating to their new environment, they nevertheless established distinct ethnic communities based on shared conceptions of religion, ethnicity, language, and point of origin.

For French Jews the situation was somewhat different: the country in which they rebuilt their communities had stripped them of their rights despite a long history of Jewish inclusion inherited from the Revolution. Until the implementation of Vichy law, the French state had regarded Judaism as a private religious distinction. Although Jews maintained their particular concerns, in their public, national roles they were viewed either as French or as nationals of other lands, indistinguishable from other immigrant minorities. Whereas Vichy had challenged that relationship, the postwar French government was quick to return to time-tested policies: Jewish distinctiveness was again a private, religious matter that had no bearing on one's public, political status. For postwar French Jews, however, the matter was more complex. This state ideology certainly had a powerful impact on those Jews who traced back for generations their roots in France, causing many to downplay all but the religious distinctions as dividing them from their fellow citizens. Nonreligious affiliations, however, had never entirely disappeared.[1] Indeed, in the prewar years, the idea that Jews formed a distinct ethnic or cultural group had become increasingly acceptable as notions of French universalism came into question and waves of immigrant Jews came to France from central and eastern Europe.[2] It was only in response to the Vichy persecutions that such ideas entered mainstream Jewish life in such a way as to really transform its public face.

A comparison of the nature of Armenian and Jewish minority affiliation in their postgenocide periods thus suggests profound differences based on the makeup of the population in question. Such differences, however, should not overshadow an equally important similarity. Despite having recently been persecuted for their ethnoreligious distinctiveness, few survivors from either population opted for complete assimilation, nor did they question their ability to retain their heritage while living within a larger nation-state. Rather, in both cases we find a striking commitment to maintaining visible communities despite the assimilationist rhetoric of the state and the racist persecutions through which they had lived.

A Minority on the Margins

The first generation of Armenian survivors quickly established a relationship to the state that stressed their compliance with national law and their abilities to acculturate to national norms, but they were not necessarily rushing to become "French." Rather, as Martine Hovanessian has effectively argued, most processed their rupture with the past by reestablishing traditional patriarchal familial and communal structures. By building homes and communities outside urban settings, leaving factories for home work, and recreating religious, political, and organizational structures that had existed prior to the genocide, Armenians, like other migratory groups of the day, sought to preserve the integrity of their village life despite the disruptions that had taken place.[3]

The experience of the refugees in Camp Oddo once again provides an example of this phenomenon. Despite a clear preference to integrate peacefully into Marseille's economic and cultural landscape, these refugees had no intention of abandoning their communal identification which had proven so dangerous in the Ottoman Empire. Complying with national norms did not imply complete assimilation, nor did the recent genocidal persecutions frighten them into flight from their ethnoreligious distinctiveness.

As noted in chapter 1, Camp Oddo became increasingly distasteful to local and national officials the more it seemed to function as an independent colony. Indeed, to observers in 1920s Marseille, the camp became a tangible sign of the failure of immigrants to integrate rapidly into their new society. In 1925, therefore, officials began taking steps to close its doors, eventually appointing a special examiner to replace the Armenian administration and empty the camp. Through his efforts, Oddo was closed in 1927.[4]

But despite Oddo's dilapidated conditions, its residents did not leave without a fight. The camp's director, Hatchikian, argued vigorously for a reversal of policy on the grounds that the refugees, after having been chased from their country and stripped of all their belongings, had finally been able to establish a self-sufficient community in Camp Oddo. Unaware that national officials were motivated primarily by a desire to break down this internal administration, Hatchikian suggested that the camp's closure would force into the street a population that had been caring for itself and that "can have no other tendencies than to assimilate well and deeply into the life of this great country that had sheltered them." There they could become a burden to the state. Thus, according to Hatchikian, Oddo accelerated the very processes that the French administration feared it was preventing: the camp encouraged integration by keeping the refugees off the public dole. Similarly, he suggested that the camp's closure would deprive its four hundred schoolchildren of an essential French-language education (they were too old to attend local schools), alienating them from their adopted society. As a last appeal, he reminded officials that among the camp's residents were thirty men who had fought in the French armed forces during World War I.[5] All three of these appeals suggest that Hatchikian viewed Camp Oddo as an arena in which loyalty to and integration into the French state were cultivated.

Although Hatchikian's appeal to the government stressed the camp's important role in helping Armenians assimilate into their new home, his petition to

Armenian national and compatriot associations to help Oddo's residents underlined just the opposite. By participating in Oddo's school, church, and charity organizations, he argued, local Armenians had been able to preserve their cultural heritage. Relying on their own hard-won and limited resources, residents had formed educational, medical, and administrative services that allowed them to sustain themselves and their connection to their own culture. It was now up to Armenian organizations, Hatchikian argued, to help these "remains of a much tortured people" go to Soviet Armenia.[6] Thus, whereas his initial plea to French authorities stressed Oddo's role as an arena in which to foster loyalty to France, the petition to Armenian organizations underlined Oddo's role as a center of Armenian language and culture.

The contradiction between these two communications is noteworthy. Were camp residents in the process of adopting French language and customs, or were they uprooted refugees waiting patiently for their return to their homeland? Was Camp Oddo a stepping stone toward their ultimate assimilation, or a safe environment in which to nurture "Armenianness"? What seems like a contradiction to the contemporary eye was not, in fact, a contradiction for Hatchikian. As a naturalized citizen and former soldier himself, he believed in teaching the residents the local language and customs. Nevertheless, he hoped to maintain Oddo as an Armenian enclave within Marseille's perimeters. Indeed, the residents' ability to care for themselves while providing a space in which they could maintain their heritage was, in his eyes, the camp's main asset. While he clearly recognized and adopted many of the French government's integrationist policies, he also fought against complete assimilation into the broader society.

Resistance to abandoning the camp increased greatly when the special examiner began pushing Oddo's refugees to leave Marseille altogether.[7] Encouraged by the nation's integrationist policies, he urged even those who had bought land or rented houses in the region to accept work contracts elsewhere, hoping to disperse them throughout the country, even threatening to expel from French territory any refugee who evaded initiatives to place his family in the provinces. Hatchikian greeted this new policy with alarm, arguing that dispersing the camp's population was yet another forced exile for a group that had already been uprooted far too often.[8] In the meantime, however, the residents simply refused to leave Marseille, moving instead to private plots in the city's suburbs. In so doing, they followed the pattern of Armenians all over France who moved quickly from industrial centers and big cities to private land and their own small homes in surrounding suburbs. The special examiner saw their behavior as a combination of insurrection and laziness, but most were simply seeking to remain in the vicinity so that their children would continue to learn their native language.[9]

A focus on Camp Oddo, despite its unique position as a refugee camp for the indigent and unemployed, highlights Armenian settlement patterns throughout France. In spite of great financial difficulties, those in the camp worked quickly to establish their own community, complete with school and church. Moreover, although they could not entirely withstand French administrative attempts to integrate them into the larger population, they nevertheless fought for the right to remain close to other Armenians; relief at finding a safe haven did not necessarily dictate blind adherence to all assimilationist policies.

Such resistance emerged often at the individual level, particularly when, on arriving in France, Armenian refugees were directed by their work contracts to areas that were distant from their friends and families. Arsene Bogbad, a sixteen-year-old Armenian orphan from Tokat, had been sent to Epinal to be entrusted to the care of the Union des syndicats agricoles vosigniens. Soon after, however, he ran away to join his compatriots elsewhere in the country.[10]

Indeed, it is significant, if not surprising, that those who moved away from Oddo or from other initial points of settlement in search of better pay or living conditions rarely broke away from other Armenians.[11] Generally moving quickly from the cities into suburbs and from renting rooms and apartments to buying small plots of lands and individual homes, they nevertheless tended to remain concentrated, mirroring typical patterns of immigrant residential settlement.[12] Thus, where one went, others followed—to Beaumont in Marseille, Valensolles in Valence, or small towns surrounding Paris, such as Bagneux, Cachan, Chaville, Versailles, and Bois Colombes. These added to the larger and more well-known communities in Alfortville, Issy-les-Moulineaux, and Asnières de Courbevoie, which took shape in 1922–23 after local industries attracted refugees there.[13]

Hence, after several years of living from hand to mouth, the uprooted survivor population moved rapidly into their own suburban communities, establishing their own associations, compatriot unions, newspapers, athletic clubs, theatrical events, and concerts and thereby creating their own "villages" among their French neighbors. Here, their lifestyle, culture, marriage patterns, and birthrates distinguished them from their neighbors.[14] This is not to say that the new suburban areas homogenized the refugee population. We have already seen that political preferences, different points of origin, and religious divisions broke the population into various subgroups. Social divisions existed as well, with those from higher economic classes settled on different streets from their poorer compatriots.[15] Within the range of this diversity, however, Armenians were able to live an Armenian life in France. A glance at the *Guide to Marseille in the Armenian Language*, published for the first time in 1928 and annually thereafter, gives a sense of the extensive subculture that Armenians created. Not only did the guide list a range of available Armenian social, political, and religious organizations, but numerous advertisements displayed the network of services of which they could avail themselves. Thus Armenian lawyers, dentists, real estate brokers, builders, tailors, grocers, electricians, and hairdressers provided services to the local population, allowing them to remain largely within their own community for any number of services.[16]

Religious divisions helped consolidate this cultural isolation. Armenian communal life in France and throughout the diaspora was centered around the church.[17] Serving primarily as a house of worship, it also provided a variety of social services to all members of the community, quickly becoming the one institution in which almost all members of the population participated at one point or another. In establishing the church as an important center of communal life, the refugees imported familiar organizational structures from their past into their new, unfamiliar environment.[18] In the Ottoman Empire, where religious affiliation had been the primary factor determining the individual's relationship to the state, the function of the Armenian Apostolic Church had been much more than religious. In the fourth century C.E., when the Armenian King Tiridates was converted to Christianity, making Armenia the first "nation" to adopt Christianity as its state religion, a sacred culture was born, linking the history of the people with that of their religion.[19] Then, in the fifteenth century, when Armenians came under Ottoman rule, the sultans gave the Armenian Patriarchate in Constantinople unprecedented political, economic, and social power to oversee the administrative affairs of the Empire's Armenian population. As a result, the Constantinople Patriarchate soon evolved into a powerful body that ran Armenian affairs in the Empire, including its political and administrative life (running schools and hospitals, representing Armenians to the national leaders, etc.) and its religious life (running monasteries and churches, overseeing marriages, etc.). By the nineteenth century, this power was being questioned by a new generation of Western-educated Armenian intellectuals who challenged the clergy on its corruption and its alliance with national authorities; still, the overwhelming majority remained committed to familiar religious practices and maintained a strong link with the church. Another small minority responded to the call of Catholic and Protestant missionaries and left the national church to create their own religious institutions.[20]

By the end of the nineteenth century, then, three separate Armenian religious denominations administered the population's affairs in the Empire, each of which was represented in the refugee population that migrated to France. As in the Ottoman Empire, the Apostolic Church was by far the most influential, attracting the greatest number of adherents and serving as the most important center of communal life. Although Armenian Catholics and Protestants also established their churches, most of the refugees gravitated around the Apostolic Church, the main seat of which was located on the rue Jean Goujon in Paris. Bolstered by lay committees of observant Armenians interested in promoting religious life, the Church eventually built parishes and schools to instruct children in Armenian language and religion in all areas of the country where Armenians had settled in large numbers. In addition, a variety of social service organizations either operated from the Church or used it as a base, including a medical dispensary, a women's league, and a veterans' organization.[21] In Marseille, for example, the Association de bienfaisance des dames arméniens de Marseille operated out of the church, providing financial and medical care to indigents, widows, orphans, and the infirm. In addition, the church provided a meeting space where nonreligious groups could come together and served the French government by issuing identity cards, small financial loans, and marriage and birth certificates to the incoming refugee population.[22]

Aside from its various religious and social services, the Church provided the community with an arena in which those with differing political and regional affiliations could come together. Although conflict did occasionally break out, the Church nevertheless remained opened to everyone. For example, Armenian communists, notoriously atheistic, would often participate in major religious celebrations such as Armenian Christmas (January 6) and Easter.[23] The Church thus served as an identifiable site of Armenian affiliation and identification, even for those who did not accept or share in its religious doctrine. Moreover, like the new Armenian suburban communities that were developing, it helped isolate the newcomers from their French Catholic neighbors. As one Armenian student described contacts between his own community and the surrounding population, "Outside occupational links, there were little or no relations at all between the Parisians and the Armenians."[24]

This social and religious division was reinforced in the political arena. Indeed, despite a communal rhetoric that called on the refugees to blend in, particularly when it came to local politics, Armenian representatives actually pursued a particularistic agenda, which pointed to Armenian distinctiveness. We have already seen how this played itself out in debates surrounding Soviet Armenia. Even on the domestic front, however, Armenian representatives would take stands on issues that affected the local population. Thus, once the Treaty of Lausanne was signed and the Armenian National Delegation no longer had an official raison d'être, it was transformed into the Comité central des réfugiés arméniens, the main task of which was to resettle refugees and orphans around the world. Like the National Delegation, the Comité central's scope was international; as such, it worked with the League of Nations to relieve the Armenian plight in Syria, Lebanon, Cyprus, Greece, and Soviet Armenia. Its efforts, however, were also directed at the domestic front, where it served as the officially recognized link between the refugees and the French government, standing in place of a formal consulate.[25]

In this capacity, the Comité central pursued an agenda that distinguished Armenians from those around them. Thus, in August 1926, for example, it requested that impoverished and unemployed stateless Armenians be exempted from new taxes created for immigrant workers. Moreover, in 1931, when the government—which had welcomed immigrant labor throughout the first two decades of the century—began a process of halting immigration, strictly enforcing border controls, tightening labor laws, and encouraging foreigners to leave, representatives of the Comité central met with various sympathetic French officials to discuss the "lamentable situation" facing stateless Armenians in France. Pointing to their difficulty obtaining legal identity papers, their weak position in regard to French immigration law, and their inability to return to their point of origin, the Comité central requested that Armenian workers be treated with "clemency and indulgence," and that they be the last among foreign workers to be fired from their jobs.[26]

Such particularistic concerns were also pursued at an individual level. Comité central representatives often pointed to a particular refugee's stateless condition or status as an atrocity survivor to make a case for legal exceptions on his or her behalf. Such was the case in 1927, when the Comité central intervened on behalf of a forty-two-year-old widow who had been refused residency status, arguing that leniency should be awarded because her husband had been killed and because she had a fifteen-year-old son to support. Likewise, the Comité requested special entrance visas in cases where refugees had been separated from their family, such as when Angèle and Sirapi Erganian, who had been placed in two Lebanese orphanages, sought to reunite with their mother, who was working in a textile factory in France. Furthermore, the Comité attempted to obtain permanent papers for refugees who had arrived on temporary visitor visas. In February 1927, for example, they requested residency rights for the Mahramadians, who had come from Constantinople to visit their son. Similarly, in January that year, the Comité requested that Artin Chariguian, who had come to visit his mother and brother for three months, be allowed to stay. "His greatest desire," wrote Léon Pachalian, the secretary-general of the Comité central, "is to live near to his family whom he has finally been able to rejoin after a long separation."[27]

By promoting such Armenian issues as family reunification, the Comité central thus distinguished a distinctive political agenda for the Armenian community. As such, it served as a quasi government in exile, establishing contact with all the independent self-help organizations that the refugees had begun constructing on their own, and even offering a number of social services, such as help locating dispersed family members and aid for those in search of employment.[28] Indeed, because incoming refugees were more likely to obtain the necessary French travel visa if they had established work contracts prior to arriving, the Comité recommended Armenian workers to various employers and sought employment opportunities in all regions of France.[29]

The Comité central's activities in France, however unsystematic, remind us that no matter how strong the rhetoric of integration, those Armenians who established homes and communities in Paris, Marseille, and elsewhere saw themselves as part of a distinctive ethnocultural community with its own concerns and needs. Even the pro-integrationist paper Le Foyer, which was adamant in its refusal to take a stance on any contemporary political debate in France, used its pages to criticize national policies, when France—as one of many nations—dealt poorly with refugee questions at the League of Nations.[30] Thus, even in the highly charged political arena in which Armenian representatives adamantly insisted that cultural assimilation was paramount, we can find evidence of a distinctive Armenian voice emerging. As scholars have noted, "This first generation of Armenian immigrants, whose main preoccupation was to assure the means of subsistence, lived in an autarchic fashion on the margins of French society except when in the workplace."[31]

In making such an argument, however, one must be careful not to go too far. Although first-generation refugees remained fairly isolated, it is also true that they were not immune to the cultural influences of their new setting. Indeed, as with most migratory groups, from the moment refugees started working in French factories they began adopting the local language in their professional endeavors.[32] Traditional familial structures were also challenged, as children began attending local schools and women joined the industrial workforce.[33] Similarly, Armenian institutional structures could not simply replicate themselves in the French context. Religious life provides a useful example of this phenomenon. No matter how important the Church became as a communal center for the refugees, its power and prestige were quickly reduced in the new setting. In the context of the French secular state, where division of church and state was the presiding norm, the Church could not provide the same legally sanctioned administrative functions it had in the past. Like the synagogue—and its official administrative structure in France, the Consistoire—which was recognized solely as a *religious* institution by the Third Republic leadership, the Armenian Church had no legal power to organize communal life. Though it maintained some responsibilities linked to the arrival of the refugees, refugees' adherence to and participation in church activities remained purely voluntary. Thus, it wielded much less control over the population than it had at any time in its history. As an example of this phenomenon, we can turn briefly to the question of schools.

In the Ottoman Empire, the Patriarchate had been the primary force behind the education of Armenians, fostering a sense of nationhood/peoplehood throughout the population. Although that influence diminished somewhat in the nineteenth century, when a European-educated intelligentsia began encouraging secular education for the Armenian public, the Church still maintained its central role. In France, however, the Church was relegated to a secondary position, its schools reaching children only one or two afternoons a week, after they had already participated in the national educational system. As a result, its impact was necessarily limited.

Moreover, the French context, which had transformed the Church from a legal to a voluntary organization, also encouraged a wide range of other organizations to develop simply by providing space in which they could do so. As a result, the Church had to compete with political and compatriot unions that formed their own schools and educational agendas, and communal life became increasingly diversified. Although political parties had already begun exerting a significant impact on communal life prior to the genocide, their impact had been limited by their semilegal status and their subordinate role to the Church. In France, however, political and religious organizations were essentially the same—voluntary associations in which the immigrant population participated at their own will. The French setting, which facilitated a variety of ethnic identifications without privileging one over the other, thus encouraged the development of alternative centers of Armenian leadership. In one instance, when the Church and the pro-communist organization Haistani oknoutian gomidé (HOG) were fighting over who would provide aid to unemployed Armenian workers, the French police intervened, forcing the two to work together. In this case, the government treated the Church as one among numerous sources of communal leadership rather than the sole voice directing Armenian affairs. In this setting, it should not be surprising that numerous quarrels broke out over who spoke for the community and who represented it to the authorities.[34] The Church, though an important organizational body, did not automatically win these fights, creating a space in which other organizations and associations could take root.

As this example suggests, despite the first generation's marginal engagement with French cultural and social structures, the new context had a profound impact on the nature of their minority community. Indeed, if the shift from "being" to "feeling" Armenian was one that took two or three generations (with the first seemingly impervious to the most basic signs of acculturation, such as adopting the national language and abandoning traditional garb), these initial arrivals nevertheless were affected by their new surroundings in both conscious and unconscious ways.[35] Within a generation the population became increasingly integrated, and by the late 1940s, Armenians and Jews shared a similar ethnoreligious minority status within the polity.

In the period immediately following the genocide, however, Armenians remained far more marginal to the state in which they lived than most French Jews two decades later (new Jewish arrivals notwithstanding). As such, their distinctiveness is quite understandable. Having little in common culturally, linguistically, or religiously with native French citizens, to make their transition easier they turned to familiar traditions, institutions, and structures. Indeed, far from fleeing those traits that had proven so dangerous in the Ottoman Empire, Armenian refugees remained a people apart, doing whatever they could to avoid offending their French hosts while still remaining on the margins of French society.

The status of the post–World War II Jewish community was more complex. Whereas some incoming Jewish refugees obviously mirrored the status of those Armenians described above, a significant percentage were either French themselves or immigrants who had already lived in France for several decades. This mix of natives, new refugees, and immigrants, though differing from one another in many ways, all faced a postwar French government recommitted to viewing Jewishness as a private, religious identification, and one that had no impact on their civil status, whether as citizens or immigrants. In theory, therefore, local Jewish populations could have responded to the years of persecution by quickly disappearing into their surrounding society, shedding any traits that might have continued to mark them as "other." In fact, the Jewish population not only remained remarkably visible in the decades following World War II, but transformed the community's public face to reflect a growing ethnic consciousness among them.

Fears of a precipitous decline among French Jews after World War II were widespread. In 1949, for example, Robert Sommer, a representative of the Consistoire de Paris, voiced deep concerns over the future of Judaism in France. Claiming that 40 to 50 percent of the community had disappeared due to deportations, postwar attempts to blend into French society, and departures for Israel, Sommer worried that French Jewry was decimated beyond repair.[36] Other communal leaders shared Sommer's fears. Indeed, in the years immediately following World War II, Jewish religious and communal leaders bemoaned the demise of Judaism in France. According to them, deportations had removed the most observant sectors of the population and postwar attempts to escape Judaism "through conversions and mixed marriages, through disappearance, evaporation, [and] camouflages" were forever destroying the community.[37]

Requests from Jewish families to legally change their name to one less recognizably Jewish or foreign-sounding particularly worried the local leadership, who noted that such requests far exceeded the percentage of Jews in the population. One report indicated that from the end of January to the beginning of April 1945, Jews had registered 110 out of 173 requests for name changes. To Consistoire officials, such name changes posed one of the "most serious and troubling" problems facing French Judaism. "In the near or not so distant future," warned the chief rabbi of France, Isaïe Schwartz, "those of our coreligionists or their children who have changed their names in this way will abandon their faith; abandonment is all the more to fear for we are unfortunately not in a period of deep belief."[38]

Such fears, however, were exaggerated. Indeed, although a series of postwar ordinances simplified the process through which individuals could legally change their name, only 2,150 Jews in France asked to do so between 1945 and 1957. It is certainly possible that some of these requests were made by Jews fearing the return of antisemitic persecution and anxious to shed an "onerous identity," yet most were requested by eastern European Jews, the pronunciation of whose names proved difficult for French tongues, or by Resistance fighters who wished to maintain the clandestine names they had used during the years of fighting.[39]

This is not to say that postwar Jewish life was characterized by a vibrant interest in Judaism. Statistical accounts for Paris suggest that religious practices among Consistoire-affiliated Jews declined sharply in the postwar years.[40] In 1948, for example, 71 bar mitzvah ceremonies were performed in Paris, compared to 296 in 1926. Similarly, the number of consistorial marriages dropped dramatically in the first decade after World War II, as did the numbers of children enrolled in religious instruction.[41]

Affiliation with the Consistoire also dropped after the war. In March 1945, the Consistoire de Paris sent out 3,600 letters to former members asking that they pay their current and past dues. By June the organization had received only 600 responses. The silence could certainly be explained by the disruption of the war; most Jews were not yet in a position to pay dues to a voluntary organization, as they were only just regaining their economic foothold. Moreover, the war's dislocation had left the Consistoire with incorrect addresses for many former members.[42] Nevertheless, French Jews, even those who had been affiliated with the Consistoire prior to the war, were clearly in no hurry to reconnect with the institutions representing French Judaism, much less to seek solace for their losses in organized religion.

Moreover, although membership numbers steadily increased, they did not reach prewar levels. In 1932 the Consistoire de Paris's membership rosters listed over 7,000 families; in January 1947, only 2,632 families were affiliated. Evidence suggests that some families were attending religious services without paying membership dues, yet numbers were still under the 5,000 that Consistoire officials believed should be listed on their rosters. By December 1948, the Consistoire reported 588 new members, bringing the total to 3,339. Nevertheless, in 1950, the president complained after a poor turnout for Consistoire elections, "We can estimate [approximately] 20,000 Jewish families in Paris and in the department; [yet] we do not have 4,000 registered in the Association and we do not have 700 who demonstrate any interest in us during elections; this is truly a failure!"[43]

How can we understand such numbers? To Consistoire officials, they indicated a crisis in Jewish life brought on by the war and the subsequent flight from visible signs of Jewish affiliation. And yet, such disaffiliation from Jewish religious life had begun long before the war. Indeed, religious observance had consistently declined for both Jews and non-Jews since the Enlightenment, particularly in Paris.[44] Given that the majority of Jews lived in the French capital, the secular instincts of the city had a wider impact on Judaism than on other religions in France. If by the first decades of the twentieth century "religion remained the technical basis for Jewish identity in France, it had clearly lost hold over most French Jews." Indeed, while immigrant religious organizations had flourished during the interwar years, consistorial influence had decreased continually since the separation of church and state in 1906, when it lost its monopoly over religious life. From 1905 to 1931, therefore, organized Jewish communities dropped from seventy-four to fifty and the number of rabbis dropped significantly as well.[45]

Although these decreasing numbers can be explained partially by the continual migration of Jews from the provinces to Paris, it is also clear that the daily practice of Judaism was in decline.

The post–World War II figures thus suggest that the Consistoire itself was in crisis rather than Jewish life as a whole. Although some of the postwar disaffiliation may have been caused by fear that active participation in Jewish institutions could prove dangerous, most was probably caused by the continued impact of the secular state on new generations of Jews. Unlike Armenians, for whom the church served as the center of communal affiliation, postwar French Jews did not view the synagogue the same way. Certainly, first-generation immigrant Jews and their children tended to remain more religiously observant than those whose ancestry in France went back several generations, meaning that both Orthodox and Hassidic congregations and yeshivas were represented in Paris and the provinces. These institutions, however, tended to be peopled by incoming Jews from eastern Europe.[46]

Indeed, for most French Jews, public religious observance was not strong. And yet to assume, as communal leaders did, that Jews were fleeing their ancestral religion in a desperate attempt to assimilate in the wake of the persecution seems misguided. In fact, not all religious participation had disappeared. Attendance at high holiday services, for example, continued to fill synagogues to capacity.[47] Even more important, however, was that even those French Jews who had abandoned the synagogue entirely had not necessarily opted for total assimilation. Rather, the nature of their identification with Jewish life was continuing to shift to ever more nonreligious forms. This shift had already begun several decades before the Holocaust in response to the Dreyfus Affair and to the integration of the first waves of eastern Jewish immigrants into French Jewish life. In light of these challenges, notions of Jewishness had become increasingly diverse, with religious practice becoming only one of numerous ways that individual Jews expressed their Jewish affiliation.[48]

Such changes were all the more apparent after World War II. Harry Rosen, a representative of the American Joint Distribution Committee, recognized as much when he arrived in 1948. Expecting to find a devastated Jewish population unwilling and uninterested in maintaining any link with its ancestral heritage, Rosen had a pleasant surprise. After meeting with a wide variety of individuals, including native and immigrant Jews from various class backgrounds, he concluded that the disaffiliated French Jewish population was *not*, in fact, alienated: "There *is* [in France] identification by a substantial number of Jews with things

Jewish, with Jewish hopes and aspirations. . . . I am not suggesting that French Jewry has suddenly become extremely Jewish-conscious or nationalist. I am suggesting, however, that Hitler has left his mark. I am suggesting further that the birth of *Medinat Israel* [the State of Israel] has captured the imagination and fired the hearts of the vast majority of Jews in France. I am suggesting that given something with which to identify, the greatest number of Jews here will identify."[49]

As Rosen's comments suggest, postwar French Jews were not in flight from their Jewishness any more than the Armenians discussed above felt driven to hide their roots. To the contrary, within a year of the restoration of peace, Jewish institutional life was once again in visible operation, with nearly two hundred organizations in Paris alone representing all religious, political, cultural, and social perspectives.[50] Moreover, new institutional frameworks took shape, which allowed ever larger numbers to express their Jewishness in nonreligious ways. Rosen himself took part in forming the Fonds social juif unifié (FSJU), a united fund modeled on American Jewish conceptions of centralized fundraising. The FSJU, in turn, devoted itself to rebuilding Jewish communal life. By directing its resources to the establishment of numerous Jewish community centers around France, this new institution provided the population with a number of new arenas in which to express their Jewishness. By placing emphasis on *cultural* connections to Jewishness rather than highlighting religious expression as the sole means of identification, the FSJU continued to reinforce a century-long shift to secular definitions of Jewish participation.

For the FSJU's particular vision of communal development to prevail, however, deeply divided segments of French Jewish life first had to come together. These divisions were established in the decades preceding the war, as immigrant and native representatives as well as subgroups of both bickered over communal priorities and political outlooks. Such enmity was underlined during the occupation as differing interpretations about the nature and depth of the threat as well as contrasting views over methods of response continued to alienate various factions from one another.[51] These ideological divisions became well entrenched in its aftermath. The emotionally charged field of child care provides a case in point. As has been well documented, Jewish war orphans captured the communal imagination in the mid-1940s. Viewed as the "wards of Israel," these young survivors were a central concern of those most committed to ensuring Jewry's future. Postwar child care agencies, such as the Zionist organization OPEJ, built numerous *maisons d'enfants* to take care of those children whose parents had been deported or killed or who had fled, as well as of those whose families found themselves financially or physically unable to care for their children.[52] The largest agency, the Oeuvre de secours aux enfants (OSE), established twenty-five such homes with fifteen hundred children by 1947.[53]

All such homes shared one goal: to provide the children with an education that might, one day, turn them into the new leaders of their beleaguered people. As one commentator of the day put it, "Maybe from among these children will come a great philosopher, scholar, or artist of whom we can say with pride: this is a Jew."[54] And yet, though sharing the same broad goal, few shared a vision of what that education should be. In addition to OSE and OPEJ, numerous other groups ran homes according to their own ideological or religious priorities. The Zionist Organization of France, for example, built two orphanages by 1949 with the purpose of sending Jewish orphans to Israel, and those concerned with providing children with a traditional religious education established the Maison israélite de refuge pour l'enfance and the Oeuvre israélite des sejours à la campagne.[55] Additionally, the communist UJRE, the Bundist Cercle Amicale, and the Zionist youth movement EIF also operated their own homes.

Each home, whether Zionist, Bundist, communist, or Orthodox, had its own convictions that its guardians and teachers sought to inculcate in their wards. Although the educators agreed that they should save the children for the Jewish people, they often disagreed as to the nature of that Jewish identity. For example, the secretary-general of the FSJF complained of the UJRE's communist-based homes, "The education in these children's homes is not carried on in a Jewish spirit, and the instruction of Yiddish, for instance, is a vague formula applied only for the sake of form." As cold war attitudes took root, such anticommunism became further entrenched.[56]

And yet, while certain ongoing political battles continued to be waged among various subgroups of the population, a profound desire for cooperation also began emerging in response to the persecutions of World War II. Georges Wormser noted of Jewish solidarity in 1946, "We will stand close together. Racism made no distinctions between us, destroying the illusions that, one has to admit, were nursed in some of our consciences." Another Consistoire official commented of his internment at Drancy that no distinction had been made among Jews of different rites: "They were Jews; that was all."[57] Such comments suggest that the Jewish leadership, aware of the attitudes that had created divisions in previous decades, was now publicly committed to fighting against "exclusivism or intolerance." As a result, a far greater acceptance of the diverse forms of Jewish expression was soon apparent in the ranks of the communal elite. As one Consistoire official noted in 1946, "All children of Israel are our spiritual brothers:

those who claim the Torah, those who speak French, Yiddish, or Hebrew as well as the peaceful Parisian merchant or the heroic Palestinian soldier. . . . We listen to the opinions of these spiritual brothers to the same extent as those of the original members of our Community. Because the solidarity of Israel endures beyond persecution. We did not need the ashes of Auschwitz to teach us that."[58] In truth, however, it was precisely the "ashes of Auschwitz" that had inspired this new rhetoric of solidarity among the previously standoffish native Jewish leadership.

Such sentiments were immediately translated into action, as various communal leaders looked to establish new cooperative institutions that de-emphasized previous sectarianism. The founding of the Conseil représentatif israélite de France is a case in point, as is the FSJU.

If, however, French Jews were predisposed to create new unified structures in the postwar period, the FSJU's birth was also the product of another postwar development: the involvement of American Jews in the reconstruction of French Jewish life. Motivated by a guilty conscience over having not done enough during the war and by an increasingly centralized and efficient fundraising operation, American Jews donated millions of dollars to European relief efforts; $14,318,000 of these funds went to France, largely through the auspices of the AJDC, the main American Jewish philanthropic organization to involve itself in international relief programs. The AJDC used these resources to fund a wide range of children's homes, hospitals, schools, refugee relief organizations, and other social welfare agencies, irrespective of their ideological or political concerns.[59] Thus, with the aid of the AJDC's subventions, the Fédération des sociétés juives, for example, provided an extensive network of housing aid and property protection for returning deportees and new immigrants as well as a variety of professional, educational, financial, medical, cultural, and legal services. Through such channels, the AJDC was soon providing for most of the community's economic needs.[60] In May 1945, Guy de Rothschild thus reported that the Joint Distribution Committee was caring directly for one third of the population. "Frankly," he remarked, "we could do nothing without the Joint."[61]

No matter how willing they were to participate in the rebirth of French Jewry, however, AJDC officials assumed from the beginning that French Jewry would eventually care for its own. As soon as the most pressing emergencies had been addressed, therefore, they began pushing local Jewish institutions to raise their own money. It was from these endeavors that the idea for the FSJU was born. Believing that centralization was not only the most efficient way to raise funds but also the best model for future communal development, AJDC officials imported American Jewish institutional models to their French setting.

Centralized fundraising as a nonsectarian activity through which diverse groups could work together toward a common end had emerged among American Jews at the end of the nineteenth century as a means of solidifying the increasingly diversified community. Although initially the call for centralization was more rhetorical than real, as various subsets of the population continued to rely on their own resources and efforts, the depression and the crisis in Europe soon forced a new economic cooperation to emerge. Then, following World War II, an unprecedented economic boom brought American Jewish philanthropy into a new era. In 1946 alone, the recently created United Jewish Appeal raised over $130 million. Even more staggering, in 1948, during Israel's war of independence, the UJA raised over $200 million.[62] With these successes, fundraising soon became a central tenet of American Jewish communal organization. By donating funds annually to the UJA or to Jewish philanthropic federations, Jews otherwise disconnected from communal life took part in its endeavors.[63] Furthermore, a centralized fundraising organization provided the Jewish American population with unprecedented ability for communal growth. Although Jews made up only 3 percent of the U.S. population, the UJA was the most successful of all postwar American philanthropies.[64]

It was the successes of American Jewish fundraising that convinced AJDC leaders that centralization was the answer to communal development in France. Generally put off by the "politically minded" infighting among French Jewish institutions, they turned to fundraising as a way to transcend division. "It is quite clear," remarked one AJDC official, "that if and when the French Jews will succeed in organizing their own united fund-raising for their own needs, they will be well along on the road to a kind of unified communal system."[65] Clearly, for AJDC officials, communal cooperation and centralized fundraising were inseparable; by participating in the latter, the former was inevitable. From the beginning, then, they pushed a centralized model that mirrored their own operations.

Unlike in the United States, centralized fundraising proved far harder to sustain in France, where notions of collective responsibility at times gave way to revolutionary ideals that celebrated the individual's relationship with the state.[66] This inability to unify philanthropic efforts effectively is all the more ironic given the highly centralized nature of communal life under the Consistoire, the body established by Napoleon to coordinate and maintain Jewish life in France. Although the Consistoire created the Comité de bienfaisance in 1809 in an effort to bring all charitable activities under one organizational umbrella, its efforts largely failed. Because of this body's critical stance toward the Jewish poor—denying aid to the drunk or idle, placing residency requirements on those receiving aid, and generally linking philanthropy with moral improvement—most philanthropic activities in the early part of the century were driven by those critical of the Consistoire for not doing enough for the Jewish poor. Thus, as in nineteenth-century America, most charitable operations arose from private contributors and from local mutual aid societies. The Consistoire tolerated their presence and even developed a system whereby it received charitable contributions from them in exchange for the favor of approving prayer meetings. It then used the funds to support the Parisian Jewish poor. Such efforts meant that by the end of the nineteenth century, French Jews had created a philanthropic structure that "extended from cradle to grave." And yet most of these efforts came under no centralizing framework despite a significant unifying philanthropic discourse.[67]

With the influx of eastern European Jewish immigrants in the 1880s and 1890s, the native Jewish leadership made new efforts to coordinate philanthropy in the hopes that such efforts would prevent overlapping services and allow for a greater investigation into the worthiness of the recipients. These efforts, much like those of the American philanthropists dedicated to aiding eastern European Jewish migration to the United States, were shaped by a profound ambivalence on the part of the givers toward the receivers. Indeed, in both countries the native Jewish establishment initially proved reluctant to welcome the eastern European Jews—whom they viewed as an embarrassment—into previously established Jewish communities. In the United States, however, although this contemptuousness never entirely dissipated and Jewish philanthropies remained committed to using their resources to transform the newcomers in their own image, communal leaders became increasingly convinced that their country provided the only viable option for Jews fleeing oppression abroad. As a result, they began working tirelessly to oppose efforts to restrict the immigration flow and devoted considerable resources to settling the incoming Jewish population. In France, however, the ambivalence toward the newcomers shaped the native Jewish leadership longer and in more profound ways. Strained community resources and a fear among community members of a resurgence of the antisemitism of the Dreyfus years interfered with the kind of centralized philanthropic and political activities that existed in the United States. This is not to suggest that French Jews remained any less moved by the eastern European Jewish plight than their American coreligionists. Indeed, wealthy French Jews provided substantial support to their charitable institutions. However, no centralized effort succeeded in coordinating them all into one national initiative. In addition, as in the United States, divisions between immigrants and natives as well as political and religious differences among the immigrants themselves served as a disincentive to unified fundraising efforts.

Unlike in the United States, however, the worldwide economic depression did not force immigrants and natives to coordinate efforts in France. Indeed, in these difficult years, new waves of refugees kept arriving, leading to new tensions and a wider proliferation of immigrant self-help organizations.[68]

In was only in the aftermath of the war, then, with a new drive for unification on the part of organized French Jewry and with the encouragement of American Jewish agencies, that a new model of communal development was born. Creating such a structure, however, was no easy task. By 1947, 82 percent of the funds on which French Jewish agencies depended came from abroad. Of the remaining 18 percent, 12 came from the government and only 6 came from local sources. Nevertheless, local fundraising practices, though disorganized and haphazard, had been able to raise considerable funds, particularly for Jewish fighting forces in Palestine, suggesting that French Jews could indeed support their entire social welfare network.[69]

Over the course of 1948 and 1949, therefore, various French Jewish organizations began working together to tap into these resources, although due to some hesitation it took nearly eight months for the "revolutionary endeavor" to take place. Initially, some were nervous about losing their independence. In addition, a handful of Zionist and communist organizations attempted to derail the process. Clearly, ideological divisions had not entirely disappeared. Nevertheless, a growing population of "neutrals" in the community, frustrated by the constant wrangling among political groups, began looking to a united campaign "almost wistfully as the possible source of 'peace.'" As a result, the major Jewish organizations, such as the Consistoire, the Alliance israélite universelle, and the Fédération des sociétés juives, were quite cooperative from the outset, as were several pro-Israeli organizations. Others joined once centralized fundraising got underway. Thus, by 24 October 1949, a general assembly composed of 250 representatives of Jewish communities in France adopted the charter of the Fonds social juif unifié.[70] For the first few years, a large percentage of the FSJU's resources came from the AJDC and the wealthiest members of French Jewish society, but its income increased annually, indicating its growing success. By 1955, the united Jewish fund collected 200 million francs, providing the bulk of all funds for cultural and social welfare institutions.[71]

By establishing a centralized fund that distanced itself from the political and ideological voices that had previously dominated local Jewish life, a new vision of communal organization was born that reflected the realities of post-1945. *Quand même*, the journal of the Fédération des sociétés juives, editorialized in June 1949,

"From all points of view, the creation of the FSJU responds to the vital needs of the Jewish community in France with an eye toward preparing the solid financial groundwork for its social and cultural activities *and for creating a climate of fraternal solidarity among all the organizations.*" Indeed, a mere ten years after its birth, the FSJU had become, according to its president, Guy de Rothschild, the principal social and cultural representative of organized French Judaism *because* of its nonsectarian approach to communal organization. "We have succeeded . . . in making all affiliations co-habitate, co-exist, while reserving a place for each one in such a way that no one can reproach us for favoritism."[72] Evidently, for Rothschild, as well as for other FSJU leaders, the Fonds had achieved what no other organization had before; it had provided room for diverse expressions of Jewish identity and as such had widened the base of communal affiliation outside the confines of traditional political and religious groupings.

This is not to suggest that political division ceased to exist. Until the late 1950s, the "great families" of the native French Jewish population, rather than representatives of the eastern European immigrants or their descendants, ran most of French Jewry's central institutions, including the FSJU, and largely funded its endeavors.[73] Moreover, splits between communists and their opponents worsened as the cold war divided West and East.[74] Nor was the FSJU welcomed with open arms by every member of the local Jewish population. As noted above, some communist and Zionist organizations attempted to block its creation. Nevertheless, the new unified fund came to control the great bulk of community assets and, thus, soon became extremely powerful. Indeed, within a short time, over two hundred organizations depended on the FSJU's annual fundraising drive (with the extensive financial help of the AJDC) to maintain themselves. Hence, the umbrella organization could entice various and often opposing Jewish groups to work together to create child care programs, old-age homes, summer camps, medical facilities, youth movements, schools, study centers, conferences, and libraries. By controlling the community's resources it thus became a significant force in communal affairs.

This is evident in the shift from the Consistoire to the FSJU as the most important body of native French Jews. While the former continued to direct religious affairs and regained some of its previous influence after the more observant North African Jews begin migrating to France following French decolonization in the late 1950s and early 1960s, its relevance decreased dramatically in the decade after World War II.[75] Indeed, some Consistoire representatives predicted such an outcome in the late 1940s as they watched the new fundraising organ develop with wary curiosity. Generally supportive of the FSJU's goals, they worried that those who had responded to its appeals might feel it unnecessary to donate to the Consistoire.[76]

As predicted, by June 1950 the Consistoire was showing a considerable reduction in its charitable donations, and by 1952 the Consistoire's budget had been "dangerously amputated," to the point where its leadership was turning to the FSJU for aid. That year the secretary of the Consistoire remarked wryly, "If the organizations that have agreed to group together under the aegis of the Fonds social claim all of Judaism, do you think they will be able to do it; do you think there will still be Judaism in France if we have no more synagogues, if our communities have no means to assure the functioning of the religion, of paying the rabbis — whose mission is as much religious as cultural and social — if the Consistoire Centrale is no longer able to fulfill its mission of centralization and representation?" The local Jewish population, however, seemed unconcerned and continued to send the better part of their donations to the FSJU. By 1956, Consistoire officials were actively campaigning for the FSJU to keep their own operations afloat.[77] Despite such efforts, as well as attempts to broaden its appeal by instituting a range of religious reforms, the Consistoire's influence on communal affairs remained secondary throughout the 1950s.

The establishment of the FSJU thus continued the process of moving the focal point of native French Jewish life away from the synagogue. With its dedication to being "sufficiently large enough to gather all those who intended to maintain their attachment to Judaism in whatever form," the Fonds social gave institutional legitimacy to cultural and social expressions of Jewish identification.[78]

This shift became all the more apparent in 1954, when Germany began providing massive financial restitutions to national and international Jewish agencies. The point of these funds was "to bring back to life, as much as is possible, French and European Judaism so culturally stricken by the war and occupation."[79] As a sign of its centrality in French Jewish affairs and because of its broad administrative structure, the FSJU took control of the distribution of these sums in France. Finally provided with regular resources, the FSJU used the income to implement a program of cultural renovation by creating the Commission du plan d'action culturelle. The members of the Commission, run by Vidal Modiano, then president of CRIF, represented all Jewish religious, political, and ideological groups in France. Together they worked to revitalize French Jewish cultural life and to rebuild small and midsize provincial communities cut off from Jewish life since World War II by funding a number of community centers.[80] These centers were designed to provide spaces in which Jewish youth could flourish and stood as physical symbols of the new commitment to unifying the diverse groups of Jewish life.

Ironically, like the FSJU itself, the idea of building community centers came from an AJDC initiative. This is not to suggest that the idea was entirely foreign to the local scene. Indeed, as early as the 1920s, the first Jewish youth group in France, the Union Scolaire, had created a library and a game and conference room for its members, becoming the first Jewish community center in France. Likewise, the Association amicale des israélites saloniciens (AAIS), an organization created by Jewish Salonican immigrants to France in 1923, built its headquarters around a cafeteria, library, reading rooms, and recreation rooms.[81] Nevertheless, the model for the new centers was that of the American Jewish community center, an organizational structure that had evolved out of the particular nature of Jewish affiliation in the United States.

The Jewish community center in the United States was born out of fears over low levels of synagogue attendance among America's Jews. Originally conceived of by Mordecai Kaplan of the Jewish Theological Seminary, the synagogue-center was to serve as more than a place of worship. It was to provide educational, recreational, social, and cultural activities as a means of invigorating Jewish life. The construction of such centers really took off, however, when eastern European Jewish immigrants, having achieved a measure of material success and having moved away from the ghetto neighborhoods in which they had originally settled, began building a new type of synagogue to reflect the realities of their new setting. These huge edifices reflected the middle-class status and social aspirations of their congregants and generally housed all the recreational and social needs of their members, including schools, gymnasiums, pool tables, game rooms, and other nonreligious facilities. This building surge took on a new momentum following World War II, when entire Jewish communities joined the larger movement from urban to suburban America. Now living in integrated populations rather than in the insular Jewish communities from which they had come, the newly established suburban communities sought outlets to express their Jewishness. The synagogue-center was one such outlet, allowing congregants to affirm their Judaism while also providing them with a variety of secular activities. In this regard, however, the synagogue-center never fulfilled Kaplan's original hopes: many new suburbanites chose to affiliate with the synagogue, but the numbers of those participating in religious services did not increase. Soon, suburban America saw the birth of the Jewish community center, a social, recreational, and educational facility with no religious component.[82]

In postwar France, which shared neither the American Jewish tradition of religious innovation nor the spread of middle-class suburban settlement, community centers in the form so familiar to American Jews by the 1950s were non-existent. Synagogues had remained sites for religious worship and, if once centers of communal life, had lost that role with increasing secularization. Nor had the native Jewish population created new secular arenas in which to express their Jewishness, the two small community centers noted above notwithstanding. While immigrant Jews maintained their *shuls*, political organizations, and landsmanshaftn, the differing priorities between immigrants and natives in the 1930s prevented cooperative communal development. Moreover, the arrival of World War II and the subsequent disruption of Jewish life made *any* further growth impossible.

It was not until the early 1950s, therefore, that local communal leaders began to look to such centers as an arena in which to expand Jewish affiliation, and under the guidance of the AJDC's Director of Cultural and Educational Reconstruction Judah Shapiro, these American institutions were now adapted to their French setting. For Shapiro, the community center offered new ways for French Jews to express their connection to Jewish life. As he argued at a 1953 FSJU meeting:

> Let us consider for a moment the fact that our western world, and for our purposes Paris itself, offers little opportunity for the daily life of a Jew to be characteristically Jewish. The largest part of his day involves activities which conform to the general pattern of the society with no distinguishing features that are Jewish. It is rare to find the neighborhood where the very atmosphere is Jewish and where by living alone, one may acquire Jewish information patterns and an outlook on life. We must provide for the Jew to be Jewish in specific places at specific times for it is no longer possible to live a life in isolation from the culture as a whole. We do not seek a return to the ghetto and do not wish to remove ourselves from the richness of the world around us but we can enrich ourselves with all the greatness that the Jewish tradition and culture has to offer.

For Shapiro, the community center was the perfect antidote to the disaffiliation of French youth, because there the person with "vague loyalties" could find a home. In addition, those who had the desire to participate in communal life but no clear idea how to do so would find in the center a welcome space to meet with other Jews.[83]

Such views proved convincing to French Jewish leaders already predisposed to focus attention on disaffiliated youth, and the first center opened in Paris in 1955. Estimated to serve approximately one thousand people, within a few months nearly eight hundred youth were already using it. With funds from the Claims Conference, the FSJU built youth centers in Belfort, Roanne, and Lens, soon followed by others in Metz, Grenoble, Lyon, and Nancy.[84]

The goal of these centers was not to educate per se—at least not in a strictly traditional sense. Rather, as one FSJU official noted, "[The center] leans toward methods of popular education" by providing leisure activities, organizing conferences, and creating study groups, summer camps, and travel groups. Most important, however, "[the center] does not take the place of either Jewish organizations or Jewish youth movements. It creates a new form of co-existence and hopes to enrich them by opening itself to all, youth and adult, without distinction of ideology, inclination, or origin. Its ambition is to be a rallying point, a common home, a place where a new style of community relations can form adapted to a profoundly secular century."[85] In other words, the community center, like the FSJU itself, was to reinvent Jewish affiliation along neither sectarian nor religious lines.

Thanks to the AJDC and FSJU, then, and with active support from other international Jewish organizations, by 1965 fifty-two community centers were spread out over the French map, providing Jews with new spaces in which to develop secular Jewish identities.[86] France's chief rabbi Jacob Kaplan noted, "The creation of . . . community centers, according to the model of the [American] Jewish community centers, offers opportunities for meeting and for contact that were not permitted in the synagogues of the nineteenth century, limited to places of worship."[87] As Kaplan's remark suggests, even religious leaders were impressed by the new centers, a fact most clearly reflected in the Consistoire de Paris's own campaign, Chantiers de Consistoire, to raise money for the construction of synagogue-centers in early 1960. The first two such centers were built in Massy Antony and Sarcelles, two Parisian suburbs where many incoming North African Jewish immigrants settled. As one brochure insisted, the "enormous beautiful consistorial synagogues" of earlier eras no longer corresponded to the population's needs. New communities no longer needed unidimensional places of worship. Rather, they required sanctuaries that could be transformed with the aid of mobile partition walls into conference rooms, projection halls, or classrooms. For the Consistoire, then, the synagogue was no longer just that, but an "ensemble, a communal home regrouping religious worship, instruction, youth group activities, cultural programs, etc."[88] Thus, by the early 1960s, even the Consistoire de Paris was adopting institutional forms that encouraged many kinds of communal participation.

The development of such community centers is symbolically important for two reasons. First, their growth and development transformed the postwar French Jewish institutional landscape. Whereas synagogues had provided communal gathering spaces throughout the nineteenth century, the new community centers were expressly built to provide cultural and social outlets. Groups with differing political views and religious rites could intermingle and participate in communal life without observing religious traditions. The centers reflected the realities of the postwar era, as the Jewish leadership not only recognized but endorsed the shift away from a strictly religious definition of French Jewish identity. Second, the centers represented in concrete, physical form a French Jewish presence in their local landscape. Far from fleeing their distinctive minority status, Jews participated in creating new structures that not only reasserted their right to exist but promoted nonreligious forms of communal development.

Comparing Minority Status

A comparison of Armenian and Jewish understandings of their minority status yields quite different responses based largely on their position within the state. As refugees, Armenians remained on the margins of French society. Unable to avoid its acculturating influence, they nevertheless turned to the insularity of their own community as a means of processing their dislocation. As a result, their institutional forms, familial structures, and settlement choices all reinforced a sense of their distinctiveness. Indeed, far from fleeing their ethnoreligious roots as a means to move past the genocidal attack, they repeatedly asserted their particularity. Such a move may not have been conscious, but it nevertheless suggests that for these survivors, the recent persecutions had not led to a radical reevaluation of the nature of their community. Until World War I, Armenians in the Ottoman Empire had experienced little conflict between their position as subjects in a multiethnic empire and their Armenian heritage. Regarded not as equal citizens but as members of a Christian minority in a larger Islamic empire, their affiliation to this community defined their relationship to the state. Although periodic violence against them had characterized their long history in the Empire, most had been able to pursue a lifestyle that was entirely Armenian, constructing their own schools, religious institutions, and welfare networks. Despite the great upheaval of World War I—or maybe because of it—most new refugees to France sought to recreate their autonomous communities in their French context. They hated the Turkish authorities who had persecuted them, and believed that France would provide the stability they needed to reestablish their devastated communities.

For French Jews, however, the situation was altogether different. Unlike Armenians, a significant percentage of the Jewish population had roots in France prior to the Holocaust. Although the recent past had included a period of marginalization, post–World War II French political culture had welcomed them back to the national fold. In the state's eyes, this meant that Jews were once again viewed primarily as a religious minority, distinguished from other citizens and immigrants only by the nature of their private religious practices. For those who had lived through World War II and Vichy persecutions, however, such a designation no longer made sense. Notions of Jewish identity had begun to expand before the Holocaust; in its aftermath, these changes gathered steam. Aided by the infusion of American Jewish money and influence, French Jews began exploring new ways of identifying that placed their ethnic and cultural distinctiveness in the foreground. Indeed, if, as some have argued, the past two decades have seen French Jews move away from universalistic conceptions of citizenship and toward an ever greater emphasis on their own particularism, I would argue that this change began taking root immediately after World War II, as those who had lived through the upheaval began to redefine the nature of Jewish identity in France.[89]

6 Genocide Revisited: Armenians and the French Polity after World War II

One of the most illuminating ways by which to compare the impact of genocide on the ethnic and national affiliations of Armenian and Jewish survivors is to look at the chronological moment when the two stories temporarily merged—after the establishment of the Vichy government in summer 1940. Given their own recent history of state-sponsored persecution, it is instructive to consider how Armenians responded to the transformation of their "safe haven" into the more restrictive Vichy regime and, parenthetically, how they reacted to the persecution of their Jewish neighbors at the hands of the Germans and French. Did they see parallels between their own plight fifteen years previously and that of European Jewry in the early 1940s? In other words, did they understand the persecution and deportation of the Jews as a "shared fate"? If so, did it shape their behavior during the war, and did their own understanding of their position in French society shift as a result? What impact did these events have on their connection to Soviet Armenia and to a broader diaspora identity?

Unfortunately, although the first of these questions is fascinating, it is virtually impossible to answer and must thus remain at the margins of this chapter and book. Certain anecdotal evidence suggests that some Armenians were well aware of the Jewish plight and even defended them, but the evidence is too spotty to allow for any generalizations about the Armenian response to Jewish victimization.[1] What can be said with certainty, however, is that the arrival of the war, which cut off diaspora allegiances by placing Armenians on opposite sides of the international conflict, and the new regulations on foreigners forced not only Jews to reevaluate their position in their surrounding society. Armenians, too, faced the tumultuous period by reconsidering their relationship to the French state. Evidence for this comes most clearly after the war when, on the one hand, a great naturalization wave transformed most Armenians into French citizens and, on the other, approximately seven thousand more, or 10 percent of the French Armenian population, heeded the Soviet Union's call for Armenians throughout the diaspora to return "home."[2] Although becoming a citizen or leaving France altogether were mutually contradictory impulses, they stemmed from a wider common realization born of the war, the economic crisis of the 1930s, and its accompanying xenophobia: Armenians in France, despite being "welcomed" and "saved" by their new patrie, actually had little protection without a permanent national affiliation.

This chapter considers the war's impact on Armenians' notions of their place in the French polity. As will become clear, the fear and dislocation of the Vichy years disrupted more than Jewish life in France. Although the Vichy government never directly persecuted Armenians (indeed, the response to Armenians stands in stark contrast to the much harsher policies toward Jewish refugees), the Armenian refugees nevertheless responded to the upheaval by seeking a permanent national solution to their apatride status. Indeed, ironically, Armenian responses in the postwar years contrast sharply with Jewish responses as far more reactive. Unlike the majority of native French Jews who saw the arrival of de Gaulle's forces as an opportunity to return to their former national status, Armenians actively sought to transform their position in the polity as soon as possible.

Thus, in the years immediately following World War II, Armenians negotiated a new relationship to the state in which they were living. An explosion in associational life accompanied this shift, as various groups sought different means of being both French and Armenian. Indeed, even though a large number chose naturalization over repatriation, their decision to become French was accompanied by a surge in public demonstrations of loyalty to and identification with Soviet Armenia. This shift was due, in part, to the coming of age of a second generation, who had arrived in France as small children or had been born there and who had a different relationship to the past and to Soviet Armenia than did their parents. More important, however, was the role of the Soviet Union on the side of the Allies during the latter half of World War II, temporarily removing its status as a pariah nation. The active participation of Armenian communists in the Resistance movements gave Soviet supporters a new moral high ground from which to argue their position once the conflict had ended. In this pro-Soviet environment, traditional party splits began to break down, and Armenians of all religious and political affiliations began actively articulating a new patriotism, one linked directly to the Armenian territory within the Soviet borders. This period of more open allegiances ended in 1947 when the cold war put old party alignments back into place more tightly than ever. Thus ended nearly a decade of flux for French Armenians, when their political allegiances and loyalties were tested and retested, ultimately forcing them to abandon their stateless status and choose between remaining in France—but now as citizens—or leaving altogether for the Soviet Union.

World War II and the Armenians

Neither the German occupation nor the indigenous Vichy anti-immigrant policies had the impact on Armenians that it had on Jews. While the latter were subjected to systematic state-sanctioned oppression in the form of loss of citizenship, property, and civil rights and ultimately deportation, Armenians suffered no particular loss in status. Indeed, as we saw in chapter 1, the refugees were at times even looked on favorably by some of the most virulent antisemites.

Nevertheless, racial stereotyping, the occupation, and accompanying xenophobia affected Armenians as well. Anti-immigrant attitudes, so prevalent during the period, influenced the environment in which they lived and worked, making them fear for their jobs and safety. Moreover, like most of those living in France during these years, Armenians also suffered great losses due to the war and the resulting atmosphere. Some lost jobs and closed their shops; others fled Paris for the Unoccupied Zone. Homes were destroyed in bombardments and various communal associations shut their doors.[3] Compatriot unions, for example, began suffering as early as 1939, when laws restricting foreign associational life led many to stop holding meetings. Political parties also suffered, particularly those favorable to the Soviet Union. Hence, the Hnchaks were ordered to disband by Vichy authorities (the HOG had been shut down in 1937), and in 1940 censorship regulations muzzled the pro-Soviet Armenian press. Likewise, the war was a tremendous blow to the vibrant Armenian intellectual life that had developed during the interwar years. Haratch, for example, was not published from 1940 to 1945, when its antifascist editor decided to shut its doors.[4]

In addition, Armenian families were caught up in national defense activities as efforts to increase the size of the French military led to the increasing recruitment of the foreign-born. As early as 1937, military leaders had made arrangements to integrate four hundred thousand Nansen refugees into the French armed forces. Then, in April 1939, a decree designed to augment those numbers required all those enjoying the right of asylum to fulfill the same two-year tour of duty required of all Frenchmen. As a result, numerous Armenians were incorporated into the French fighting forces, both in the regular infantry and the Foreign Legion, many of whom remained German prisoners for the war's duration.[5]

Those who remained in Paris had to negotiate various interventions by German officials and French police. Particularly debilitating was the Service du travail obligatoire (STO), which sent those caught in its web to forced labor in Germany or to certain French industrial areas routinely bombed by the allies.[6] In February 1944, for example, 150 Armenians from Valence were rounded up for the STO. To avoid such engagements, Armenian laborers often joined the Organisation Todt (OT), which promised its volunteers that they would not be taken from France.[7] Others avoided forced labor by using more behind-the-scenes methods. When Edouard Khédérian was called up by the STO, for example, he bribed a French officer to make his folder "disappear."[8]

Moreover, all Armenians under German occupation were watched closely as potential supporters of the Soviet Union. After Germany attacked the Caucasus, Armenian refugees were instructed to report periodically to the Office des émigrés caucasiens en France. Those who failed to do so were automatically considered citizens of the Soviet Union and henceforth subject to all actions taken against them.[9] In addition, as the German army penetrated further into the Caucasus, local authorities began recruiting pro-German administrators from among Armenian university students, forcing some to go to the front.[10] In short, Armenians in France, despite being "welcomed" and "saved" by their new patrie, experienced deep insecurity during the war years as a result of their status as "outsiders."

Thus, even if Armenians were not the "villains" of French society during World War II, their precarious position kept them on the defensive throughout the Vichy years. Prominent Armenians watched racial debates closely and responded quickly to any perceived attack on the Armenian character. To cite one example: in 1943, a week after the immigrant expert Georges Mauco publicly criticized local Armenians for a variety of physiological, social, and economic flaws, the Armenian anthropologist Kherumian defended his people, insisting that Armenians came from a genetic stock similar to that of western and central Europeans, and as such they constituted "a valuable ethnic contribution."[11] His defense echoed the chorus of previous Armenian spokespeople who had argued that Armenians made up a hardworking, stable, law-abiding, healthy, and brave population that would continue to serve France well. Elsewhere, Kherumian argued that Armenians were a "race" of warriors who had never given up the fight for freedom. This warrior culture, combined with their Christianity and their "profound spiritual kinship" with the West, justified their protected place in French society.[12]

In such arguments we can see the intensification of the pro-Armenian propaganda campaign used to garner French support for the apatrides in the 1920s. Still concerned about ensuring their safety in an increasingly insecure environment, Armenian representatives continued to insist that Armenians could make a significant contribution to French society. Some went so far as to adopt the racial tone of the day by insisting on the Armenians' "ARYAN and CHRISTIAN" heritage.[13] Such defense activities were seconded by other, more material attempts to safeguard the Armenians' place in French society. The Office des réfugiés arméniens, for example, now merged with the Comité central des réfugiés arméniens de Paris, handed out certificates to the local Armenian population attesting that the holder was of Armenian origin and, "like his parents, of the Armenian race."[14] And, throughout the war, communal representatives made vocal pledges of loyalty to the French state and backed these pledges with financial contributions. Most indicative of this relationship was the 909,885 franc gift from the Comité central des réfugiés arméniens to Marshal Pétain in 1943 "to benefit the Marshal's social works."[15]

If, some, however, chose to safeguard their position by pledging loyalty to the state, others chose the opposite path and became actively involved in the Resistance. For Armenian communists this was a particularly easy decision, because once the Germans turned against the Soviet Union, those in the Resistance were fighting not only to protect the land that had provided them shelter but against the threat to their national homeland. Thus, theirs was a double mission, concerned with freeing both France and Armenia from the German peril. The most famous figure of this Resistance was Nissak Manouchian, or "Manouch," a genocide orphan who arrived in France in 1925. To support himself as a poet, Manouchian worked first in the factories of Marseille and Paris, joining both HOG and the French Communist Party in 1934 and ultimately becoming head of the latter's immigrant section, the Main d'œuvre immigrée (MOI). In 1935, he was named editor of the Armenian paper *Zangou*, which discussed problems of immigrant life, contemporary political questions, and life in the Soviet Union. The paper's principal mission, however, was its anti-Nazism. According to Manouchian's wife, Mélinée (who wrote a book about his life many years after the Nazis executed him), Manouchian's anti-Nazism developed out of his own losses during World War I. Having experienced oppression firsthand, he felt a personal obligation to fight against fascism wherever it arose.[16]

This anti-Nazi sentiment, coupled with a sincere loyalty to his adopted land, led Manouchian to join the Resistance immediately after returning from the front. Indeed, despite his pro-Soviet tendencies, Manouchian was also a French patriot. As with many of his generation, loyalties to France and to Armenia were not mutually exclusive, even when actively agitating on behalf of the Soviet Union in the 1930s. During World War II, these loyalties merged even more completely as communists and noncommunists worked together to free France. According to Mélinée, for both her and her husband the choice to resist arose from their loyalty to their adopted land: "We lived in France, and our combat had to be carried out at the side of the people of this country against the most terrifying thing that could exist: Nazism."[17]

Manouchian encountered no trouble linking himself to the Resistance. Already a member of MOI before the war and well-known to the leaders of the Union populaire franco-arménienne (the organization that took over after HOG was closed in 1938) and the French Communist Party, he was asked to organize resistance and distribute literature among Parisian Armenians. Then in 1943, he was named military head of the Francs-Tireurs et partisans immigrés in the Parisian region, otherwise known as the "Groupe Manouchian." From 17 March to 12 November 1943, Manouchian's group carried out over one hundred actions in the Parisian region, for which twenty-three of the group's members were ultimately caught and executed on 21 February 1944.[18] The Germans carried out the execution with great publicity, hanging large red posters with pictures of ten of the condemned men. Although there were French citizens among the group, the posters indicated that they were primarily foreign bandits, most of whom were Jewish, working for Moscow and London. With this, the Germans hoped to provoke additional xenophobia and antisemitism among the native population, but the publicity campaign instead provided a certain notoriety for the condemned men, a notoriety that lasted well after the war ended.[19]

In the postwar years, the organized Armenian community celebrated and mourned Manouchian's Resistance activities and high-profile death as an indication of their patriotism, resistance, and loyalty to France throughout the occupation. That several other Armenians had seconded Manouchian's activities simply provided additional proof that the population as a whole had risen up against the Germans and helped restore freedom to France. According to Mélinée Manouchian, who herself remained active in the Resistance until the war's end, fellow Armenian communists "from Lyon to Marseille and Grenoble to Loiret" fought against the Nazis by distributing tracts in Armenian neighborhoods. Even noncommunists, she insists, were overwhelmingly anti-Nazi, actively supporting Resistance activities throughout the war. Indeed, according to her, only a tiny minority refused to support the Resistance movement, not so much because they were pro-Hitler as because they were so actively opposed to the Soviet Union and communism.[20]

Similarly, a book published shortly after the war, *Sur le chemin de la libération, 1940–44: Réseau Liban*, claimed that a sizable Armenian Resistance had fought under the name *réseau liban* [Lebanese group]. According to its leader, Haig Stephan, Armenians in France sought revenge on the Germans for allowing the massacres of World War I when, as Turkey's ally, they could have offered resistance. Nor, claimed the book, were French Armenians able "to accept the presence of racial hatred on the soil of their adopted country."[21] Turning to their history of resistance, born at the turn of the century when their own country had come under attack, French Armenians fought to protect the land that had welcomed and sheltered them by joining together in a complex Resistance network.

Further research has suggested that, in fact, there was no réseau liban. As the well-known Resistance historian Henri Michel has written, "A certain number of Armenians who played a role in the resistance collecting money, tracts, false papers, and transporting arms wanted to be recognized after the war for their efforts. They gave a framework to their group but evidence of the group's activities is both slim and imprecise." Michel contends that after the war, clandestine fighters sometimes came together by profession, nationality, or religion claiming to have resisted as a coherent group when in fact they had fought in entirely different units.[22]

The extent of Armenian participation in the Resistance thus remains under debate. Certainly there were those who collected money, wrote and distributed anti-German tracts and false papers, and transported arms. In 1940 some concerned Armenians in Paris, for example, created the Institut Arménien, which under the cover of its activities as a sporting association worked to prevent German propaganda from attracting Armenian youth.[23] Elsewhere, Armenian communists came together in 1941–42 into the Front national arménien (FNA) and the Association des jeunes patriots arméniens (which later became the Jeunesse arménienne de France) to recruit and organize the refugee population into fighting units. Both of these organizations also worked after the war with the Comité d'épuration to arrest traitors and collaborators. The FNA was particularly important in Marseille, where some if its members also participated in the Francs-Tireurs et Partisans français.[24] Moreover, certain Armenians fought with de Gaulle under the banner of the Forces françaises libres and others worked with the Travail allemand to undermine the German forces from within. What should by now be evident, however, is that the picture is more complex than postwar testimonies may have suggested. Whereas some Armenians joined the active Resistance, about fifty dying in the struggle, and many others supported its goals, most sought to negotiate a safe space for themselves in what had become an unsettling and volatile environment. For some this meant rejecting the status quo and joining the Resistance; for others it meant participating in the racial debates of the day to secure a safe place for Armenians in French society; for still others it meant profiting from the German occupation.[25] Perhaps for the majority, however, it meant simply lying low, trying to make ends meet, and waiting to see how the political winds would shift next.

Whatever their response to the events of World War II, however, there is little doubt that the occupation and the new regime transformed how the majority of Armenians understood their position in their host society. This transformation is evident in the years immediately following the war, when most abandoned their apatride status for the safety of naturalized citizenship, and when a new explosion in associational life attested to the development of a new Franco-Armenian identity, particularly among those who had been born in France or had come there as young children.

Politics and Participation after World War II

Although for many in France the restoration of republican government after World War II meant a return to familiar patterns and structures of the past, for Armenians the situation was quite different. The preceding years had posed new questions as to their place in France, and few felt comfortable maintaining their unprotected, stateless position of the interwar period. In this atmosphere the vast majority applied for and received French citizenship.[26]

Prior to World War II, very few Armenians made the decision to become French citizens, despite the liberal naturalization law of 1927. According to official French figures, there were 29,227 nonnaturalized Armenians living in France in 1931 versus 5,114 who opted for citizenship. The overall figures are undoubtedly too low, but the gap between them still gives a sense of the large numbers who did not follow through on the naturalization process.[27] In part, this reluctance can be explained by their protected status as Nansen refugees, which made naturalization seem somewhat redundant, particularly after 1936, when the French government ratified the League of Nations' convention expanding the rights of Nansen refugees. Moreover, a certain "aversion on the part of the French to naturalize Armenians, who are regarded as Asiatics," may have also played a role.[28] As such a comment suggests, a general xenophobia in France influenced the number of naturalizations despite liberal laws to the contrary. Thus in 1930, only 11 percent of the foreign population had been naturalized compared to 55 percent in the United States, and rates dropped dramatically between 1933 and 1935.[29]

Whatever the reason, the great majority of the French Armenian population entered World War II without the protection of citizenship, and for most these few years suggested that a change in status was of the utmost importance. This impulse had three broad sources, the first of which was largely external to the Armenian population and originated from inside the French government, which committed itself to a broad campaign of pushing citizenship requests through as quickly as possible. Immediately following the war, demographers, economists, and politicians believed that intensive recruitment of foreign labor was the fastest means to ensure France's full recovery. Worried over repeating the mistakes of the 1930s, however, the government introduced even greater state supervision of the immigration process. By carefully overseeing the growth of the foreign work-force, "according to the criteria of ethnic and cultural 'balance,' assimilation and national cohesion," officials hoped to promote the rapid integration of the new-comers and to prevent any one foreign group from predominating.[30] Naturaliza-tion was one means to ensure that immigrants would rapidly join the surrounding society, and as a result the Ministries of Justice and the Interior worked together to decentralize the process, giving greater authority to individual departments to carry out naturalizations, thereby ensuring that citizenship would be granted more quickly and efficiently. Here too, however, the government sought to con-trol the balance of the incoming population; officials in both ministries stressed that the naturalization process should favor "Nordic elements" as well as agricul-tural workers and miners, with limits placed on those "less desirable" elements of the foreign population, such as artisans, those in commercial and liberal pro-fessions, and those coming from the big cities. "This measure," commented one circular, "is aimed at reducing the considerable proportion of naturalized citi-zens in the cities and distributing naturalizations more normally throughout the whole of the foreign population and in all regions."[31]

Given their artisanal professions and urban concentration, Armenians seem-ingly fit into those "less desirable" members of the foreign population. Never-theless, their naturalization requests were granted over the course of the next few years. Because of the increased commitment to integrationist policies, the government could find no good reason to prevent these former refugees from be-coming citizens, particularly as the children of the first arrivals, on reaching the age of eighteen, were already able to declare themselves citizens.[32] Naturalizing their parents was a way to facilitate the integration of entire families and thereby promote the national cohesion so sought for in the immediate postwar years. The police still kept a close eye on Armenian associations and particularly monitored their political activities, but with each passing year these refugees were becoming less "foreign"; naturalization brought them into the national fold all the more completely.[33]

As the discussion above suggests, a second push for naturalization came as a result of demographic change and reflects the coming of age of a second generation of Armenians who had either come to France at a very young age or were born there. By obtaining citizenship, their status could now reflect their increasing integration into the heart of the nation.

But although governmental receptivity and demographic change were primarily responsible for the wave of Armenian naturalization requests, the impact of the war years on the sensibilities of those who had been living as apatrides should not be discounted. Although the Vichy government had revoked the rights of both French-born and foreign Jews, those without citizenship had proven far more vulnerable. Indeed, if citizenship provided no *guarantee* of safety, it certainly afforded more than that available to the apatride. As we have seen, non-Jewish foreigners were treated poorly during the war years, often conscripted into forced labor battalions. Likewise, the nonnaturalized could claim no protection as prisoners of war, even if they had fought for the French. Indeed, this very fact had encouraged mobilized Armenians to seek French citizenship as quickly as possible after being drafted.[34] After the war, such logic continued to influence refugee behavior as they and their descendants sought to ensure their position in their adopted home.

Moreover, the decision to naturalize oneself was the ultimate declaration of loyalty to France. World War II had certainly not brought an end to Armenian assertions of allegiance, as was clear at the memorial service that the Armenian Church in Paris held for those who had fallen in the fight to free France. Similarly, in October 1944, two months after liberation forces retook control of the country, a delegation from the Union Franco-Arménienne met with de Gaulle, giving "a moving address of loyalty and devotion to France." Because the vice president of this organization, Archag Tchobanian, a well-known Armenian intellectual who had been actively involved in communal life since the days of the Armenian Delegation, had also pledged Armenian support to Pétain, his new pledge indicated that Armenian loyalty was to the French nation writ large rather than to any particular regime.[35] Like Jewish leaders who, throughout the politically unstable nineteenth century, had formally congratulated each new French government in the hopes of protecting their community's civil rights, Armenians sought to protect themselves from one regime to the next by publicly pledging their loyalty.[36] Now, however, individuals seconded the declarations of their representatives by opting for citizenship.

Not all, however, responded to the war's upheaval by applying for citizenship. A significant minority chose instead to leave France altogether for the "homeland." To understand the new wave of public support for Soviet Armenia that encouraged this "repatriation," it is first necessary to consider the impact of the Armenian Resistance movement, however small its numbers, on the postwar relationship to politics and nationalism.

Manouchian's Resistance efforts and high-profile death immediately transformed him into an ethnonational hero for all French Armenians. In the weeks and months following liberation, his example came to symbolize the entire population's sentiments and actions throughout the war. One author noted in 1945, "Many of the Armenian youth in France, after having completed their military obligations during the war of 1939–40, joined the ranks of the Francs-Tireurs partisans (FTP) after the armistice of 10 June, courageously organizing armed revolts against the invaders and falling heroically on the fields of honor." As evidence, he cited Manouchian, Tavitian (another Armenian, shot with Manouchian in February 1944), as well as three others executed by the Germans for their Resistance activities.[37]

By exaggerating stories of their Resistance activities, Armenians simply mirrored the surrounding population. As we have already seen, the post–World War II French popular imagination was quick to celebrate French Resistance as the continuation of republicanism and French patriotism, overemphasizing its demographic significance.[38] In constructing their own Resistance myth, Armenians proved that they too had protected France's honor and, as such, deserved to be considered loyal Frenchmen. Manouchian's visibility made him an ideal hero for the whole population, as communists and noncommunists alike pointed to him as their reigning icon. As a self-declared communist and a member of HOG *and* as a symbol of the Resistance, Manouchian's hero status transcended politics. Indeed, he was not only an Armenian communist but also a genocide orphan *and* a French patriot. The conflation of these three characteristics made him the perfect hero for the postwar years. Having successfully straddled the triple loyalties that divided the population — to France, Armenia, and the Soviet Union — Manouchian served as a unifying symbol. Memorials to him stressed these triple identifications equally, noting his enduring attachment to his ancestral past, his love for the new Soviet state, and his status as an immigrant hero of France. The newspaper *Notre Voix*, organ of the pro-Soviet French Armenian youth organization Jeunesse arménienne de france (JAF), for example, published an annual testament to Manouchian's group. Typically these would include a short biography of his past as a survivor, a description of his Resistance activities for France, and a poem expressing his love for Soviet Armenia.[39]

Manouchian's role in the communist Resistance also provided pro-Soviet Armenians with greater legitimacy in the eyes of their compatriots. Armenian communists who had fought for recognition and support in the decade preceding the war suddenly had a new moral high ground from which to launch their appeals, blurring the boundaries between left and right, communists and "loyal" French. France's immediate postwar climate favored such a blurring of political allegiances. With all of the Second World War's twists and turns, the Soviet Union had ended on the side of the Allies and, thus, of the provisional government. Moreover, the communists' important role in leading the general Resistance movement encouraged a new respect for them among the nation as a whole. Vichy had discredited the right wing of the political spectrum and, though it did not take long for it to regain its footing, in the immediate postwar years public opinion moved toward the left. In the euphoria of the war's end, for example, communist, socialist, and Resistance newspapers accounted for over half the circulation of the daily press, and the readership of communist dailies quadrupled compared to the prewar period.[40]

A similar shift to the left occurred within Armenian organizations, particularly in the first two years after the war. The example of organizations of former combatants provides a helpful case in point. Following World War I, Armenians who had fought under French command in the Légion d'Orient came together in August 1917 to form the Association des anciens combattants volontaires arméniens de l'armée française (originally under the name Union des Volontaires Arméniens de l'Armée Française). Generally mirroring other such commemorative groups of the era, this association sought to maintain and develop the links of camaraderie and mutual aid among its members, while also "defending" their moral, social, and material interests. In addition, the association organized commemorations for Armenian soldiers who had died for France. On 11 July 1926, for example, its members presented a commemorative plaque to the church on rue Jean Goujon in memory of those volunteers who had fallen during their armed service.[41] Then, in 1935, a commemorative monument was added to the church's entrance; an Armenian soldier dressed in French uniform now greeted all newcomers to the church.[42] Through such monuments and commemorative events, including annual participation in the November Armistice Day commemorations, the members of the association continued to link their own patriotic and national interests with those of their adopted home. Following World War II, however, another group of combatants took shape, the Anciens combattants de la guerre 1939–45, Forces françaises de l'interieur (FFI) à résistants arméniens. Whereas the former was made up of those of mostly moderate political sympathies unwilling to question French policies or participate in national political life, the newer members were products of the Resistance and held political sympathies with the left and even the extreme left.[43] This latter group remained pro-French, having fought to free the country from Hitler, but their politics were more radical than their predecessors' and, in the postwar atmosphere, more popular.

In this environment, support for the Soviet Union flourished under the banner of the FNA and the Association des jeunes patriotes. Claiming to be the official representatives of those who had fought in the Resistance (it was largely due to the FNA's efforts that Manouchian's Resistance activities became so celebrated), these two organizations capitalized on the enthusiasm born of the war's end.[44] Attempting to straddle the differences that had once divided the community, the FNA took advantage of the more open postwar atmosphere to call for unity. To cite one example: in January 1945 the FNA helped found a federation of Armenian youth associations, which included, among others, the Union des jeunes gens arméniens, the Cercle de la jeunesse arménienne, the Union des jeunes patriotes arméniens, and the Scouts arméniens. By bridging different political and religious affiliations, this federation sought to bring together diverse youth groups into one larger association dedicated to teaching Armenian culture, art, and language, as well as providing youth with a sense of Armenian continuity. According to its own literature, "More than ever we are obliged to unite and to act. We must enter into this action with a new breath, an increased energy, and fertile dreams and accomplish our noble mission toward our youth, our people, and our country with spirit and enthusiasm."[45]

Such efforts did not necessarily change the structure of organized communal life; as prior to the war, regional and local associations continued to break the population into smaller subgroups. Moreover, although it established itself in all areas of the country where Armenians congregated, the FNA's membership remained small. In Lyon, for example, they numbered about 150 in 1946. In Aix, police reported that most of the population did not want to join an expressly political organization, thus mirroring communal behavior from before World War II. Yet even without a huge membership, the FNA made its mark by participating in a postwar explosion of Armenian associational life and by capitalizing on the more open environment to push its own leftist, activist, pro-Soviet agenda. As the HOG had done in the interwar period, the FNA organized anniversary celebrations for Soviet Armenia during which several thousand people would gather to listen to the Soviet ambassador and the president of the FNA toast the Armenian homeland.[46] In addition, the organization regularly showed propaganda films to promote life in the Armenian Republic and to attract new adherents. Through these efforts, the FNA also became the primary force behind organizing the large "repatriation" wave in 1946 and 1947.

Equally interesting was the FNA's relationship to activist politics. Because of its links to the Resistance and its acceptance in Armenian associational life, the FNA, as opposed to its more cautious predecessor, was actively engaged in French political life wherever it related to issues affecting Armenian life. Hence, the FNA took part in Centre d'action et de défense des immigrés (CADI), an organization formed to protect immigrant rights after the war, and defended Armenian political rights on the public stage. It fought, for example, to ensure that citizenship was provided to all Armenian combatants of 1939–40 and for the suppression of foreign workforces organized under Vichy. Thus, despite its pro-Soviet stance and its later push to repatriate Armenians, the FNA did not shy away from local political debates.[47] Rather, as distinct from organizations of the prewar period, the FNA showed a willingness to organize as Armenians on the domestic scene. This new active ethnopolitical stance, as we have seen, also developed among France's postwar Jewish population, suggesting that Vichy had sparked a more public and vocal ethnopolitical consciousness among various local minority groups. This willingness to work as a pro-Armenian advocate strengthened the FNA's standing in the eyes of the refugee community, as did organizational efforts to celebrate and enhance the Armenian Resistance record. The greatest evidence of this influence came in 1946, when the Soviet government convinced seven thousand Armenians to leave France for a new life in the USSR.

Nerkaght

In September 1943, Archag Tchobanian published an apologetic article in *Marseille-Soir* arguing that Armenian refugees were not, in fact, stateless but rather *displaced*.[48] Responding to the prevalent antirefugee sentiment of the day, Tchobanian argued that if the Soviet Union would simply open its doors as it had in the 1920s, Armenians from across the diaspora would opt to return "to the land of their ancestors." In closing, however, he conceded that not all Armenians were prepared to leave French territory: "A part of the Armenian population, profoundly attached to France and integrated into French life, will want to remain and live in the nation that they have made their adopted home."[49] For Tchobanian, who supported the notion of Armenian resettlement in the Soviet Republic and who cited Armenian attachment to this land as proof of their nonapatride status, migration was not an option. Only those not yet integrated into French life should be expected to make such a move.

Although published at the height of the Vichy years, Tchobanian's article cannot be dismissed as wartime propaganda. His 1945 republication of the article as a pamphlet suggests that the question of the Armenians' place in France still remained a salient topic after the occupation ended. Moreover, the pamphlet pointed to the tension that still surrounded the question of national affiliation as soon as the Soviet government opened Armenia's borders to refugees throughout the diaspora. Where was the Armenian homeland? Was it in the Soviet Republic, a country that was in name their own but that was far removed from the ancestral lands of most refugees living in France? Was it their "adopted home," the place where they found safe haven but that had proven unsafe? The intensity of the repatriation campaign of the 1940s and the strong opposition it ultimately inspired suggests that the question of national allegiance remained as complex after World War II as it had in the years before the conflict began. Certainly, as Martine Hovanessian has suggested, the repatriation movement provided the community with a tangible political project after years of what had been theoretical if charged debates over the nature of political allegiances.[50] Yet, whatever the enthusiasm surrounding the national movement in the initial months after liberation, it did not take long for intense debates to resurface over where Armenians really belonged and which nation deserved their primary loyalty.

Repatriation had arisen as an issue well before World War II. Immediately following the Sovietization of Armenia, the new state's relationship to displaced genocide refugees remained undefined. Shortly thereafter, however, the Soviet government began encouraging the "return" of western Armenians to the Republic. These first migration waves brought approximately forty thousand to the Caucasus between 1921 and 1936, mostly from countries such as Greece and Bulgaria, where their settlement had been hindered by poor conditions and lack of resources. Members of the long-settled French Armenian community, as well as wealthy Armenians throughout the diaspora, supported these efforts with funds from the AGBU, but, as we saw in chapter 4, very few opted to leave France at this juncture.[51] Only after World War II, when the Soviet government claimed land from Turkey, did attempts to organize a massive relocation of diaspora Armenians gain widespread support. While similar attempts to attract Russians, Ukrainians, and Georgians failed, approximately one hundred thousand Armenians, or about 10 percent of the diaspora, responded to the Soviet state's appeal. The disillusionment that most of these "returnees" felt on arriving in Armenia during the last years of Stalin's rule prevented most from entering the new society with ease. Nearly all of the approximately seven thousand Armenians who left France for Soviet Armenia between 1946 and 1947 and their descendants tried to return in the late 1950s.[52] Such figures do not, however, discount the importance of the initial migration wave when it occurred. During the immediate postwar years and prior to the solidifying of cold war allegiances, Soviet Armenia served as a focal point for Armenian national aspirations, even for those of opposing political views.

Great hope spread throughout the diaspora immediately following World War II as the Soviet Union began encouraging Armenian settlement. As part of its policy to establish a sphere of influence in the countries along its borders, the government sought to extend southward into Turkish lands. By settling new refugee populations in what had been Armenian lands in eastern Turkey, the Soviet government hoped to protect itself from what it saw as a growing Turkish threat. Though not particularly dedicated to satisfying Armenian nationalist aspirations (or those of other national groups in the region), Stalin's attempts to extend his influence brought those on all sides of the Armenian political spectrum into agreement. Hopes for the recovery of ancestral lands lost during the genocide and their incorporation into a larger and stronger Armenian state allowed political organizations and religious leaders of various affiliations to mobilize in support of Soviet demands.[53] Immediately after liberation, for example, the Comité de défense des droits de l'émigration arménienne published a pamphlet attacking the Armenian massacres of 1914 and demanding reparations that would allow the Armenian provinces to regenerate themselves. "We have great hope," commented the Comité, "that in the near future we will be able to join together with our brothers who have remained in the country to commence the reconstruction of our dear fatherland."[54] Such sentiments blended the issue of land restitution with repatriation; new immigrants could settle in the recovered territories. As a result, representatives of all political parties as well as the Church leadership agreed to support repatriation drives in the hopes that they would reunite Armenians and end the period of exile brought on by World War I. After several years of hostility between Soviet Armenia and those in the diaspora, a new relationship developed. Now all were fighting in coordination to raise and solve the Armenian Question for good.[55]

In France, as elsewhere, repatriation received the support of the Church and the wealthier, more established members of the community regrouped around the Ramgavar Party and the AGBU. But support also came from the Hnchaks, the communists, and even the Dashnaks, who, despite their anti-Soviet stance, were attracted by the hope that Turkey would finally release Armenian territory. The new political agenda, therefore, attracted more than the ardent communists among the population, and even Dashnaks — the most fervent anticommunists of the interwar years — put aside their quarrels to collaborate with the FNA; for a time, Dashnaks even sat at the highest levels of the FNA's organizational structure.[56]

This political collaboration did not last, however, and the issues that divided the most ardent supporters of the Soviet Union from those who strove for an independent Armenian state began to break apart as international politics began to crystallize into the cold war. Fearing Soviet expansion into the Middle East and an imminent invasion of Turkey, the United States began actively supporting Turkish resistance to Stalin's plans. By early 1946, having achieved little more than the creation of a widespread hostility on the part of Turkish and American authorities, the Soviet government began to back away from its claims to Armenian and Georgian lands. In March of that year, relations between East and West deteriorated further, inspiring Winston Churchill to make his famous "Iron Curtain" speech, and the Soviet Union saw most of its attempts to attain Turkish concessions end in failure. While repatriation plans continued for the rest of 1946, expansion into the Middle East became a lower priority, and by the end of that year the United States had become the most important power in the region. From that point on, all chances for the recovery of Armenian lands came to an end as relations between East and West continued to deteriorate.[57]

The beginning of the cold war and the end to Soviet claims on Turkish Armenian lands spelled doom for the previous two years of cooperation among divergent political groups throughout the Armenian diaspora. In France, the split was dramatized as early as June 1946, when two Dashnak Party leaders from Paris attended a celebration of Armenian independence in Marseille. There they faced great hostility from Soviet supporters, all members of the FNA, who promoted a boycott of the meeting and even accused one of the two visitors of being Nazi collaborators. This incident, as well as a subsequent brawl between Dashnaks and members of the FNA, led to the immediate resignation of the Dashnak representative from the FNA's directing committee. In addition, the Dashnaks announced a definitive break with their rivals, demanding that all Party members refrain from participating in any organization affiliated with the FNA.[58]

This split between the two organizations intensified during the repatriation campaign of the next six months. Indeed, Dashnaks were notably absent from a 1 July 1946 symposium on the Armenian Question in which the FNA was actively involved, as political turmoil split the two organizations apart. During this meeting, attended by nearly two thousand people and sponsored by the Défense des revendications des arméniens de Turquie, an umbrella organization that united those political parties interested in Armenian concerns, participants insisted that Armenian zones in Turkey be attached to Soviet Armenia and encouraged those in the diaspora to "repatriate."[59] By now, however, the Dashnaks refused to work with the FNA or to cooperate in any repatriation efforts.

Nevertheless the repatriation drive continued to pick up steam, and from the summer of 1946 until its abrupt conclusion in 1947, Soviet propaganda bombarded the Armenian population. In France, the Soviet embassy in Paris established the Comité central d'immigration, which, with the help of the FNA, initiated a major propaganda campaign to encourage Armenian departures. Well before the Soviet government was ready to load boats with immigrants, the propaganda worked to convince the local population that life would be good for them in their "homeland." An Armenian diplomat working for the Soviet embassy in Paris and also serving as the Soviet's official representative to the FNA was responsible for the repatriation. He organized conferences throughout the country to convince hesitant Armenians to pack their bags and established local and regional offices to facilitate the process and carry out the necessary paperwork.[60]

Supplementing the propaganda activities of these local committees for repatriation was the newspaper *Joghovourt*, the main organ of the pro-Soviet contingent of the French Armenian population. For months its pages published articles encouraging readers to join the repatriation movement and attacking those who would leave their descendants "ignorant of their origins." Seconding these efforts was the pro-Soviet youth organization JAF, which reported in its organ *Arménie* that no effort would be spared in executing the decisions of the Comité central d'immigration and in facilitating the massive departure of young Armenians to the "motherland."[61]

As the repatriation effort intensified, the FNA, which had spent much of the first two years after liberation stressing the Armenian commitment to France, began insisting that the refugees' real home was in Soviet Armenia. Proclaiming that the surrounding population held Armenians in disdain, organizational propaganda attacked the French government for the slow speed with which naturalization requests were being carried forward, particularly of those prisoners of war who, despite five years in captivity in service for France, had not yet obtained citizenship. Within a few months, the FNA backed away from the more open and unifying rhetoric of 1944 and 1945. Now Armenians would have to choose between their nation of refuge and their "homeland." Those who discouraged repatriation were labeled fascists who were preventing their compatriots from finding a happiness that they had never before known.[62]

Initial attempts to lure Armenians away held little appeal. For those established businessmen and artisans, many of whom were naturalized or on their way to becoming so, leaving was never a viable option. Those regrouped around the Ramgavar Party and the AGBU helped fund the migration, but they never considered moving themselves.[63] Not unlike postwar French Zionists who supported the creation of a Jewish homeland for their less fortunate brethren, these financially comfortable and settled Armenians continued to feel no contradiction between supporting the Armenian state for others while opting to live in the diaspora themselves. Nor did they insist that all new refugees settle only in Armenia, hoping instead that France would open its doors to *more* Armenians seeking to leave the Middle East.[64] If repatriation seemed a viable option for some unfortunate refugees, it was not the only solution to their problems.

The most organized resistance to the repatriation movement unsurprisingly came from the Dashnak Party, which, after its split from the FNA in the summer of 1946, did its best to counter the pro-Soviet propaganda. Its own Party paper, *Haratch*, though increasingly geared to presenting news without commentary, nevertheless published numerous anti-Soviet articles and protested FNA policies. In addition, the paper reemphasized the Armenians' historical commitment to France, for example, the role of young Armenians in French military service. In its 29 October edition, *Haratch* went so far as to condemn the repatriation propaganda: "We owe it to ourselves not to influence those Armenians who are well aware of the reception that France has offered them and who prefer to finish their days in their second homeland rather than to attempt the Soviet adventure." *Haratch* thus countered appeals for repatriation by reminding its readers of the hospitality of their "second homeland." The assumption underlying such articles was that Armenians would be more at home in France than in the Soviet Republic. Indeed, in its next edition *Haratch* questioned whether Armenians in the diaspora could ever consider Soviet Armenia a motherland as most had originated from Turkey, not from the Soviet state.[65]

Other local Armenian organizations, such as the Institut arménien de France, once so committed to its anti-German propaganda, now worked to counter the impact of repatriation by encouraging students from Armenia to come to France to complete their education. Indeed, the issue became so charged that in September 1946 the director's life was threatened by his political opponents. Such incidents suggest that the fight over repatriation quickly became a battle over communal leadership. The FNA, anxious to elevate its position in the eyes of its compatriots, worked for two years to receive official recognition from the French government for its role in the Resistance. Finally obtaining such recognition in November 1946, the FNA used its new legitimacy to further the repatriation cause, organizing more informational meetings, showing films, and collecting names of those interested in repatriation.[66]

In a December 1946 attempt to consolidate its drive for communal control, the FNA's president and the director of *Joghovourt*, Henri Marmarian, attempted to replace the director of the Office des réfugiés arméniens with someone sympathetic to the repatriation movement. This move backfired because those unaffiliated with the FNA supported the leadership of the Office des réfugiés arméniens and were angered by Marmarian's attempt to extend his own control. Nevertheless, the incident attests to the degree to which repatriation became a power struggle among various factions within the communal leadership. Soon organizations were divided between those opposed to the repatriation efforts and those who believed Armenians belonged in the Soviet Republic. In October 1946, for example, the Marseille chapter of the Union générale arménienne, a sporting club with a twenty-year history, nearly split into factions. The organization's central office in Paris had chosen to fuse with the FNA's youth association, JAF, and a core of those in Marseille demanded autonomy.[67] Repatriation was now becoming a dividing line across which members of the community situated themselves.

Nor could the Church escape the battle over repatriation that raged throughout Armenian associational life. In August 1946, Ardavast Sumeian, a representative from the Central Gregorian Church in Etchmiadzine, came to western Europe with instructions from the Grand Catholicos to reorganize the Church throughout the region. Supporters of the Front national arménien welcomed him, but the Dashnaks greeted him coldly, seeing in him an official representative of Moscow. In France, the central leadership of the Armenian Church was made up primarily of Dashnak sympathizers who remained hostile to all Soviet influence. Sumeian hoped to change the makeup of this leadership and to reconstitute the Armenian Church according to a new base. Delaying Church leadership elections for several months, despite the fact that no new elections had taken place since 1939 and the terms of those already in office had long expired, he attempted to influence its makeup. Soon, however, the battle over Church leadership became fused with the battle over repatriation, when Sumeian participated in the Front national's efforts to prepare Armenians for departure.[68]

Thus, from the summer of 1946 to early 1947, a fever of excitement surrounded the whole issue of repatriation as defenders and critics of the Soviet Union fought for influence in the community, and as seven thousand Armenians chose to leave the relative security of their new land to rejoin their compatriots in the homeland. Who were these migrants, and why did they decide to go? By and large, the passengers on the boats were younger and less well off than those they left behind in Paris and Marseille. As Edouard Khédérian described those waiting at the ports to board the boats, "They were, for the most part, people of modest means who were poorly assimilated in France and who believed that the Soviet Union was a socialist country." Many came from poorer areas of the city where workers concentrated.[69] The prorepatriation campaign waged throughout the diaspora had created a fervent idealism among them about the path that lay ahead and assuaged the fears of those initially hesitant to leave. As one Egyptian repatriate described it:

> In 1947, the Armenians who lived in Egypt and who wished to go back to the motherland would tear out letters from our compatriots who had left the preceding year republished in the daily papers. If these letters emphasized the warm clothes we should pack for our departure (which left us a little worried), they stressed above all the large sums the Soviet government delivered to each immigrant who wanted to build a house or provided us with names of young people that we had known in exile and who had just been received brilliantly at the University of Yerevan where they were pursuing their studies at the cost of the State. Our correspondents assured us that unemployment was unknown in the USSR and that each new arrival could count on finding work. In contrast, the anti-Soviet press warned us against the fate that awaited us in Armenia, but we did not give credit to remarks that contradicted our desires and that proposed nothing in exchange for our renouncement of the return to the old country. The arrival of a delegation sent by Moscow succeeded in strengthening our convictions. These men who spoke our language and responded kindly, fraternally to all our questions reassured us.[70]

In France, such propaganda had an important impact in shaping how young Armenians understood their link to the "motherland." Describing how he justified his departure Jacques Parvanian recounts, "My parents had made this voyage in the other direction twenty-five years previously. . . . They were fleeing their persecutors. I am returning to the homeland. They were poor. I am also poor but I sense a difference. I am rich in faith, in energy. I know what I want. I am not going adrift. I am returning home, I have been told. Very well; so be it!" Ironically, Parvanian was in no way returning home, as he was a native-born Parisian. Nor did animosity toward France fuel his departure. His descriptions of how he and his shipmates viewed their native land display a sense of loss over what they were leaving behind: "We are leaving [France] forever. We know that we are not to see it again. We are a little regretful. She had been our foster mother for our entire lives. We abandon her with a little heartache. But we know we are going to a country where everything is better, more fair." [71]

The regret that accompanied leaving France behind was intensified by the difficulty of leaving loved ones on its shores. Only twenty-two years old when he left France on 23 December 1947, Parvanian was the only member of his family to repatriate. His parents, having come to France in the early 1920s, had no interest in uprooting again. As a result, Parvanian set sail with forty-two hundred strangers to return "home," leaving behind everything he had ever known. Thus, the choice to repatriate divided not only communal organizations but families as well. During his voyage Parvanian befriended a family, one side of which decided to migrate while the other remained in Marseille. In another case, Dikran Iranyan, a repatriate to the USSR from Egypt who had studied in Paris in the early 1930s, where he had become a devoted Marxist, left his wife and children to return to the "homeland." Despite his sadness over leaving his family, he opted "to see my homeland again and to construct my life on the land to which my body and soul belonged. In addition, my faith in the communist gospel remained intact." [72]

Thus, a youthful idealism that the Soviet Union could provide new opportunities encouraged those in the diaspora to depart for the unknown. As noted above, for most the repatriation proved to be a tremendous disappointment. In the international arena, the years 1947–49 saw the beginning of the cold war, bringing an end to alliances forged during World War II. As relations between the Soviet Union and France deteriorated, the Ministry of the Interior began forbidding naturalized French citizens and those born in France from departing, while giving authorization quickly to those nonnaturalized Armenians who had not fought in the French army, had criminal records, or had not paid their taxes or rent (much to the anger of some of those still hoping to depart who did not fall into these categories).[73] In the Armenian diaspora, antagonism and resentment between partisans and opponents of Soviet Armenia continued to fester. The end of repatriation and the reports of the conditions that new immigrants to the USSR faced on their arrival led anticommunists to accuse repatriation proponents of deception. Thus, the arrival of the cold war brought old party alignments back into position more firmly than ever and ultimately forced the FNA to close its doors in 1948.

It should not be assumed, however, that the end to this overtly pro-Soviet Armenian political organization brought an end to sympathies for their cause. Indeed, World War II, the notoriety of the Armenian Resistance movement, the postwar atmosphere of collaboration among various groups of divergent political affiliations, and the calls for unity had made support for the Soviet Armenian state respectable. Previous attempts to downplay connections to the Republic were now balanced by a newfound dedication to celebrating links between those in the USSR and those in the diaspora. Within a year of closing its doors, the FNA was replaced by the Union culturelle française des arméniens de France, an organization with less overtly political goals but still dedicated to strengthening the bonds between the French and Armenian peoples and to teaching both local Armenians and the French population more generally of Armenia's culture, history, and development. Despite these cultural goals, however, the Union's raison d'être was to establish and maintain connections with their national homeland and to keep a vibrant Armenian identity alive among the French population through organizing commemorative evenings that celebrated the anniversary of Soviet Armenia and, later, through coordinating tours to the Republic.[74]

Similarly, the youth organization JAF, founded in the postwar enthusiasm for Soviet Armenia, continued to flourish after 1948, rapidly spreading throughout French Armenian communities and dedicating itself to promoting cultural exchanges of all kinds with Soviet Armenia. Through activities such as dances, bazaars, film viewings, and theatrical evenings for the communities' youth, the JAF served as a site where patriotic links to Soviet Armenia could be explored and developed without demanding an overtly supportive stance in favor of the regime. Through JAF's efforts, Armenian youth could thus maintain an emotional link to Soviet Armenia without having to repudiate their position as French citizens. In addition, the organization provided an arena in which youth could embrace a sense of ethnic identification with their Armenianness. Born in France, many of these youth did not share the same direct link with their ancestral heritage as their parents. Participation in JAF's many activities allowed them, now often French by birth, to maintain or create such a link.[75]

The popularity of JAF should not suggest that other political positions faded or disappeared. To the contrary, cold war divisions brought the political parties into sharp contrast with one another once again. Not only did the Dashnak leaders continue to work against pro-Soviet tendencies in the Armenian population, but they founded their own youth movement, Nor-Seround, in 1945 to enlarge their anti-Soviet base. Despite their different political stances, however, the youth affiliated with Nor-Seround, like those in JAF, expressed their Armenian affiliation through a variety of cultural activities, such as sporting clubs, dances, choirs, and debates, organized to inculcate a sense of Armenian patriotism in a new generation of militants. Indeed, no matter how starkly opposed these two groups were in political terms, evidence suggests that most students joined Nor-Seround or JAF less for their political ideologies than for the variety of social activities they offered. In both cases, although the groups may have been organized primarily as a means to instill a particular relationship to the Armenian Question and to the nature of a national homeland, both served to create a local Armenian sociability, priority being given to the social rather than to the political. A struggle for leadership and power in the community thus did not necessarily divide the larger agenda. While one faction remained pro-Soviet and another remained actively opposed, their suborganizations often remained devoted to the same broad cultural goals, cultivating a sense of Armenianness among their compatriots either through celebrating a link with the "motherland" or through cultivating a link to the "Armenian nation" writ large.[76]

Beginning in the 1940s, the international Armenian press, which had used the term "colonies" to designate the various Armenian communities throughout the world, shifted to the term "diaspora," indicating a changing sensibility as to the permanence of their dispersion.[77] This shift was particularly clear in France, where World War II and the accompanying regulations on foreigners, followed quickly by the nerkaght, forced a reevaluation of the community's minority status. If, in the immediate post–World War I years, most sought to rebuild the autonomous communities of their Ottoman Armenian past, by World War II it had become clear that something fundamental had changed. The irony is that although some chose to leave France for Soviet Armenia, most opted for citizenship in a state that had just proven itself intolerant of ethnic distinctiveness and willing to de-emancipate its own citizens without question.

If Armenians—whose lack of persecution under Vichy stands out so starkly next to the far more brutal treatment of French Jews—responded so radically to the questions posed by World War II, one would surely have expected native French Jews to have also sought radical transformations in their minority status. And yet, as we have seen, most French Jews were not anxious to do so. Rather, their responses more closely mirrored those of Armenians immediately after World War I as they attempted to reconstruct their disrupted communities. Nevertheless, as for Armenians in the early 1940s, major international events, well beyond the confines of the Jewish community, soon unfolded that showcased the long-term impact of the Holocaust in shaping the community's minority affiliations.

Conclusion

In his 1996 book *Vanishing Diaspora*, Bernard Wasserstein argues that the Jews of Europe are in the process of a rapid and steady decline. Pointing to the central role of Nazism in creating this state of affairs, Wasserstein places most of the "blame" on broader cultural and social factors. Due to diminishing birthrates, increasing migrations from eastern Europe, secularizing trends that have undermined the centrality of Judaism, and the rapid disappearance of "authentic" Jewish culture—its languages, scholarship, literature, music, and so on—Wasserstein predicts that the Jews of Europe are "slowly but surely . . . fading away." "Soon," he insists, "nothing will be left save a disembodied memory."[1]

Whether or not one accepts Wasserstein's most dire predictions about the current state of Jewish life, a close study of postwar French Jewry seems to confirm the position that, aside from substantial demographic consequences, World War II did not in and of itself pose a definitive threat to the continuation of Jewish life in France. Not only did nearly two-thirds of the population survive, but because of American Jewish aid and the continued involvement of surviving native and foreign-born communal leaders, organizational life was rapidly reconstituted and, in some cases, enhanced. Although affiliation in organized religious activities continued to dwindle in the decades after the war, this seems to have been driven more by liberal forces that had long sought to pull Jews into their surrounding societies than by Jews' persecution during World War II. To put it another way, despite the devastating ways the Holocaust played itself out in France, its occurrence had little immediate impact on stemming the tide of Jewish integration. Neither driving Jews from their ancestral heritage, as some communal leaders feared, nor encouraging them to maintain a greater affiliation with communal life, the Holocaust did not force most surviving native French Jews to question their place in French society.

In making such a point, I am not trying to downplay the significance of the Holocaust in shaping and, in most cases, destroying European Jewish life. Studies on the extent of the devastation have well documented its horrific impact. Rather, my main interest here has been to trace how that persecution was understood in France by those who lived through it by asking what impact, if any, it had on their notions of national identity and communal solidarity. In considering these issues, the comparison with Armenian genocide survivors in France after World War I has been instructive. This population faced a considerably greater disjuncture with the past than that faced by most Jews in France (if more closely resembling that of "displaced persons" who found refuge in France after World War II). Neverthe-less, those Armenians who struck roots in France sought quickly to reestablish those traditions and institutions that had existed in their villages further east. In-deed, even a superficial comparison of the two cases suggests that in the immedi-ate aftermaths of their respective genocides, neither Armenian refugee popula-tions in France nor Jewish Holocaust survivors responded to the attacks against them by questioning the possibility of maintaining a successful diasporic exis-tence. Although both experienced a surge of support for their own nationalistic movements and although some opted to leave France for their "homeland," the overwhelming majority chose to remain in their dispersed communities without engaging in much sustained public dialogue on the question.

This is not to suggest that Armenians and Jews followed identical paths when rebuilding from genocide. Indeed, in both cases, the questions that drove communal life were dictated by concerns internal to each and shaped by each group's specific history and relationship to France. Such specificity is most evi-dent when we consider the impact of genocide on communal politics and self-expression. For native-born French Jews, particularly the Jewish leadership, the most significant impact of the Holocaust was an increasing willingness to mo-bilize politically as Jews and to acknowledge a growing appreciation of the ethnic links binding Jews to one another across national borders. Although the events of World War II did not force an immediate self-conscious exploration of the effect of genocide on communal life or on group self-identification — except perhaps among some communal leaders who feared that French Jewry would never re-cover — the shift in status from that of equal citizens within the polity to that of a subject and hounded minority had an enduring legacy.

In particular, notions of Jewish ethnic and political participation continued to expand, a shift that is particularly clear when we consider the native Jewish institutional leadership. Before the occupation, the native leadership, shaped by their assimilationist culture, had participated in attempts to gallicize eastern European Jewish refugees. Reluctant to stand out as distinct, they sought to ease the newcomers' settlement while trying to prevent them from calling attention to themselves or engaging in political activities that focused on their Jewishness. After the war, many of these leaders remained committed to former institutions and practices. Shifts, however, are evident in their notions of ethnic bonds and political engagement. During the occupation, many of these same leaders had been forced by the Nazis and Vichy alike to participate in the policing of French Jewry. Others spent the war years hiding Jews, fighting in the Resistance, forging passports, and engaging in clandestine activities to sabotage the Nazis' extermination effort. As such, they were forced to confront certain unquestioned assumptions they had maintained about the place of Jews in French society.

These same Jewish leaders led the reconstruction effort in the postwar years. The institutions they established and directed reflected the lessons they had learned. Particularly interesting was a new willingness to accept and even embrace the legitimacy of diverse expressions of Jewish identity evident in the community centers and fundraising institutions they helped develop. In cooperating with the American Joint Distribution Committee to build new arenas of communal expression, they displayed a willingness to move away from the traditional religious and benevolent societies that had characterized institutional life and to embrace models of communal organization that encouraged broader conceptions of Jewish participation and ethnic diversity.

In addition to such internal changes, a new commitment to ethnic politics also characterized postwar French Jewish life. By embracing a more overtly pro-Zionist and pro-Israeli stance as well as becoming more actively involved in fighting for Jewish rights in France, Jews in France, like their coreligionists throughout the Western world, began to articulate a more politically defined notion of Jewish identity. Even here, however, national context played a significant part in shaping articulations of this politicization. As we saw, an initial caution characterized how some French Jews viewed the founding of the State of Israel; familiar refrains echoed the necessity to prove that the primary loyalty of French Jews remained firmly embedded at home. Nevertheless, it is clear that the Holocaust and persecutions of the Vichy regime tempered previous inclinations to downplay a political aspect to Jewish identity, creating ever-broader notions of communal solidarity and ethnic participation among French Jews.

Similarly for Armenian refugees, the genocide and the subsequent flight to France profoundly influenced internal conceptions of Armenianness. Unlike most of the Jews under study, however, whose efforts to rebuild took place on the land in which they had been persecuted, Armenians fled attacks abroad. Their political expressions and self-conceptions were as much shaped by their integration into a foreign land as by the genocide itself. Whereas the agendas of particular political parties had been influenced by the events of World War I, this was less true for those not actively involved in political life. For them, whatever the genocide's lessons, they were relevant to a country in which the refugees no longer lived. As long as they behaved inconspicuously and obeyed French laws, their position in France was assured and they could reestablish their traditional familial and communal structures in the new setting. However, they initially sought to establish communities that closely resembled those they had left behind, although their status had changed dramatically from that of a subject religious minority in a multinational empire to that of stateless refugees in a homogenizing nation-state. This shift in status affected communal development from the moment the refugees arrived in France. It was only with the outbreak of World War II that French Armenian populations took stock of the tremendous changes that had occurred. Like French Jews, a new generation of Armenians, generally all French nationals, began articulating a more ardent Armenian nationalism and a self-conscious perception of diaspora solidarity. Now safely protected as citizens of France, they could express a more vocal connection to Soviet Armenia. Countering this trend, however, was an ever-increasing integration into the French state that pushed many away from communal activities altogether.

As the above discussion suggests, the genocide and Holocaust shaped these two survivor populations quite differently. In both cases the surviving population more or less sought to pick up where it had left off; for French Jews this remained a real possibility, whereas for Armenian refugees, the ruptures were too great to allow any sustained link with communal structures of the past. As a result, communal development in both populations differed substantially. Nevertheless, it is interesting to note that in both cases, genocide, in and of itself, did not force survivors to make a clean break with the past. Moreover, in neither case did the recent history of genocide suggest to survivors and escapees that integration into the surrounding nation-state was a potentially dangerous choice. Indeed, a striking silence on this question is notable in both populations.

The nation in which they settled did much to ensure that such discussions remained muted. The power of France's integrationist heritage shaped the relationship between both minorities to their respective pasts and to their national allegiances. For Armenian refugees grateful to find a haven after years of flight and massacre, their apatride status — and not their particular position as genocide survivors — shaped how they integrated into their surrounding society. Although certain French authorities expressed sympathy for the uprooted population, most were more focused on integrating the large foreign and refugee populations as rapidly as possible than on the particularities of their past. Such attitudes on the part of government representatives encouraged most Armenians to avoid any activities that would undermine their chances of being allowed to remain, including those that might suggest that their loyalties lay primarily with Soviet Armenia. In this case, then, their political choices were determined as much by their current relationship with the French government as by their recent past of massacre and deportation.

Similarly, governmental policies toward French Jews *after* World War II — and not the shadow of the previous four years of government-sponsored persecution — shaped how survivors and escapees understood their position in the polity. In this case, the postwar commitment to restoring republican order and national stability prevented authorities from supporting initiatives that singled out Jewish particularism. Thus, even in an atmosphere in which the right wing had been discredited, the government proved uninterested in addressing the challenges that Vichy had posed to its assimilationist approach to ethnic distinctiveness. Local Jewish populations, frustrated by efforts to stonewall the return of their property and belongings, nevertheless took heart in the return of familiar republican norms and thus accepted the provisional government and the later Fourth Republic as the legitimate heirs of the fallen Third Republic, rejecting Vichy as an aberration. However dramatic and disturbing the persecutions they had faced, French Jews, whether born in France or the product of the massive prewar migrations, did not, by and large, respond by reassessing their position in the polity.

What, then, can we conclude about the impact of genocide on the ethnic and national affiliations of survivors? Recent reflections have interpreted these events as major turning points in Armenian and Jewish history. Can the same be said for survivors and escapees themselves? Did they experience the ideological and physical attacks as transformative? The answer is both yes and no. Clearly, for both Armenians and Jews, the loss of family members, friends, homes, economic security, communal support systems, and — in the Armenian case — their ancestral lands was brutally destructive. Survivors of both populations were thus well aware of a systematic, violent attempt to be rid of them forever. Nor were the recent pasts stifled and suppressed in some kind of postgenocidal communal decision to silence what had happened because of a collective inability to understand or process those events. Rather, they commemorated their losses and threw themselves into recovering from the upheaval in ways that, at times, transformed the face of their communities.

And yet, in both cases, the nature and extent of this transformation was limited by the particular context in which they found themselves. Indeed, for both populations the immediate present was at least as important in establishing communal priorities as was the recent past. And for both, this "immediate present" was promising. Quickly benefiting from the complex interaction among government, culture, and ethnic distinctiveness that characterized much of twentieth-century French history, survivors of both populations saw few threats to their desire to reconstitute their homes and communities. This feeling of security was so powerful that in many cases it overshadowed the fears of the previous years of destruction. A comparative study of these two cases thus directs our attention to the importance of context in shaping minority culture. Armenians and Jews rebuilt their communities amid the distinctly different conditions of pre- and post–World War II France and faced distinct problems related to the nature of the aggression that had been directed against them, to their particular position in the polity, and to their historical relationship with the French state. Nevertheless, a comparison between them suggests that the common denominator, integration into the French state, was at least as significant as the genocides themselves in directing the shape and direction of communal life for the next several decades.

Notes

Introduction

Unless otherwise noted, all translations are mine.

1 A growing literature on the topic of genocide has emerged in recent years. In general, this literature has fallen into one of two broad categories. The first tends to be specific historical studies that detail the cultural, social, political, and economic causes and consequences of a given case of genocide. Examples of such literature are cited throughout this introduction, where appropriate, with regard to both the Armenian and Jewish cases. The second category tends to be larger comparative studies focusing on a number of sociological, psychological, and political questions pertaining primarily to the origins, prevention, and international implications of genocide. For a recent discussion of the dimensions of this literature and its limitations, see Alex Alverez, *Governments, Citizens and Genocide: A Comparative and Interdisciplinary Approach* (Bloomington: Indiana University Press, 2001), pp. 1–7, 14–18.

2 A small body of psychological literature on the impact of trauma on genocide survivors has addressed this issue from a different angle. See, most recently, Antonius C. G. M. Robben and Marcelo M. Suàrez-Orozco, eds., *Cultures under Siege: Collective Violence and Trauma* (Cambridge, England: Cambridge University Press, 2000). Literary scholars have also turned to this topic. For example, Rubina Peroomian, *Literary Responses to Catastrophe: A Comparison of the Armenian and Jewish Experience* (Atlanta, Ga.: Scholars Press, 1993), p. 1, sets out to "assess the impact of the Genocide on the collective psyche of the Armenian people" by comparing Armenian literary responses to genocide to those of Jewish Holocaust survivors. Although this project is interesting from the standpoint of assessing the two genocides' impact on individual intellectuals, it is less convincing in its attempt to explore the "collective psyche" of Armenian survivors. For literary examinations of the Holocaust's impact on postwar French

Jewish intellectuals, see Seth L. Wolitz, "Imagining the Jew in France from 1945 to the Present," *Yale French Studies* 85: *Discourses of Jewish Identity in Twentieth Century France* (1994): 119–34; Lawrence D. Kritzman, "Critical Reflections: Self-Portraiture and the Representation of Jewish Identity in French," in *Auschwitz and After: Race, Culture, and "the Jewish Question" in France,* ed. Lawrence D. Kritzman (New York: Routledge, 1995), pp. 98–118; also interesting is Jeanine Parisier Plottel's article "Jewish Identity in Raymond Aron, Emmanuel Berl, and Claude Lévi-Strauss," in the same volume. The historical investigation of *particular* survivor communities has also begun to emerge in certain cases. Some notable examples in the case of the Holocaust include Michael Brenner, *After the Holocaust: Rebuilding Jewish Lives in Postwar Germany,* trans. Barbara Harshav (Princeton: Princeton University Press, 1997); Hanna Yablonka, *Survivors of the Holocaust: Israel after the War,* trans. Ora Cummings (New York: New York University Press, 1999); William Helmreich, *Against All Odds: Holocaust Survivors and the Successful Lives They Made in America* (New York: Simon and Schuster, 1992). In the case of Armenians, historical accounts of various postgenocide communities have, by necessity, documented the great upheaval of the genocide on these communities. See, for example, Anny Bakalian, *Armenian-Americans: From Being to Feeling Armenian* (New Brunswick, N.J.: Transaction Publishers, 1993); Susan Paul Pattie, *Faith in History: Armenians Rebuilding Community* (Washington, D.C.: Smithsonian Institution Press, 1997).

3 Michael Marrus, *The Unwanted: European Refugees in the Twentieth Century* (New York: Oxford University Press, 1985), pp. 3–13; Gérard Noiriel, *Réfugiés et sans-papiers: La République face au droit d'asile* (Paris: Hachette Littératures, 1998), pp. 84–100, 154–55 (originally published as *La Tyrannie du national: Le droit d'asile en Europe (1793–1993)* (Paris: Calmann-Levy, 1991); John Hope Simpson, *The Refugee Problem: Report of a Survey* (London: Oxford University Press, 1939), pp. 227–30.

4 For a comparison of the two genocides, see Robert Melson, *Revolution and Genocide: On the Origins of the Armenian Genocide and the Holocaust* (Chicago: University of Chicago Press, 1992).

5 The major text tracing Vichy policies toward Jews still remains Michael Marrus and Robert Paxton, *Vichy France and the Jews* (New York: Basic Books, 1981). For other important works on the subject, see André Kaspi, *Les Juifs pendant l'Occupation* (Paris: Seuil, 1991); Serge Klarsfeld, *Vichy Auschwitz: Le Rôle de Vichy dans la solution finale de la question juive en France, 1943–1944* (Paris: Fayard, 1983); Donna Ryan, *The Holocaust and the Jews of Marseille: The Enforcement of Anti-Semitic Policies in Vichy France* (Urbana: University of Illinois Press, 1996); Susan Zuccotti, *The Holocaust, the French, and the Jews* (New York: Basic Books, 1993).

6 Paula Hyman, *The Jews of Modern France* (Berkeley: University of California Press, 1998), p. 185. Others place the number closer to two hundred thousand. See Annette Wieviorka, "Despoliation, Reparation, Compensation," in *Starting the Twenty-First Century: Sociological Reflections and Challenges,* ed. Ernest Krausz and Gitta Tulea (New Brunswick, N.J.: Transaction Publishers, 2002), p. 205. Of those deported, approximately

one third were French citizens. The rest were Jewish immigrants who had come to France in the interwar period. About 3 percent survived deportations and later returned to France. Marrus and Paxton, *Vichy France and the Jews*, p. 343.

7 Jacqueline Mesnil-Amar, *Ceux qui ne dormaient pas: 1944–46, Fragments de journal* (Paris: Éditions de Minuit, 1957), p. 119.

8 For information on the denaturalization of those who had recently acquired citizenship, see Marrus and Paxton, *Vichy France and the Jews*, pp. 4, 323–30. For a discussion of Vichy internment policies, see Vicki Caron, *Uneasy Asylum: France and the Jewish Refugee Crisis, 1933–1942* (Stanford: Stanford University Press, 1999), pp. 341–45. For a discussion of the state's legal maneuvering, see Richard H. Weisberg, *Vichy Law and the Holocaust in France* (New York: New York University Press, 1996).

9 For a thorough overview, see Vahakn N. Dadrian, *The History of the Armenian Genocide: Ethnic Conflict from the Balkans to Anatolia to the Caucasus* (Providence, R.I.: Berghahn Books, 1995). For a discussion of the attack against Armenian cultural and religious sites, see Vahé Oshagan, "The Impact of the Genocide on West Armenian Letters," in *The Armenian Genocide in Perspective*, ed. Richard Hovannisian (New Brunswick, N.J.: Transaction Books, 1986), p. 169; Dickran Kouymjian, "The Destruction of Armenian Historical Monuments as a Continuation of the Turkish Policy of Genocide," in *A Crime of Silence: The Armenian Genocide—The Permanent People's Tribunal*, ed. Gerard Libaridian (Cambridge, Mass.: Zoryan Institute, 1985), pp. 173–83. Ara Sarafian, "The Absorption of Armenian Women and Children into Muslim Households as a Structural Component of the Armenian Genocide," in *In God's Name: Genocide and Religion in the Twentieth Century*, ed. Omer Bartov and Phyllis Mack (New York: Berghahn Books, 2001), pp. 209–21.

10 The one exception was new Jewish populations who migrated to France after World War II from further east. For statistics on these, see Doris Bensimon and Sergio Della Pergola, *La Population juive de France: Socio-démographie et identité* (Jerusalem: Institute of Contemporary Jewry, 1984), p. 36. Gary S. Cross, *Immigrant Workers in Industrial France* (Philadelphia: Temple University Press, 1983), provides a useful overview of the history of interwar immigrant labor in France.

11 Martine Hovanessian, *Le Lien communautaire: Trois générations d'Arméniens* (Paris: Armand Colin, 1992), and *Les Arméniens et leurs territoires* (Paris: Les Éditions Autrement, 1995).

12 Melson, *Revolution and Genocide*, p. 29, argues that the Holocaust and the Armenian genocide were "total domestic genocides," which he distinguishes from other "partial" genocides in terms of the extent of the perpetrators' intent. Also see Yehuda Bauer, "The Place of the Holocaust in Contemporary History," in *Holocaust: Religious and Philosophical Implications*, ed. John K. Roth and Michael Berenbaum (New York: Paragon House, 1989), pp. 16–42. For Bauer's most recent thoughts on comparing the Holocaust to other genocides, see Yehuda Bauer, *Rethinking the Holocaust* (New Haven: Yale University Press, 2001), pp. 39–67. For another interesting comparison,

see Christopher Simpson, *The Splendid Blond Beast: Money, Law, and Genocide in the Twentieth Century* (New York: Grove Press, 1993). Certain authors, convinced of the historical "uniqueness" of the Holocaust, have attempted to prove its distinctiveness. Most notable in this regard is Steven Katz's monumental work, *The Holocaust in Historical Context* (New York: Oxford University Press, 1994). Such works have inspired great polemical debates over the value of comparative research in the field. For an overview of these debates, see Alan S. Rosenbaum, ed., *Is the Holocaust Unique?* (Boulder, Colo.: Westview Press, 1996). Also helpful is Vahakn N. Dadrian, "The Tripartite Edifice of the Holocaust and the Imagery of Uniqueness," *International Network on Holocaust and Genocide* 1, no. 2 (April 1996): 13–21, and Gav Rosenfeld, "The Politics of Uniqueness: Reflections on the Polemical Turn in Holocaust and Genocide Scholarship," *Holocaust and Genocide Studies* 13, no. 1 (1999): 28–61.

13 As noted, some psychological and literary studies have begun to explore this question, as has the historical investigation of *particular* survivor communities.

14 Rogers Brubaker, *Citizenship and Nationhood in France and Germany* (Cambridge, Mass.: Harvard University Press, 1992); Gérard Noiriel, *The French Melting Pot: Immigration, Citizenship, and National Identity*, trans. Geoffroy de Laforcade (Minneapolis: University of Minnesota Press, 1996).

15 Todd Endelman, ed., *Comparing Jewish Societies* (Ann Arbor: University of Michigan Press, 1997), pp. 1, 3, 14.

16 Nancy Green, "The Comparative Method and Poststructural Structuralism: New Perspectives for Migration Studies," *Journal of American Ethnic History* 13, no. 4 (1994): 4. Also of interest is her article, "L'Histoire comparative et le champ des études migratoires," *Annales ESC* 6, no. 6 (1990): 1335–50.

17 Laura Lee Downs, *Manufacturing Inequality: Gender Division in the French and British Metalworking Industries, 1914–1939* (Ithaca, N.Y.: Cornell University Press, 1995), p. 12, compares two different political and cultural contexts, interwar France and Britain, to examine the occupational gender inequality present in both countries.

18 Nancy Green, *Ready to Wear, Ready to Work* (Durham, N.C.: Duke University Press, 1997), p. 283.

19 Anahide Ter Minassian, "Les Arméniens de Paris depuis 1945," in *Le Paris des étrangers depuis 1945*, ed. Antoine Marès and Pierre Milza (Paris: Publications de la Sorbonne, 1994), pp. 219–25. Numerous studies have documented the relationship of Jews to the memory of the Holocaust, with scholars disagreeing over its significance in the immediate postwar years. Nevertheless, most agree that it was not until the late 1960s, in the aftermath of the Eichmann trial, that public commemorations of the Holocaust began playing a central role in defining the nature of contemporary Jewish identity. Particularly controversial in both describing and condemning the nature and history of these commemorations has been Tom Segev, *The Seventh Million: The Israelis and the Holocaust*, trans. Haim Watzman (New York: Hill and Wang, 1993), and Peter Novick, *The Holocaust in American Life* (Boston: Houghton Mifflin, 1999). For a

less polemical and more comparative discussion, see essays in *Thinking about the Holocaust: After Half a Century*, ed. Alvin H. Rosenfeld (Bloomington: Indiana University Press, 1997).

20 See, for example, Saul Friedlander, ed., *Probing the Limits of Representation: Nazism and the "Final Solution"* (Cambridge, Mass.: Harvard University Press, 1992).

21 Doris Bensimon, *Les Juifs de France et leurs relations avec Israel, 1945–1988* (Paris: Éditions L'Harmattan, 1989), p. 15.

22 A quickly growing literature, too vast to list here, has documented this process in many European countries, as well as in Israel and even the United States. In France, the defining text in the field is Henry Rousso's *Le syndrome de Vichy: De 1944 à nos jours*, 2d ed. (Paris: Seuil, 1990). Also important is Annette Wieviorka's *Déportation et génocide: Entre la mémoire et l'oubli* (Paris: Plon, 1992).

23 Bruno Bettelheim, postface to Claudine Vegh, *I Didn't Say Goodbye*, trans. Ros Schwartz (New York: Dutton, 1984), p. 164. For comparative overviews of Holocaust memorials, see Sybil Milton, *In Fitting Memory: The Art and Politics of Holocaust Memorials* (Detroit: Wayne State University Press, 1991); James E. Young, *The Texture of Memory* (New Haven: Yale University Press, 1993) and *At Memory's Edge* (New Haven: Yale University Press, 2000). For France, see Serge Barcellini and Annette Wieviorka, *Passant, souviens-toi! Les lieux du souvenir de la Seconde Guerre mondiale en France* (Paris: Plon, 1995), pp. 451–81; Caroline Wiedmer, *The Claims of Memory: Representations of the Holocaust in Contemporary Germany and France* (Ithaca, N.Y.: Cornell University Press, 1999). For a discussion of the historiographical silence, see Pierre Vidal-Naquet, "The Holocaust's Challenge to History," in Kritzman, *Auschwitz and After*, pp. 25–34.

24 Novick, *The Holocaust in American Life*, p. 83. Wieviorka, *Déportation et génocide*, pp. 161–69, makes a similar point about survivors in postwar France.

25 Henri Verneuil, for example, describes his childhood impressions of a meeting in Marseille on 24 April 1927 at which two thousand people gathered to "commemorate their dead." Henri Verneuil, *Mayrig* (Paris: Robert Laffont, 1985), pp. 54–59.

26 By 1939, approximately half of the French Jewish population was made up of recent immigrants. See Nancy Green, *The Pletzl of Paris: Jewish Immigrant Workers in the Belle Epoque* (New York: Holmes and Meier, 1985); Paula Hyman, *From Dreyfus to Vichy: The Remaking of French Jewry, 1906–1939* (New York: Columbia University Press, 1979); David Weinberg, *A Community on Trial: The Jews of Paris in the 1930s* (Chicago: University of Chicago Press, 1974).

27 Béatrice Philippe, *Être juif dans la société française du moyen-âge à nos jours* (Paris: Éditions Montalba, 1979), p. 281.

28 William Safran, "France and Her Jews: From 'Culte Israelite' to 'Lobby Juif,' " *Tocqueville Review* 5, no.1 (1983): 104.

29 In recent years, sociologists, political scientists, ethnographers, and demographers have taken great interest in the transforming French Jewish population, which more than doubled as a result of the decolonization of North Africa. The bulk of this litera-

ture takes the 1960s, and not the 1940s, as its point of departure and is interested in the "renouvellement juif" that emerged in the changing political culture of post-1968 France. For discussions of the North African Jewish migration, see Doris Bensimon-Donath, *L'intégration des Juifs nord-africains en France* (Paris: Mouton, 1971); Bensimon and Della Pergola, *La Population juive de France*; Véronique Poirier, *Ashkénazes et Séfarades: Une étude comparée de leurs relations en France et en Israel (années 1959–1990)* (Paris: Cerf, 1998); Claude Tapia, *Les Juifs sépharades en France (1965–1985): Études psychosociologiques et historiques* (Paris: Éditions L'Harmattan, 1986). For discussions of shifting notions of French Jewish identity since 1968, see Chantal Benayoun, *Les Juifs et la politique* (Paris: Centre national de recherche scientifique, 1984); Pierre Birnbaum, *Jewish Destinies: Citizenship, State, and Community in Modern France*, trans. Arthur Goldhammer (New York: Hill and Wang, 1999); Judith Friedlander, *Vilna on the Seine: Jewish Intellectuals in France Since 1968* (New Haven: Yale University Press, 1990); André Harris and Alain Sédouy, *Juifs et Français* (Paris: Éditions Grasset and Fasquelle, 1979); Dominique Schnapper, *Jewish Identities in France: An Analysis of Contemporary French Jewry*, trans. by Arthur Goldhammer (Chicago: University of Chicago Press, 1983); Simon Sibelman, "Le Renouvellement juif: French Jewry on the Eve of the Centenary of the Affaire Dreyfus," *French Cultural Studies* 3 (1992): 263–76; Sylvie Strudel, *Votes juifs* (Paris: Presses de la Fondation nationale des sciences politiques, 1996); Henry Weinberg, *The Myth of the Jew in France, 1967–1982* (Oakville, N.Y.: Mosaic Press, 1987).

30 David Weinberg, "The Reconstruction of the French Jewish Community after World War II," in *She'erit hapletah, 1944–1948: Rehabilitation and Political Struggle: Proceedings of the Sixth Yad Vashem International Historical Conference, Jerusalem 1985* (Jerusalem: Yad Vashem, 1990), p. 174. Bensimon, *Les Juifs de France et leurs relations avec Israel*, p. 17, also argues that the Holocaust did not bring an end to French Jews' identification with their heritage, although, she claims, most relegated their attachment to the private sphere. For other discussions of the period, see David Weinberg, "France," in *The World Reacts to the Holocaust*, ed. David S. Wyman (Baltimore: Johns Hopkins University Press, 1996); Annette Wieviorka, "Les Juifs en France au lendemain de la guerre: État des lieux," *Archives juives: Revue d'histoire des Juifs de France* 28, no. 1 (1995): 4–22 and *Déportation et génocide*, part 3. For a brief overview of the literature on the period, see Hyman, *The Jews of Modern France*, pp. 186–91.

31 Elie Wiesel, *Memoirs: All Rivers Run to the Sea* (New York: Schocken Books, 1995), p. 115.

32 Although the Armenian genocide technically occurred during the last gasps of the Ottoman Empire, the massacres and elimination of the Armenian minority did not stop with the establishment of Turkey. Indeed, one could argue that the genocide was an integral step in the creation of the new nation, as Ataturk continued efforts to create a state of and for Turks. Ronald Suny, "Empire and Nation: Armenians, Turks, and the End of the Ottoman Empire," *Armenian Forum* 1, no. 2 (1998): 51, writes, "The genocide of the Armenians took place between empire and nation-state, before the idea of an Anatolian nation-state for the Turks had developed, in the context of the

last desperate attempt to save the empire in the age of nationalism. At the same time, however, the Genocide provided a base for a Turkish republic in Anatolia, cleansing the now-purported 'homeland' of the Turks of one of their major competitors."

33 Bensimon and Della Pergola, *La Population juive de France*, p. 36. Information on France's prewar Armenian populations comes from J. Mathorez, "Les Arméniens en France de 1789 à nos jours," *Revue des études arméniennes* 2, no. 2 (1922): 293–314.

34 Green, *The Pletzl of Paris*, pp. 201–16; Hyman, *The Jews of Modern France*, p. 137.

35 See particularly Brubaker, *Citizenship and Nationhood*, chaps. 2, 4, 5.

36 Eugene Weber, *Peasants into Frenchmen: The Modernization of Rural France, 1870–1914* (Stanford: Stanford University Press, 1976), emphasizes a state-centered formulation of French national identity that became disseminated particularly effectively in the 1880s and 1890s under the Third Republic. Subsequent scholarship has challenged this "top-down" perspective. See, for example, Theodore Zeldin, *France 1848–1945*, 2 vols. (Oxford: Clarendon Press, 1973–77); Hervé le Bras and Emmanuel Todd, *L'Invention de la France: Atlas anthropologique et politique* (Paris: Livre de Poche, 1981), who argue that local and national cultures came together to form a modern French identity. More recent scholarship has echoed this criticism while still pointing to the significance of the state's universalist model. See Peter Sahlins, *Boundaries: The Making of France and Spain in the Pyrenees* (Berkeley: University of California Press, 1989); Noiriel, *The French Melting Pot*.

37 Emancipation was not immediate, as there was considerable debate over the Jews' ability to integrate as citizens. Thus, it was not until 1790 that the small population of acculturated Sephardim in France's southwest were emancipated, followed in 1791 by the larger population of more traditional, Yiddish-speaking Ashkenazim concentrated primarily in Alsace and Lorraine. For an overview of the debates and consequences of the Revolution's emancipation of French Jews, see Robert Badinter, *Libres et égaux . . . L'émancipation des Juifs sous la Révolution française (1789–1791)* (Paris: Fayard, 1989); Birnbaum, *Jewish Destinies*, p. 4; David Feuerwerker, *L'Émancipation des Juifs en France, de l'Ancien Régime à la fin du Second Empire* (Paris: A Michel, 1976); Arthur Hertzberg, *The French Enlightenment and the Jews: The Origins of Modern Anti-Semitism* (New York: Columbia University Press, 1968, 1990); Hyman, *The Jews of Modern France*, pp. 17–35; Frances Malino, *The Sephardic Jews of Bordeaux: Assimilation and Emancipation in Revolutionary and Napoleonic France* (Tuscaloosa: University of Alabama Press, 1978).

38 For a discussion of the Consistoire, see Phyllis Cohen Albert, *The Modernization of French Jewry: Consistory and Community in the Nineteenth Century* (Hanover, N.H.: Brandeis University Press, 1977). The classic study of Napoleon and the Jews is still Robert Ancel's *Napoléon et les Juifs* (Paris: Presses Universitaires de France, 1928). See also Simon Schwarzfuchs, *Napoleon, the Jews and the Sanhedrin* (London: Routledge and Kegan Paul, 1979). For a recent synthesis, see Hyman, *The Jews of Modern France*, pp. 37–52.

39 Historians of French Jewry have devoted considerable attention to exploring the re-

lationship of Jews to the polity in the postrevolutionary and Napoleonic eras. Earlier studies argued that in light of state incorporation, Jewish ethnic distinctiveness quickly lost ground. Recent work, however, has suggested otherwise. For an example of earlier arguments, see Michael Marrus, *The Politics of Assimilation: A Study of the French Jewish Community at the Time of the Dreyfus Affair* (New York: Oxford University Press, 1982). Works stressing the complexities of the acculturation process include three important articles by Phyllis Cohen Albert, "Ethnicity and Jewish Solidarity in Nineteenth-century France," in *Mystics, Philosophers, and Politicians: Essays in Jewish Intellectual History in Honor of Alexander Altman*, ed. Jehuda Reinharz and Daniel Swetschinski (Durham, N.C.: Duke University Press, 1982), pp. 249–74; "The Right to Be Different: Interpretations of the French Revolution's Promises to the Jews," *Modern Judaism*, no. 12 (1992): 243–57; and "L'Intégration et la persistance de l'ethnicité chez les juifs dans la France moderne," in *Histoire politique des Juifs en France*, ed. Pierre Birnbaum (Paris: Presses de la Fondation nationale des sciences politiques, 1990), pp. 221–43. Also see Jay R. Berkovitz, "The French Revolution and the Jews: Assessing the Cultural Impact," *AJS Review* 20, no. 1 (1995): 25–86; Pierre Birnbaum, *Les Fous de la République: Histoire politique des Juifs d'état, de Gambetta à Vichy* (Paris: Fayard, 1992); Pierre Birnbaum, ed., *Histoire politique des Juifs de France: Entre universalisme et particularisme* (Paris: Presses de la Fondation nationale des sciences politiques, 1990); Michael Graetz, *Les Juifs en France au XIXe siècle: De la Révolution à l'Alliance israélite universelle*, trans. Salomon Malka, 2d ed. (Paris: Éditions du Seuil, 1989); Paula Hyman, *The Emancipation of the Jews of Alsace: Acculturation and Tradition in the Nineteenth Century* (New Haven: Yale University Press, 1991); Hyman, *The Jews of Modern France*. For an overview of the different schools in this debate, see Birnbaum, *Jewish Destinies*, chap. 2.

40 In the French colonies themselves any dedication to policies of assimilation was more rhetorical than real. Alec G. Hargreaves and Mark McKinney, *Post Colonial Cultures in France* (New York: Routledge, 1997), p. 21.

41 Brubaker, *Citizenship and Nationhood*, p. 109.

42 Herman Lebovics, *True France: The War over Cultural Identity* (Ithaca, N.Y.: Cornell University Press, 1992), argues that it was precisely in these years that essentialized notions of French nationalism began to exert a profound influence over French society, challenging concepts of universal citizenship at the cultural level. In the political arena, however, discourses of universalism remained hegemonic. The historiography on French immigration has been growing since the late 1980s, after years of relative indifference to the issue. For an analysis of this lacuna, see Noiriel, *The French Melting Pot*, chap. 1. Recent work has attempted to fill in the gap by addressing the history of one particular wave of migration or another or by examining the impact of various migrants on a particular locale. For the best recent general overview, see Ralph Schor, *Histoire de l'immigration en France de la fin du XIXe siècle à nos jours* (Paris: Armand Colin, 1996).

43 Such a discussion should not suggest that immigration policies functioned smoothly and seamlessly in this period. Indeed, as Patrick Weil, *La France et ses étrangers: L'aventure d'une politique de l'immigration de 1938 à nos jours* (Paris: Gallimard, 1994), p. 36, demonstrates, prior to the late 1930s French immigration policies were often incoherent and ineffective. Nevertheless, such an integrationist outlook dominated the relationship between all minorities and the state. Thus, for example, when France won Alsace back from the Germans in 1918, promises to observe local customs were ignored in an active attempt to eliminate German language and culture from the region. Stephen L. Harp, *Learning to Be Loyal: Primary Schooling as Nation Building in Alsace and Lorraine, 1850–1940* (DeKalb: Northern Illinois University Press, 1998). Noiriel, *The French Melting Pot*, p. 87. Dominique Schnapper, *La France de l'intégration: Sociologie de la nation en 1990* (Paris: Éditions Gallimard, 1994).

44 Patrick R. Ireland, *The Policy Challenge of Ethnic Diversity: Immigrant Politics in France and Switzerland* (Cambridge, Mass.: Harvard University Press, 1994), p. 35. For a discussion of the ruptures and continuities of French immigration policies during World War II, see Weil, *La France et ses étrangers*, pp. 54–74.

45 Report, Direction générale de la sûreté national to Ministre de l'intérieur, "Le statut des étrangers," 7 February 1945, F/1a/3345, AN.

46 I have been influenced here by Noiriel's *The French Melting Pot*, pp. 265–78, in which he argues that integration in the state cannot be forcibly imposed by a democratic government, and that immigrants themselves slowly adopt those national norms that allow them to improve their position in their host nation. Indeed, most contemporary scholars agree that while universalistic notions of French citizenship remained powerful, individual minority communities also maintained a distinctive cultural presence. See Rogers Brubaker, "The Return of Assimilation? Changing Perspectives on Immigration and Its Sequels in France, Germany, and the United States," *Ethnic and Racial Studies* 24, no. 4 (July 2001): 534, where he notes that although states can adopt assimilationist policies, these policies do not necessarily have assimilationist outcomes.

47 According to Khachig Tölölyan, "Rethinking Diaspora(s): Stateless Power in the Transnational Moment, *Diaspora* 5, no. 1 (1996): 3–36, until the late 1960s, Western scholars considered the Jewish dispersion to be the paradigmatic case of a diaspora, and the Armenian and Greek dispersions as two other important examples. Recently, however, there has been a transformation toward "re-naming as diasporas the more recent communities of dispersion, those that were formed in the five centuries of the modern era and which were known by other names until the late 1960s: as exile groups, overseas communities, ethnic and racial minorities, and so forth." For a discussion of the expansion of the term diaspora and a call for a more specific definition, see Michel Bruneau, "Espaces et territoires de diasporas," in *Diasporas*, ed. Michel Bruneau (Montpellier: Reclus, 1995), pp. 5–23.

48 Liliana R. Goldin, "Transnational Identities: The Search for Analytical Tools," in *Identities on the Move: Transnational Processes in North America and the Caribbean Basin*, ed. Liliana R. Goldin (Albany, N.Y.: Institute for Mesoamerican Studies, 1999), p. 2.

49 Much of the early work on transnationalism tended to focus on distinguishing contemporary immigration waves from those earlier in the century. See, for example, Linda Basch, Nina Glick Schiller, and Christina Blanc Szanton, "Transnationalism: A New Analytic Framework for Understanding Migration," in *Towards a Transnational Perspective on Migration: Race, Class, Ethnicity, and Nationalism Reconsidered*, ed. Linda Basch, Nina Glick Schiller, and Christina Blanc Szanton (New York: New York Academy of Sciences, 1992), pp. 1–24. Recent critiques have sought to broaden its usage in chronological terms while narrowing its theoretical reach. See, for example, Peter Kivisto, "Theorizing Transnational Immigration: A Critical Review of Current Efforts," *Ethnic and Racial Studies* 24, no. 4 (2001): 549–77.

50 For a discussion of how international connections influenced the Armenian fate, see Vahakn N. Dadrian, "Genocide as a Problem of National and International Law: The World War I Armenian Case and Its Contemporary Ramifications," *Yale Journal of International Law* 14, no. 2 (1989): 221–334. The literature on how the perceived threat of Jewish multinationalism shaped antisemitic discourse throughout Europe is too vast to cite here. For a recent discussion of how such fears shaped refugee policy toward Jewish refugees who sought shelter in France in the 1930s, see Caron, *Uneasy Asylum*, pp. 19–21, 162–63, 191–92.

51 Avtar Brah, *Cartographies of Diaspora: Contesting Identities* (New York: Routledge, 1996), pp. 190–95. Brah points out that not all diasporas sustain an ideology of return. Nevertheless, the "concept of diaspora places the discourse of 'home' and 'dispersion' in creative tension." For other conceptualizations of the relationship of "homelands" and diaspora communities, see Bruneau, "Espaces et territoires," pp. 12–14; Walker Conner, "The Impact of Homelands upon Diasporas," in *Modern Diasporas in International Politics*, ed. Gabriel Sheffer (New York: St. Martin's Press, 1986), pp. 16–46; William Safran, "Diasporas in Modern Societies: Myths of Homeland and Return," *Diaspora* 1, no. 1 (1991): 83–99; Gabriel Sheffer, "Ethnic Diasporas: A Threat to Their Hosts?" in *International Migration and Security*, ed. Myron Weiner (Boulder, Colo.: Westview Press, 1993), pp. 263–85. For Armenian links to homeland, see Ronald Grigor Suny, *Looking toward Ararat: Armenia in Modern History* (Bloomington: Indiana University Press, 1993), pp. 213–17. On diaspora nationalism and its relationship to the homeland, see Anthony D. Smith, "Zionism and Diaspora Nationalism," in *Myths and Memories of the Nation* (Oxford: Oxford University Press, 1999), pp. 203–24.

52 Khachig Tölölyan, "The Nation-State and Its Others: In Lieu of a Preface," *Diaspora* 1, no. 1 (1991): 5.

53 Ibid., p. 6.

54 Hyman, *From Dreyfus to Vichy*, p. 236.

1 Aram Turabian, *La France, Les Arméniens, et les Juifs* (Paris, 1938), pp. 3–4; emphasis added.

2 John Hope Simpson, *The Refugee Problem: Report of a Survey* (London: Oxford University Press, 1939), p. 3; Michael Marrus, *The Unwanted: European Refugees in the Twentieth Century* (New York: Oxford University Press, 1985), pp. 3–13; Gérard Noiriel, *Réfugiés et sans-papiers: La République face au droit d'asile* (Paris: Hachette Littératures, 1998), pp. 98–101.

3 Marrus, *The Unwanted*, p. 52.

4 Robert H. Johnston, *"New Mecca, New Babylon": Paris and the Russian Exiles, 1920–1945* (Montreal: McGill-Queen's University Press, 1988), p. 21. Timothy P. Maga, *America, France, and the European Refugee Problem, 1933–1947* (New York: Garland Publishing, 1985), p. 13, claims that France had accepted the largest majorities of all refugee migrations of the 1920s. The government maintained a conservative estimate of 180,000–250,000. J. Simpson, *The Refugee Problem*, pp. 297–336, provides a helpful overview of early French refugee policies.

5 For a discussion of immigrant labor in France, see Gary S. Cross, *Immigrant Workers in Industrial France* (Philadelphia: Temple University Press, 1983). For more on the historiography of French immigration, see Gérard Noiriel, *The French Melting Pot: Immigration, Citizenship, and National Identity*, trans. Geoffroy de Laforcade (Minneapolis: University of Minnesota Press, 1996).

6 William H. Schneider, *Quality and Quantity: The Quest for Biological Regeneration in Twentieth-Century France* (Cambridge, England: Cambridge University Press, 1990), p. 234.

7 Statistics on the Russian presence varied enormously, with some international officials declaring it as high as 400,000. According to Johnston, *"New Mecca, New Babylon,"* pp. 23–25, calculating Russian presence (and that of other refugees) was a problem due to definitional questions (who was a Russian?), émigré mobility, bureaucratic error, and inertia. By his count, the number was probably closer to 120,000. For a discussion of the open-door policy France maintained toward refugees, see Marrus, *The Unwanted*, 113–14. For a brief but interesting comparison of Russian and Armenian refugees to France, see Gérard Noiriel, "Russians and Armenians in France," in *The Cambridge Survey of World Migration*, ed. Robin Cohen (Cambridge, England: Cambridge University Press, 1995), pp. 145–47.

8 Determining the exact number is difficult. At the time, local Armenian representatives complained about the inaccuracies of national census data, which considered as Armenian only those who had been officially recognized as stateless refugees and ignored those holding Turkish, Syrian, Lebanese, Greek, Iranian, or French citizenship. In 1938, one newspaper published 63,346 as the official number, and subsequent accounts have continued to put the number at approximately 65,000 or 70,000.

This number reflected statistics put out by the French government. See "Marsēyli hayots' t'iwĕ," *Hay Sirt* [Marseille, France], 23 July 1936; "Le Nombre des Arméniens en France," *Le Foyer*, 1 November 1929; "Le Nombre des Arméniens en France," *Le Foyer*, 15 January 1930; "Fransabnak hayeru t'iwĕ," *Pahak* [Romania], 20 March 1938; J. Simpson, *The Refugee Problem*, pp. 318–19. For a discussion of the difficulties of obtaining reliable estimates, see Aïda Boudjikanian-Keuroghlian, "Un Peuple en exil: La Nouvelle diaspora (XIXe–XXe siècles)," in *Histoire des Arméniens*, ed. Gérard Dédéyan (Toulouse: Éditions Privat, 1982), pp. 635–41. For the percentage of Armenians in Europe and the Near East, see J. Simpson, *The Refugee Problem*, p. 44.

9 Johnston, "*New Mecca, New Babylon*," p. 10.

10 Aby Harari, *Situation de l'apatride et du réfugié dans la législation française actuelle* (Paris: Librairie du Recueil Sirey, 1940), p. 7.

11 The phrase "orphans of the nation" comes from Pierre Audiat, "L'Absurde cruauté," *Paris-Midi*, 8 July 1935. Many of the immigrants who came to France in the post–World War I years traveled back to their native land on a regular basis. Yves Lequin, "L'Etrangeté française," in *Histoire des étrangers et de l'immigration en France*, ed. Yves Lequin (Paris: Larousse, 1992), p. 343, suggests that most immigrants maintained a strong link with their country of origin, often living in both places and never settling permanently in either.

12 Marrus, *The Unwanted*, p. 94.

13 Of particular interest on this question is Rogers Brubaker, *Citizenship and Nationhood in France and Germany* (Cambridge, Mass.: Harvard University Press, 1992), and Noiriel, *The French Melting Pot*.

14 Unless otherwise noted, the following discussion on Armenian history during and after World War I is drawn from Richard G. Hovannisian, "The Historical Dimensions of the Armenian Question, 1878–1923," in *The Armenian Genocide in Perspective*, ed. Richard G. Hovannisian (New Brunswick, N.J.: Transaction Publishers, 1986), pp. 19–41. Also see Anahide Ter Minassian, *La Questionne arménienne* (Roquevaire: Éditions Parenthèses, 1983).

15 Vahakn N. Dadrian, "Genocide as a Problem of National and International Law: The World War I Armenian Case and Its Contemporary Legal Ramifications," *Yale Journal of International Law* 14, no. 2 (1989): 221–334.

16 Vahakn N. Dadrian, *The History of the Armenian Genocide: Ethnic Conflict from the Balkans to Anatolia to the Caucasus* (Providence, R.I.: Berghahn Books, 1995).

17 Richard G. Hovannisian, *Armenia on the Road to Independence* (Berkeley: University of California Press, 1967).

18 Mary Mangigian Tarzian, *The Armenian Minority Problem, 1914–1934: A Nation's Struggle for Security* (Atlanta, Ga.: Scholars Press, 1992), pp. 75–97.

19 Yves Ternon, "Le Génocide de Turquie et la guerre (1914–1923)," in *Histoire des Arméniens*, pp. 483–523; Claude Mutafian, "La France en Cilicie: Histoire d'un échec,

1919–1939," *Les Temps modernes*, nos. 504–6 (1988): 90–108. Cyril le Tallec, *La Communauté arménienne de France, 1920–1950* (Paris: L'Harmattan, 2001), pp. 16–22.

20 Hovannisian, "The Historical Dimensions," p. 37; Tarzian, *The Armenian Minority Problem*, pp. 158–63.

21 The Treaty of San Stephano, ending the Russo-Turkish War in 1878, as well as the Treaty of Berlin brought the Armenian Question international recognition. Although the Treaty of Berlin stipulated that European powers would intervene on behalf of the Armenians if the situation deteriorated, no such help came. As the situation became increasingly precarious for Ottoman Armenians, pro-Armenian movements developed throughout Europe with the aim of forcing the various governments to follow through on the terms stated in the Treaty of Berlin. Throughout the early 1920s, such pressure groups continued to assume that European governments had not only a right but an obligation to act on behalf of the Armenians. It is only with this in mind that we can understand why the pro-Armenian movements achieved a degree of legitimacy. For some responses to the first wave of massacres, see Maurice Leveyre, "Les Massacres de Sasounkh," *La Revue de Paris*, 1 September 1895; *La Vérité sur les massacres d'Arménie: Documents nouveaux ou peu connus — Rapports de témoins oculaires, correspondances particulières, extraits de journaux* (Paris: P. V. Stock, Éditeur, 1896); Malcolm MacColl, *L'Arménie devant l'Europe: Le Gouvernement turc est une théocratie* (Paris: Typographie A. Davy, 1897); Pierre Quillard and Louis Margery, *La Question d'Orient et la politique personnelle de M. Hanotaux* (Paris: P. V. Stock, Éditeur, 1897); P. Pisani, *Les Affaires d'Arménie: Extrait du correspondant* (Paris: De Soye et Fils, 1895); *Sassoun et les atrocités hamidiennes: Interpellation des atrocités, rapport officiel* (Genève: L'Union des étudiants arméniens de l'Europe, 1904); *Les Massacres d'Arménie: Témoignage des victimes* (Paris: Mercure de France, 1896); Victor Bérard, *Le Sultan et l'Europe* (Paris: Calmann-Lévy, 1896); Le P. Charmetant, *Martyrologe arménien* (Paris: Oeuvre d'Orient, 1896). Several works were also translated from Armenian and English into French. For discussions of the French pro-Armenian movement, see Edmond Khayadjian, *Archag Tchobanian et le mouvement arménophile en France* (Marseille: Centre national de documentation pédagogique, 1986); Madeleine Rebérioux, "Jean Jaurès and the Armenians," *Armenian Review* 44, no. 2-174 (1991): 1–11; and some excerpts in Ter Minassian, *La Question arménienne*.

22 Minutes, Société France-Arménie, 19 February 1918, v. A.5, Bibliothèque Nubar. A list of members is included in the Minutes, 25 February 1918, same folder. It is interesting to note that there are no Armenian names on the list. As is clear from the minutes of that meeting, certain prominent Armenians believed that an association made up entirely of French nationals would have more authority with the government than one that included Armenians. The intention of the Armenian leaders was to form an Association Arméno-Français as soon as an autonomous Armenian region could be established.

23   *Hommage à l'Arménie: Compte-Rendu de la manifestation qui eut lieu le 9 avril 1919 dans la grand amphithéâtre de la Sorbonne* (Paris: Éditions Ernest Leroux, 1919), pp. i, v.

24   Minutes, Société France-Arménie, 16 October 1916, V.A.5., Bibliothèque Nubar. In the Minutes of 15 January 1917, it was reported that five hundred copies of this pamphlet were printed, two hundred of which were distributed to the Directeur de l'enseignement primaire and another three hundred of which were given to the Directeur de l'enseignement secondaire. Another pamphlet, "La Nation arménienne," was written later and also distributed in the schools.

25   Minutes, Assemblé générale extraordinaire, Société France-Arménie, 14 October 1918, V.A.5, Bibliothèque Nubar; Declaration of purpose and program for the Association Franco-Arménienne, undated, V.A.5, Bibliothèque Nubar; Minutes, Association Franco-Arménie, 17 November 1918, V.A.5, Bibliothèque Nubar.

26   Hovannisian, *Armenia on the Road to Independence*, pp. 250–51.

27   Rapport sur l'activité de l'Association France-Arménie, undated [1922], V.A.5, Bibliothèque Nubar.

28   Review of *Andradnik*, *La Comoedia*, 4 April 1929; Emile Pipert, "Les Arméniens et la Provence," *Le Petit Marseillais*, 31 December 1929.

29   L. G. Guerdan, "Les Arméniens et la France," *La Vie*, July 1939; "Les Actions de secours en faveur des Arméniens," *Revue internationale de la Croix-Rouge* 2, no. 15 (15 March 1920): 241. C. Delmas, "Rapport sur le fonctionnement des services d'assistance française aux populations réfugiées en Syrie et au Liban," 27 July 1923, B32936, Archives du Ministère de Finance (same carton is listed in the AN as f/30/2043). In this report, Delmas also speaks about the aid that France provided in transporting Armenian refugees from Cilicia to the French mandatory areas of Syria and Lebanon in the early 1920s. J. Simpson, *The Refugee Problem*, pp. 35–36, 39, 43 documents French participation in a number of international initiatives to help them settle. Also see Noiriel, *Réfugiés et sans-papiers*, pp. 110–11.

30   Philippe Bernard and Henri Dubief, *The Decline of the Third Republic, 1914–38*, trans. Anthony Forester (Cambridge, England: Cambridge University Press; Paris: Éditions de la Maison des sciences de l'homme, 1988), p. 37.

31   The largest waves came in 1926. All migration had stopped by 1934. See Aïda Boudjikanian-Keuroghlian, *Les Arméniens dans la région Rhône-Alpes: Essai géographique sur les rapports d'une minorité ethnique avec son milieu d'accueil* (Lyon: Association des Amis de la Revue de géographie de Lyon, 1978), p. 27, and "Un peuple en exil," pp. 627–30, 648.

32   Noiriel, *Réfugiés et sans-papiers*, pp. 31–36, 65–67, 78.

33   Noiriel, *The French Melting Pot*, pp. 54–59; Noiriel, *Réfugiés et sans-papiers*, pp. 166–76.

34   Ministère de l'Agriculture, Service de la Main-d'œuvre et de l'immigration agricoles, *Conventions et règlements relatifs à l'immigration et à l'émigration* (Paris: Imprimerie nationale, 1928), p. 288; Cross, *Immigrant Workers in Industrial France*, pp. 45–70; Noiriel,

The French Melting Pot, pp. 81–82; Ralph Schor, Histoire de l'immigration en France de la fin du XIXe siècle a nos jours (Paris: Armand Colin, 1996), pp. 45–79.

35 Georges Mauco, Les Étrangers en France: Leur rôle dans l'activité économique (Paris: Librairie Armand Colin, 1932), p. 68. Although Mauco's work on foreign populations in France has been criticized for its antisemitic and xenophobic tendencies, it still provides a useful overview as well as an invaluable perspective on prevailing administrative attitudes of the day. For a critical reading of Mauco's work, see Patrick Weil, La France et ses étrangers: L'aventure d'une politique de l'immigration de 1938 à nos jours (Paris: Gallimard, 1991), pp. 42–47.

36 Noiriel, Réfugiés et sans-papiers, p. 92. He notes that keeping tabs on refugees had always caused problems for the French administration (pp. 68–74).

37 Many of the earliest Russian apatrides still had passports, but only those issued by the former tsarist government or by local military commanders. In addition, Russian diplomatic or consular representatives often continued to issue identity papers on prerevolutionary authority. Receiving countries, however, were reluctant to recognize these documents, and also hesitated to acknowledge those issued by their Soviet successors. Marrus, The Unwanted, pp. 93–94.

38 Noiriel, The French Melting Pot, pp. 56–66; J. Simpson, The Refugee Problem, pp. 274–75.

39 Mauco, Les Étrangers en France, pp. 129–30. French officials did attempt to crack down on illegal immigration, if not very successfully. Evidence of such attempts can be found, for example, in Marseille, where the Commissaire spécial de Marseille reported to the Directeur de la sûreté générale, 23 October 1923, 4M957, Bouches-du-Rhône, "My personnel are conducting a very rigorous inspection on board the foreign ships coming from the Orient and taking the necessary measures to return illegal aliens [clandestins] and those passengers without visas from French consulates."

40 It is worth noting that the League of Nations established small assistance offices for various refugee groups in France (Russian, Armenian, and later German and Spanish) to ensure that refugees knew their rights under French and international law. Unfortunately, most refugees were unaware that such services existed. However inefficient, these refugee assistance offices existed only in France, which, despite its early failures with regard to refugee policy, remained one of the most concerned countries with respect to solving international refugee problems. Maga, America, France, and the European Refugee Problem, pp. 17–18.

41 The recruiting system itself was flawed, with various recruiters seeking to take advantage of Armenian refugees by charging large fees to procure labor contracts. The French administration finally sought to take charge of the process in 1926, causing some consternation among those Armenians already in France who had been profiting from the recruitment business. Confidential Report, 22 November 1926, Associations arménophiles, Délégation nationale, Bibliothèque Nubar. Other information about individual Armenians who were led astray by recruiters can be found

in an exchange between Pachalian (Secrétaire général, Comité central des réfugiés arméniens) and Berron (Action Chrétienne en Orient), 9–30 June 1925, same file. For more on the holes in the recruiting system, see Boudjikanian-Keuroghlian, *Les Arménines dans la region Rhône-Alpes*, p. 33.

42 Commissaire spécial to the Préfet des Bouches-du-Rhône, 23 October 1923, no. 4.011, 4M957, Bouches-du-Rhône.

43 Louise Holborn, "The League of Nations and the Refugee Problem," *Annals of the American Academy of Political and Social Science* (May 1939). For a discussion of international interventions on behalf of Armenian and Russian refugees, and the ultimate granting of the Nansen passport, see J. Simpson, *The Refugee Problem*, pp. 34–36, 62–116, 197–221, 239–45; Marrus, *The Unwanted*, chap. 2; Noiriel, *Réfugiés et sans-papers*, pp. 101–4. Noiriel argues compellingly on p. 107 that the reason the Nansen passport was accepted so quickly was because most European nations believed that this measure would facilitate the massive repatriation of those displaced by the war and end the refugee problem for good.

44 Even when the government had accepted the Nansen passport, most Armenians already living in France did not get one initially. Once settled, they only sought the documentation if they wanted to leave the country. Thus, all attempts to count how many Armenians lived in France were hampered. An official list of those registering for Nansen passports from 1926 to 1946, for example, cites fewer than 100 in most years, the largest number being 162 in 1930. Certificats Nansen, (registre) 1926–1946, 4M1138, Bouches-du-Rhône.

45 Telegram, Ministère de l'Intérieur to Préfet des Bouches du Rhône, 21 September 1922, 4M957, Bouches-du-Rhône. The initial arrival of Armenians in Marseille is covered in Marie-Françoise Attard-Maraninchi and Emile Temime, *Histoire des migrations à Marseille*, vol. 3: *Le Cosmopolitisme de l'entre-deux-guerres (1919–1945)* (Marseille: Edisud, 1990). It is worth noting that the refugees were not all Armenian. Upheaval in Smyrna sent those of all nationalities fleeing. One early boatload contained 251 French, 4 Armenians, 9 Swiss, 11 Italians, 1 Spaniard, 25 Greeks, 4 Yugoslavians, and one nine-month-old British child. Telegram, Ministère de l'Intérieur to Préfet des Bouches du Rhône, 26 September 1922, 4M957, Bouches-du-Rhône. In a "note de service," 23 September 1922, 4M957, Bouches-du-Rhône, a French general describes the division of the two thousand refugees into four camps: Caserne des Incurables, Ste. Marthe, Camp Oddo, and Camp Mirabeau.

46 This did not, however, prevent the French government from requesting such funding. Indeed, the prefect requested 1,524 francs from the Armenian consulate to cover the lodging costs of refugees at the Camp de Ste-Marthe. Préfet des Bouches du Rhône to Trésorier payeur général, 30 October 1922, 4M957, Bouches-du-Rhône.

47 In cases of guardianship, wills, and inheritance, for example, immigrants were expected to go to their own consulate to adjudicate disputes. In other words, in these matters the immigrants were still subject to the laws of the country from which they

had come. The Turkish consulate, however, refused to recognize Armenians as Turkish citizens, leaving all their personal affairs unresolved. Correspondence between Berron and Pachalian, 17 and 22 July 1925, Associations arménophiles, Délégation national, Bibliothèque Nubar.

48 Ministre de l'Intérieur to les Préfets, 27 July 1925, 4M957, Bouches-du-Rhône. From that point on, they were to be called "citoyens de l'URSS — d'origine arménienne" if they recognized the Soviet government and "Réfugiés russes, d'origine arménienne" if they did not. Those from the Turkish provinces were labeled "Turcs d'origine arménienne." Despite specific instructions from the Ministry of the Interior, in some areas local officials continued recording Armenian refugees as "Turkish" on their identity papers, causing problems for the refugees when they needed to turn to government services. Secrétaire générale (Comité central des réfugiés arméniens) to Ministre des affaires étrangères, 3 Novembre 1925, Fransa gtnoworֲ gaghtʿaknner, Délégation nationale, Bibliothèque Nubar.

49 One of the first boats, the Lamartaine, arrived on 19 September 1922. It contained over one hundred Armenian refugees fleeing battles between Turks and Greeks in Smyrna. It was in response to these first arrivals that the Armenian colony in Marseille established the Comité de secours aux réfugiés arméniens. Commissaire Spécial de Marseille to Ministère de l'Intérieur, no. 3316, 19 September 1922, 6M9770, Bouches-du-Rhône. Mirzayantz was unable to care effectively even for these few refugees. By 26 October, the refugee camp Ste. Marthe still had seven families (twenty-three people) because of the overflow of Armenians at the Hotel du Levant. "Relevée des journées passées au Camp St. Marthe par les sujets Arméniens," 26 October 1922, 4M957, Bouches-du-Rhône. Material on initial aid from Armenian sources is drawn from Tigran S. Mirzayantz to Préfet des Bouches-du-Rhône, 12 October 1922, same carton. Simeon Mirzayantz to Préfet des Bouches du Rhône, 17 November 1922, 4M957, Bouches-du-Rhône. Telegram, Préfet des Bouches-du-Rhône to Ministère de l'Intérieur, 17 November 1922, 4M957, Bouches-du-Rhône. For a discussion of the establishment of Camp Oddo, see Attard-Maraninchi and Temime, Le Cosmopolitisme de l'entre-deux-guerres (1919–1945), pp. 47–54. Also see Edmond Khayadjian, "La communauté arménienne de Marseille," Marseille, Revue municipale trimestrielle, no. 118 (1979): 32–39.

50 Not all Armenians needed government aid. Many arrived with adequate resources to take care of themselves, often leaving Marseille for other areas of France. Of the 707 refugees to arrive on the Phrygie, for example, 103 were Armenians "[who] have resources and for the most part are not staying in Marseille." Commissaire spécial de police des chemins de fer et de ports to Préfet des Bouches-du-Rhône, 28 October 1923, 4M957, Bouches-du-Rhône.

51 Information on the 80,000 franc contribution was noted in Préfet des Bouches-du-Rhône to the Trésorier Payeur Général, 11 December 1924, 4M957, Bouches-du-Rhône. The citation comes from René Renoult to Président de la Ligue français pour

la défense des droits de l'homme et du citoyen, 29 July 1924, in Correspondance, Délégation Nationale—1921, Bibliothèque Nubar.

52 Général de Division Breton, "Réfugiés arméniens," 25 November 1922, 4M957, Bouches-du-Rhône.

53 As Noiriel, *The French Melting Pot*, p. 81, explains, different treaties revolved around the length and regularity of the immigrant's residency. As a result, in some cases medical care would be provided only if a worker had lived in France for five consecutive years.

54 Two Armenian doctors estimated that over one thousand Armenians died of tuberculosis in 1926 alone. Dr. Cololian and Dr. Krikorian, *Le Foyer*, 15 January 1929.

55 Eugène Prat-Flottes, *Ce qu'il est utile de connaître a fin de pouvoir mener une lutte active contre la Tuberculose dans les milieux Arméniens* (Toulon: Imprimerie G. Rougeolle, 1929), p. 17. Interestingly, the two Armenian doctors who responded to Prat-Flottes's piece in the Armenian paper *Le Foyer* insisted that Armenians should not build their own sanitarium and should rely instead on French medical care. They proposed, however, that an organization be founded to pay for Armenian care in these already established sanitariums. Dr. Cololian and Dr. Krikorian, *Le Foyer*, 15 January 1929.

56 Préfet to René Paux, Comité de secours aux victimes des événements d'orient, 13 March 1924, 4M957, Bouches-du-Rhône. In September 1923, the Union nationale arménienne was founded to take over this role from the Comité de secours aux réfugiés arméniens de Marseille under the leadership of Aram Turabian. Préfet des Bouches-du-Rhône to Ministre de l'Intérieur and Ministre des Affaires étrangères, 21 September 1923, 4M957, Bouches-du-Rhône. The High Commission for Refugees refused the request because its resources were also quite limited and, in turn, asked the delegation for aid for Armenians in Greece and elsewhere. De Moteville, Haut-Commissaire Adjoint pour les réfugiés, to Président de la Délégation de la République Arménienne, 17 October 1922, Correspondance, Délégation Nationale—1921, Bibliothèque Nubar.

57 Général Havard, Commandant de la base de Marseille, to Préfet des Bouches-du-Rhône, 2 October 1923, 4M957, Bouches-du-Rhône. Commissaire spécial to Préfet des Bouches-du-Rhône, 18 October 1923, 4M957, Bouches-du-Rhône. Sénateur Flaissières, Maire de Marseille, to Préfet des Bouches-du-Rhône, 19 October 1923, 4M957, Bouches-du-Rhône. The threat that the refugees posed to hygiene greatly worried local officials. Fears that they would contaminate the city surfaced repeatedly, and local commissions were established to deal with the threat. Siméon Flaissières, *Le Petit Provençal*, 21 October 1923, cited in Khayadjian, *Archag Tchobanian*, p. 294.

58 Ministre de l'Intérieur to Préfet des Bouches-du-Rhône, 5 December 1923, 4M957, Bouches-du-Rhône. Ministre de l'Intérieur to Préfet des Bouches-du -Rhône, 31 October 1923, 4M957, Bouches-du-Rhône, and Ministre du Travail to Ministre de l'Intérieur, 4 July 1925, same carton. Although the numbers decreased from November 1923 forward, the flow was not completely interrupted, and new Armenians kept

arriving until 1926. Attard-Maraninchi and Temime, *Le Cosmopolitisme de l'entre-deux-guerres (1919–1945)*, p. 48. Préfet to René Paux, 13 March 1924, 4M957, Bouches-du-Rhône. It is worth noting, however, that the government gave 11,000 francs to the Alliance française in Marseille to help pay for the costs of settling Armenians in 1923. Préfet to Mme Thibon, Président du Comité de l'Alliance française à Marseille, 5 May 1924, 4M957, Bouches-du-Rhône.

59 Président du Conseil and Ministre des Affaires Étrangères to Préfet des Bouches-du-Rhône, 3 March 1925, 4M957, Bouches-du-Rhône. Ministre du Travail to Ministre de l'Intérieur, 4 July 1925, 4M957, Bouches-du-Rhône. Details of the liquidation of Oddo can be found in Attard-Maraninchi and Temime, *Le Cosmopolitisme de l'entre-deux-guerres (1919–1945)*, pp. 54–55.

60 Ministre du Travail to Ministre de l'Intérieur, 4 July 1925, 4M957, Bouches-du-Rhône.

61 Ludovic Nadeau, "Enquête sur la population de France," *L'Illustration*, 24 August 1929.

62 Commissaire spécial de Valence to Secrétaire général du Ministère de la sûreté générale, "Renseignements concernant les Arméniens," 10 May 1926, f7/13436, AN.

63 Cited in Noiriel, *Réfugiés et sans-papiers*, p. 227.

64 "La Maison aux mille et un Arméniens," *Le Paris-Midi*, 17 July 1929. Raymond Petit, "À Alfortville, dans l'Ile-Saint-Pierre, 4000 Arméniens ont fondé un village où ils vivent selon les traditions et les lois de leurs ancêtres," *Paris-Soir*, 18 December 1933.

65 Brubaker, *Citizenship and Nationhood*, chap. 5.

66 Martine Hovanessian, *Le Lien communautaire: Trois générations d'arméniens* (Paris: Armand Colin, 1992), p. 38.

67 J. Simpson, *The Refugee Problem*, pp. 239–45.

68 Circular no. 39, Ministre de l'Intérieur to Messieurs les Préfets, 28 January 1926, 4M954, Bouches-du-Rhône. In response, the prefect reported nine thousand Armenians, seven thousand of whom were capable of working. Préfet des Bouches-du-Rhône to Ministre de l'Intérieur, 12 February 1926, same carton. It is interesting to note that much of the information on Armenian refugees was sketchy, whereas that regarding Russians was much more fully developed. This was largely due to the sophistication of Russian refugee organizations, which operated more successfully than their Armenian counterparts.

69 Circulaire no. 59 (91), from Ministre de l'Intérieur to Messieurs les Préfet, 28 August 1926, 4M965 Bouches-du-Rhône.

70 Noiriel, *Réfugiés et sans-papiers*, p. 210.

71 For refugee expulsions in international law and in France, see J. Simpson, *The Refugee Problem*, pp. 246–61.

72 There is no heading or date on this report, but there are citations in it from a letter from the Ministère de l'Intérieur to the Préfets de Police, 5 October 1926, f/7/13518, AN.

73 This law dated from 1849 but was followed with much greater rigor in the interwar period. This and other laws regarding immigrants are noted in "État actuel de la

législation des étrangers," Ministère de l'Intérieur, no date, f/7/13518, AN. Flyers reminding various prefectures of their rights in this regard circulated throughout the departments. One example is Circulaire, Ministère de l'Intérieur, no date, dossiers des expulsions nos. 51351–51400, 4M1698, Bouches-du-Rhône. See also J. Simpson, *The Refugee Problem*, pp. 252–56.

74 Report, 26 February 1925, f/7/13436, AN. In the same folder (1922–1928), there are several documents having to do with this expulsion, including the initial report of the arrest, 15 January 1925. Most police interest in the Armenians focused on their relationship with Soviet Armenia and their Soviet/Bolshevik groups in France. Indeed, if looking only at police files, one would assume the spread of communism went much further than it actually did in the refugee population. Various reports on Armenian communist activity can be found in f/7/13436, AN, as can files on the pro-Soviet newspaper *Erivan*.

75 Armenian officials, for example worried about possible expulsions among Armenians who did not fulfill their initial work contracts. Evidence of such concern was found in Comité central des réfugiés arméniens to L. Berron, 18 December 1924, Associations Arménophiles, Délégation nationale, Bibliothèque Nubar.

76 "La Justice sanctionne une fois de plus un état de fait stupide et cruel," *L'Œuvre*, 2 July 1935. Dossiers des expulsions nos. 51351–51400, 4M1698, Bouches-du-Rhône. Information on a young Armenian expelled for living in France under a false name was found in the exchange between Pachalian and Berron, 9–30 June 1925, Associations arménophiles, Délégation national, Bibliothèque Nubar. In contrast, Agop Keledian never understood why he had been asked to leave French territory. Agop Keledian to Préfet de Marseille, 14 March 1925, *Fransa gtnowoṛ gaghtʻaknner*, Délégation nationale, Bibliothèque Nubar.

77 The more the numbers of immigrants rose in France, the more complicated expulsions became, and the more poorly they were actually carried out. Complaints to this effect are occasionally evident in the archives. For one example, Report from Préfet, Ville de Nice, to Commissaire principal chargé du contrôle général des services de recherches judiciaires, 4 June 1912, f/7/14711, AN.

78 I say "theoretically" because there were times when the adjoining state would not transport the individual home. Thus, one Yugoslav, Gjuc Roksandie, was forced to walk back and forth over the bridge between France and Switzerland with neither side willing to let him in. The official complaining of this incident noted that it was not an isolated case. Commissariat spécial de Pontarlier, 7 February 1933, no. 167, f/7/14711, AN.

79 Report, Préfecture des Bouches-du-Rhône, 13 December 1926, Dossiers des expulsions nos. 51351–51400, 4M1698, Bouches-du-Rhône. This file includes many letters back and forth from the woman's son to the prefect and from the prefect to the Ministry of the Interior, as well as a copy of the expulsion order.

80 Pierre Audiat, "L'Absurde cruauté," *Paris-Midi*, 8 July 1935.

81 A report on the numbers of foreigners expelled for political reasons from 1 January 1927 until 10 October 1927 is surprisingly low. Of 408 foreigners expelled during those months, only 2 were Armenians. The largest group was Italian (196), followed by 58 Spanish and 50 Polish. "État, par nationalités, des 408 étrangers expulsés de France pour faits politiques du 1er Janvier 1927 au 10 Octobre 1927," f/7/13518, AN. The low figure here suggests that many more foreigners than rhetoric of the time suggested were expelled for crimes that were not political. In the same file, a report from 1 March 1928 lists the number of foreigners expelled from France from 21 July 1926 to 28 February 1928 as 1,555 by the administrative police and 11,675 by the judicial police. The same report indicates that from 21 July 1926 to 20 October 1927, the administrative police expelled 1,211 foreigners and the judicial police 8,165.

82 État signalétique des étrangers expulsés de France, February 1926–July 1928, f/7/14655, AN. I obtained these figures from two books intended for customs officials policing French borders, which listed the physical characteristics of expelled individuals. The subtotals for each month were provided, allowing me to come to the total figure listed above. I obtained the Armenian figure by counting the Armenian last names listed in the book. I cannot, of course, be certain that all the individuals with traditional Armenian names were actually Armenian; some may have been Persian or Turkish. Likewise, there may have been some Armenians expelled who did not have traditional Armenian names. In other files, I found evidence of expelled Armenians whose names were not included in the books, suggesting that the expulsion books were not comprehensive and that the number of Armenians expelled may have been larger.

83 "Autour d'un Suicide," Le Foyer, 15 Juillet 1929.

84 Ibid.; "Clémence et Amnistie," Le Foyer, 1 September 1931. Président du Conseil, Ministre de l'Intérieur, to Préfet des Bouches-du-Rhône, 11 April 1930, 4M965, Bouches-du Rhône.

85 For a thorough history of French refugee policy in the 1930s and the rising anti-Jewish sentiment, see Vicki Caron, Uneasy Asylum: France and the Jewish Refugee Crisis, 1933–1942 (Stanford: Stanford University Press, 1999).

86 Michael Marrus and Robert Paxton, Vichy France and the Jews (New York: Basic Books, 1981), pp. 34–44. For a general overview of French political and economic life in the 1930s, see Gordon Wright, France in Modern Times: From Enlightenment to the Present, 4th ed. (New York: Norton, 1987), pp. 357–89. For a discussion of French responses to foreigners in the 1920s and 1930s, see Ralph Schor, L'Opinion française et les étrangers, 1919–1939 (Paris: Publications de la Sorbonne, 1985). A helpful overview of this material can be found in Eugene Weber, "Foreigners," in The Hollow Years: France in the 1930s (New York: Norton, 1994).

87 Caron, Uneasy Asylum, p. 10. Caron successfully demonstrates a much greater fluctuation in refugee policy in the 1930s than previous scholars have suggested.

88 Circular, A. Bussissères, Directeur générale de la Sûreté nationale to Gouverneur
Général de l'Algérie; Monsieur le Préfet de Police, Messieurs les Préfets, no date,
no. 162, f/7/14711, AN. Circular, no. 114, "IIème instruction au sujet du régime ad-
ministratif des étrangers qui se trouvent dans l'impossibilité de quitter le territoire,"
25 August 1938, f/7/14711, AN.

89 Here I follow Caron *Uneasy Asylum*, p. 6, who argues that policies toward Nansen refugees were distinct from those for other refugee groups. As such, she argues against
those who have painted French refugee policy with broader strokes. See, for example, Noiriel, *Réfugiés et sans-papiers*, pp. 114–16, and Barbara Vormeier, "La Situation
administrative des exilés allemandes en France (1933–1945): Accueil-répression-
internement-déportation," *Revue d'Allemagne* 18, no. 2 (1986): 185.

90 As well as for those possessing German citizenship. Caron, *Uneasy Asylum*, p. 34.

91 Ibid., pp. 6, 17, 43–63, 136–38; Noiriel, *Réfuigés et sans-papiers*, p. 111; J. Simpson, *The
Refugee Problem*, pp. 252–56, 567–95.

92 Anahide Ter Minassian, "Les Arméniens et le Paris des libertés," in *Le Paris des étrangers depuis un siècle*, ed. André Kaspi and Antoine Marès (Paris: Imprimerie nationale,
1989), p. 130.

93 Lucien Rebatet, "L'Invasion: Les Étrangers en France," *Je suis partout*, 23 March 1935,
and "L'Invasion: Les Étrangers en France," *Je suis partout*, 2 March 1935. In response,
some local Armenians organized a meeting to debate his controversial statements
with him; Rebatet declined to attend. Aram Terzian, "Growth of the Armenian Community in Paris during the Interwar Years, 1919–39," *Armenian Review* 27, no. 3-107
(1974): 275. Le Tallec, *La Communauté arménienne de France*, p. 102, notes that in 1938,
Je suis Partout published a corrigendum recognizing that Armenians were not Jews.

94 Roland Destel, "Promenades et visites: Notre colonie arménienne, elle n'est pas as-
sez connue des Marseillais," *Le Marseillaise*, 10 May 1930, and "Promenades et visites:
Notre colonie arménienne, une ère de prospérité s'ouvre pour elle," *Le Marseillaise*,
24 May 1930.

95 François-Paul Raynal, "Cœurs en Exil: Soixante mille émigrés arméniens ont été
accueillis par la France fraternelle," *Le Petit Journal*, 6 June 1936; Camille Mauclair,
"Un noble peuple méconnu—les Arméniens," *L'Indépendant*, 5 August 1939.

96 Cited in Weber, *The Hollow Years*, p. 88. A translation of the term used by ancient
Greeks to designate aliens with no citizenship or other rights, *métèques* was adopted
by French nationalists as a pejorative term for aliens in France. For more on this and
on Maurras, see Weber, chap. 4.

97 In "The Antisemitic Revival of the 1930's: The Socioeconomic Dimension Reconsidered," *Journal of Modern History* 70 (March 1998): 22–73, Vicki Caron contests recent
arguments suggesting that 1930s French antisemitic campaigns were either part of
a wider xenophobia or a symbolic protest by which enemies of the Third Republic
could attack the state. For other discussions of French antisemitism in the 1930s,
see Pierre Birnbaum, *Un Mythe politique: "La République juive," De Léon Blum à Pierre Men-*

dès France (Paris: Fayard 1988); Marrus and Paxton, *Vichy France and the Jews*, pp. 25–71; Ralph Schor, *L'Antisémitisme en France pendant les années trente: Prélude à Vichy* (Brussels: Ed. Complexes, 1992); Richard Millman, *La Question juive entre les deux guerres: Ligues de droite et antisémitisme en France* (Paris: Armand Colin, 1992); Stephen A. Schuker, "Origins of the 'Jewish Problem' in the Later Third Republic," in *The Jews in Modern France*, ed. Frances Malino and Bernard Wasserstein (Hanover, N.H.: University Press of New England, 1985), pp. 135–80; Zeev Sternhell, "The Roots of Popular Antisemitism in the Third Republic," in Malino and Wasserstein, *The Jews in Modern France*, pp. 103–34.

98   Weber, *The Hollow Years*, p. 105.

99   Ministre de l'Intérieur, 4 September 1939 and 17 September 1939, f/7/14711, AN.

100 Marrus and Paxton, *Vichy France and the Jews*. The best overview of Vichy France remains Robert O. Paxton, *Vichy France: Old Guard and New Order, 1940–1944* (New York: Columbia University Press, 1972).

101 "Quarante-cinq Juifs, Arméniens, Turcs, et mauvais Français avaient créé une officine de marché noir," *Le Matin*, 14 October 1942. J. H. Probst, "Ce que doit être notre politique d'immigration dans une France rénovée," *Echo des étudiants*, 18 August 1943.

102 Louis Reynaud, "Race et nation," *Illustration*, 28 November 1942.

103 Nicholas Kossovitch, *Relations entre les groupes sanguines des Arméniens et les autres caractéristiques anthropométriques de cette race*, Institut international d'anthropologie, IIIe session, Amsterdam, 20–29 September 1927 (Paris: Librairie E. Nourry, 1928). See Schneider, *Quality and Quantity*, pp. 224–26.

104 "A Propos de métis et d'apatrides," *Illustration*, 16 January 1943. See Schneider, *Quality and Quantity*, pp. 231–55. According to John M. Efron, *Defenders of the Race: Jewish Doctors and Race Science in Fin-de-siècle Europe* (New Haven: Yale University Press, 1994), p. 10, despite France's long scientific tradition and sophisticated community of anthropologists, it contributed relatively little to racial debates about Jews. This, he explains, was due to the more secure position that Jews held in French society when compared to those in central and eastern Europe and to the nature of French antisemitism, which rarely existed for the sole aim of combating Jews but rather was co-opted into larger political causes such as royalism. Efron is certainly right to note the relatively small output of French race scientists on the Jewish Question, but it would be wrong to assume that Germans "displaced Jews as the principal target of French hostility" after the Franco-Prussian War. Antisemitism in France was certainly bound up in wider xenophobic sentiments and French Jews did, at times, escape the racial characterizations of non-French Jews; nevertheless, immigration theorists turned race science against the local Jewish population, particularly as the tensions of the 1930s and early 1940s mounted.

105 Georges Montandon, "Le Passeport ancestral et le discrimination entre citoyens et habitants en France, "*Le Soir*, 26 June 1942. See Schneider, *Quality and Quantity*, pp. 257–60.

106 Efron, *Defenders of the Race*, p. 4.

107 "Pour nos amis arméniens," *Appel*, 23 July 1942.

108 The Jewish race scientist Samuel Weissenberg conducted his own study of comparisons between Armenians and Jews. See Efron, *Defenders of the Race*, pp. 119–20.

109 A discussion of Armenian proclamations of loyalty is covered in chapter 3. For a more detailed discussion, see Maud Mandel, "In the Aftermath of Genocide: Armenians and Jews in Twentieth-Century France" (Ph.D. diss., University of Michigan, 1998), pp. 83–99. For a discussion of the most striking examples of French Jewish identification with the state, see Pierre Birnbaum, *Les fous de la République: Histoire politique des Juifs d'état de Gambetta à Vichy* (Paris: Fayard, 1992).

110 Sander L. Gilman, *Jewish Self-Hatred: Anti-Semitism and the Hidden Language of the Jews* (Baltimore: Johns Hopkins University Press, 1986), p. 2.

111 Caron, "The Antisemitic Revival of the 1930's," convincingly argues that antisemitism in France was "the last ditch effort of those groups seeking to preserve some vestige of the ancien régime, a vision of state and society based on corporate economic privilege, an authoritarian political order, and Christian values." In other words, antisemitism arose as a response to emancipation and was thus distinct from other xenophobic tendencies. Pierre Birnbaum, *Jewish Destinies: Citizenship, State, and Community in Modern France*, trans. Arthur Goldhammer (New York: Hill and Wang, 1999), pp. 178–88, also distinguishes compellingly between xenophobia and antisemitism in modern France, although he suggests that racism against Jews has been far less violent than that directed at foreign residents. However, he makes an exception of the Vichy years, when the republican state collapsed. To make this case, Birnbaum also points to the "enemy from within" paradigm, which in his view helps explain the particular nature of anti-Jewish rhetoric.

2 The Strange Silence: France, French Jews, and the Return to Republican Order

1 The phrase is that of Emanuel Mournier, the editor of *Esprit*, who devoted the journal's 1 September 1945 issue to the Jewish Question.

2 Eric Conan and Henry Rousso, *Vichy and Ever-Present Past*, trans. Nathan Bracher (Hanover, N.H.: University Press of New England, 1998), pp. 19–20, 51–52, make this point emphatically when discussing contemporary calls for memorialization on behalf of the victims.

3 Joseph Billig, *Le Commissariat Général aux questions juives, 1941–44* (Paris: Éditions du Centre, 1954–60).

4 Annie Kriegel, postface to Béatrice Philippe, *Être juif dans la société française du moyen-âge à nos jours* (Paris: Éditions Montalba, 1979), pp. 405–6, cited in Seth L. Wolitz, "Imagining the Jew in France from 1945 to the Present," *Yale French Studies 85: Discourses of Jewish Identity in Twentieth Century France* (1994): 119.

5 A precise Aryanization figure is hard to come by. The only two systematic counts

disagree with one another somewhat significantly due to the methodology used in obtaining the figures. The first study, Billig's *Le Commissariat Général aux questions juives, 1941–44*, vol. 3 (1960), was based on the files of the Commissariat-Général aux questions juives and counted assets (shops, companies, shares, etc.). The second, more recent study of Aryanization figures was conducted by the Mattéoli Commission (the 1997 study group established in France to consider the theft and restitution of Jewish property during and after World War II) and included Aryanization files that might have related to one or more assets. For a discussion of the Commission's methodology, see Mission d'étude sur la spoliation des Juifs de France, "Rapport d'étape," Paris, 1997. For the Commission's final approximation of Aryanization figures, see Mission d'étude sur la spoliation des Juifs de France, "Rapport général," Paris, 2000, pp. 163–64.

6   Michael Marrus, and Robert Paxton, *Vichy France and the Jews* (New York: Basic Books, 1981), p. 153.

7   Some prominent Jews, such as René Mayer, Pierre Mendès France, and René Cassin, were themselves involved in the liberation effort and in attempts to establish a new government in the postwar years.

8   In his initial analysis of French restitution policies, Zosa Szajkowski, *Analytical Franco-Jewish Gazetteer: 1939–1945* (New York: American Academy for Jewish Research, Lucius N. Littauer Foundation, Gustav Wurzweiler Foundation, 1966), chap. 32, argues that economic competition in the postwar era made the population extremely hostile to returning Jews. He concludes that the governmental bureaucracy, though not itself antisemitic, tended first and foremost to the needs of the larger population and catered to their prejudices. David Weinberg adopts a similar argument in "The Reconstruction of the French Jewish Community after World War II," in *She'erit Hapletah, 1944–1948: Rehabilitation and Political Struggle: Proceedings of the Sixth Yad Vashem International Historical Conference, Jerusalem 1985* (Jerusalem: Yad Vashem, 1990).

9   Recent reports from the Mattéoli Commission confirm this analysis: "Analysis of restitution and reparation measures demonstrates in fact that, unlike the original looting, which was based on a set of discriminatory legal criteria, restitution and reparation were handled in the main without reference to the notion of what is 'Jewish' arbitrarily applied by the occupation forces." Mission d'étude sur la spoliation des Juifs de France, "Rapport d'étape." Annette Wieviorka, "Despoliation, Reparation, Compensation," in *Starting the Twenty-First Century: Sociological Reflections & Challenges*, ed. Ernest Krausz and Gitta Tulea (New Brunswick, N.J.: Transaction Publishers, 2002), pp. 201–17, who served on the Mattéoli Commission, makes a similar point. Tony Kushner, *The Holocaust and the Liberal Imagination: A Social and Cultural History* (Cambridge, Mass.: Blackwell, 1994), chap. 7, has described a similar phenomenon in Britain and the United States. In these two countries, he argues, a dedication to liberal universalism prevented British and American society from coming to terms with the specificity of the Jewish plight during World War II.

10 Henry Rousso, *The Vichy Syndrome*, trans. Arthur Goldhammer (Cambridge, Mass.: Harvard University Press, 1991), pp. 15–27.

11 Recent historical exploration of the purges include Henri Amouroux, *La Grande Histoire des Français après l'Occupation*, vol. 9: *Les Règlements de comptes, septembre 1944–janvier 1945* (Paris: Robert Laffont, 1976–93); Philippe Buton and Jean-Marie Guillon, eds., *Les Pouvoirs en France à la Libération* (Paris: Belin 1994); Herbert R. Lottman, *L'Épuration, 1943–1953* (Paris: Fayard, 1986); François Rouquet, *L'Épuration dans l'administration française: Agents de l'État et collaboration ordinaire* (Paris: Éditions du CNRS, 1993); Henry Rousso, "L'Épuration en France: Une histoire inachevée," *Vingtième siècle revue d'histoire* 33 (1992): 78–105. Megan Koreman, *The Expectation of Justice, France 1944–1946* (Durham, N.C.: Duke University Press, 1999), argues that although a unified story of national liberation can be told, the process was actually quite complex and differed according to locale.

12 Jean-Pierre Rioux, *The Fourth Republic, 1944–58*, trans. Godfrey Rogers (Cambridge, England: Cambridge University Press, 1987), pp. 44–45. It should not be assumed that by returning to pre-Vichy forms of governing de Gaulle and his followers sought to reestablish the Third Republic. Indeed, as Andrew Shennan, *Rethinking France: Plans for Renewal, 1940–1946* (Oxford: Clarendon Press, 1989), p. 54, argues, de Gaulle's belief in "the primacy of national interest, the importance of collaboration between social classes, and the necessity of a post-war renewal of parliamentary institutions and political elites" displayed a dissatisfaction with both Vichy and the prewar regime.

13 Rioux, *The Fourth Republic, 1944–58*, pp. 17–28; Michael Kelly, Elizabeth Fallaize, and Anna Ridehalgh, "Crisis of Modernization," in *French Cultural Studies*, ed. Jill Forbes and Michael Kelly (New York: Oxford University Press, 1995), p. 105.

14 "Thousands of Jews in France Need American Assistance to Survive Winter, Arthur Greenleigh, J.D.C. Representative Declares," *News*, 23 August 1945(?), 311, American Joint Distribution Committee [AJDC]. The year of the article is not indicated on the document, but its content strongly suggests 1945.

15 Note concerning "Biens juifs," 2 September 1944, B10934, Archives du Ministère de Finance. As of 30 August 1944, the banks were asked to return any Jewish holdings that were *not* under the administration of an administrateur provisoire. This ruling also forbade banks from retaining 5 percent on the withdrawal of cash and securities, as they had done in the Unoccupied Zone since August 1942.

16 In 1943, the prefect of the Seine had decreed that all abandoned Jewish apartments should be given to war victims (*sinistrés*), repatriated prisoners, or functionaries named to Paris. Contrôleur général des administrateurs provisoires de biens israélites to Ministre de la Justice, Direction des affaires civiles, 7 August 1945, AJ/38/1111, AN.

17 Mme T. to Services des restitutions, 4 December 1945, Procès Verbal—5877, B41507, Archives du Ministère de Finance.

18 Préfet du Bas-Rhin to Pisani, Directeur du cabinet du Ministre de l'Intérieur, 3 March

1946, f/1a/3346, AN. The situation in Strasbourg was particularly difficult. One Jewish lawyer working on behalf of the dispossessed reported, "Strasbourg is a city that lost one third of its lodgings through bombings. Now [we face] housing one hundred percent of the population in sixty percent of the apartments without speaking of those occupied by innumerable civil and military officials." Housing problems, he reconfirmed, were leading to tensions between returning Jews and those already comfortably settled in their apartments. B. to M. Sarfaty, Service de restitution des biens spoliés, 25 July 1945, Dossier 11, AJ/38/1138, AN. For examples of such hostility throughout France, see Szajkowski, *Analytical Franco-Jewish Gazetteer*, pp. 107–11.

19   "Bagarres provoquées par des antisémites à l'occasion de la réintégration de locataires israélites évincés," *Bulletin d'information*, May 1945, 13/ 2–2, Jewish Theological Seminary (JTS).

20   Nina Gourfinkel, *Aux Prises avec mon temps: L'Autre patrie* (Paris: Éditions du Seuil, 1953), p. 314.

21   By-laws, Association française des propriétaires de biens aryanisés, AJ/38/1134, AN.

22   Pamphlet, Association nationale intercorporative du commerce, de l'industrie et de l'artisanat, AJ/38/1134, AN.

23   M. Y. to Service des domaines, 17 March 1945, Procès Verbal—1171, B41489, Archives du Ministère de Finance. Ets M., Manufacture d'appareils orthopédiques to Séquestre de l'ex-Commissariat aux questions juives, 15 March 1945, Dossier M., 139, AJ/38/1137, AN.

24   This "rational" response to Vichy's discriminatory policies was born during the war itself, when the policies were initially implemented. As Richard Weisberg argues in his study of Vichy's legal structure, *Vichy Law and the Holocaust in France* (New York: New York University Press, 1996), when the state adopted categorical distinctions between Jews and non-Jews, even those who did not display openly antisemitic attitudes were quick to implement the new legislation. A rational and bureaucratic approach to the legal system made persecution of Jews a "normal" part of the functioning of government.

25   Robert O. Paxton, *Vichy France: Old Guard and New Order, 1940–1944* (New York: Columbia Press, 1972), pp. 330–52.

26   Ibid., p. 342.

27   Michel F. to Ministre de l'Intérieur, 22 May 1946, f/1a/ 3345, AN.

28   L. W., 7 October 1944, AJ/38/1135, AN. The letter is not addressed to anyone in particular but is in a folder with other letters to the Commissaire de la république in Limoges.

29   E. Montel, President, Conseil général du département de la Haute Garonne to Ministre de l'Intérieur, 22 May 1946, f/1a/3345, AN.

30   Victor M. Bienstock, "Do the Jews of France Have a Future?" Jewish Telegraphic Agency, Inc., 1945, 311, AJDC. In many cases, public displays of antisemitism were countered by equally public attempts to suppress them. For example, the efforts of

a well-known café owner to keep antisemitic flyers in the window of his café were thwarted by indignant pedestrians who would tear them down. *Fraternité*, 4 May 1945. Some hostility was still directed at immigrant Jews and other non-French citizens, such as in an article in *France Revolution*, 3 December 1944, that warned against the dangers of bringing foreigners onto national territory. However, there was also a strong alternative voice; the Resistance paper *Unir*, for example, ran an article entitled "Il faut préparer le retour des prisonniers immigrées," 28 October 1944, which spoke of the importance of immigrants to France and of their role in liberating the country.

31 Ministre de l'Intérieur to les préfets, 6 December 1946, AJ/38/1135, AN.

32 Idith Zertal, *From Catastrophe to Power: Holocaust Survivors and the Emergence of Israel* (Berkeley: University of California Press, 1998), pp. 61–65, 86, points to the strong connections between the Ministry of the Interior and various prominent Jewish activists after the war as well as to the tremendous support and sympathy that that Ministry felt with regard to Jewish concerns, particularly Zionism.

33 Circulaire signed by Henri Viguier, Directeur du cabinet pour le Ministre de l'Intérieur, 31 January 1947, Dossier M., AJ/38/1137, AN. For further discussion of the destruction of these archives, which did indeed take place in 1948, see Conan and Rousso, *Vichy*, pp. 46–73.

34 Rousso, *The Vichy Syndrome*, pp. 15–27.

35 This is not to say that the government entirely ignored Jewish suffering under occupation. On 21 July 1946, the government participated in a commemoration of the thirty thousand Jews arrested on 16 July 1942 who were taken to the Vélodrome d'Hiver and then deported. On this occasion, a memorial plaque was hung and Laurent Casanova, the minister representing the government, mourned the deported Jews, denounced Vichy propaganda, and chastised the collaborators. Report, "Inauguration d'une plaque à la mémoire des 30.000 Israélites arrêtés le 16 Juillet 1942 et parqués au Vélodrome d'Hiver," 21 July 1946, f/1a/3368, AN.

36 Report, "Last Quarter 1944," 311, AJDC.

37 Annette Wieviorka, *Déportation et génocide: Entre la mémoire et l'oubli* (Paris: Plon, 1992), pp. 25–157; Koreman, *The Expectation of Justice*, pp. 74, 88.

38 Wieviorka, *Déportation et génocide*, pp. 20–21.

39 Those deportees who had not lived in France prior to the war but who sought shelter there in its aftermath faced a more difficult situation, as government officials tended to mistrust them. One example of such mistrust is evident in a circular from the Ministre de l'Intérieur to the commissaires régionaux et les préfets, "Étrangers rapatriés ou introduits en France à la suite de l'avance des armées alliés," 5 May 1945, f/1a/3346, AN.

40 Koreman, *The Expectation of Justice*, p. 79.

41 The government legislated pensions for political and racial deportees by placing them in the category of civilian war victims. Such pensions were awarded only to

French citizens and not to those of foreign birth who happened to be living in France at the time of their deportation. Until this day, French children of foreign parents have been refused compensation on the grounds that their parents were not citizens when they were deported. Mission d'étude sur la spoliation des Juifs de France, "Rapport d'étape."

42 Report, "Relief Situation in France, January through June 1945," 17 August 1945, 311, AJDC.

43 Arthur Greenleigh to Moses Leavitt, 7 April 1945, 311, AJDC.

44 Other Jewish agencies believed that antisemitic propaganda had proven less successful in France than in any other country under German occupation (with the possible exception of Holland and Belgium). While cautioning that the years of anti-Jewish rhetoric had left some impression on the native population, one report stressed that it "should not be an insuperable task to eliminate anti-Jewish feeling after the liberation of France and the restoration of her republican liberties before such sentiment has had time to naturalize itself on the French spirit." Report on the French Jewish community, Consultative Conference of the AIU, AJC, and AJA, June 1955, Anglo Jewish Association papers, AJ37/6/6/6/6, Parkes Library (although this report is located in the 1955 Consultative Conference file, its content suggests that it was written before France was entirely liberated).

45 Only one out of every one hundred Jews living in France in 1945 was a concentration camp survivor. Wieviorka, *Déportation et génocide*, p. 434.

46 Mission d'étude sur la spoliation des Juifs de France, "Rapport général," pp. 35–40.

47 Memoranda 3, Restitutions and Compensation, prepared in connection with the London Conference of Jewish Organizations, Anglo Jewish Association papers, AJ95/148, Parkes Library.

48 Directeur de l'aryanisation économique au Commissariat-Général aux questions juives to Général de Gaulle, 25 September 1944, AJ/38/1134, AN.

49 Pamphlet, Association nationale intercorporative du commerce, de l'industrie et de l'artisanat, AJ/38/1134, AN.

50 The pamphlet, "Pas de victimes privilégiées," is reprinted in *Bulletin d'information*, May 1945, 13/ 2–2, JTS.

51 For a list of the twelve most important of these pressure groups of Jewish property owners, see Szajkowski, *Analytical Franco-Jewish Gazetteer*, pp. 108. Complaints over government procrastination were echoed throughout the Jewish community. See, for example, the Centre de documentations des déportés et spoliés juifs' publication concerning the juridical position of Jews in France, in Jacques Rabinovitch and Raymond Sarrauté, *Examen succinct de la situation actuelle juridique des Juifs* (Paris: Centre de documentation des déportés et spoliés juifs, 1945), pp. 30–31. Also see André Weil Curiel and Raymond Castro, *Spoliation et restitution: Commentaire théorique et pratique de la législation relative aux spoliations* (Paris: Éditions R.G., 1945). Similarly, in a pamphlet directed at the National Assembly, the Mouvement national contre le racisme requested

that the government move more rapidly to restitute the losses of the twelve thousand families it calculated were dispossessed or unemployed. "Mouvement national contre le racisme s'adresse à l'Assemblée consultative," no date, 17/1–2, JTS.

52 Buton and Guillon, *Les Pouvoirs en France à la Libération*. For a discussion of the complexity of this power shift, see Koreman, *The Expectation of Justice*, pp. 8–47.

53 Arrêté, Commissariat de la république pour le Languedoc et le Roussillon, 22 September 1944, B10934, Archives du Ministère de Finance. Other regions followed similar patterns: Arrêté, Commissariat de la république d'Angers, 9 October 1944, B10935, Archives du Ministère de Finance. Délégué à la sauvegarde des biens israélites to the Comité d'unité et défense des Juifs de France, 30 October 1944, AJ/38/1138, AN. The folder entitled "Administrateurs séquestres, Arrêtés de nominations," AJ/38/1139, AN, is also relevant. The Service de la sauvegarde des biens israélites took charge of 164 dossiers concerning the pillaging in the department of Hérault.

54 In some cases, the new managers were Jewish themselves. In the reports by Gabriel D., he makes reference to "nos coreligionnaires," AJ/38/1139, AN.

55 L. to Préfet de l'Hérault, 26 October 1944, AJ/38/1138, AN, and Délégation à la sauvegarde des biens israélites to Préfet de l'Hérault, 16 November 1944, same folder.

56 Szajkowski, *Analytical Franco-Jewish Gazetteer*, p. 108.

57 Ordonnance du 14 Novembre 1944 portant application de l'ordonnance du 12 Novembre 1943 sur la nullité des actes de spoliations accomplis par l'ennemi ou sous son contrôle, B10934, Archives du Ministère de Finance. One measure preceding that of November 14 is worth noting. On 16 October 1944, the state property management agency was authorized to restore assets of all businesses and securities that had been confiscated and escrowed. In addition, another order was passed on 29 November 1944 which reinstated judges, civil servants, and military or civil personnel who had been recalled, forced into retirement, dismissed, or demoted under antisemitic laws. Mission d'étude sur la spoliation des Juifs de France, "Rapport d'étape."

58 Szajkowski, *Analytical Franco-Jewish Gazetteer*, p. 109. Szajkowski cites the publication of a 1945 handbook written by a French lawyer providing advice on how to avoid returning Jewish property and apartments: Roger Dalle, *Réintégration des Israélites* (Paris, 1945). Inside the book, an inscription in bright red letters reads, "Tenants, small merchants threatened with eviction, read this book!"

59 Rabinovitch and Sarraute, *Examen succinct de la situation actuelle juridique des Juifs*, p. 13. The Mouvement national contre le racism argued that the laws seemed more geared to prolonging the status quo than to providing justice for Jews or punishing the guilty. "Mouvement national contre le racisme s'adresse à l'Assemblée consultative," no date, 17/1–2, JTS.

60 "Rapport sur l'activité des Services de la sauvegarde des B.I. du département de l'Hérault depuis le 20 Novembre 1944 jusqu'au 20 Décembre," 20 December 1944, AJ/38/1138, AN.

61 Ordonnance du 14 Novembre 1944 concernant la réintégration de certains locataires,

AJ/38/1134, AN. These exceptions were disallowed in cases where the rented space was also originally used for a business or when the current occupant had collaborated with the Nazi government. In April 1945 a new law prevented all foreign nationals from claiming an apartment in which the present tenant had not yet found a new home. This new law reduced the effectiveness of the 14 November ordinance even further. Wieviorka, "Despoliation, Reparation, Compensation," p. 211, notes of these laws, "This decree during the bitter and chronic apartment crisis that started in France after the First World War illustrates the Republic's desire not to establish a special category concerning the deported people, which is present in the later legislation. This put within brackets something that was not properly understood: the uniqueness of the situation of the Jews during the war and after the Liberation." One report claimed that a full two months later "no single Jew had regained his former apartment because of the stringency of the qualifying conditions and the complexity of the procedures involved." Memoranda 3, Restitutions and Compensation, prepared in connection with the London Conference of Jewish Organizations, Anglo Jewish Association papers, AJ95/148, Parkes Library. In addition, even in cases where dispossessed Jews were able to obtain a judgment by the courts that their homes should be evacuated, they often encountered great difficulties in trying to evict the new occupants. *Bulletin d'information*, May 1945, 13/ 2–2, JTS.

62 Szajkowski, *Analytical Franco-Jewish Gazetteer*, p. 109. See also Renée Poznanski, "L'Héritage de la guerre: Le Sionisme en France dans les années 1944–1947," in *Les Juifs de France, le sionisme et l'état d'Israel*, ed. Doris Bensimon and Benjamin Pinkus (Paris: Publications Langues'O, 1989), p. 242.

63 *Le Front national*, 25 October 1945, for example, reported the story of a Mme W., who, after returning from Auschwitz and having lost her daughter and husband during the war, was unable to reclaim her apartment. The new owners not only refused to move but also rejected a proposal that she be allowed to use simply two rooms of the apartment. Mme. W. took the new owners to court, but a long delay in a decision kept her "in the street." D. Weinberg, "The Reconstruction of the French Jewish Community," p. 171, estimates that by 1951 only half of the estimated sixty-five thousand Jews in Paris whose homes had been occupied or sold had their apartments returned to them. The situation was worse, claims Szajkowski, *Analytical Franco-Jewish Gazetteer*, pp. 109–10, for poorer Jews because during the occupation it had been difficult to liquidate large holdings, and it was easier to arrange restitution when the purchaser had been the government or a large cooperation. For Jewish owners of small businesses or workshops, however, the situation was more difficult and harder to enforce. Moreover, the problems facing nonnaturalized Jews were particularly grave because they did not benefit from the November decrees.

64 Suzanne W., avocat à la Cour to M. Sarfaty, Séquestre de l'ex-Commissariat aux questions juives, Limoges, 23 January 1945, Dossier T., AJ/38/1137, AN.

65 Ordonnance 45–770 du 21 Avril 1945, AJ/38/1140, AN. The government did write laws

concerning the rights and obligations of the provisional administrators somewhat sooner. Décret 45–171 du 2 février 1945, AJ/38/1134, AN.

66 This included the issue of property confiscated from Jews detained and deported from internment camps. However, the implementation of the restitution of such assets followed a somewhat different course from property that could be claimed by those who had never been interned or deported, because at times entire families were deported together and no heirs came forward. Details of the restitution of property confiscated in such camps can be found in Annette Wieviorka, *Les Biens des internés des camps de Drancy, Pithiviers et Beaune-La-Rolande* (Paris: Mission d'étude sur la spoliation des Juifs de France, 2000) and Serge Klarsfeld, André Delahaye, and Diane Afoumado, *La Spoliation dans les camps de Province* (Paris: Mission d'étude sur la spoliation des Juifs de France, 2000).

67 Mission d'étude sur la spoliation des Juifs de France, "Rapport d'étape."

68 *Bulletin d'information*, May 1945, 13/ 2–2, JTS.

69 Several letters complaining about this missing legal text are located in "Courier: Service des restitutions du 1er Janvier au 31 Décembre," 1945, AJ/38/1134, AN. Jewish organizations also complained about the inequities of the April legislation. Conseiller juridique, Conseil Réprésentatif Israélite de France (CRIF), to Térroine, 17 October 1945, B10934, Archives du Ministère de Finance. Restitution of these accounts was extremely complex because several thousand accounts had been emptied to pay the 1 billion franc fine that the Germans imposed on France's Jewish population. Beginning in 1943, a tax of 5 percent was withheld on each transaction and paid to the Union générale des israélites de France to pay this collective debt. For more information on the restitution of the banking and financial sector, see Mission d'étude sur la spoliation des Juifs de France, "Dossier d'information sur les travaux en cours," Paris, 1998.

70 Térroine, Chef du service des restitutions des biens des victimes des lois et mesures de spoliations, to M. K., 4 February 1946, B10934, Archives du Ministère de Finance. K.'s original letter to the Minister of Finance, 18 January 1946, is in the same folder. Bour, Chef de cabinet, Ministre de finance to Térroine, 10 August 1945, B13097, Archives du Ministère de Finance. Térroine's response to Bour, 16 August 1945, is in the same carton.

71 Ministre de l'Intérieur to Ministre des Finances, 18 May 1946, B10934, Archives du Ministère de Finance.

72 Mission d'étude sur la spoliation des Juifs de France, "Rapport d'étape."

73 A copy of the laws creating the CGQJ and its by-laws is available in AJ/38/123, AN. For a detailed discussion of its history, see Marrus and Paxton, *Vichy France and the Jews*, chap. 4. On 21 August 1944, officials loyal to the last director of the CGQJ, Jean Antignac, destroyed files related to his tenure. Nevertheless, most remained available for scrutiny. Direction du Commissariat-Général aux questions juives to Ministre de la Justice, undated, AJ/38/1134, AN.

74 Directeur des domaines de la Seine to Térroine, 11 February 1946, B10934, Archives du Ministère de Finance. On 18 August, immediately after the liberation of Paris, Armillon, the Directeur des Services juridiques et du statut des personnes at the Commissariat-Général aux questions juives, took over for the former director, Jean Antignac. Armillon communicated directly with the Comité de libération de la région parisienne over how to proceed with the affairs of the Commissariat. Situation du Commissariat à la libération de Paris, AJ/38/1134, AN.

75 In early September, the provisional government named the Directeur des domaines de la Seine to take charge of the office. He saw his role as "purely administrative." As such, he managed personnel expenditures, rent, and all other managerial tasks connected to the occupation of the premises but was uninvolved in restitution activities of any kind. Ordonnance sur requête, Tribunal civil de la Seine, 2 September 1944, B10934, Archives du Ministère de Finance. On 13 October 1944, the Ministry of Finance authorized M. Janicot, Directeur des domaines du département de la Seine, to sign ordinances dealing with personnel and other expenses concerning the former Commissariat-Général aux questions juives. Arrêté, 13 October 1944, and Directeur des domaines to Térroine, 11 February 1946, in the same carton.

76 Not all restitution services were coordinated by this office. Those who had been pillaged by the CGQJ came to this office, whereas anyone who had been pillaged by the Germans requested aid from the Service de la reconstruction (dommages de guerre).

77 André Braun, Report, Service des restitutions, 6 September 1946, B13097, Archives du Ministère de Finance. Braun, a lawyer, took over for Térroine in May 1946.

78 Service de restitution des biens des victimes des lois et mesures de spoliation to Commissaire de la république, Marseille, 30 March 1945, B10934, Archives du Ministère de Finance. Térroine to Chef de la délégation régionale du service de restitution des biens des victimes des lois et mesures de spoliation, 30 October 1945, AJ/3/1135, AN. Those in Limoges, Lyon, Marseille, Nice, and Toulouse were already established by October 1945, but the other four still had to be set up. All other departments worked through the Parisian delegation.

79 Reports on the delegations of Limoges, Toulouse, Marseille, Nice, and Lyon can be found in "Rapports sur l'inspection des délégations régionales," B10934, Archives du Ministère de Finance. The central government's attempts to regulate and coordinate the different regions' activities faced some resistance. Occasionally local officials would implement their own policies, which were at odds with the restitution legislation being written in Paris. M. Calvet to Commissaires régionaux de la république, 21 April 1945, B10934, Archives du Ministère de Finance; M. Calvet to Commissaires régionaux de la république, 17 August 1945, B10935, Archives du Ministère de Finance. Such blatant dismissal of Parisian directives was rare, however. In most cases, regional delegates cooperated with national policies, even when they saw little purpose in being linked to the central administration. Such was the case of the Tou-

louse delegation that saw Paris's involvement as unnecessary and irrelevant. Délégué régionale de Toulouse to Térroine, 28 May 1945, AJ/38/1140, AN.

80 Fine artworks abandoned in this way were not handled by Térroine's office. Rather, a Commission de récupération artistique under the Ministry of Fine Arts, founded in November 1944, took responsibility for this task. The Commission dealt with all works of art, historical objects, archives, books, and manuscripts stolen by the enemy or under its control. Of the 61,527 artworks that France was able to recover, the Commission was able to return 45,441 to their rightful owners by 31 December 1949, the date when the Commission was disbanded. Mission d'étude sur la spoliation des Juifs de France, "Rapport d'étape."

81 Much of this property was the subject of a large-scale reparations program settled with Germany in the 1950s and administered by the Fonds social juif unifié in France.

82 Service des restitutions to all prefectures, 1 June 1945, B10934, Archives du Ministère de Finance; Ordonnance 45.624 du 11 Avril 1945, AJ/38/1140, AN.

83 Térroine to all prefectures and delegation heads, 1 June 1945, AJ/38/1140, AN.

84 Mme Alfred W. to Service des restitutions, 9 October 1945, B41491, Archives du Ministère de Finance. R. to Services des restitutions, 3 August 1945, Procès Verbal—1332, B41490, Archives du Ministère de Finance. The letter dated 13 September in the same file is also relevant. Those who had been dispossessed had two years to make a claim to the Ministry of Finance. At that point, all that had not been claimed was sold, with first priority going to those who had been despoiled during the war. Nevertheless, there were those unable to take advantage of restitution laws within the allotted time frame. Chef du Service des restitutions to M. S., 20 November 1947, Procès Verbal 1502, B41487, Archives du Ministère de Finance. In this case, S., who worked in London, was unable to pursue his restitution claims in Paris. He wrote in 1947 asking about his books and piano.

85 Préfet de la Moselle to Service des restitutions des biens, 9 January 1947, B13097, Archives du Ministère de Finance.

86 Note pour la presse et la radio, 8 June 1945, B13097, Archives du Ministère de Finance. For an example of one man who found and then "lost" his possessions: G. to M. Herzog, 30 June 1945, Procès Verbal—1062, B41487, Archives du Ministère de Finance. For a similar example where the client ultimately found much of her lost property: Procès Verbal—1112, B41488, Archives du Ministère de Finance.

87 P. for L. to Service des restitutions, 27 August 1947, Procès Verbal—1222, B41489, Archives du Ministère de Finance. W. to Service des restitutions, 13 August 1945, Procès Verbal 1213, B41489, Archives du Ministère de Finance. Mme W. to Services des restitutions, 26 May 1945, Procès Verbal 1369, B41491, Archives du Ministère de Finance.

88 Braun to M. Henri L., 17 March 1947, Procès Verbal—1410, B41491, Archives du Ministère de Finance, and complaint letter from Henri L. to Ministre des Finances, 27 February 1947, same file. L. claims to be a political deportee (not a racial deportee),

although this does not mean he was not Jewish; many of the initial deportees were called political deportees when they were actually being deported as Jews. He claims in his letter that his original inventory was written from a hospital bed in June 1945 where he was recovering from typhus after having survived twenty months in Auschwitz. The lack of detail, he argues, was quite justifiable given his physical and mental condition of the time.

89 Procès Verbal—1070, B41487, Archives du Ministère de Finance. Procès Verbal—1173, B41489, Archives du Ministère de Finance. In this case, the client submitted a second inventory after visiting the depots several times. The head of restitution services dismissed this client's claims, but the battle between them raged until the 1950s, when the Ministry of the Interior got involved. Some did not consider a court battle worth their time. An example of a client who decided that "in light of all the administrative complications, I'd prefer not to lose my time" can be found in Procès Verbal—1429, B41491, Archives du Ministère de Finance.

90 Mme G. to Ministre des Finances, 10 July 1945, Procès Verbal—1013, B41487, Archives du Ministère de Finance.

91 On one occasion, Térroine asked the Minister of Finance to forward to the Ministry of the Interior some antisemitic literature he had received. He forwarded the same report to the police, urging both to keep a close eye on antisemitic groups. Térroine to Ministre des Finances, 17 May 1945, B13097, Archives du Ministère de Finance.

92 Chef de Service des restitutions to G., 30 March 1945, Procès Verbal 1092/1237, B41488, Archives du Ministère de Finance. In response to G.'s complaint, Térroine could only reiterate those laws. While expressing regret that she had found so little of her property, he insisted that most of the objects that had disappeared had been sent to Germany. All unidentifiable belongings, he added, had been given to Entr'aide française, who was distributing them to those in need; Madame G. would have to return there if she wanted help. Térroine to Auguet, 25 September 1945, Procès Verbal—1013, B41487, Archives du Ministère de Finance.

93 Térroine to Rampon, Directeur du Cabinet, 19 March 1946, B13097, Archives du Ministère de Finance. Report by Braun, 6 September 1946 B13097, Archives du Ministère de Finance.

94 The Limoges office, for example, was closed as of April 1 1947. Chef du service des restitutions to Chef de la délégation régionale du service des restitutions, 15 January 1946?, AJ/38/1135, AN. The Toulouse office was closed earlier, on 1 October 1946. Délégué régional to chef du service des restitutions, 2 September 1946, AJ/38/1140, AN.

95 Mission d'étude sur la spoliation des Juifs de France, "Dossier d'information sur les travaux en cours." Remis à Lionel Jospin, en novembre 1998.

96 Mme C. to Services des restitutions, 18 October 1945, Procès Verbal—4704, B41502, Archives du Ministère de Finance.

97 For a discussion of the administrateurs provisoires, see Marrus and Paxton, *Vichy*

France, pp. 152–60. For a more detailed examination of their standing in French law, see Weisberg, *Vichy Law*, pp. 251–56, 281–92. Information on the dismissal of Jewish employees was found in Report on the French Jewish community, Consultative Conference of the AIU, AJC, and AJA, June 1955, in Anglo Jewish Association papers, AJ37/6/6/6/6, Parkes Library.

98 Mission d'étude sur la spoliation des Juifs de France, "Dossier d'information sur les travaux en cours."

99 In Hérault, for example, the prefect instructed local bank directors to block all accounts open in the name of those administrateurs provisoires who had managed Jewish property. Préfet de l'Hérault to bank directors, 22 September 1944, AJ/38/1138, AN.

100 Exploitation générale de chiffons pour papeteries et effilochage to Séquestre de l'ex-Commissariat aux questions juives, 8 March 1945, Dossier S., 178, AJ/38/1137, AN. Dossier J., 92, AJ/38/1136, AN.

101 Billig, *Le Commissariat Général aux questions juives*, p. 282, cited in Weisberg, *Vichy Law*, p. 282. Le rapport Formery, 12–23 May 1944, cited in Marrus and Paxton, *Vichy France*, p. 157. While Louis-Gabriel Formery, the inspector of finances under Vichy, examined the administrateurs provisoires looking for means to improve on Aryanization (not to obstruct it), he concluded that a number of them were dishonest and were working to defraud Jews and the state (although some were covering and concealing Jewish property as well).

102 Zélick J. to Service des restitutions, 21 August 1945, B10934, Archives du Ministère de Finance. Felix B., Manufacture strasbourgeoise de chemises pour hommes, to Séquestre du Commissariat aux questions juives, Limoges, 24 March 1945, Dossier B., Felix, 19, AJ/38/1136, AN. L'Union de résistance et d'entr'aide des Juifs de France to M. Sarfaty, 22 March 1945, Dossier B., 25, AJ/38/1136, AN.

103 B. to the Séquestre de l'ex-Commissariat aux affaires juives, Limoges, Dossier B., 16, AJ/38/1136, AN. Armand L. to Union de résistance et d'entr'aide des Juifs de France, Dossier L., 127, AJ/38/1137, AN.

104 Circulaire, Association des administrateurs provisoires de France, 23 September 1944, AJ/38/1134, AN. This organization was actually founded in February 1944, several months before the war ended. During its first few months (prior to liberation) its goals included facilitating the carrying out of the administrateurs' functions; defending their rights against any claims; and representing them to the Commissariat-Général des questions juives as well as to the entire national administration. By-laws, Association des administrateurs provisoires de France, AJ/38/1134, AN. Marrus and Paxton, *Vichy France*, p. 296. There were also advocacy groups pleading for the "other side," such as the Association national pour les victimes des persécutions nazies. This group had "no political or confessional character." It is also worth noting that the Association de défense des français israélites dépossédés par les allemands was established in September 1944. Documents concerning all three groups are located

in "Situation des administrateurs provisoires," AJ/38/1134, AN. Even broader was the work of the Secours français, which fought for, among other things, reparations for "all victims of fascism, the war, poverty, social injustices and natural calamities." By-laws, Secours français, 13/2–1, JTS.

105 Association des administrateurs provisoires de France to Fremont, Directeur du blocus, Ministère des Finances, October 1944, AJ/38/1134, AN. This letter is followed by an Exposé relatif aux administrateurs provisoires, which continues to defend their actions in some detail.

106 Albert Neuville, "Rapport sur la situation des administrateurs provisoires des entreprises ayant pour objet le commerce de banque ou les fonctions d'intermédiaires dans les bourses de valeurs qui ont été mises dans l'impossibilité de faire de nouvelles operations de banque ou de bourse," 25 June 1945, B13097, Archives du Ministère de Finance.

107 Such was the opinion of the Minister of Finance. Projet de note au Ministre des Finances, no date, AJ/38/1134, AN. It is clear that this proposal was written in response to requests made by the Association des administrateurs provisoires, 30 September 1944.

108 Contrôleur général adjoint des administrateurs provisoires de biens israélites to Mme la Concierge, 39 avenue de la république, 8 June 1945, Classeur 2, AJ/38/1110, AN.

109 Some administrateurs, for example, were known to have compelled former Jewish proprietors to turn over profits from months before the trusteeship had been installed by threatening to have them declared guilty of fraudulent bankruptcy. Report on the French Jewish community, Consultative Conference of the AIU, AJC, and AJA, June 1955, in Anglo Jewish Association papers, AJ37/6/6/6/6, Parkes Library.

110 Weisberg, Vichy Law, pp. 281–88.

111 Memoranda 3, Restitutions and Compensation, prepared in connection with the London Conference of Jewish Organizations, Anglo Jewish Association papers, AJ95/148, Parkes Library.

112 Report, Albert Neuville, "Rapport sur la situation des administrateurs provisoires des entreprises ayant pour objet le commerce de banque ou les fonctions d'intermédiaires dans les bourses de valeurs qui ont été mises dans l'impossibilité de faire de nouvelles operations de banque ou de bourse," 25 June 1945, B13097, Archives du Ministère de Finance.

113 One example is noted in André Weiss, Préfet de l'Hérault, to Etienne W., 2 September 1945, AJ/38/1138, AN. Due to a socialist amendment in the Assembly in May 1945, a compromise ordinance was adopted that softened the impact of trusteeship on Jewish victims by voiding all confiscations and false sales. As a result, legitimate profits were to be returned to the owner and damage made good by the persons who had acquired the property. If the latter was insolvent or had disappeared, the rightful owner could ask the state for compensation on the same terms as if he had suffered war

losses. Memoranda 3, Restitutions and Compensation, prepared in connection with the London Conference of Jewish Organizations, Anglo Jewish Association papers, AJ95/148, Parkes Library.

114 Contrôleur des administrateurs provisoires de biens israélites to Commissaire de police, 18 September 1945, Classeur 4, AJ/38/1112, AN. Examples of such cases against different administrateurs provisoires are available in "Rapport d'activité du Séquestre de l'ex-Commissariat aux questions juives, mois de Mai et Juin 1945," AJ/38/1135, AN. This report, which deals only with the Limoges region, also includes some cases where the former administrateur did restitute all required sums.

115 Contrôle des administrateurs provisoires de biens israélites to Ministre du travail, Office régional de la main d'œuvre, 2 March 1945, Classeur 1, AJ/38/1109, AN. Former administrateurs provisoires often misunderstood the purpose of this office, believing it would advocate on their behalf. Many, for example, wrote requesting aid or information regarding remuneration. One example is noted in Contrôleur des administrateurs provisoires de biens israélites to Daniel K. et fils, 12 March 1945, Classeur 1, AJ/38/1109, AN. Many cases never went before the courts. Sometimes, the administrator and the dispossessed French Jews settled among themselves. One such case can be found in Contrôleur général adjoint des administrateurs provisoires de biens israélites to Mme P., 11 June 1945, AJ/38/1110, AN. In this case, the administrateur offered to settle out of court.

116 In June 1945, the office established delegations in Lyon, Grenoble, Clermont-Ferrand, Bourges, and Orleans. At the end of July, they added Marseille, Nice (which included Cannes, Grasse, and Toulon), Nîmes, and Montpellier. Then at the end of September, delegations were set up in Poitiers, Bordeaux, Agen, Toulouse, Pau, and Limoges and shortly thereafter in Angers, Nantes, Rennes, Caen, and Rouen. In October 1945, Lille and Amiens were added to the list. The regions differed dramatically from one another. Toulouse, for example, had 3,500 dossiers to sort through, while in Poitiers there were few Jewish businesses placed under administration and those few had already been restituted by fall 1945. In Agen, "the Israélites in the region were mostly refugees and did not possess much property," hence the number of cases was quite small. Contrôleur des administrateurs provisoires de biens israélites to Ministre de la Justice, Direction des affaires civiles, 21 September, 1945, AJ/38/1112, AN. Information concerning the establishment of the other delegations are in this carton as well as in AJ/38/1110.

117 Note sur l'organisation du Service de contrôle des administrateurs provisoires et liquidateurs des biens israélites: création–attributions–situation actuelle du service, 16 February 1948, Classeur 24, AJ/3/1132, AN. Contrôleur général des administrateurs provisoires de biens israélites to Ministre de la Justice, 14 April 1945, Classeur 1, AJ/38/1109, AN, and Contrôleur général des administrateurs provisoires de biens israélites to Chef du Service des restitutions, 17 May 1945, same file. Rapport sur la situation du Service du contrôle des administrateurs provisoires de biens israélites à

la date du 10 Novembre 1945, Classeur 5, AJ/38/1113, AN. Note sur l'organisation du Service de contrôle des administrateurs provisoires et liquidateurs de biens israél- ites: création - attributions - situation actuelle du service, 16 February 1948, Classeur 24, AJ/3/1132, AN.

118 Report on Affaire Benjamin L. c/ C., 16 April 1945, Classeur 1, AJ/38/1109, AN.

119 Report on Affaire H-A., Vêtement moderne et Ste parisienne du vêtement c/ P-G., 16 April 1945, Classeur 1, AJ/38/1109, AN. Report on E. c/V., 6 November 1945, Clas- seur 5, AJ/38/1113, AN.

120 For one example of the comptroller's attempts to settle such a case, Contrôleur des administrateurs provisoires de biens israélites to the Chef du Service des restitutions, 15 March 1945, AJ/38/1109, AN. Contrôleur des administrateurs provisoires de biens israélites to Térroine, 3 April 1945, Classeur 1, AJ/38/1109, AN.

121 This is not to say that no restitution activity took place after that date. For example, an act of 16 June 1948 made the state liable for reimbursing victims for withholdings handed over to the Treuhand or the Commissariat-Général as well as fees charged by the administrateurs provisoires. Mission d'étude sur la spoliation des Juifs de France, "Dossier d'information sur les travaux en cours." Such efforts at restitution petered out at the beginning of the 1950s. Note sur l'organisation du Service de con- trôle des administrateurs provisoires et liquidateurs de biens israélites: Création– Attributions–Situation actuelle du service, 16 February 1948, Classeur 24, AJ/3/1132, AN. When the service was closed, it had investigated nearly all of the six thou- sand complaints filed against administrators (in some cases, several claims were filed against the same administrator). Mission d'étude sur la spoliation des Juifs de France, "Extraits du deuxième rapport d'étape." Remis à Lionel Jospin, en jan- vier 1999.

122 Victor M. Bienstock, "Do the Jews of France Have a Future?" Jewish Telegraphic Agency, Inc., 1945, 311, AJDC.

123 *Bulletin du Centre israélite d'information,* 15 November 1945, 12/5, JTS.

124 Not surprisingly, recently arrived Jewish immigrants were those who had the hard- est time reclaiming stolen assets. Of course, the reason much property was never claimed was because widespread deportation had led to the deaths of entire families, with nobody left to search for stolen property. Mission d'étude sur la spoliation des Juifs de France, "Dossier d'information sur les travaux en cours."

125 Maud Mandel, "Philanthropy or Cultural Imperialism? The Impact of American Jew- ish Aid in Post-Holocaust France," *Jewish Social Studies* 9, no. 1 (2002): 53–94.

3 Integrating into the Polity: The Problem of Inclusion after Genocide

1 Anthony Smith, "Ethnic Nationalism and the Plight of Minorities," in *Myths and Memories of the Nation* (Oxford: Oxford University Press, 1999), p. 198.

2 Aïda Boudjikanian-Keuroghlian, "Un peuple en exil: La Nouvelle diaspora (XIXe–

XXe siècles)," in *Histoire des Arméniens*, ed. Gérard Dédéyan (Toulouse: Éditions Privat, 1982), pp. 627–31; S. Andesian and M. Hovanessian, "L'Arménien: Langue rescappée d'un génocide," in *Vingt-cinq communautés linguistiques de la France*, ed., Genevieve Vermès (Paris: L'Harmattan, 1988), 2: 66–67. Paris quickly became the center of Armenian life, with approximately 30,000 establishing roots there between 1922 and 1925. Marseille also had well over 20,000. Lyons counted the third largest Armenian population. See Levon Ch'ormisean, *Fransahayeru patmut'iwně*, Vol. 1: *Hay sp'iwṛk'ē* (Beirut: Imprimerie G. Doniguian, 1975), p. 233; John Hope Simpson, *The Refugee Problem: Report of a Survey* (London: Oxford University Press, 1939), p. 318.

3 Exchange between Pachalian (Secrétaire général, Comité central des réfugiés arméniens) and Berron (Action Chrétienne en Orient), 9–30 June 1925, Associations arménophiles, Délégation national, Bibliothèque Nubar.

4 Ch'ormisean, *Fransahayeru patmut'iwně*, pp. 233–34; Anahide Ter Minassian, "Les Arméniens et le Paris des libertés," in *Le Paris des étrangers depuis un siècle*, ed. André Kaspi and Antoine Marès (Paris: Imprimerie nationale, 1989), p. 123.

5 Jean Der Sarkissian and Lucie Der Sarkissian, *Les Pommes rouges d'Arménie* (Paris: Flammarion, 1987), p. 13.

6 André Sernin, *L'Homme de Tokat* (Paris: Editions France-Empire 1987), pp. 78–80. This book is based on interviews that Sernin did with his neighbor, Edouard Khédérian, in which the author took certain narrative liberties. Nevertheless, the story provides enough rich detail about Khédérian's experiences that it remains a useful source.

7 Secrétaire general, Comité central des réfugiés arméniens to Préfet de Police, 2 march 1927, Délégation national, Bibliothèque Nubar.

8 Martine Hovanessian, *Le Lien communautaire: Trois générations d'arméniens* (Paris: Armand Colin, 1992).

9 "Relevé des journées passées au Camp Ste Marthe par les sujets Arméniens," 26 October 1922, 4M957, Bouches-du-Rhône. Of the total camp population, 178 were designated "Assyro-Chaldéens." Préfet des Bouches-du-Rhône to Ministre de l'hygiène, de l'assistance et de la prévoyance sociales, 12 December 1923, 4M957, Bouches-du-Rhône. The demographic breakdown reflected the makeup of Marseille's Armenian population, half of whom were women, according to one press account, and half men. "Fransabnak Hayeru t'iwě," *Pahak*, 20 March 1938. The number is particularly striking when compared to other immigrant groups. According to another article, women made up only 57,585 of the 206,647 foreigners in Marseille. "Ōtarakanner Marsilioy mēj," *Haṛaj*, 1 March 1933. For more on the large numbers of Armenian women and children, see Aïda Boudjikanian-Keuroghlian, *Les Arméniens dans la région Rhône-Alpes: Essai géographique sur les rapports d'une minorité ethnique avec son milieu d'accueil* (Lyon: Association des Amis de la Revue de géographie de Lyon, 1978), pp. 87–88.

10 Attard-Maraninchi and Temime, *Le Cosmopolitisme de l'entre-deux-guerres*, p. 51. Directeur des réfugiés arméniens du Camp Oddo to Chef de Division à la préfecture des Bouches-du-Rhône, 26 November 1923, 4M957, Bouches-du-Rhône. Many of the

agricultural workers worked only seasonally and found themselves without income in the winter months. Préfet des Bouches-du-Rhône to Ministre de l'hygiène, de l'assistance et de la prévoyance sociales, 12 December 1925, 4M957, Bouches-du-Rhône.

11 Letters regarding the increasing camp population are located in 4M957, Bouches-du-Rhône. For a discussion of the establishment and functioning of Camp Oddo, see Marie-Françoise Attard-Maraninchi and Emile Temime, *Le Cosmopolitisme de l'entre-deux-guerres (1919–1945)*, vol. 3: *Histoire des migrations à Marseille* (Marseille: Edisud, 1990), pp. 47–55. Also helpful is Edmond Khayadjian, "La Communauté arménienne de Marseille," *Marseille, Revue municipale trimestrielle* 118 (1979): 32–39.

12 In November 1923, as many as five hundred of the camp's residents were destitute. Préfet to Président du Conseil, Ministre des affaires étrangères, Ministre de l'intérieur, 23 October 1923, 4M957, Bouches-du-Rhône. Reports on theft come from Commissaire spécial to Préfet des Bouches-du-Rhône, "Arrivées d'orientaux provenant de Constantinople de la Mer Noire," 6 September 1923, 4M957, Bouches-du-Rhône.

13 Police report, 2 June 1927, f/7/13436, AN. Ter Minassian, "Les Arméniens et le Paris des libertés," p. 121. Not surprisingly, these employers where highly invested in their laborers and thus proved quite determined that they complete the terms of their contract. In cases where the refugee refused, the employer expected repayment for any investment. Such was the case, for example, when one young Armenian refugee was brought to France as an agricultural worker. After arriving at the reception center in Bayon, however, he refused to work, arguing that he already had a profession that he wanted to practice. He was allowed to leave but only after having given his passport to his employers as a guarantee that he would pay back the cost of his travel expenses to France and his lodging in Bayon once he found other employment. Administrateur Délégué, Registre du Commerce, Cooperative Agricole de Bayon, 29 September 1923, Fransa gtnowoṛ gaght'aknner, Délégation Nationale, Bibliothèque Nubar.

14 Boudjikanian-Keuroghlian, *Les Arméniens dans la region Rhône-Alpes*, p. 94. According to Ter Minassian, "Les Arméniens et le Paris des libertés," p. 133, these figures tapered off during the economic crisis of the 1930s.

15 Ludovic Nadeau, "Enquête sur la population de la France," cited in "Comment les autres nous voient," *Le Foyer*, 1 September 1929. "Les Enquêtes du 'Radical,' M. le Préfet sait-il que le Camp Oddo où s'entassent Syriens et Arméniens est une véritable honte pour notre cité," no date, "Réfugiés du Camp Oddo, 1922–7," previously M6 9770 but not currently classified, Bouches-du-Rhône. Attard-Maraninchi and Temime, *Le Cosmopolitisme de l'entre-deux-guerres*, p. 52.

16 The Comité de secours, which later transformed itself into the Union national arménienne de Marseille, also sought to preserve a sense of union among local Armenians and to serve as their intermediary to the government. Statuts, Union national arménienne de Marseille, 26 June 1924, 4M693, Bouches-du-Rhône. Residents

also received funds from Armenians living outside the camp and from local charity organizations, particularly the Alliance française. Sources on camp funding include Commissaire spécial to Préfet des Bouches-du-Rhône, "Arméniens," 18 September 1923 and Préfet to Ministre de l'hygiène, et l'assistance et de la prévoyance sociales, 15 March 1924, 4M957, Bouches-du-Rhone; Commissaire spécial chargé du Camp Oddo to Préfet des Bouches-du-Rhône, 28 May 1926, 4M964, Bouches-du-Rhône; Attard-Maraninchi and Temime, *Le Cosmopolitisme de l'entre-deux-guerres (1919–1945)*, pp. 51–55.

17   For information on Armenians in the Légion d'Orient, see Cyril le Tallec, *La Communauté arménienne de France, 1920–1950* (Paris: L'Harmattan, 2001), pp. 12–16.

18   Note II, "Réfugiés arméniens," Général de division, Breton, Commandant d'armes délégué, 25 November 1922, 4M957, Bouches-du-Rhône. Takvor Hatchikian to Président du Conseil, 2 July 1925, Fransa gtnowoṛ gaght'aknner, Délégation Nationale, Bibliothèque Nubar.

19   Michael Marrus and Robert Paxton, *Vichy France and the Jews* (New York: Basic Books, 1981).

20   Edouard B. to Sarfaty, Service de restitution des biens spoliés, Limoges, 12 October 1945, Dossier avocats, B., AJ/38/1136, AN. *Activité des organisations juives en France sous l'occupation, Études et monographies* (Paris: Centre de Documentation juive contemporaine, 1947), p. 28.

21   Reprinted in Samuel René Kapel, *Au Lendemain de la Shoa: Témoignage sur la naissance du Judaïsme de France et d'Afrique du Nord, 1945–1954* (Jerusalem: Diffusion, R. Mass, 1991), p. 9. More information on the postwar situation in Alsace can be found in Jacob Kaplan, "La Renaissance du judaïsme français," in *Reconstruction of European Jewish Life and the Conference of European Rabbis*, ed. Rabbi Maurice Rose (London: Conference of European Rabbis, Standing Committee, 1967), pp. 59–60.

22   Jacques Adler, *The Jews of Paris and the Final Solution: Communal Response and Internal Conflicts, 1940–44* (Oxford: Oxford University Press, 1985), p. 14, indicates that of the 76,000 Jews deported to concentration camps, 16,000 were of French descent; 60,000 were either naturalized or immigrants.

23   Minutes, 7 March 1945, AA26, Consistoire de Paris.

24   Paul B., 23 October 1944, Procès-verbal 1444, B41492, Archives du Ministère de Finance. Camille C. to Directeur de l'administration des domaines, 6 December 1944, Procès-verbal 1161, B41489, Archives du Ministère de Finance.

25   Report for France for Last Quarter 1944, 311, AJDC.

26   The records of the Ministry of Finance provide several examples of well-known Jews applying for restitution. Two examples are Procès-verbal 1225, B441489, and Procès-verbal 1750, B41495, Archives du Ministère de Finance. Edouard B. to Sarfaty, 25 July 1945, Dossier 11, AJ/38/1136, AN. "Economic Reconstruction and Rehabilitation in Europe: Some Notes and Statistics on Reconstruction Activities, 1944–8," Reconstruction Department, European Executive Council, no date, 3462, AJDC.

27   Annette Wieviorka, "Les Juifs en France au lendemain de la guerre: État des lieux," *Archives juives: Revue d'histoire des Juifs de France* 28, no. 1 (1995): 5–6. Wieviorka notes that although most did return to Paris, some opted to remain in the provinces, modifying the geographical spread of Jews in France permanently.

28   Report for France for Last Quarter 1944, 311, AJDC. René C., Comptabilité to Préfet de l'Hérault, 18 October 1944, AJ/38/1138, AN.

29   Arthur Greenleigh, "Comments on Program for France" 3 December 1945, 311, AJDC.

30   Berthe R. to Service des restitutions biens des victimes des lois et mesures de spoliations, 7 August 1945, AJ/38/1134, AN. Jules D. to Ministre des Finances, 30 November 1944, AJ/38/1134, AN. L., 24 October 1944, Procès-verbal 1222, B41489, Archives du Ministère de Finance. The L. family had migrated to Germany from Poland in 1933, only to flee again shortly thereafter. Hardly had they settled in Paris when war broke out. They escaped deportation but lost their apartment and entire extended family. See also Jacquiline C. to the Union de résistance et d'entr'aide des Juifs de France, 24 April 1945, AJ/38/1136, AN.

31   Guy de Rothschild to Mr. Baerwald, 8 May 1945, 311, AJDC. "Pour nos déportés," Union des Juifs pour la résistance et l'entr'aide, 8 March 1945, French Jewish Communities, 13/2–1, JTS. Renée P. to Ministre des Finances, 8 November 1944, B41487, Archives du Ministère de Finance. "Relief Situation in France, January through June 1945," 17 August 1945, 311, AJDC.

32   According to estimates, approximately 11 million displaced Europeans were seeking repatriation or a new home when the Nazis were finally defeated. In the subsequent months, great masses of people headed for their former countries and were able to repatriate surprisingly rapidly given the collapse of most normal communication and transportation systems. For surviving Jews, however, returning home was rarely an option, as in many regions hostility toward Jews continued to flare even after the war's end. Michael Marrus, *The Unwanted: European Refugees in the Twentieth Century* (New York: Oxford University Press, 1985), pp. 297–98, 331–39.

33   In some cases, Jewish organizations worked with French immigration authorities to bring handicraft and unskilled workers into the national labor force. Mazor to Leftwich, 15 November 1947, Federation of Jewish Relief Organizations (FJRO) 62/1, Parkes Library. Jewish officials estimated that by the end of 1946, 10,000 Jewish refugees had migrated legally to France and another 15,000 had come without proper papers. Minutes, 7 December 1946, AA26, Consistoire de Paris. According to numbers issued by the AJDC, 1,500 to 2,000 refugees were coming to France each month in 1946. Report 369, "Current activities with respect to immigration from Poland to France," October 1946, 328, AJDC.

34   Doris Bensimon and Sergio Della Pergola, *La Population juive de France: Socio-démographie et identité* (Jerusalem: Institute of Contemporary Jewry, 1984), p. 36. Mazor, FJRO, to Dr. Cymerman, 25 March 1949, FJRO 61, Parkes Library.

35 Mazor to Dr. Cymerman, 25 March 1949, FJRO 61, Parkes Library. Robert Gamzon, "The Fight for Survival Goes On," 1946, 311, AJDC.

36 By 1935, the FSJF pulled together eighty-five loosely affiliated mutual aid and charitable organizations dedicated to serving the intellectual and practical needs of Jewish immigrants. Paula Hyman, *From Dreyfus to Vichy: The Remaking of French Jewry, 1906–1939* (New York: Columbia University Press, 1979), p. 86.

37 Report, Office for France Activities, May 1948 through September 1948, 310, AJDC.

38 In Limoges, for example, the UJRE was active helping Jews regain apartments. Union de résistance et d'entre'aide des Juifs de France to Commissaire de la République à Limoges, 26 October 1944, AJ/38/1135, AN. The UJRE also helped many Jews reclaim stolen goods. H. to Union de résistance et d'entr'aide des Juifs de France, 12 March 1945, Dossier 89, AJ/38/1136, AN. Examples of their attempts to lobby on behalf of Jewish interests are evident in a letter from the UJRE to Directeur du service économique et du blocus, Marseille, 25 October 1944, B10934, Archives du Ministère de Finance.

39 Sabine Zeitoun, *L'Œuvre de secours aux enfants (OSE) sous l'occupation en France* (Paris: L'Harmattan, 1990).

40 An example of a Jewish man who could not return to Paris because his former apartment was occupied can be found in Procès-verbal 1281, B41490, Archives du Ministère de Finance. Also see Wieviorka, "Les Juifs en France au lendemain de la guerre," pp. 4–22.

41 In Edouard B.'s above-cited letter, he remarks that 90 percent of the lawyer's professional work in Strasbourg "consists of attending to problems caused by the war."

42 Marcel L.'s claim on behalf of his deported brother-in-law, for example, took a year and a half to settle. Dossier 13, AJ/38/1136, AN.

43 The folder "Jugements," AJ/38/1140, AN, for example, holds records of thirty-five such cases, most of which date from summer 1945.

44 Edward A., 11 June 1945, Procès-verbal 1492, B41492, Archives du Ministère de Finance. L.'s struggle to regain her belongings after a four-and-a-half-year forced absence stretched at least until May 1946 and maybe far longer. Procès-verbal 1272, B41490, Archives du Ministère de Finance.

45 Kaplan, "La Renaissance du Judaïsme français," p. 60, reported in 1963 that the decade after the war was characterized by numerous marriages and high birthrates.

46 Henri Verneuil, *Mayrig* (Paris: Robert Laffont, 1985), pp. 13–14. Marig Ohanian, *Un Arménien parmi les autres* (Paris: Back, 1988), p. 152.

47 Verneuil, *Mayrig*, p. 40.

48 Anahide Ter Minassian, "Les Arméniens de France," *Les Temps modernes*, nos. 504–6 (1988): 194.

49 J. Mathorez, "Les Arméniens en France de 1789 à nos jours," *Revue des études arméniennes* 2, no. 2 (1922): 293–314; Ch'ormisean, *Fransahayeru patmut'iwnĕ*, pp. 22–52.

50 The Armenian Question actually comprised numerous "questions" that took shape over the course of the late nineteenth and early twentieth centuries. All centered on how the international community (particularly leaders in western Europe) would address the various problems facing Armenians in the Ottoman and Russian Empires as well as under the Soviet regime. Anahide Ter Minassian, *La Questionne arménienne* (Roquevaire: Éditions Parenthèses, 1983), p. 9.

51 Archag Tchobanian, *L'Arménie sous le joug turc* (Paris: Plon-Nourrit, 1916), pp. 34–35.

52 Aram Turabian, *L'Eternelle victime de la diplomatie européenne* (Paris: Sous le patronage des anciens volontaires arméniens des armées alliés, 1929), pp. 214–30, 210. For more on his life, see Aram Turabian, *Trente ans en France: Ma vie* (Marseille: Imp. Nouvelle, 1928).

53 Although economic problems and rising unemployment in the 1930s were primarily responsible for France's rising anti-immigrant sentiment, xenophobic currents existed there already in the previous decade. William H. Schneider, *Quality and Quantity: The Quest for Biological Regeneration in Twentieth-Century France* (Cambridge, England: Cambridge University Press, 1990), chap. 8.

54 Ministre de l'Intérieur to Ministre des Affaires étrangères, "Des Travailleurs arméniens," 12 December 1922, f/7/12976, AN.

55 Turabian, *L'Éternelle victime*, p. 10.

56 Société de bienfaisance, *Comptes rendus de la 37ème année: Société de bienfaisance des Arméniens de Paris* (Paris: Société de bienfaisance des Arméniéns de Paris, 1928). This tradition of praising France had a long history within the local Armenian community, who saw their new home as a stark contrast to the "backward" Ottoman Empire. Maud Mandel, "In the Aftermath of Genocide: Armenians and Jews in Twentieth-Century France" (Ph.D. diss., University of Michigan, 1998), chap. 2.

57 The Société, which had operated on a small scale from 1890 to 1894, expanded its operations when Armenian refugees began fleeing a wave of massacres in the Ottoman Empire. *Aghkʿadtakhnamě ěnkerutʿiwn Pʿarizi Hayotsʿ: Hogelianakan hishatanaranj: 1890–1930* (Paris: Société de bienfaisance des Arméniens de Paris 1932), p. 42.

58 "Prix de vertu," *Le Foyer*, 1 December 1929, and "Pris de vertu," *Le Foyer*, 1 November 1930. This is not to suggest that the Société was uninterested in helping Armenian refugees. To the contrary, the Société went out of its way to stress communal solidarity. As the fortieth-anniversary booklet noted, "Do not break this chain that our predecessors built with their hearts. Remember that fidelity to one's promises was never a vain word for Armenians; remain faithful to these noble virtues of solidarity that were always the honor of the Armenian nation." *Aghkʿadtakhnamě ěnkerutʿiwn Pʿarizi Hayotsʿ*, p. 52.

59 Numerous examples of this rhetoric surface throughout the paper. For one of the earliest examples, see "Notre nouvelle patrie," *Le Foyer*, 1 November 1928.

60 "Traitement de faveur," *Le Foyer*, 15 November 1928.

61 "Notre nouvelle patrie," *Le Foyer*, 1 November 1928.

62 "Des Faits," *Le Foyer*, 1 December 1928.

63 *Le Foyer*, 15 November 1928. "Mer npatak," *Le Foyer*, 1 November 1928. "La France," *Le Foyer*, 1 November 1928.

64 Hovh. Varzhapetean, *Ughets'oyts' Marsēyli: Patkeradzard ev k'artisawor B. Tpagrut'iwn/Guide de Marseille en langue arménienne* (Marseille: Tpagrut'iwn "ALIS," 1930). "Le Décalogue du réfugié arménien," *Le Foyer*, 1 May 1929.

65 Hyman, *From Dreyfus to Vichy*, p. 116. For more on the relationship between native and immigrant Jews, see Nancy Green, *The Pletzl of Paris: Jewish Immigrant Workers in the Belle Epoque* (New York: Holmes and Meier, 1986); David H. Weinberg, *A Community on Trial: The Jews of Paris in the 1930s* (Chicago: University of Chicago Press, 1977). It is worth noting that similar assimilationist tendencies were expressed in every major Western Jewish community where eastern European Jews migrated in large numbers, playing itself out differently in each context. For a helpful comparative discussion, see Todd Endelman, "Native Jews and Foreign Jews in London, 1870–1914," in *The Legacy of Jewish Migration: 1881 and Its Impact*, ed. David Berger (New York: Columbia University Press, 1983), pp. 109–21; Jack Wertheimer, *Unwelcome Strangers: East European Jews in Imperial Germany* (New York: Oxford University Press, 1987), pp. 176–81.

66 "Pat'shachut'ean hamar," *Hay Sirt*, 3 December 1931.

67 Statuts, Union arménienne des amis du progrès, 22 October 1925, 4M693, Bouches-du-Rhône.

68 Cited in Commissaire spécial de Valence to Secrétaire général du Ministère de l'Intérieur, "Renseignements concernant les Arméniens, "10 May 1926, f/7/13436, AN.

69 Verneuil, *Mayrig*, p. 40.

70 In Lyon, for example, the Armenian population opened a nursery school that taught both Armenian and French. "Lyon," *Le Foyer*, 1 November 1929. Moreover, in some regions of the country, French industrialists provided funds for those Armenians working for them to start small schools. *L'Amitié française*, 10 February 1929. "Hay tsprots'neru khndirē Fransai mēj," *Hay Sirt*, 27 August 1931.

71 Attard-Maraninchi and Temime, *Le Cosmopolitisme de l'entre-deux-guerres*, p. 101.

72 Ter Minassian, "Les Arméniens de Paris," p. 130.

73 Hyman, *From Dreyfus to Vichy*, pp. 8, 11.

74 Pierre Birnbaum, *Jewish Destinies: Citizenship, State, and Community in Modern France*, trans. Arthur Goldhammer (New York: Hill and Wang, 1999), p. 4.

75 Nadia Malinovich, "Le Réveil d'Israel: Jewish Identity and Culture in France, 1900–1932" (Ph.D. diss., University of Michigan, 2000), p. 30. Malinovich suggests that a renewed interest in Jewish life and culture was not simply a knee-jerk response to antisemitism, but a reaction to the "new networks and social spaces [the Dreyfus Affair] created." For an overview of the history of Alfred Dreyfus's trial for treason, his eventual pardon, and the antisemitic outcries that accompanied the whole affair, see André Brendin, *The Affair: The Case of Alfred Dreyfus* (New York: George Braziller, 1986);

Stephen Wilson, *Antisemitism in France at the Time of the Dreyfus Affair* (Rutherford, N.J.: Farleigh Dickinson Press, 1982).

76 Hyman, *From Dreyfus to Vichy*, pp. 33–35.

77 Philippe Landau, "Les Juifs de France et la Grande Guerre 1914–1941: Un Patriotisme républicain" (Ph.D. diss., Université Paris 7, 1991); Hyman, *From Dreyfus to Vichy*, pp. 49–54; Malinovich, *Le Réveil d'Israel*, pp. 121–27.

78 Vicki Caron, *Uneasy Asylum: France and the Jewish Refugee Crisis, 1933–1942* (Stanford: Stanford University Press, 1999), p. 2. For discussions of rising antisemitic discourse in the interwar years, see Pierre Birnbaum, *Une Mythe politique: "La République juive" de Léon Blum à Pierre Mendès France* (Paris: Fayard 1988); Richard Millman, *La Question juive entre les deux guerres: Ligues de droite et antisémitisme en France* (Paris: Armand Colin, 1992); Ralph Schor, *L'Antisémitisme en France pendant les années trente: Prélude à Vichy* (Paris: Éditions Complexes, 1992); Robert Soucy, *French Fascism: The Second Wave, 1933–1939* (New Haven: Yale University Press, 1995). For discussions of popular attitudes toward Jews during these years, particularly middle-class socioeconomic concerns, see Caron, *Uneasy Asylum*.

79 Green, *The Pletzl of Paris*; Hyman, *From Dreyfus to Vichy*; D. Weinberg, *A Community on Trial*. Vicki Caron, "Loyalties in Conflict: French Jewry and the Refugee Crisis, 1933–1935," *Leo Baeck Institute Yearbook* 36 (1991): 336, argues that there was not one single native French Jewish voice on the refugee issue. Rather, members of the Jewish leadership debated whether their primary loyalties should lie with the refugees or the French state. Nevertheless, even those most sympathetic to the refugee plight "vehemently opposed mass colonization, fearing that the creation of unassimilated ethnic enclaves would prevent the successful integration of the refugees and would offend French sensibilities."

80 In "Le Réveil d'Israel," pp. 143–49, Malinovich argues that divisions between "natives" and "immigrants" have been too starkly drawn. She contends that certain sectors of the native Jewish population were in fact interested in contact with the immigrants. Moreover, by the late 1930s, many of those eastern European Jews who had migrated to France in the earlier decades of the twentieth century—particularly those who had come as children—were becoming integrated into French society. Hence, the division here between "native" and "immigrant" refers less to birthplace and more to degree of integration into French cultural and social norms.

81 D. Weinberg, *A Community on Trial*, pp. 53, 54.

82 Ibid., chap. 5.

83 Richard Cohen, *The Burden of Conscience: French Jewish Leadership during the Holocaust* (Bloomington: Indiana University Press, 1987), pp. 21–24; Adler, *The Jews of Paris and the Final Solution*.

84 Whereas the Statut des Juifs discriminated against all Jews, the position of foreign Jews was far more precarious, as special legislation gave police the right to intern them or to place them under police supervision in assigned residences. R. Cohen, *The*

Burden of Conscience, p. 24. Both Cohen and Adler argue that it took the native Jewish leadership several years to accept that their own fate was tied to that of immigrant Jews. Initially trusting that all citizens would be protected from the worst antisemitic legislation, they were not inclined to link their fate to that of non-French Jews. As the war progressed, however, and anti-Jewish measures became more stringent, the native Jewish leadership became increasingly intent on preventing the complete disintegration of communal life, eventually leading them to call for united defense activities.

85 Guy de Rothschild to Mr. Baerwald, 8 May, 1945, 311, AJDC. "Au Lendemain de la défaite totale de l'Allemagne, le Judaïsme fait le bilan des 5 dernières années de persécutions, "Bulletin d'information, May 1945, French Jewish Communities, 13/ 2–2, JTS. Kapel, *Au Lendemain de la Shoa*, p. 9.

86 Kapel, *Au Lendemain de la Shoa*, pp. 10–16.

87 "Nos problèmes," *La Terre retrouvée*, 18 September 1944.

88 Jean-Jacques Bernard, "Réflexions d'un français juif," *Revue juive de Genève* (October 1934): 23–27. Bernard's conversion did not, in his mind, distance him completely from other Jews. In a 1955 biography of his father, for example, he reflected, "My entrance into the Catholic church brought me much closer with those Jews faithful to the mother religion than to those who converted opportunistically or to those Christians unfaithful to the spirit of Christianity. . . . From this perspective, one can understand perhaps that baptism rather than distancing me brought me closer to a father who, without having returned to Judaism, never became totally detached from it." Yet, despite such musings, Bernard could not help but speculate/hope that his father was on the verge of converting on his deathbed. Jean-Jacques Bernard, *Mon Père: Tristan Bernard* (Paris: Éditions Albin Michel, 1955), pp. 257–65. Jean-Jacques Bernard, *Le Camp de la mort lente: Compiègne 1941–1942* (Paris: Albin Michel, 1944). It should be noted that Bernard's experience in Compiègne was not typical of what most arrested Jews faced. Like Drancy, Compiègne was a detention camp from which Jews were deported eastward. Annette Wieviorka, *Déportation et génocide: Entre la mémoire et l'oubli* (Paris: Plon, 1992), p. 447, notes, "For those who knew Dachau or Mauthausen, Compiègne became 'a paradise,' a sort of privileged time between prison and the death camp." Bernard's experiences there were even more atypical than most others, as he was arrested with several other leading public figures (who were treated somewhat better than other interns) and freed after becoming dangerously ill.

89 Jean-Jacques Bernard, "Autour du drame juif," *Le Figaro*, 14 April 1945, p. 2.

90 *Droit et Liberté*, 27 April 1945. Jean Paul, "Une Opinion sur le problème des Juifs étrangers," *La Revue des Éclaireurs israélites de France* (April 1945).

91 Marc Jarblum, "En Lissant J.J. Bernard: *Le Camp de la mort lente*," *La Terre retrouvée*, 1 February 1945, p. 1.

92 André Spire, *Souvenirs à bâtons rompus* (Paris: Éditions Albin Michel, 1962), pp. 239–

47; Encyclopedia Judaica, 8: 396–97. For more on Hertz's early Zionism, see Malinovich, "Réveil d'Israel," p. 139. His most explicit exploration of a Jewish "soul" can be found in Henri Hertz, "Ceux de Job," in *Tragédies des temps volages: Contes et poèmes, 1906–1954* (Paris: P. Seghers, 1955).

93 Henri Hertz, "Être ou ne pas être juif," *Esprit*, n.s. (September 1945): 513. The *Esprit* issue also included articles on the state of the catastrophe throughout Europe, the postwar position of French Jews, and a more lyrical piece describing one Jewish writer's disillusionment with his society.

94 Importantly, as we'll see, these views were precisely those espoused by the French Zionist movement in the period *preceding* World War II, when French Zionists "centered on discourses of dualism." Malinovich, "Réveil d'Israel," p. 255.

95 Georges Wormser to M. Feldmann, 12 March 1951, republished in Georges Wormser, *Français Israélites: Une Doctrine-une tradition-une époque* (Paris: Les Éditions de minuit, 1963), p. 112. Minutes, 6 November 1946, AA26, Consistoire de Paris.

96 Wieviorka, *Déportation et génocide*, pp. 347–52, has demonstrated that most of the consistorial leaders preferred to view the Vichy years "as a parenthesis which never encroached on the image that the Jews had forged of France since their emancipation."

97 *Bulletin du Centre israélite d'information*, October 1945, French Jewish Communities, 12/5, JTS.

98 Bernard Wasserstein, *Vanishing Diaspora: The Jews in Europe since 1945* (Cambridge, Mass.: Harvard University Press, 1996), p. 92. For assessments of postwar conversion, see Maud Mandel, "Faith, Religious Practices, and Genocide: Armenians and Jews in France following World War I and II," in *In God's Name: Genocide and Religion in the Twentieth Century*, ed. Omer Bartov and Phyllis Mack (New York: Berghahn Books, 2001), pp. 292–94.

99 Pino [Ginsburg] to Mossad Center, Genf, 16 November 1945, HHA 14/160, cited in Idith Zertal, *From Catastrophe to Power: Holocaust Survivors and the Emergence of Israel* (Berkeley: University of California Press, 1998), pp. 76–77.

100 Jules C. to Ministre de l'Intérieur, 10 January 1945, AJ/38/1138, AN. Maurice P. to Terroine, 5 May 1945, AJ/38/1134, AN. Zyzek M. to Commissaire de la République Limoges, 29 November 1944, AJ/38/1135, AN.

101 R&S S. to Séquestre de l'ex-Commissariat aux questions juives, 8 March 1945, Dossier 178, AJ/38/1137, AN.

102 Robert Gamzon, "The Fight for Survival Goes On," 1946, 311, AJDC.

103 Susan Zuccotti, *The Holocaust, the French, and the Jews* (New York: Basic Books, 1993). Renée Poznanski, *Être juif en France pendant la Seconde Guerre mondiale* (Paris: Hachette, 1994), p. 708, also stresses how Jewish placement in pre–World War II France played a role in their high survival rates.

104 Guy de Rothschild, *The Whims of Fortune: The Memoirs of Guy de Rothschild* (New York: Random House, 1985), p. 124. Rothschild does nevertheless acknowledge the trans-

formative impact the war had on his self-understanding: "Under the surface of the social privileges from which I'd benefited since the day I was born, I could be nothing more than just another Jew."

105 Jean-Paul Sartre, *Anti-Semite and Jew*, trans. George J. Becker (New York: Schocken Books, 1976), p. 71.

106 Henry Rousso, *The Vichy Syndrome*, trans. Arthur Goldhammer (Cambridge, Mass.: Harvard University Press, 1991).

107 Wieviorka, *Déportation et Génocide*, p. 436, argues that in the immediate postwar period, Jews had little interest in dredging up memories of the immediate past.

108 This shift had already begun by the late 1920s. See Malinovich, "Le Réveil d'Israel," pp. 143–49.

109 Annette Wieviorka, "Despoliation, Reparation, Compensation," in *Starting the Twenty-First Century: Sociological Reflections and Challenges*, ed. Ernest Krausz and Gitta Tulea (New Brunswick, N.J.: Transaction Publishers, 2002), p. 208. Given that immigrant Jews were persecuted more aggressively than the native-born, naturalization may have seemed the safest route to pursue. This alone cannot explain the high naturalization rates, however, because during the war even the newly naturalized had been singled out.

110 Boudjikanian-Keuroghlian, "Un peuple en exil," pp. 650–51; Andesian and Hovanessian, "L'Arménien: Langue rescapée d'un génocide," p. 67. This transformation was intensified during World War II, when certain large industries were closed because of bombings. Hovanessian, *Le Lien communautaire*, pp. 141–46.

111 J. Simpson, *The Refugee Problem*, p. 319, notes that Armenians often escaped the 10 percent quota rule.

112 Hovh. Varzhapetean, *Guide de Marseille/Ughetsʿoytsʿ Marsēyli* (Marseille: Imprimerie Daron, 1939), pp. 8–9, 17–39. Such statistics should not, however, suggest that all Armenians abandoned manual labor in the early 1930s. As late as 1936, one Armenian paper placed the number of Armenian day laborers in Marseille as high as 5,350, and tailors, shoemakers, carpenters, and other artisans added up to 4,155. Although this estimate may be inaccurate, unskilled labor was still a significant source of income for some. "Marsēyli Hayutʿiwnē," *Zhoghovurti Dzayn*, 30 July 1936. Boudjikanian-Keuroghlian, *Les Arméniens dans la region Rhône-Alpes*, p. 123, confirms such findings in the Rhône-Alpes, where, according to her, a significant percentage of Armenians remained laborers in the 1920s and 1930s. Ter Minassian, "Les Arméniens de Paris," p. 129, confirms this diversity in Paris.

113 Hovanessian, *Le Lien communautaire*, pp. 141–46; Boudjikanian-Keuroghlian, "Un peuple en exil," pp. 650–51; Andesian and Hovanessian, "L'Arménien: Langue rescapée d'un génocide," p. 67; and Ter Minassian, "Les Arméniens de Paris," p. 134. Ter Minassian notes that certain sectors of the population remained quite poor, including widows, the infirm, and certain Armenian intellectuals who refused to pursue

manual labor. In *Le Lien communautaire*, pp. 172–73, Hovanessian argues that the departure of women from the factories into the patriarchal framework of the home provided a sense of continuity between the "new life" in France and the "old world" of Armenian village life in the Ottoman Empire.

114 Minutes, 7 January 1946, AA26, Consistoire de Paris.

115 Procès-verbal 1235, B41489, Archives du Ministère de Finance. In one case, "After liberation, I reclaimed my place as head of the business without any difficulty." The business had been sold with the owner's consent to the widow of his former business associate and three former employees to avoid its being sold to strangers. Gustave B. to Service des restitutions, 28 August 1945, Dossier 22, AJ/38/1136, AN. Sadia L. to Chef du Service des restitutions, 17 May 1945, Procès-verbal 1091, B41488, Archives du Ministère de Finance. Délégué régional du service des restitutions to Terroine, 15 March 1946, AJ/38/1140, AN.

116 Mission d'étude sur la spoliation des Juifs de France, "Rapport général" (Paris, 2000), pp. 165–66.

117 Report on situation in France, 311, AJDC. "Economic Reconstruction and Rehabilitation in Europe: Some Notes and Statistics on Reconstruction Activities, 1944–8," Reconstruction Department, European Executive Council, no date, 3462, AJDC.

118 This number includes the families of the borrowers. Report on western Europe, May 1951, 309, AJDC.

119 Founded in Russia in 1880, ORT's goal was to advance vocational schooling in agriculture, craft, and industry among the international Jewish population. After the Bolshevik Revolution, its headquarters moved to Berlin (in 1921) and an American branch was founded as well. Following Word War II, ORT members began organizing courses in carpentry, mechanics, tailoring, and more for Jewish refugees across Europe. Yehuda Bauer, *Out of the Ashes: The Impact of American Jews on Post-Holocaust European Jewry* (Oxford: Pergamon Press, 1989), chap. 8. "Economic Reconstruction and Rehabilitation in Europe: Some Notes and Statistics on Reconstruction Activities, 1944–8," Reconstruction Department, European Executive Council, no date, 3462, AJDC.

120 Jean-Pierre Rioux, *The Fourth Republic, 1944–58*, trans. Godfrey Rogers (Cambridge, England: Cambridge University Press, 1987), pp. 63–80, 112–50.

121 *European Jewry Ten Years after the War: An Account of the Development and Present Status of the Decimated Jewish Communities of Europe* (New York: Institute of Jewish Affairs of the World Jewish Congress, 1956), pp. 213–14, 197. Country Report: France, Country Directors Conference, Paris, 1954, 309, AJDC.

122 Report on Jewish community in France, Georges Wormser, Consultative Conference of the AIU, AJC, and AJA, June 1955, Anglo Jewish Association papers, AJ37/6/6/6/6, Parkes Library.

1 Rogers Brubaker, *Nationalism Reframed: Nationhood and the National Question in the New Europe* (Cambridge, England: Cambridge University Press, 1996), pp. 4–7, 55–76.

2 For a history of the modern Armenian diaspora and its transformation after World War I, see Aida Boudjikanian-Keuroghlian, "Un peuple en exil: La Nouvelle diaspora (XIXe–XXe siècles)," in *Histoire des Arméniens*, ed. Gérard Dédéyan (Toulouse: Éditions Privat, 1982), pp. 601–68; Anahide Ter Minassian, "La diaspora arménienne," in *Diasporas*, ed. Michel Bruneau (Montpellier: Reclus, 1995), pp. 24–41.

3 Boudjikanian-Keuroghlian, "Un peuple en exil," p. 626.

4 André Sernin, *L'Homme de Tokat* (Paris: Éditions France-Empire, 1987), p. 28.

5 The Armenegan Party was founded in Van in 1885. For a general overview of the political parties and their positions, see Anahide Ter Minassian, *Nationalism and Socialism: The Armenian Revolutionary Movement, 1887–1912*, trans. A. M. Berrett (Cambridge, Mass.: Zoryan Institute, 1984); Louise Nalbandian, *The Armenian Revolutionary Movement* (Berkeley: University of California Press, 1967); Christopher J. Walker, *Armenia: The Survival of a Nation*, 2d ed. (New York: St. Martin's Press, 1980). For the spread of political ideologies in eastern Armenia, see Ronald Grigor Suny, "Populism, Nationalism and Marxism among Russia's Armenians," and "Labor and Socialism among Armenians in Transcaucasia," in *Looking Toward Ararat: Armenia in Modern History* (Bloomington: Indiana University Press, 1993), pp. 63–93.

6 J. Mathorez, "Les Arméniens en France de 1789 à nos jours," *Revue des études arméniennes* 2, no. 2 (1922): 293–314; Anahide Ter Minassian, "Les Arméniens de France," *Les Temps modernes*, nos. 504–6 (1988): 189–234; Aram Terzian, "Growth of the Armenian Community in Paris during the Interwar Years 1919–1939," *Armenian Review* 27, no. 3-107 (1974): 260–76; Levon Ch'ormisean, *Fransahayeru patmut'iwně*, Vol. 1: *Hay sp'iwṛk'ě* (Beirut: Imprimerie G. Doniguian, 1975), pp. 22–52. For a discussion of France's dynamic Armenian intellectual and cultural elite before and after World War I, see Cyril le Tallec, *La Communauté arménienne de France, 1920–1950* (Paris: Harmattan, 2001), pp. 78–87.

7 Richard G. Hovannisian, *Armenia on the Road to Independence: 1918* (Berkeley: University of California Press, 1967), p. 32.

8 In 1919, Nubar summoned a congress in Paris made up of representatives from all the major Armenian communities. For a discussion of the congress, see Richard Hovannisian, *The Republic of Armenia*, Vol. 1: *The First Year, 1918–1919* (Berkeley: University of California Press, 1971), pp. 250–60; Mary Mangigian Tarzian, *The Armenian Minority Problem, 1914–1934: A Nation's Struggle for Security* (Atlanta. Ga.: Scholars Press, 1992), pp. 120–23.

9 Unsurprisingly, the two delegations disagreed on numerous issues. The Republic's delegation was particularly interested in protecting the Republic's weak and undefended position on Turkey's border. In contrast, Nubar, as representative of all

diaspora Armenians, sought much greater concessions from Turkey. Ultimately, Aharonian, unable to communicate efficiently with the Armenian capital, agreed to tailor his own delegation's aims to those of the national delegation. Although the two did not completely merge, they agreed to unite on the most important issues as the Delegation of Integral Armenia, with Nubar primarily representing Turkish and diaspora Armenians and Aharonian representing Russian Armenians and the independent Republic. Hovannisian, *The Republic of Armenia*, 1: 254–59.

10 Until 1924, an exiled Armenian government officially functioned in France. After France recognized the Soviet Union, the delegation nevertheless maintained its presence in Paris until 1965. For the Republic's demise and its transformation into a Soviet state, see Richard Hovannisian, *The Republic of Armenia*, Vol. 4: *Between Crescent and Sickle: Partition and Sovietization* (Berkeley: University of California Press, 1996).

11 For a general schematic of Armenian parties in France, see Martine Hovanessian, *Le Lien communautaire: Trois générations d'arméniens* (Paris: Armand Colin, 1992), pp. 98–104.

12 "Des Menées communistes étrangères à Paris," 17 February 1926; "L'Activité du H.O.G à Marseille" [January 1927]; "Comité de Secours pour l'Arménie," 20 November 1933; Commissariat spécial de Saint-Etienne, "Réunion du Comité de secours à l'Arménie Soviétique," 14 September 1932, f/7/13436, AN.

13 Boudjikanian-Keuroghlian, "Un peuple en exil," p. 634; Hovanessian, *Le Lien communautaire*, p. 108.

14 For example, in 1932, members of the most prominent Armenian benevolent organization, the AGBU, were furious when the Soviet Armenian government diverted funds they had designated for the construction of an official building in Armenia to support a new procommunist Armenian paper in France. Report, 13 January 1932, f/7/13436, AN.

15 "Des Menées communistes étrangères à Paris," 17 February 1926, f/7/13436, AN. According to police speculations, HOG leaders sought naturalization in order to carry out their procommunist activities without fear of expulsion. "Organisation des Arméniens de France," 15 September 1932, f/7/13436, AN.

16 "Réunion du Comité intersyndical arménien affilié au comité departmental de la main d'œuvre étrangère," 12 April 1925, f/7/13436, AN. Report, Contrôle générale des services de police administrative de Marseille, "Arméniens, République soviétique arménienne," 30 December 1925, f/7/13436, AN.

17 Boudjikanian-Keuroghlian, "Un peuple en exil," p. 661.

18 "Comité central des réfugiés arméniens; journal Haratsch; Issahakian, Arachak," 6 February 1933, f/7/13436, AN. "A.S. du journal arménien Haratsch," May 1933, f/7/13436, AN; "A.S. du journal arménien Haratsch," 17 January 1928, same file. Préfet du département de la Drome to Ministre de l'Intérieur, 9 October 1925, f/7/13436, AN. A new pro-Soviet paper, *Mer Ughin*, was published and then suppressed by the French government, to be followed by *Darbnots'*, suppressed in April 1932,

and *Arshav*, suppressed in December 1932. Numerous other procommunist Armenian papers also went into publication for short runs. "Au sujet du journal arménien l'Abaka," 12 March 1928, f/7/13436, AN.

19   Le Tallec, *La Communauté arménienne de France*, p. 115.

20   Commissaire spécial to Secrétaire général du Ministère de l'Intérieur, "Comité révolutionnaire arménien 'Tachnak,' " 8 April 1932, f/7/13436, AN. Hovanessian, *Le Lien communautaire*, p. 122.

21   "L'Activité du H.O.K. à Marseille," [January 1927], f/7/13436, AN; Commissaire divisionnaire de police spéciale to Préfet des Alpes Maritimes, 15 December 1930, same carton. Boudjikanian-Keuroghlian, "Un peuple en exil," p. 663, demonstrates that similar debates raged throughout all diaspora communities, particularly those of Lebanon, France, and the United States, where the Dashnaks had strong bases of support. For an in-depth discussion of the importance of such symbols in Armenian American life, see Jenny Phillips, "Symbol, Myth, and Rhetoric: The Politics of Culture in an Armenian-American Population," (Ph.D. diss., Boston University, 1978).

22   Contrôle générale des services de police administrative, "Communistes: République soviétique arménienne," 24 December 1925, f/7/13436, AN. Other reports in the same file provide information on anniversary celebrations each year in Marseille, Lyon, and Paris. *Inch'pēs tsnay: Azat u ankakh Hayastanē* (Paris, 1930). Ideological differences meant that genocide commemorations became divisive as well. According to Hovanessian, *Le Lien communautaire*, p. 130, the Dashnaks monopolized these commemorations until World War II, after which time the pro-Soviet Armenian organization Jeunesse arménienne de France (JAF) became the primary force behind the commemorations. No coordinated efforts succeeded until 1965.

23   "Arméniens réunion de la rue Tapis Vert," 2 June 1926, f/7/13436, AN. Reports on other anniversary celebrations are also available in this folder.

24   Commissaire spécial de Lyon to Directeur de la sûreté générale, 3 May 1926, f/7/13436, AN. Similarly, in January 1926, French and Armenian communists disrupted Aharonian's presentation in Marseille. Contrôle général des services de police administrative, "Arméniens," 25 January 1926, same carton. Tract cited in Commissaire spécial, "Renseignements concernant les Arméniens, Incidents d'ordre politique," 17 May 1926, f/7/13436, AN. "L'Anniversaire de la République arménienne donne lieu, à Lyon, à de sanglants incidents," *Le Petit Parisien*, 3 December 1928. Another example of such violence in Lyon took place in February 1933, when four Armenians were wounded during a fight. Commissariat spécial de Lyon, "Réunion de la colonie arménienne de Lyon et bagarre à la sortie," 14 February 1933, f/7/13436, AN. Not all cases led to violence, however. In Lyon in 1929, the Dashnaks organized festivities for the anniversary of the Armenian Republic, during which no violent outbursts took place. "A/s. de l'organisation de la fête nationale arménienne," 1 June 1929, same carton. Commissaire spécial Brun, "Fête organisée par la colonie arménienne à la Marie du 3° arrêt.," 13 June 1932, f/7/13436, AN.

25   "Une Bagarre entre Arméniens et gardiens de la paix avenue d'Iéna," *Le Matin*, 29 April 1930. Frédéric Bourgade, *Les Arméniens de Valence: Histoire d'une integration réussie* (Valence: Éditions "Les Bonnes Feuilles," 1991), p. 41.

26   Commissaire spéciale to Directeur de la sûreté générale, "Commémoration du 8e anniversaire de la République arménienne," 1 June 1926, f/7/13436, AN. "Patker," Haṛaj, 22 April 1935.

27   For material on the brawl in Grenoble, see Commissaire central to Préfet de l'Isère, 28 March 1933, f/7/13436, AN. More information on the same event is included in Commissaire central to Directeur de la sûreté général, 27 February 1933 and 4 March 1933, "Comité de secours pour l'Arménie dit le Hog," same file. For Valence, see "Patker," Haṛaj, 22 April 1935. For a helpful discussion of Armenian life in Lebanon, see Nikola Schangaldian, "The Political Integration of an Immigrant Community into a Composite Society: The Armenians in Lebanon, 1920–1974" (Ph.D. diss., Columbia University, 1979).

28   "Organisation des Arméniens de France," 15 September 1932, f/7/13436, AN.

29   Ministre de l'Intérieur to juge d'instruction de Grenoble, 20 July 1933, "Comité de secours pour l'Arménie dit le Hog," f/7/13436/, AN. Commissaire spécial [Marseille], "Arméniens," 25 January 1926, f/7/13436, AN; and Commissaire spécial de Marseille, "Arméniens," 1 February 1926, same carton. Commissaire spécial de Marseille, "Arméniens: Réunion de la rue Tapis Vert," 2 June 1926, f/7/13436, AN.

30   *Le Foyer*, for example, published numerous articles in Armenian condemning the HOG.

31   "A.S. d'un meeting de révolutionnaires arméniens," 13 October 1933; "Comité de secours pour l'Arménie dit le Hog," f/7/13436, AN. Report, 26 February 1925, f/7/13436, AN. Police tailed those they suspected of communist sympathies. One report, for example, details the activities of several Armenian communists who participated in the Section centrale de la langue arménienne du P.C., December 1929, f/7/13436, AN.

32   In its place, the Association franco-arménienne was born; it disappeared with World War II. *Fransahay mshakutʻayin miutʻiwn: 30 Tari i tsaṛayutʻiwn fransahay hamaynkʻin* (Paris: Union culturelle française de France, 1980), p. 87; Suny, *Looking toward Ararat*, p. 223.

33   Commissaire spécial to Secrétaire général du Ministère de l'Intérieur, "Comité révolutionnaire arménien 'Tachnak,'" 8 April 1932, f/7/13436, AN. "Organisation des Arméniens de France," 15 September 1932, f/7/13436, AN.

34   Mampré Calfayan, 16 December 1925, included with report by the Commissaire spécial de Marseille, 31 December 1925, f/7/13436, AN.

35   Mélinée Manouchian, *Manouchian* (Paris: France Loisirs, 1974), pp. 17, 27.

36   Copy of pamphlet found in "Report," Contrôle général des services de police administrative, 3914, 8 December 1925, f/7/13436, AN. "Le 1er Août et les Arméniens," Le Foyer, 1 August 1929. Le Tallec, *La Communauté arménienne de France*, p. 134. Commissaire divisionnaire de police spéciale to Préfet des Alpes Maritimes, 15 December 1930, f/7/13436, AN. Commissaire spécial, "Renseignements concernant les Armé-

niens," 14 May 1926, f/7/13436, AN. In some cases, HOG members were able to convince unemployed Armenians to join their organization, such as in 1927, when five hundred of Marseille's two thousand Armenian unemployed workers came together to form a local chapter. Ministre de l'Intérieur to Ministre de Travail, 24 March 1927, f/7/13436, AN. Préfet de l'Ardèche to Président du Conseil, Ministre de l'Intérieur, 31 May 1930, f/7/13436, AN.

37 For example, By-laws, Union compatriotique de Palou, 7 September 1928, 3496, 4M761, Bouches-du-Rhône.

38 Brubaker, *Nationalism Reframed*, pp. 4–7, 55–76. Brubaker's discussion of the "triadic nexus," although better suited to a discussion of the relationship between newly formed central and eastern European states and their national minorities than to the long-established French state, nevertheless provides an interesting theoretical perspective from which to explore the impact of "external national homelands" on national minorities everywhere.

39 An overview of such organizations in Marseille can be found in Marie-Françoise Attard-Maraninchi and Emile Temime, *Le Cosmopolitisme de l'entre-deux-guerres (1919–1945)*, vol. 3: *Histoire des migrations à Marseille* (Marseille: Edisud, 1990), pp. 103–5. Report on annual dinner of the Union des Arméniennes de Russie in "Nouvelles," *Le Foyer*, 1 January 1929. By-laws, Union arménienne de Constantinople, 21 October 1931, 4177, 4M693, Bouches-du-Rhône. It is worth noting that many of these groups declared themselves to local authorities only upon needing a bank account or after requiring some other official notarization. Thus, they may have existed for several years before appearing in the archives. To cite one example, the Union compatriotique de la ville de Zara Sivas declared itself to the government in 1929, but it was formed in 1924. By-laws, Union compatriotique de la ville de Zara Sivis, 9 July 1929, 3645, 4M761.

40 By-laws, L'Union d'Arabkir, 7 March 1935, 6716, 4M694, Bouches-du-Rhône; By-laws, "Union compatriotique de Erzenga, 13 May 1939, 7139, 4M761, Bouches-du-Rhône; By-laws, Union des compatriotes Arméniens de Ghantaroz, 31 August 1927, 3270, same carton. In Camp Oddo in 1924 residents from Bithynie formed their own compatriotic union and their entire governing board was from the camp. By-laws, Union compatriotique des arméniens de Bithynie à Marseille, 26 January 1925, 2746, 4M761, Bouches-du-Rhône.

41 In Paris, for example, there were seventy-eight landsmanshaftn proper and eighty-three other Jewish mutual aid societies in the 1930s. These organizations offered communal welfare to their members by providing them with free loans and medical benefits as well as by organizing social gatherings and intervening on behalf of illegal immigrants in dealings with French police and immigration authorities. Jonathan Boyarin, *Polish Jews in Paris: The Ethnography of Memory* (Bloomington: Indiana University Press, 1991), pp. 17–20.

42　"A.S. de l'Association des Arméniens originaires de Tchépni (Sivas), 14 January 1930, f/7/13436, AN. Statuts, Union "Senekerimain" des Arméniens de Sivas à Marseille, 20 August 1924, 9503, 4M693, Bouches-du-Rhône.

43　"Patker," Haṛaj, 22 April 1935. By-laws, Union de Bienfaisance du Arménienne de Marache, 11 May 1928, 3433, 4M698, Bouches-du-Rhône. "Cours de soir," Le Foyer, 15 April 1929.

44　By-laws, Union compatriotique de Tomarza et ses environs, 8 February 1933, 4578, 4M761, Bouches-du-Rhône. The treasurer and the president of the Papert compatriot union lived at the same address, as did the president and treasurer of the Tchkhan union. By-laws, Union compatriotique de Babert, 11 May 1939, 7138, 4M761, Bouches-du-Rhône; By-laws, Union compatriotique de Tchkhan (de l'Everek), 17 December 1930, 3956, same carton.

45　Not all mutual aid/compatriot unions were based on a link to a particular physical territory. Some, such as the Association de l'entr'aide arménienne, created in May 1933, were life insurance organizations that provided financial aid to the beneficiary of its members upon their death. A/s. Association de l'entr'aide arménienne qui sollicite l'autorisation de fonctionner comme société de secours mutuels, July 1933, f/7/13436, AN.

46　By-laws, Union de reconstruction compatriotique de Yeni-Han de Sivas, 19 November 1935, 3424, 4M761, Bouches-du-Rhône; By-laws, Union compatriotique des Arméniens d'Ak-Chéhir, 4 September 1929 and 3 June 1936, 3683, same carton. By-laws, Union compatriotique de Tcharsandjak, 22 August 1929, 3674, 4M761, Bouches-du-Rhône.

47　Boyarin, Polish Jews in Paris, p. 18.

48　By-laws, Union compatriotique des arméniens de Sivri-Hissar, 21 April 1927 and 29 June 1936, 3186, 4M761, Bouches-du-Rhône. Another reconstruction attempt was implemented by Armenians from Dikranagerd. By-laws, Association compatriotique et reconstruction de Dikranagerd, 1 October 1932, 4485, same carton.

49　Hovanessian, Le Lien communautaire, pp. 63–64.

50　Two examples are By-laws, Société de bienfaisance des Arméniens de la ville d'Ankara, 10 février 1932, 4170, 4M698, Bouches-du-Rhône; By-laws, Union des compatriotes arméniens d'Amassia, 10 June 1927, 3219, 4M761.

51　By-laws, Association compatriotique de Palou, 8 September 1928, 3497, 4M761, Bouches-du-Rhône; By-laws, Union de Bienfaisance de Palou, Okou, et Tepe, 12 December 1928, 3541, 4M698, Bouches–du-Rhône. Attard-Maraninchi and Temime, Le Cosmopolitisme de l'entre-deux-guerres, p. 104.

52　Le Tallec, La Communauté arménienne de France, p. 120.

53　1 August 1925, Haṛaj, cited in Anahide Ter Minassian, "Les Arméniens et le Paris des libertés," in Le Paris des étrangers depuis un siècle, ed. André Kaspi and Antoine Marès (Paris: Imprimerie nationale, 1989), p. 138.

54 Ter Minassian, "La diaspora arménienne," pp. 29–30.

55 Ibid., p. 37.

56 "Explications," *Le Foyer*, 1 March 1930. Various articles in *Le Foyer* attest to the AGBU's patterns of donations as well as to those of individual benefactors who gave to both the AGBU and refugee relief throughout the Near East.

57 Le Tallec, *La Communauté arménienne de France*, p. 141.

58 Between 1965 and 1971, for example, 6,852 French Jews migrated from France to Israel, and since that time, Israel has received between 1,000 and 1,500 French Jews each year (due, in part, to the influx of North African Jews to France). Doris Bensimon, *Les Juifs de France et leurs relations avec Israel, 1945–1988* (Paris: Éditions l'Harmattan, 1989), p. 171.

59 For an overview comparing early responses of Jews to Israel's birth, see Bernard Wasserstein, *Vanishing Diaspora: The Jews of Europe since 1945* (Cambridge, Mass.: Harvard University Press, 1966), pp. 85–102.

60 Most important among them were André Spire and Edmond Fleg. See Aron Rodrigue, "Rearticulations of French Jewish Identities after the Dreyfus Affair," *Jewish Social Studies* 2, no. 3 (1996): 1–24; Nadia Malinovich, "Le Réveil d'Israel: Jewish Identity and Culture in France, 1900–1932" (Ph.D. diss., University of Michigan, 2000), pp. 77–91.

61 Although the organized Zionist movement was generally rejected by the majority of Jews in most western and central European Jewish communities, scholars have nevertheless begun to trace its impact on notions of Jewish identity in various places. For some examples, see Michael Brenner, *The Renaissance of Jewish Culture in Weimar Germany* (New Haven: Yale University Press, 1996), pp. 22–31; Hillel J. Kieval, *The Making of Czech Jewry: National Conflict and Jewish Society in Bohemia, 1870–1918* (New York: Oxford University Press, 1988); Marsha Rozenblit, *Reconstructing a National Identity: The Jews of Habsburg Austria during World War I* (New York: Oxford University Press, 2001), pp. 36–38.

62 Malinovich, "Le Réveil d'Israel," pp. 134, 254. Whereas earlier accounts of Zionist history in France point to the institutional weakness of the movement, recent studies have stressed its impact in inspiring a more ethnic definition of Jewishness among a population previously committed to religious definitions of Jewish identity. For discussions of Zionism's weakness prior to 1945, see Catherine Nicault, *La France et le Sionisme, 1897–1945: Une rencontre manquée?* (Paris: Calmann Lévy, 1992). Works that stress the movement's impact include Michel Abitbol, *Les Deux terres promises: Les Juifs de France et le Sionisme, 1897–1945* (Paris: Orban, 1989); Paula Hyman, *From Dreyfus to Vichy: The Remaking of French Jewry, 1906–1939* (New York: Columbia University Press, 1979), chap. 6; Malinovich, "Le Réveil d'Israel," pp. 253–71. Also see Doris Bensimon and Benjamin Pinkus, eds., *Les Juifs de France, le Sionisme et l'État d'Israel* (Paris: Publications Langues'O, 1989).

63 David H. Weinberg, *A Community on Trial: The Jews of Paris in the 1930s* (Chicago: University of Chicago Press, 1977), 34.

64 Conseil représentatif des Juifs de France, no date (received at the Board of Deputies on 18 December 1944), CII/7/3b/I, Greater London Records Office (GLRO). Examples of some of CRIF's restitution activities are detailed in a letter to Professor Terroine, 17 October 1945, BIO934, Archives du Ministère de Finance. Evidence of their attempts to prevent the resurgence of antisemitism in Germany and elsewhere are evident in "Mémoire concernant les revendications juives à l'égard de l'Allemagne," May 1951, Anglo Jewish Association papers, AJ37/6/6/5/2, Parkes Library.

65 Pierre Birnbaum, *Jewish Destinies: Citizenship, State, and Community in Modern France*, trans. by Arthur Goldhammer (New York: Hill and Wang, 1999), p. 217, points to the birth of CRIF as evidence of French Jews' profound loss of faith in the state following World War II. He writes, "Like disappointed lovers, they abandoned the state they had once adored." As I argue in chapter 3, such a position is too stark; most French Jews did not in fact "abandon" the state. Nevertheless, he is right to point to CRIF as evidence of a new consciousness among French Jews that the state was not infallible and that they must organize on their own behalf.

66 Annette Wieviorka, "Les Juifs en France au lendemain de la guerre: État des lieux," *Archives juives: Revue d'histoire des Juifs de France* 28, no. 1 (1995): 9.

67 *European Jewry Ten Years after the War: An Account of the Development and Present Status of the Decimated Jewish Communities of Europe* (New York: Institute of Jewish Affairs of the World Jewish Congress, 1956), p. 209. Even the cooperation among different Zionist groups eventually broke down, as political differences divided revisionists, general Zionists, and others. Occasionally such divisions turned violent, as when the revisionists attempted to disrupt other Zionist rallies. "Réunion organisée par la Histadrouth (CGT Palestinienne), le 10 octobre," 11 October 1946, dossier Palestine—Zionism, f/1a/3368, AN.

68 Renée Poznanski, "Le Sionisme en France pendant la deuxième guerre mondiale: Développements institutionnels et impact idéologique," in Bensimon and Pinkus, *Les Juifs de France, le Sionisme et l'État d'Israel*, p. 212.

69 In the United States, for example, the anti-Zionist rhetoric of the prewar years virtually disappeared. See Edward S. Shapiro, *A Time for Healing: American Jewry since World War II* (Baltimore: Johns Hopkins University Press, 1992), pp. 201–12.

70 Michael Graetz, *Les Juifs en France au XIXieme siècle: De la Révolution française à l'Alliance israélite universelle*, trans., Salomon Malka (Paris: Seuil, 1989); Michael M. Laskier, *The Alliance Israélite Universelle and the Jewish Communities of Morocco, 1862–1962* (Albany: State University of New York Press, 1983); Aron Rodrigue, *French Jews, Turkish Jews: The Alliance Israélite Universelle and the Politics of Jewish Schooling in Turkey, 1860–1925* (Bloomington: Indiana University Press, 1990).

71 For discussions on the Alliance's rejection of the nationalist agenda as well as the subtle ways in which this discourse influenced its position, see Malinovich, "Le Réveil d'Israel," pp. 129–32, 268.

72 Memorandum de l'Alliance israélite universelle sur le problem palestinien, 30 June 1947, Anglo Jewish Association papers, AJ37/6/6/5/2, Parkes Library.

73 Hyman, *From Dreyfus to Vichy*, pp. 160–70. For background on the Consistoire, see Phyllis Cohen Albert, *The Modernization of French Jewry: Consistory and Community in the Nineteenth Century* (Hanover, N.H.: University Press of New England, 1977).

74 Richard Cohen, *The Burden of Conscience: French Jewish Leadership during the Holocaust* (Bloomington: Indiana University Press, 1987), p. 57, chap. 7.

75 Minutes, 7 February 1946, AA26, Consistoire de Paris.

76 Immigrant groups (Bundist, Zionist, and communist) also de-emphasized Jewish particularity by constructing monuments that celebrated Jewish heroes fighting an antifascist war rather than Jewish deportees. Annette Wieviorka, *Déportation et génocide: Entre la mémoire et l'oubli* (Paris: Plon, 1992), pp. 391–411.

77 M. Sachs, Consistoire Centrale, 5 November 1944, French Jewish Communities, 13/2–1, JTS.

78 Leon Meiss, Consistoire Centrale, 5 November 1944, French Jewish Communities, 13/2–1, JTS.

79 Minutes, 2 December 1947, AA27, Consistoire de Paris. Minutes, 6 April 1949, AA28, Consistoire de Paris.

80 Rapport sur les relations entre l'état d'Israel et les Juifs de la diaspora, Grand Rabbin Kaplan, [June 1949], Assises du judaïsme français, 1949, Consistoire de Paris. Prior to World War II, Caen was actively involved in communal affairs, serving as a member of the Consistoire de Paris and as president of the assimilationist Union Scolaire. In both capacities he advocated an active native Jewish institutional involvement in the assimilation of immigrant Jews (rather than waiting for the process to occur naturally). Hyman, *From Dreyfus to Vichy*, pp. 147–50.

81 Malinovich, "Le Réveil d'Israel," pp. 275–78; Hyman, *From Dreyfus to Vichy*, p. 172; D. Weinberg, *A Community on Trial*, pp. 52–53. A short sketch of Kaplan's life can be found in Maurice Rose, ed., *Reconstruction of European Jewish Life and the Conference of European Rabbis* (London: Conference of European Rabbis, Standing Committee, 1967), p. 69.

82 Here too Kaplan expanded on prewar pro-Zionist arguments that insisted that support for Zionism was perfectly compatible with a loyalty and love for France. Malinovich, "Le Réveil d'Israel," pp. 254–55.

83 Rapport sur les relations entre l'état d'Israel et les Juifs de la diaspora, Grand Rabbin Kaplan, [June 1949], Assises du judaïsme français, 1949, Consistoire de Paris.

84 Minutes, 26 May 1948, AA27, Consistoire de Paris. Cited in report by the President, "Position du Consistoire vis-à-vis de l'état d'Israel," Minutes, 2 June 1948, AA27, Consistoire de Paris.

85 Pierre Birnbaum, *Les Fous de la République: Histoire politique des Juifs d'état, de Gambetta à Vichy* (Paris: Fayard, 1992), pp. 341–44.

86 Report by the President, "Position du Consistoire vis-à-vis de l'état d'Israel," Minutes, 2 June 1948, AA27, Consistoire de Paris.

87 Weill Goudchaux, "Israel et la diaspora," *Journal des communautés* (28 April 1961): 5, cited in Bensimon, *Les Juifs de France*, pp. 164–65.

88 Minutes, 7 June 1948, AA27, Consistoire de Paris. Minutes, 2 June 1948, AA27, Consistoire de Paris.

89 Minutes, 7 December 1948, AA27, Consistoire de Paris.

90 Z. 4/10.300, Central Zionist Archives, cited in Renée Poznanski, "Héritage de la guerre: Le Sionisme en France dans les années 1944–1947," in *Les Juifs de France, le Sionisme et l'état d'Israel*, ed. Doris Bensimon and Benjamin Pinkus (Paris: Publications Langues'O, 1989), p. 238. M. et L. Benaroya, " 'Lève-toi et va dans la ville du massacre,' " *La Terre retrouvée*, 1 February 1945. "Traduction en langue française de la réunion de l'organisation des 'Sioniste révisionnistes unifiés,' tenue en langue yiddish le 20 Juin à la Maison de la mutualité," 1 July 1946, dossier Palestine—Zionism, f/1a/3368, AN.

91 "Arrivé de convois d'Israélites en provenance d'Europe centrale," 23 December 1946, f/1a/3368, AN. "Question étrangères" and "Entrée clandestine en France de Juifs en provenance de camps de concentration allemands," Direction générale de la sûreté nationale, 13 September 1946, f/1a/3368, AN. For a discussion of disagreements among French policymakers toward those Jewish refugees passing through the country, see Idith Zertal, *From Catastrophe to Power: Holocaust Survivors and the Emergence of Israel* (Berkeley: University of California Press, 1998), pp. 52–92. For the response from Jewish agencies, see Laura Margolis to Henrietta Buchman, 31 December 1948, 316, AJDC. AJDC Office for France to Robert Pilpel, 13 December 1948, 325, AJDC, and Office for France Activities, May 1948 through September 1948, 310, AJDC. Other organizations, such as Bahad Hapoel Hamizrachi, operated their own holding camps as well. Charles Passman to AJDC—New York, 2 September 1949, 325, AJDC.

92 In the last quarter of 1948, for example, 852 children passed through the Aliyah European Transient Center in Marseille. European Executive Council, Welfare Department Report Number 3, June 1949, 310, AJDC. From its inception in fall 1946, Youth Aliyah brought 1,899 children from Poland, Bulgaria, Germany, Austria, Holland, and Hungary into France. By April 1949, 1,250 of them had already left for Israel. Lena Meyer, "European Executive Council, Welfare Department Report Number 2," April 1949, 314, AJDC. In one instance, an entire orphanage that had been relocated from Poland to Paris when persecution had become too great in the east relocated to Israel in 1949. Letter requesting aid, 1 June 1948, papers of the Federation of Jewish Relief Organisations of Great Britain (FJRO) 61, Parkes Library. According to AJDC reports, as of 1948 there were 1,846 men, women, and children living in eleven rab-

binical and yeshiva installations around Paris. European Executive Council, Welfare Department Report Number 3, June 1949, 310, AJDC; Memorandum, Laura Margolis to Judah Shapiro, "Rabbinical and Yeshiva Groups," 6 December 1949, 316, AJDC.

93 "Discours prononcé ne Yiddish par trois orateurs juifs au cours de la réunion organisée le 12 juillet, salle Lancry, par l'Union juive de la résistance et de l'entr'aide," 20 July 1946, dossier Palestine—Zionism, f/1a/3368, AN; "Meeting de protestation contre les 'pogroms' de Pologne, organisée par l'Association des juifs polonais en France," 12 July 1946, same folder. "Réaction des milieux israélites après les évènements de Palestine," 11 July 1946, dossier Palestine—Zionism, f/1a/3368, AN. "Les Israélites de Strasbourg protestant contre l'attitude adoptée à l'égard de leurs coreligionnaires de Palestine par le gouvernement anglais," 13 July 1946, dossier Palestine—Zionism, f/1a/3368, AN. Report on réunion de protestation contre la politique britannique en Palestine, organisée par l'organisations sioniste de France, 5 July 1946, dossier Palestine—Zionism, f/1a/3368, AN.

94 "Réunion organisée par l'Organisation sioniste," 28 July 1946, dossier Palestine—Zionism, f/1a/3368, AN. Newsletter from Keren Hayessod, distributed by Keren Hayessod de France, 17 August 1945, French Jewish Communities, 13/2–2, JTS. Zertal, From Catastrophe to Power, pp. 77–79.

95 Cited in Poznanski, "Le Sionisme en France pendant la deuxième guerre mondiale," p. 213.

96 "Les Milieux israélites lyonnais craignent que l'activité déployée par les dirigeants sionistes en vue de favoriser l'immigration juive en France ne suscite un nouveau mouvement antisémite," 29 July 1946, dossier Palestine—Zionism, f/1a/3368, AN. For pro-Zionist sentiment in Lyon," Lyon, Centre de la propagande sioniste, 24 July 1946, same folder.

97 "La Propagande anti-britannique dans les milieux juifs de Paris," 11 July 1946, dossier Palestine—Zionism, f/1a/3368, AN.

98 Guy de Rothschild, The Whims of Fortune: The Memoirs of Guy de Rothschild (New York: Random House, 1985), p. 306. Dossiers non-inventoriés: Dossier généralités - Comité d'études des affaires juives, Archives du Ministère des relations extérieures, April and May 1945, cited in Poznanski, "L'Héritage de la guerre," p. 247.

99 Harry M. Rosen to Joseph J. Schwartz, "United Fund-Raising for French Jewish Community," 30 June 1948, 357, AJDC. European Jewry Ten Years after the War, p. 44.

100 Harry M. Rosen to Joseph J. Schwartz, "United Fund-Raising for French Jewish Community," 30 June 1948, 357, AJDC. Country Directors Conference Report: France, 1956, 309, AJDC.

101 Brubaker, Nationalism Reframed, p. 67. For a similar point about the impact of "homelands" on diaspora populations, see Michel Bruneau, "Espaces et territoires de diasporas," in Diasporas, ed. Michel Bruneau (Montpellier: Reclus, 1995), p. 14.

102 Gabriel Sheffer, "Ethnic Diasporas: A Threat to Their Hosts?" in International Migration

and *Security,* ed. Myron Weiner (Boulder, Colo.: Westview Press, 1993), pp. 263–85, shows the significant economic impact of ethnic diasporas on their homelands.

103 Brubaker, *Nationalism Reframed,* p. 60.

5 Maintaining a Visible Presence

1 Phyllis Cohen Albert argues that even in the nineteenth century Jews expressed their identity in characteristically "ethnic" ways. "Ethnicity and Jewish Solidarity in Nineteenth-century France," in *Mystics, Philosophers, and Politicians: Essays in Jewish Intellectual History in Honor of Alexander Altman,* ed. Jehuda Reinharz and Daniel Swetschinski (Durham, N.C.: Duke University Press, 1982), pp. 249–74.

2 Nadia Malinovich, "Le Réveil d'Israel: Jewish Identity and Culture in France, 1900–1932" (Ph.D. diss., University of Michigan, 2000). For a discussion of the challenge to notions of French universalism, see Rogers Brubaker, *Citizenship and Nationhood in France and Germany* (Cambridge, Mass.: Harvard University Press, 1992), pp. 98–102.

3 Martine Hovanessian, *Le Lien communautaire: Trois générations d'arméniens* (Paris: Armand Colin, 1992). As the copious literature on immigration documents, most new arrivals deal with the culture shock of migration by turning inward as much as possible. Ralph Schor's *Histoire de l'immigration en France de la fin du XIXe siècle à nos jours* (Paris: Armand Colin, 1996), pp. 92–97, offers a helpful synthesis of this process in interwar France.

4 Président du Conseil, Ministre des Affaires étrangers to Préfet des Bouches-du-Rhône, 2 March 1925, 4M957, Bouches-du-Rhône. Marie-Françoise Attard-Maraninchi and Emile Temime, *Le Cosmopolitisme de l'entre-deux-guerres (1919–1945),* vol. 3: *Histoire des migrations à Marseille* (Marseille: Edisud, 1990), pp. 54–55.

5 Takvor Hatchikian to Président du Conseil, 2 July 1925, Fransa gtnoworֲ gaght῾aknner, Délégation Nationale, Bibliothèque Nubar.

6 Marsēyl kʻēmb Ōttō i hay gaghtʻakannerun Azg. Pashtōnakan marminneru ev Hayrenasēr azgayinneru, 24 June 1925, Fransa gtnoworֲ gaghtʻaknner, Délégation Nationale, Bibliothèque Nubar.

7 Conflict broke out among the residents themselves over who should have to leave first, with several complaining that wealthier residents were being "protected" in the camp. T. Nazarian, N. Missakian, and O. Tomassian to Directeur du dépôt des travailleurs étrangers de Marseille, 4 July 1925, 4M957, Bouches-du-Rhône.

8 Tnōrēn kʻēmb Ōttō gaghtʻakayani to Prn. Pʻashalean, Kʻartughar gaghtʻakanatsʻ Hantsnakhumbi, 26 May 1926, Fransa gtnoworֲ gaghtʻaknner, Délégation Nationale, Bibliothèque Nubar.

9 Commissaire spécial chargé du Camp Oddo to Préfet des Bouches-du-Rhône, 14 June 1926, 4M964, Bouches-du-Rhône. Tnōrēn kʻēmb Ōttō gaghtʻakayani to Prn. Pʻashalean, Kʻartughar gaghtʻakanatsʻ Hantsnakhumbi, 26 May 1926, Fransa gtnoworֲ

gaght'aknner, Délégation Nationale, Bibliothèque Nubar. Hatchikian himself remained in Marseille and set up a printing press. Hovh. Varzhapetean, *Guide de Marseille/Ughets'oyts' Marsēyli* (Marseille: Imprimerie Daron, 1939), p. 8.

10 Commissaire de Police—ville d'Epinal to Commissaire spécial de la gare St. Lazare chargé des services d'émigration à Paris, 15 February 1924, Fransa gtnowor̲ gaght'aknner, Délégation Nationale, Bibliothèque Nubar.

11 Levon Ch'ormisean, *Fransahayeru patmut'iwnē* Vol. 1: *Hay sp'iwr̲k'ē* (Beirut: Imprimerie G. Doniguian, 1975), p. 80. It is instructive to note that in this regard they mirrored most of the immigrant propulations of the era, who tended to group by neighborhood or street. See Schor, *Histoire de l'immigration*, pp. 93–94.

12 An example of such patterns is clear in police reports from Courbevoie, 2 June 1927, f/7/13436,AN. Hovanessian, *Le Lien communautaire*, pp. 55–56, 76, calls the preoccupation with building such homes a "common fever" among the refugees.

13 Aïda Boudjikanian-Keuroghlian, "Un peuple en exil: La Nouvelle diaspora (XIXe–XXe siècles)," in *Histoire des Arméniens*, ed. Gérard Dédéyan (Toulouse: Éditions Privat, 1982), pp. 648–49; Martine Hovanessian, "Soixante ans de présence arménienne en région parisienne (Le Cas d'Issy-les-Moulineaux)," *Revue européenne des migrations internationales* 4, no. 3 (1988): 73–90.

14 Attard-Maraninchi and Temime, *Le Cosmopolitisme de l'entre-deux-guerres*, p. 100. Anahide Ter Minassian, "Les Arméniens et le Paris des libertés," in *Le Paris des étrangers depuis un siècle*, ed. André Kaspi and Antoine Marès (Paris: Imprimerie nationale, 1989), pp. 132–33, discusses the insular nature of the Armenian family in Paris in the interwar years and the low rate of intermarriage. Birthrates for Armenians were also considerably higher. In Valence in 1926, for example, Armenians gave birth at a rate three times that of the local French population. Aïda Boudjikanian-Keuroghlian, *Les Arméniens dans la region Rhône-Alpes: Essai géographique sur les rapports d'une minorité ethnique avec son milieu d'accueil* (Lyon: Association des Amis de la Revue de géographie de Lyon, 1978), p. 94. According to Ter Minassian (p. 133), these figures tapered off during the economic crisis of the 1930s. She also argues that the interwar years were characterized by an Armenian cultural renaissance, with eighty-seven Armenian periodicals taking shape in Paris alone from 1919 to 1939 as well as a half dozen Armenian presses and thousands of novels, essays, historical works, poems, and essays being published in Armenian.

15 Hovanessian, *Le Lien communautaire*, pp. 55–56, 80. Ter Minassian, "Les Arméniens et le Paris des libertés," pp. 124–25.

16 Varzhapetean, *Guide de Marseille/Ughets'oyts' Marsēyli*.

17 The Church's role maintaining an "Armenian identity" in the diaspora has been traced in most scholarly studies of twentieth-century Armenian communities. See, for example, Anny Bakalian, *Armenian-Americans: From Being to Feeling Armenian* (New Brunswick, N.J.: Transaction Publishers, 1993), chap. 2; Susan Paul Pattie, *Faith in History: Armenians Rebuilding Community* (Washington, D.C.: Smithsonian Institution

Press, 1997), chap. 13. For a general theoretical discussion of the link between the Church and the diaspora, see Khachig Tölölyan, "The Role of the Armenian Apostolic Church in the Diaspora," *Armenian Review* 41, no. 1-161 (1988): 55-68.

18 Hovanessian, *Le Lien communautaire*, pp. 116-22.

19 The isolation of the Armenian Church in the fifth century (over doctrinal disagreements with neighboring Christian sects) intensified the link between Church and people because it prevented their potential merging with other Christian groups. "Affirmation de l'Arménie chrétienne," in *Histoire des Arméniens*, ed. Gérard Dédéyan (Toulouse: Éditions Privat, 1982), pp. 141-84.

20 Christopher J. Walker, *Armenia: The Survival of a Nation*, 2d ed. (New York: St. Martin's Press, 1980), pp. 125-26.

21 *Le Guide des étrangers* (Paris: A-DER, 1937), pp. 5-24. The Armenian Red Cross, an international organization, and one branch of the Union des dames arméniennes de Paris ran the dispensary where needy Armenian refugees could obtain free medical help. This organization also devoted much of its work to aiding orphans. P'arizi hay tiknants' miut'iwně: Ir keank'n u gortsě–hngewtasnameay hobeleanin aṛt'iw, 1913–1929 (Paris, 1929). Between them, Armenian Protestants and Catholics make up less than 10 percent of the French Armenian population. For discussions of their activities, see Hovanessian, *Le Lien communautaire*, pp. 118-20; René Leonian, ed., *Les Arméniens de France sont-ils intégrés ou assimilés* (Issy-les-Moulineaux: Imprimerie IMEAF, 1986); Cyril le Tallec, *La Communauté arménienne de France, 1920–1950* (Paris: l'Harmattan, 2001), pp. 60-65.

22 By-laws, Association de bienfaisance des dames arméniennes de Marseille, 7 October 1931, 4170, 4M698, Bouches-du-Rhône. Commissaire spécial [Lyon] to Préfet du Rhône, 20 November 1928, f/7/13436, AN.

23 Hovanessian, *Le Lien communautaire*, pp. 121-22.

24 Aram Terzian, "Growth of the Armenian Community in Paris during the Interwar Years, 1919–39," *Armenian Review* 27, no. 3-107 (1974): 275.

25 Ligue international philoarménienne to G. Noradounghian, 16 January 1925, Divers, Délégation Nationale, Bibliothèque Nubar. Albert Thomas (League of Nations) to Noradounghian, 12 January 1925, same file. Reports and letters regarding refugees in Greece, Syria, Lebanon, Cyprus, China, Hungary, and Soviet Armenia in Papiers divers-Comité central des réfugiés arméniens; "Docteur Melconian," Délégation Nationale; and Bureau international du travail, Délégation Nationale, Bibliothèque Nubar. John Hope Simpson, *The Refugee Problem: Report of a Survey* (London: Oxford University Press, 1939), pp. 300-301.

26 Comité central des réfugiés arméniens to Ministre des Affaires étrangères, 30 August 1926, Puissances, Délégation Nationale, Bibliothèque Nubar. "Nos réfugiés en France," *Le Foyer*, 1 December 1931. The impact on refugees of laws restricting the rights of foreign workers shifted over the course of the 1930s, with hard-line policies shaping earlier laws and more liberal policies under the Popular Front. J. Simpson,

The Refugee Problem, pp. 275–77, discusses the impact of these laws on refugees in France, noting (p. 319) that in many areas Armenians were able to retain their jobs.

27   [Comité central des réfugiés arméniens to Ministre des Affaires étrangères], 4 March 1927, Délégation Nationale, Bibliothèque Nubar. Secrétaire général (Comité central des réfugiés arméniens) to Ministre des Affaires étrangères, 21 January and 11 February 1927, Délégation Nationale, Bibliothèque Nubar. At times, the Foreign Ministry rejected the Comité central's requests. Many examples of such requests — both accepted and denied — are documented in Puissances, Délégation Nationale, Bibliothèque Nubar. Other Armenian organizations also did their best to reunite families. The representative of the Armenian Church in Paris, for example, wrote to the Comité central asking them to bring five orphans living in Lebanese orphanages to Paris to live with their parents. Kat'oghikosakan Patuirakut'iwn S. Ejmiatsni hayots' Ywropayi to Ĕndh. K'artughar Gaght'akanats' Kedronakan Handznazhoghovin, 25 May 1925, Azg. Marminner, Délégation Nationale, Bibliothèque Nubar.

28   Ĕhdh. Kartughar to Harut'iwn Dēr Pōghosean, 2 February 1925, Divers, Délégation Nationale, Bibliothèque Nubar. For example, the Comité central helped locate Joseph Hasaoumian and Bogosse Baliyan for their families. Several letters back and forth regarding this issue between 30 December 1924 and 8 April 1925, Fransa gtnowor gaght'aknner, Délégation Nationale, Bibliothèque Nubar. Other examples can be found in letters between the Comité central des réfugiés arméniens and the Service international d'aide aux émigrants, in Associations arménophiles, Délégation Nationale, Bibliothèque Nubar.

29   Comité central des réfugiés arméniens to Société de mécanique de Clichy, 2 September 1925, Fransa gtnowor gaght'aknner, Délégation Nationale, Bibliothèque Nubar; Secrétaire Général (Comité central des réfugiés arméniens) to L. Antériou (Député de l'Ardèche) 12 February 1925, in same carton.

30   "L'Office international Nansen pour les réfugiés," *Le Foyer*, 1 March 1931, and "Le Président Paul Doumer," *Le Foyer*, 1 June 1931. Even then, however, the criticism was directed primarily at the international community as a whole. Indeed, if anything, France was portrayed as the best of the bunch because it at least had let in numerous refugees both at home and in Syria and Lebanon.

31   S. Andesian and M. Hovanessian, "L'Arménien: Langue rescapée d'un génocide," in *Vingt-cinq communautés linguistiques de la France*, vol. 2, ed. Genevieve Vermès (Paris: L'Harmattan, 1988), pp. 66–67.

32   Schor, *Histoire de l'immigration*, pp. 98–102, points out that rates of integration varied among migrant groups. For example, those who worked with their compatriots, as Armenians began doing early on, resisted integration longer. Nevertheless, no immigrant population was immune, particularly as a younger generation began to be educated in French schools. Likewise, for those who ended up in mines and factories working alongside French citizens, integration was more rapid.

33   For the impact of the migration on traditional Armenian families and the role of

women, see Hovanessian, *Le Lien communautaire*, pp. 172–74; Ter Minassian, "Les Arméniens et le Paris des libertés," pp. 127–28, 131–32. This pattern was replicated throughout immigrant communities. For a helpful discussion of the relationship between gender and immigrant labor in interwar France and the United States, see Nancy Green, *Ready to Wear and Ready to Work: A Century of Industry and Immigrants in Paris and New York* (Durham, N.C.: Duke University Press, 1997), pp. 161–87.

34 Ministre de l'Intérieur to Ministre de Travail, 24 February 1927, f/7/13436, AN. Hovanessian, *Le Lien communautaire*, pp. 131–32. Such conflicts broke out *within* institutions as well. In one instance, a conflict over the Armenian Church's voting procedure was taken to the French courts. Commissaire spécial [Lyon] to Préfet du Rhône, 20 November 1928, f/7/13436, AN.

35 Bakalian, *Armenian-Americans*, traces the integration of Armenian immigrants into American society and argues that for the first generation, Armenian identity was not a choice but exclusive and all-encompassing. In subsequent generations, however, with increased acculturation, it became tangential and, hence, sentimental and symbolic. Thus, the first generation "was" Armenian, whereas the third "felt" Armenian.

36 Robert Sommer, "Où va le Judaïsme français?" *L'Amandier fleuri* 1, no. 1 (1949): 9, cited in Roger Berg, "La Pratique du Judaïsme en France," *Yod* 21 (1985): 83.

37 Pierre Lowell, "Les Foyards," *Évidences* 27 (1952): 36.

38 "Demandes de changements de nom," *Bulletin d'information* (May 1945): 3, French Jewish Communities, 13/ 2–2, JTS. "Rapport sur les changements de noms," Gaston Hildenfinger, June 1947, Législation et demandes de changements de noms, Consistoire de Paris.

39 Paul Levy, *Les Noms des israélites de France: Histoire et dictionnaire* (Paris: PUF, 1960), cited in Annette Wieviorka, *Déportation et génocide: Entre la mémoire et l'oubli* (Paris: Plon, 1992), p. 365. "Note sur les demandes de changement de nom (d'après le J.O. depuis le 1er Janvier 1945)," in Législation et demandes de changements de noms, Consistoire de Paris.

40 Wieviorka, *Déportation et génocide*, p. 353, compiles some figures on Jewish marriages, bar mitzvah ceremonies, and confirmations from different figures in the consistorial archives. Also see Berg, "La Pratique du Judaïsme en France."

41 In 1947, 440 marriages were performed; the number dropped consistently thereafter and by 1953 had reached an all-time low of 253. Simon Schwarzfuchs, "Un Aspect démographique de la communauté parisienne," *Journal des communautés* (22 January 1954): 3. Edgard Spira, "Compte rendu financier," *Journal des communautés* (24 June 1960), reported that from 1950 to 1954 the number of students in Talmud Torah never exceeded 750 and hit a low in 1953 of 473. In 1955 the number jumped to 1,265 and by 1959 had reached 2,400. According to Berg, "La Pratique du judaïsme en France," p. 95, this jump was evidence of the progress that the French Jewish leadership had made in encouraging the rebirth of Jewish faith since World War II. Berg, however, ignores the impact of North African Jews, which he claims did not have an effect

until 1960. In fact, North African Jews were already coming in large numbers by the mid-1950s. The dramatic jump in numbers undoubtedly reflects their impact.

42 Minutes, 7 March and 6 June 1945, AA26, Consistoire de Paris.

43 Minutes, 23 April 1947, AA26, Consistoire de Paris. Also see Roger Berg, "La Communauté juive de Paris en 1957," Bi-tefutsot ha-golah (Dispersion et Unité) 1 (1960): 343. Minutes, 7 December 1948, AA27, Consistoire de Paris. Minutes, 4 January 1950, AA28, Consistoire de Paris.

44 Historians of religion have argued that the de-Christianization of France was not, in fact, a linear process, and that Catholicism in particular experienced periods when religious sentiment was more intense. In particular, they note the mid-1930s to mid-1960s as several decades when renewed interest in Catholicism took hold, followed by a period of religious crisis. See Gérard Cholvy et al, Histoire religieuse de la France contemporaine, vol. 3 (Paris: Bibliothèque historique private, 1988); Gérard Cholvy, La Religion en France de la fin du XVIIIe à nos jours (Paris: Hachette, 1991). Judaism and Catholicism followed different paths in the twentieth century; for French Jews a period of renewed interest in Judaism came in the late 1960s and 1970s, after the arrival of North African Jewish immigrants and just when Catholicism was entering a period of "crisis." It is still true, however, that both felt the impact of the secular state, which—with the exception of the Vichy years—militantly enforced a separation of public life and private religious practices. For statistics on religious practices in twentieth-century France, see Fernand Boulard, Gérard Cholvy, and Yves-Marie Hilaire, eds., Matériaux pour l'histoire religieuse du peuple français, XIXe–XXe, 3 vols. (Paris: Ed. du CNRS, EHCSS, FNSP, 1982–92).

45 Paula Hyman, From Dreyfus to Vichy: The Remaking of French Jewry, 1906–1939 (New York: Columbia University Press, 1979), p. 30.

46 European Jewry Ten Years after the War: An Account of the Development and Present Status of the Decimated Jewish Communities of Europe (New York: Institute of Jewish Affairs of the World Jewish Congress, 1956), p. 203; File Yeshivoth A-Z, AJDC.

47 In 1947 estimates of attendance at Kol Nidre services in Paris reached fifteen thousand. In certain synagogues these numbers were made up of newly arrived Egyptian and North African Jewish refugees, but it is also clear that the native Jewish population had clearly not completely abandoned their ancestral religion. Minutes, 2 October 1946, AA26, Consistoire de Paris; Minutes, 8 October 1947, AA27, Consistoire de Paris.

48 For a discussion of the impact of the Dreyfus Affair, World War I, and immigration waves on broadening notions of French Jewish identity in the early twentieth century, see Malinovich, "Le Réveil d'Israel" and Hyman, From Dreyfus to Vichy. For ethnic Jewish affiliations even in the previous century, see Albert, "Ethnicity and Jewish Solidarity in Nineteenth-century France."

49 Harry M. Rosen to Joseph J. Schwartz, "United Fund-Raising for French Jewish Com-

munity," 30 June 1948, file 357, AJDC. David Weinberg, "The Reconstruction of the French Jewish Community after World War II," in *She'erit hapletah, 1944–1948: Rehabilitation and Political Struggle: Proceedings of the Sixth Yad Vashem International Historical Conference, Jerusalem 1985* (Jerusalem: Yad Vashem, 1990), p. 174, argues that far from destroying Jewish communal affiliation, the Holocaust enticed certain of those with assimilationist tendencies to reconsider their Jewish heritage and to take a "growing pride in the dual heritage of Frenchmen and Jew." Studies on the 1920s, such as Malinovich's, however, suggest that this pride in a dual heritage was already a significant part of communal discourse prior to the Holocaust. Doris Bensimon, *Les Juifs de France et leurs relations avec Israel, 1945–1988* (Paris: Éditions l'Harmattan, 1989), p. 17, also argues that most Jews remained committed to their ethnic heritage despite the Holocaust, although, she claims, most relegated their attachment to the private sphere. The argument here is that this attachment was less private than previously understood.

50 *Tableau des organisations juives*, 15 May 1946, Consistoire israélite de Paris, cited in Annette Wieviorka, "Les Juifs en France au lendemain de la guerre: État des lieux" *Archives juives: Revue d'histoire des Juifs de France* 28, no. 1 (1995): 9.

51 Jacques Adler, *The Jews of Paris and the Final Solution: Communal Response and Internal Conflicts, 1940–44* (Oxford: Oxford University Press, 1985); Richard Cohen, *The Burden of Conscience: French Jewish Leadership during the Holocaust* (Bloomington: Indiana University Press, 1987).

52 "Le Problème des enfants de déportés et la question des conversions," *Bulletin d'information* (May 1945): 2, French Jewish Communities, 13/ 2–2, JTS. In 1947 OPEJ had fourteen children's homes, but by 1950 it was supporting only approximately five hundred children. L. Zupraner to Brodie, 19 September 1950, papers of the Chief Rabbinate, E1196, GLRO. For a discussion of OPEJ and other child care agencies after the war, see Wieviorka, *Déportation et génocide*, pp. 369–90. Paula Hyman, *The Jews of Modern France* (Berkeley: University of California Press, 1998), pp. 187–189, nicely synthesizes the literature on Jewish war orphans.

53 Like OPEJ, the numbers decreased throughout the late 1940s, and by 1950, OSE had only nine such homes with five hundred children. Sabine Zeitoun, *L'Œuvre de secours aux enfants (OSE) sous l'occupation en France* (Paris: L'Harmattan, 1990).

54 Rachel Cheigman, "Maison d'enfants," *La Terre retrouvée*, 1 February 1945.

55 As of February 1949, they had sent 240 Jewish orphans out of France. Secours national juif to Mr. Cristal, 16 February 1949, FJRO 61, Parkes Library. Request for aid from Rabbi B. Apeloig, Secretary General of the Maison israélite de refuge and the Oeuvre israélite des séjours à la campagne, 18 October 1945, French Jewish Communities, 13/2–1, JTS.

56 Kelman to Jews from France, Inc., 30 May 1947, 314, AJDC. One organizer complained, "We are obliged to struggle against the Jewish Communists whose pro-

paganda is intense and whose corrupting influence is growing every day." Judah
Shapiro, Fondation Roger Fleishman, to President, American Joint Distribution
Committee, 23 August 1950, 347, AJDC.

57 Georges Wormser, "Le Leçon des évènements," introduction to *La Communauté de
Paris après la libération* (Paris: Consistoire israélite de Paris, 1946), pp. 6–7. Despite
this new rhetoric of solidarity, old biases died hard. While the Consistoire de Paris
took an active part in aiding eastern European Jewish migration to France in the late
1940s, certain members insisted that only those who would "benefit" French Jewry
should be encouraged to migrate, as well as those who were "useful" and would assimilate rapidly into French society. Minutes, 4 December 1946, AA26, Consistoire
de Paris. In addition, coordinated activities between native Jewish organizations and
those representing Jews of eastern European descent did not always go smoothly. For
example, in 1947, members of the Consistoire de Paris expressed disapproval when
Rabbi Kaplan lent his name to the FSJF's summer camp fundraising drive, worrying
that their own organization would not get the appropriate credit or financial benefit.
Others worried that the summer camps would not stringently enforce religious practices. Wormser, despite his previous rhetoric of unity, refused to sign his name to
any Fédération document written in Yiddish. Nevertheless, other Consistoire members were pleased to know that their organization and the Fédération could work
together despite their past history. Minutes, 4 June 1947, AA26, Consistoire de Paris.
Bulletin quotidien d'information de l'agence télégraphique juive, 28ème année, 307 (7 May
1946) French Jewish Communities, 13/2–1, JTS.

58 Minutes, 7 February 1946, AA26, Consistoire de Paris. As another official remarked,
the Consistoire's main goals for the new era should be "to regroup, to advise, to com-
fort, and above all to unite." Minutes, 7 January 1946, AA26, Consistoire de Paris.
Edmond Dreyfuss, "Rapport au Consistoire de Paris sur les mesures à prendre en vue
de remédier à la désaffection pour le culte," Minutes, 5 May 1946, AA27, Consistoire
de Paris.

59 British Jews also contributed to postwar reconstruction of French Jewish life, but
because of the British-Jewish conflict in Palestine and the consequent increase in
antisemitic rhetoric, Anglo-Jewry proved reluctant to become actively involved in relief efforts that might call attention to themselves. Moreover, because of their smaller
numbers, lesser financial means, and comparatively insignificant political influence,
British Jews proved far less involved in reconstruction efforts than their American
Jewish counterparts. Richard Bolchover, *British Jewry and the Holocaust* (Cambridge,
England: Cambridge University Press, 1993); Tony Kushner, *The Holocaust and the Liberal Imagination: A Social and Cultural History* (Oxford: Basil Blackwell, 1994); Bernard
Wasserstein, *Britain and the Jews of Europe, 1939–1945* (New York: Clarendon Press,
1979). Some aid was nevertheless forthcoming from the Anglo-Jewish Association
and the Federation of Jewish Relief Organizations. The archives of both organizations document their involvement and are located in the Parkes Library. Also provid-

ing aid was the Central British Fund for Jewish Relief and Rehabilitation, founded in 1933 to aid Jewish refugees. For more on the latter, see Amy Zahl Gottlieb, *Men of Vision: Anglo-Jewry's Aid to Victims of the Nazi Regime, 1933–1945* (London: Widenfeld and Nicolson, 1998). For a history of the AJDC's origins, see Yehuda Bauer, *My Brother's Keeper* (Philadelphia: Jewish Publication Society of America, 1974). For the war years, see Yehuda Bauer, *American Jewry and the Holocaust: The American Jewish Joint Distribution Committee, 1928–1939* (Jerusalem: Institute of Contemporary Jewry, Hebrew University, 1981). For the postwar years, see Yehuda Bauer, *Out of the Ashes: The Impact of American Jews on Post-Holocaust European Jewry* (Oxford: Pergamon Press, 1989). For an overview of AJDC activities in France, see Isabelle Goldsztejn, "Le Role de l'American Joint dans la reconstruction de la communauté," *Archives juives: Revue d'histoire des Juifs de France* 28, no. 1 (1995): 23–37; *Activité des organisations juives en France sous l'occupation* (Paris: Centre de documentation juive contemporaine, Série 4, Études et monographies, 1947), pp. 15–18.

60 Memorandum, Laura Margolis to Judah Shapiro, "Educational and Cultural Activities, Office for France," 7 December 1949, 316, AJDC; Report d'activité du 1er trimestre 1945, Fédération des sociétés juives de France, French Jewish Communities, 13/2–1, JTS. Evidence of the Federation's intervention on behalf of deported Jews is evident in Report, Délégation régionale du services des restitutions, Nice, Annex, 2 April 1946, B10934, Archives du Ministère de Finance. Evidence on intervention on behalf of new immigrants was found in Mazor to Leftwich, FRJO, 15 November 1947, FRJO 62/1, Parkes Library, and "Relief Situation in France, January through June 1945," 17 August 1945, 311, AJDC. Frustrated that their funds were paying for overlapping services in many organizations, in May 1945, AJDC officials initiated a fusion of several different social service agencies into the Comité juif d'action social et de reconstruction; this committee provided financial allocations, clothing, meals, lodging, convalescent and medical care, and retirement facilities to as many as 27,030 people, or 15 percent of the Jewish population. Central Office Bulletin, European Executive Council, 21 September 1949, 314, AJDC. In April 1946, the AJDC established a special branch, the Service spécial des immigrants, to deal exclusively with the incoming population.

61 Guy de Rothschild to Mr. Baerwald, 8 May 1945, 311, AJDC.

62 For Jewish charities in the 1920s and 1930s, see Daniel J. Elazar, *Community and Polity: The Organizational Dynamics of American Jewry*, revised and updated ed. (Philadelphia: Jewish Publication Society, 1995), pp. 209–19; Deborah Dash Moore, *At Home in America: Second Generation New York Jews* (New York: Columbia University Press, 1981), pp. 149–74; Beth S. Wenger, *New York Jews and the Great Depression: Uncertain Promise* (New Haven: Yale University Press, 1996), pp. 135–65; Jonathan Woocher, *Sacred Survival: The Civil Religion of American Jews* (Bloomington: Indiana University Press, 1986), pp. 22–28, 32–51. For postwar Jewish fundraising, see Edward S. Shapiro, *A Time for Healing: American Jewry since World War II* (Baltimore: Johns Hopkins University Press,

1992), pp. 62–64. For a history of the UJA and its development, see Abraham J. Karp, *To Give Life: The UJA in the Shaping of the American Jewish Community* (New York: Schocken, 1981); Marc Lee Raphael, *A History of the United Jewish Appeal* (Chico, Calif.: Scholars Press, 1982).

63 Woocher, *Sacred Survival*, pp. 51–62.

64 Shapiro, *A Time for Healing*, p. 63.

65 Arthur Greenleigh to Moses Leavitt, 7 April 1945, 311, AJDC. Leon Shapiro to Harry Rosen, 7 May 1948, 357, AJDC.

66 Nancy Green, "To Give and to Receive: Philanthropy and Collective Responsibility among Jews in Paris, 1880–1914," in *The Uses of Charity: The Poor on Relief in the Nineteenth-Century Metropolis*, ed. Peter Mandler (Philadelphia: University of Pennsylvania Press, 1990), pp. 215–19.

67 For an overview of nineteenth-century French Jewish philanthropy, see Phyllis Cohen Albert, *The Modernization of French Jewry: Consistory and Community in the Nineteenth Century* (Hanover, N.H.: Brandeis University Press, 1977), pp. 136–40, 197, 237–38; Derek Penslar, *Shylock's Children: Economics and Jewish Identity in Modern Europe* (Berkeley: University of California Press, 2001), pp. 99, 122; Green, "To Give and to Receive, pp. 199–226.

68 Hyman, *From Dreyfus to Vichy*, pp. 120–32; Green, "To Give and to Receive." As the refugee crisis grew in central Europe, the native Jewish leadership proved more divided on the correct response to incoming Jewish immigrants, with some calling for a broader open-door policy. Vicki Caron, "Loyalties in Conflict: French Jewry and the Refugee Crisis, 1933–1935," *Leo Baeck Institute Yearbook* 36 (1991): 305–38.

69 Sources of funds of AJDC-subventioned organizations in France in 1947, 357, AJDC. For a description of the disorganized nature of local fundraising practices, see Memorandum, Jacques Pulver to Benjamin B. Goldman, "Report on my Trip to the United States," 5 November 1946, 357, AJDC. For Rosen's comments on ample Jewish fundraising in 1948, see Memorandum, Harry M. Rosen to Joseph J. Schwartz, "United Fund-Raising for French Jewish Community," 30 June 1948, and Memorandum, Harry M. Rosen to Philip Skorneck, "Progress Report on United Campaign for France," 22 June 1948, same file.

70 Président du Comité d'action et de collecte du Fonds social juif unifié, *Note d'information du CRIF*, 10 March 1952, Anglo Jewish Association papers, AJ95/I/31, Parkes Library. Harry Rosen to Ben [Goldman], no date, 357, AJDC. Memorandum, Harry M. Rosen to Joseph J. Schwartz, "United Fund-Raising for French Jewish Community," 30 June 1948, 357, AJDC. In February 1948, the Consistoire voted to support the birth of a common fund. Minutes, 4 February 1948, AA27, Consistoire de Paris. *Jewish Telegraphic Agency News*, 25 October 1949, p. 3.

71 In January 1950, due to pressure from the Zionist organization, the FSJU joined forces with the Aid to Israel Fund to conduct an "Appel Unifié." The results of 35 million

francs for the FSJU indicated that for the foreseeable future, the Fonds social should run its own campaign. "JDC Program in France–1951," 309, AJDC. In 1951, they did run their own campaign and received 92 million francs. "JDC Program in France-1952," same file. In Paris, the growing success of the FSJU can be measured in terms of numbers of contributing donors and amount of money raised. Hence, in 1951 it raised 88,025,000 francs from 3,761 donors; in 1955, it raised 155,075,000 francs from 6,255 people. *Country Report: France,* American Joint Distribution Committee, Country Directors Conference, Paris, 1956, 309, AJDC. Georges Wormser, Report on the Jewish community in France, Consultative Conference of the AIU, AJC, and AJA, June 1955, Anglo Jewish Association papers, AJ37/6/6/6/6, Parkes Library.

72 "Nos problèmes: Le FSJU," *Quand même,* June 1949; emphasis added. Guy de Rothschild, "Pour un judaïsme ouvert," in *Assemblée générale du Xe anniversaire du Fonds social juif unifié* (Paris: FSJU, 1960), p. 14.

73 Bernard Wasserstein, *Vanishing Diaspora: The Jews in Europe since 1945* (Cambridge, Mass.: Harvard University Press, 1996), p. 63.

74 In the early 1950s, the AJDC came under attack in the Parisian Yiddish and Zionist press for providing funds to the communist organization, the UJRE. *Unzer vort,* 2 December 1952. In addition, Rabbi Zalmon Schneerson, formerly deeply involved in directing Orthodox Jewish affairs in France, sent a telegram to the AJDC deploring the fact that the "growth of the French Communist organizations have been indirectly nurtured by JDC funds" and urging the AJDC to "rid itself of all Communist and pro-Communist elements responsible for the abandonment of their faith and heritage by thousands of our children." Rabbi Zalmon Schneerson to Edward M. Warburg, 20 January 1953, 371, AJDC. In response to the pressure and to accusations that the AJDC employed communists, the AJDC cut off funds to the UJRE. M. W. Bekelman to Moses Leavitt, 23 and 25 February 1953, 371, AJDC.

75 For the resurgence of the Consistoire in the 1960s, after the North African Jews arrived, and its greater cooperation with the FSJU, see Maud Mandel, "In the Aftermath of Genocide: Armenians and Jews in Twentieth-Century France" (Ph.D. diss., University of Michigan, 1998), chap. 8.

76 Consistoire leaders provided campaign lists early in the FSJU's formation, thereby cooperating with its organizers; moreover, some members of the Consistoire were actively involved in building and creating the new organization. Georges Wormser, for his part, remained supportive of the "risky initiative," hoping it would attract unaffiliated Jews. He insisted, however, that potential donors be reminded to preserve some of their funds for the community's religious activities. Rabbis, therefore, used their position to call for support for the new united fund, but the contribution forms that were distributed noted in red that religious institutions were excluded from receiving FSJU funds. Minutes, 5 October 1949; Minutes, 11 January 1950; Minutes, 7 June 1950, AA28 Consistoire de Paris.

77 Minutes, 7 June 1950, AA28 Consistoire de Paris. Rapport moral, 1952, Assises du Judaïsme français, Consistoire de Paris. Unmarked report [Rapport moral, Henri Levi, Secrétaire du Consistoire central], Assises du Judaïsme français 1956, Consistoire de Paris. Such trends are also evident in Projet de rapport moral, 22 June 1958, Assises du Judaïsme français 1958, Consistoire de Paris.

78 Julien Samuel, "Rapport moral: Regard sur 10 années d'activité du fonds social juif unifié," in *Assemblée générale du Xe anniversaire du Fonds social juif unifié* (Paris: FSJU, 1960), p. 4.

79 *Le Problème des revendications matérielles juives à l'égarde l'Allemagne* (Paris: Fédération des sociétés juives de France, 1952). Edgar Abravanel, "Le Judaïsme français prend conscience de ses devoirs," *Journal des communautés*, 23 March 1956 and 13 April 1956.

80 The Consistoire, for example, used these restitution funds to strengthen a variety of provincial communities, to build or rebuild libraries, and to print prayer books and religious textbooks. Henry Levy, Untitled report, Assises du Judaïsme français 1956, Consistoire de Paris. For information on the Commission du plan d'action culturelle, see Samuel, "Rapport moral," pp. 3–12; Berg, "La Pratique du Judaïsme en France," pp. 83–84, 91–92. For information on communal centers, see Abravanel, "Le Judaïsme français prend conscience de ses devoirs," p. 7.

81 Malinovich, "Le Réveil d'Israel," pp. 154, 168. In addition to youth centers, the AJDC requested a $50,000 grant from the Ford Foundation to build a Jewish community center in Paris in 1952 as a means "to bring about the social integration of a group of Jewish refugees." Memorandum, Judah J. Shapiro to Charles Jordan, 31 July 1952, 309, AJDC. Officials hoped that the new center would function like those in the United States in the 1920s, when "such centers and Settlement Houses had as an underlying motif the Americanization of new immigrants." In much the same way, the center in Paris was to bring immigrants into contact with "the French Community, the French language, customs, traditions and social patterns." Report, Laura Jarblum and Auren Kahn, 28 August 1952, same file.

82 David Kaufman, *Shul with a Pool: The "Synagogue Center" in American Jewish History* (Hanover, N.H.: University Press of New England, 1999); Abraham J. Karp, "Overview: The Synagogue in America—A Historical Typology," and Jack Wertheimer, "The Conservative Synagogue," in *The American Synagogue: A Sanctuary Transformed*, ed. Jack Wertheimer (Cambridge, England: Cambridge University Press, 1987), pp. 1–34, 111–49; Wenger, *New York Jews and the Great Depression*, pp. 166–96.

83 Judah Shapiro, "A Jewish Youth Center in Paris," Cultural Conference called by the Fonds social juif unifié, 22 March 1953, 316, AJDC.

84 Country Report: France, Country Directors Conference, Paris, 1956, 309, AJDC.

85 Samuel, "Rapport moral," p. 9.

86 Erik Cohen, *L'Étude et l'éducation juive en France ou L'Avenir d'une communauté* (Paris: Les Éditions du Cerf, 1991), p. 174.

87 Jacob Kaplan, "La Renaissance du Judaïsme français," in *Reconstruction of European Jewish Life and the Conference of European Rabbis*, ed. Maurice Rose (London: Conference of European Rabbis, Standing Committee, 1967), p. 61.

88 *Bâtir de nouvelles communautés* (Paris: Association consistoriale israélite de Paris, 1966). Rabbi Simon Schwarzfuchs articulated a similar position several years earlier: "The time has passed when one community can allow itself to construct a synagogue that will be used only 5 or 6 hours per week." Simon Schwarzfuchs, 13ème assemblée générale, FSJU: Journée d'études des problèmes des réfugiés et rapatriés d'Afrique du Nord, 5–6 May 1962.

89 Claude Tapia, "Religion et politique: Interférence dans le judaïsme français après l'immigration judéo-maghrébine," in *Les Juifs du Maghreb: Diasporas contemporaines*, ed. Jean-Claude Lasry and Claude Tapia (Paris: Éditions Harmattan, 1989), p. 211, also argues that after World War II, Jews in France rejected the universalistic philosophy that had characterized their position in French political life since the middle of the nineteenth century. Tapia's position is noteworthy, but he does not develop his argument nor does he provide any sources. In fact, this point precedes his more developed discussion of the intersection between religion and politics after the North African Jews migrated to France. For a discussion of more recent shifts away from universalism, see Chantal Benayoun, *Les Juifs et la politique* (Paris: Centre national de recherche scientifique, 1984); Pierre Birnbaum, *Jewish Destinies: Citizenship, State, and Community in Modern France*, trans. Arthur Goldhammer (New York: Hill and Wang, 1999); Sylvie Strudel, *Votes juifs* (Paris: Presses de la Fondation nationale des sciences politiques, 1996).

6 Genocide Revisited: Armenians and the French Polity after World War II

1 In 1942, for example, an Armenian named Badajlian publicly criticized the persecutions against Jews in a Parisian restaurant. "Métèques incorrigibles," *Pilori*, 24 September 1942. However, it is worth noting that this article, which condemned Badajlian for his behavior, identified him as a "sujet perse" and not an Armenian. An example of an Armenian who helped secure safety for two Jews can be found in André Sernin, *L'Homme de Tokat* (Paris: Éditions France-Empire 1987), pp. 104–8. For examples of parallels between the Jewish and Armenian fate made in the 1950s, see *Sur le chemin de la libération, 1940–44: Réseau Liban* (Paris: Imprimerie de Bresnik, 1952), p. 47, where the Armenian author, who had been active in the Resistance, argued that the refusal of Western powers to punish Turkey for the 1915 genocide had provided international sanction for future massacres of Jews and Poles. Likewise, Mélinée Manouchian, *Manouchian* (Paris: France Loisirs, 1974), p. 101, noted, "The Armenians had not been Nazism's direct victims . . . but what happened in Europe strangely resembled what they had known twenty-five years earlier. With superior

technical capabilities and a much wider field of activity, this was a new genocide." It is hard to know, however, how much of this consciousness was present during the war itself and how much was born in the post-Holocaust years, when the international community had already defined and condemned genocide at the International Military Tribunal at Nuremberg.

2 Yves Ternon, *La Cause arménienne* (Paris: Éditions du Seuil, 1983), p. 147, puts the number at 7,280.

3 See, for example, Jacques Parvanian, *Au-delà de l'espérance*, Vol. 1: *La Foi* (Paris: La Pensée universelle, 1979), p. 10, in which he talks in passing about his family's exodus from Paris. Martine Hovanessian, *Le Lien communautaire: Trois générations d'Arméniens* (Paris: Armand Colin, 1992), p. 170, documents the difficulties faced by individual families. Not all of her informants, however, were worse off during the war. Those with sewing machines, for example, had the right to a quota of wool and, due to the limited competition, were able to sell their products at a higher price (p. 158).

4 Anahide Ter Minassian, "Les Arméniens de Paris depuis 1945," in *Le Paris des étrangers depuis 1945*, ed. Antoine Marès and Pierre Milza (Paris: Publications de la Sorbonne, 1994), p. 216. Cyril le Tallec, *La Communauté arménienne de France, 1920–1950* (Paris: L'Harmattan, 2001), pp. 78, 100, 120, 174, 186–87.

5 Vicki Caron, *Uneasy Asylum: France and the Jewish Refugee Crisis, 1933–1942* (Stanford: Stanford University Press, 1999), pp. 6, 224. Le Tallec, *La Communauté arménienne*, pp. 155–62.

6 In September 1940, a law decreed that foreign men over the age of eighteen and under fifty could be assembled into groups of foreign workers if there was an excess participating in the national economy, or if, having sought refuge in France, they could not return to their own country. The law was suppressed in October 1945. *Bulletin du Centre israélite d'information*, 15 November 1945, 12/5, JTS. Sarah Farmer, "Out of the Picture: Foreign Labor in Wartime France," in Sarah Fishman et al., *France at War: Vichy and the Historians* (Oxford: Berg, 2000), pp. 249–60.

7 Le Tallec, *La Communauté arménienne*, p. 187.

8 Sernin, *L'Homme de Tokat*, pp. 107–8.

9 Le Tallec, *La Communauté arménienne*, p. 186. "Recensement des réfugiés d'origine arménienne," *Les Nouveaux Temps*, 24 June 1943. Relevant articles also appeared on 10 July 1943 in *Paris-Soir* and *Les Nouveaux Temps* and on 6 October 1943 in *Cri du peuple*, *Le Progrès* (Moulins), *Le Petit Comptois*, *France socialiste*, *Dépêche* (Tours), *L'Oeuvre*, *Le Matin*, *Paris-Soir*. Advertisements continued to be published reminding Armenians to register with the occupying authorities. For example, *Tribune de Seine et Oise*, 23 October 1943; "Avis aux émigrés caucasiens en France," *Pari du peuple*, 1 January 1944; *L'Œuvre*, *Le Matin*, *Paris-Soir*, and *Les Nouveaux Temps* (the latter two on 14 January 1944). In July 1944, the French authorities in the Occupied Zone noted that over seven thousand had registered. "Avis et communication," *Journal officiel de l'état français*," 7 July 1944, and "Avis aux arméniens," *France socialiste*, 21 July 1944.

10 Sur le chemin de la libération, p. 91; "La Jeunesse immigrée dans la lutte," Jeune combattant, 9 September 1944.

11 The two articles appeared in Ethnie française, the journal that Georges Montandon edited with one of his former students prior to taking the editorship of La Question juive. William H. Schneider, Quality and Quantity: The Quest for Biological Regeneration in Twentieth-Century France (Cambridge, England: Cambridge University Press, 1990), pp. 257–60.

12 R. Kherumian, "Les Arméniens en France," Ethnie française, January 1943. R. Kherumian, "Les Marches orientales de l'Europe: Le Destin de l'Arménie," La France socialiste, 2 September 1942. R. Kherumian, Les Arméniens, race, origines ethno-raciales (Paris: Vigot, 1941).

13 L'Arménie et le peuple arménien (Paris: Imprimerie H. Turabian, 1941), preface. Like Jewish race scientists in central and eastern Europe, Armenians appropriated the contemporary discourse to defend their place in their adopted society. See John M. Efron, Defenders of the Race: Jewish Doctors and Race Science in Fin-de-Siècle Europe (New Haven: Yale University Press, 1994). Prior to the 1940s, as race science took hold as a valid discourse in French public life, Armenians began asserting the purity of their racial makeup. Le Foyer, for example, published three separate articles on the "Armenian race": Dr. Kossowitz, "La Race arménienne d'après ses groupes sanguins," Le Foyer, 1 January 1929; "La Race arménienne," Le Foyer, 15 June 1929; and "Nos origines," Le Foyer, 1 January 1932.

14 Le Tallec, La Communauté arménienne, p.185.

15 "Le Président du conseil municipal de Paris reçu par le Maréchal," Paris-Soir, 13 March 1943, and Les Nouveaux Temps, the same day.

16 Varvara Basmadjian, Les Arméniens: Réveil ou fin (Paris: Édition Entente, 1979), pp. 143–44. Manouchian, Manouchian, p. 59.

17 Manouchian, Manouchian, p. 79.

18 Of the twenty-three, the one woman, Olga Bancic, was decapitated at Stuttgart because of a law in France preventing the execution of women.

19 Arsène Tchakarian, Les Fusillés du Mont Valérine (Paris: L'Écritoire pour le Comité national du souvenir des fusillés du Mont Valérine, 1991), pp. 155–57. Also see T. S. Dramp'yan, Fransahay komunistnerĕ gimagrut'yan tarinerin 1941–44 (Yerevan: "MITK'" Hratarakch'ut'yun, 1967); Basmadjian, Les Arméniens, pp. 143–44; Manouchian, Manouchian, p. 92.

20 Manouchian, Manouchian, p. 101.

21 Sur le chemin de la libération, p. 48.

22 Henri Michel, Bibliothèque critique de la résistance: Bibliographie (Paris: Institut pédagogique nationale, 1964), p. 102.

23 Sur le chemin de la libération, p. 91.

24 "Associations fédérés dans l'organisme appelle, CADI, f/1a/3345, AN. Le Tallec, La Communauté arménienne, pp. 169–73 writes about the FNA's Resistance activities dur-

ing the war, but his evidence is sketchy and pertains mostly to the waning days of the campaign in August 1944. The materials presented on the FNA's activities in Marseille (pp. 173–82), are somewhat more developed.

25 Le Tallec, *La Communauté arménienne*, pp. 162–63, 187, 189. On p. 185, he calculates the number of Armenians who died for the Resistance at fifty. This number, however, reflects those who lived in France and those who ended up on French soil during the battle because they had been incorporated into the German foreign legions when captured as Soviet soldiers. In France, some members of these battalions deserted to fight with the French underground against the German army.

26 Aïda Boudjikanian-Keuroghlian, "Un peuple en exil: La Nouvelle diaspora (XIXe– XXe siècles)," in *Histoire des Arméniens*, ed. Gérard Dédéyan (Toulouse: Éditions Privat, 1982), p. 649.

27 Le Tallec, *La Communauté arménienne de France*, p. 99. The law of 10 August 1927 was based on previously accepted principles of jus soli. All those born on French soil of foreign parents were thus French unless they explicitly renounced their citizenship upon coming of age. In addition, the law reduced residency requirements from ten years to three and to only one for those who possessed a diploma from a French university. For more on the principle of jus soli in French citizenship laws, see Rogers Brubaker, *Citizenship and Nationhood in France and Germany* (Cambridge, Mass.: Harvard University Press, 1992).

28 John Hope Simpson, *The Refugee Problem: Report of a Survey* (London: Oxford University Press, 1939), pp. 43, 321.

29 Paula Hyman, *From Dreyfus to Vichy: The Remaking of French Jewry, 1906–1939* (New York: Columbia University Press, 1979), p. 66, notes that in 1928–29, one fifth of all applications for naturalization were summarily rejected. Gérard Noiriel, *Le Creuset français: Histoire de l'immigration XIXe–XXe siècle* (Paris: Le Seuil, 1988), explains this reluctance by pointing to the ambivalence in liberal French immigration laws, which on the one hand claimed to respect a tradition of generosity to foreigners while on the other seeking to prevent them from becoming political actors in the state. For decreasing rates throughout the 1930s, see Caron, *Uneasy Asylum*, p. 57. The comparative figures come from Gary Cross, *Immigrant Workers in Industrial France: The Making of a New Laboring Class* (Philadelphia: Temple University Press, 1983), p. 178. One explanation for these differences might have arisen from the different timing of immigration to both countries, with migration to the United States coming virtually to a halt in the early 1920s.

30 Maxim Silverman, *Deconstructing the Nation: Immigration, Racism, and Citizenship in Modern France* (London: Routledge, 1992), p. 39. According to Silverman, such state-controlled immigration soon gave way to more market-driven and unorganized immigration processes.

31 Gouvernement provisoire de la république française, "Instructions complémentaires destinés au Ministre de la justice (Service des naturalisations)," 18 July 1945,

f/1a/3345, AN. Circulaire, Ministre de l'Intérieur, "Mesures relatives à la liquidation rapide des dossiers de naturalisation en instance dans les préfectures," 24 August 1945, f/1a/3346, AN.

32 Most Armenians in France were products of the interwar migration, but some newcomers arrived in the late 1940s, primarily from the Balkans and Middle East. Ter Minassian, "Les Arméniens de Paris depuis 1945," p. 209.

33 Note pour Monsieur le directeur général de la sûreté nationale, 26 August 1946, f/1a/3346, AN.

34 Hovanessian, *Le Lien communautaire*, p. 108. Caron, *Uneasy Asylum*, chaps. 10 and 11, covers debates in the 1930s over naturalizations for foreigners serving in the French army.

35 *Libération*, 11 November 1944. *Marseillaise*, 26 October 1944. The Union franco-arménienne, though primarily concerned with promoting a variety of educational, agricultural, economic, cultural, and athletic outlets for local Armenian populations, also dedicated itself to cultivating a relationship between the French and Armenian people. *Dsragir–Kanongir: Fransahay azgayin chakati* (Fransahay azgayin ĕndh. miwtʻian) (Paris: 1945) and *Dsragir–Kanongir: Fransayi hay azgayin ĕndh. miwtʻian* (Paris: 1947). For more on Tchobanian, see Edmond Khayadjian, *Archag Tchobanian et le mouvement arménophile en France* (Marseille: Centre national de documentation pédagogique, 1986).

36 Phyllis Cohen Albert, "Ethnicity and Jewish Solidarity in Nineteenth-century France," in *Mystics, Philosophers, and Politicians: Essays in Jewish Intellectual History in Honor of Alexander Altman*, ed. Jehuda Reinharz and Daniel Swetschinski (Durham, N.C.: Duke University Press, 1982), p. 250.

37 A. Atanassian, *Témoignages sur l'origine des Arméniens* (Paris: Imp. Turabian, 1945).

38 Henry Rousso, *The Vichy Syndrome*, trans. Arthur Goldhammer (Cambridge, Mass.: Harvard University Press, 1991).

39 *Notre Voix*, February 1953.

40 Rousso, *The Vichy Syndrome*, p. 18.

41 *Statuts: Association des anciens combattants volontaires arméniens de l'armée française* (Paris, 1917), V.12.3.4, Bibliothèque Nubar. Three other organizations of former soldiers also took shape in France during or just following the war, including two associations of former combatants in the Caucases and one of former officers. *Kanonadrutʻiwn: Pʻarizi hay dazmikneri khmbakutʻian/Association des combattants arméniens à Paris—Statuts* (Paris: 1922), V.12.2.5, Bibliothèque Nubar. Report, "Inauguration d'une stèle sur le fronton de l'église arménienne," 9 July 1926, f/7/13436, AN.

42 Aram Terzian, "Growth of the Armenian Community in Paris during the Interwar Years, 1919–39," *Armenian Review* 27, no. 3-107 (1974): 269.

43 For examples of such armistice activities, see "Sur la tome du soldat inconnu," *Gaulois*, May 1921. Articles also appeared in *Victoire*, *Débats*, *Temps*, and *Matin* on the same day. Elsewhere in France, wherever local commemorations took place, Armenians also participated. Report, Contrôle général des services de police administra-

tive, "Anniversaire de l'armistice," 12 November 1924, f/7/12976, AN. For reports of other commemorative events, see "Traitement de Faveur," *Le Foyer*, 15 November 1928; "Les Volontaires arméniens morts pour la France," *Le Foyer*, 1 December 1928; and "Les Volontaires arméniens," *Le Foyer*, 15 November 1929. "Discussion au sein de l'Association des anciens combattants arméniens," 9 October 1946, f/1a/3364, AN.

44 The FNA was not the only organization to focus on Manouchian as a war hero. The Centre d'action et de défense des immigrés (CADI), a postwar immigrant defense organization (of which the FNA was a member), built a monument in the cemetery of Ivry to Manouchian and others who died during that execution (including Jews, Italians, Poles, etc.) as immigrant heroes of the French Resistance. "Cérémonie organisée par le 'Front national arménien' à la mémoire de 22 Arméniens fusillées par les Allemands en Février 1944," 7 July 1946, f/1a/3364, AN; CADI to Ministre de l'Intérieur, 22 February 1946, same carton, AN.

45 Foyer culturel de la jeunesse arménienne, 12 January 1945, Bibliothèque Nubar. "Fête d'ouverture du foyer culturel de la jeunesse arménienne," 3 December 1944, Bibliothèque Nubar. Other organizations also adopted the call for unity. The Union franco-arménien, for example, committed itself to keeping an atmosphere of solidarity throughout the population. *Dsragir–Kanongir: Fransayi hay azgayin ĕndh. miwtʻian.*

46 Direction générale de la sûreté nationale, "Désaffection marquée de la colonie arménienne a l'égard de l'Union national des arméniens en France, 24 July 1946, f/1a/3364, AN. "Associations fédérés dans l'organisme appelle, CADI, f/1a/3345, AN. "Le Meeting des Arméniens de Paris," *Resistance*, 3 December 1944, and "Commémoration du 26ème anniversaire du rattachement de l'Arménie à l'Union Soviétique," 23 November 1946, f/1a/3368, AN.

47 "Associations fédérés dans l'organisme appelle, CADI, f/1a/3345, AN. G. Braun, "Qu'attend votre immigration du Congrès," *Unir*, 25 January 1945.

48 The Armenian term *nerkaght* describes better than immigration or repatriation the migration that took place in the mid-1940s to Soviet Armenia, for, like *aliyah* in the case of Jews migrating to Israel, it has particularistic connotations that imply a "gathering in" of exiles rather than simple migration.

49 Archag Tchobanian, *Les Arméniens réfugiés en France* (Paris: 1945), pp. 15–16, cited in Khayadjian, *Archag Tchobanian et le mouvement arménophile en France*, p. 299.

50 Hovanessian, *Le Lien communautaire*, p. 110.

51 "Rapatriement," *Le Foyer*, 1 October 1931. "Fonds de rapatriement," *Le Foyer*, 1 December 1931. According to J. Simpson, *The Refugee Problem*, p. 38, 1,783 Armenian refugees went to Soviet Armenia in 1936, funded primarily by a French government grant, the League of Nations' Nansen Office, and various organizations in France. He notes that another 96 went from 1931–32.

52 Claire Mouradian, "L'Arménie soviétique depuis la mort de Staline" (Ph.D. diss., École des hautes études en sciences sociales, 1982), pp. 345–46. Anahide Ter Minassian, *La Questionne arménienne* (Roquevaire: Éditions Parenthèses, 1983), p. 20.

Anahide Ter Minassian, "La diaspora arménienne," in *Diasporas*, ed. Michel Bruneau (Montpellier: Reclus, 1995), p. 30.

53　Ronald Grigor Suny, "Return to Ararat: Armenians in the Cold War" and "Looking toward Ararat: The Diaspora and the 'Homeland,'" in *Looking Toward Ararat: Armenia in Modern History* (Bloomington: Indiana University Press, 1993), pp. 164–67, 225.

54　Comité de défense des droits de l'émigration arménienne, *Bulletin N°3*, July 1944.

55　Boudjikanian-Keuroghlian, "Un peuple en exil," p. 634; Suny, "Return to Ararat," p. 167.

56　Claire Mouradian and Marc Ferro, "L'Arménie soviétique (1920–1980)," in *Histoire des Arméniens*, ed. Gérard Dédéyan (Toulouse: Éditions Privat, 1982), p. 543. Le Tallec, *La Communauté arménienne*, p. 172.

57　Suny, "Return to Ararat," pp. 170–77.

58　"Réunion organisé par le Front national arménien," 2 July 1946; "Effervescence dans la colonie arménienne des Bouches-du-Rhône," 1 July 1946; "Démission de M. Korkidian du comité directeur du Front national arménien," 1 July 1946; and "Rupture entre le Front national arménien et le parti Dachnaksoutiun," 29 June 1946, f/1a/3364, AN. Whereas most Dashnak leaders supported the Allies, a right-wing faction chose to join the Nazis in their battle against the Soviet Union. In 1943 an agreement was made public between this faction and the German government that indicated that if Nazi forces won the war and occupied Soviet lands, they would establish their own protectorate over a self-governing Armenia. Although pro-Nazi sympathies did not dominate the Dashnaktsutiun, the Party came under attack both during and following the war. Suny, "Looking Toward Ararat," p. 224. According to Le Tallec, *La Communauté arménienne de France*, p. 116, though a handful of Dashnaks tried to curry favor with the German occupation forces in France, the majority sought to remain neutral.

59　*Fransahay mshakut'ayin miut'iwn: 30 Tari i tsarayut'iwn fransahay hamaynk'in* (Paris: Union culturelle française de France, 1980), pp. 87–88.

60　"La Propagande en faveur du retour massif en Arménie soviétique des Arméniens résidant en France," 21 October 1946, f/1a/3368, AN.

61　"Commentaires sur la presse arménienne et sur le développement de la propagande soviétique dans les milieux arméniens," 10 October 1946, f/1a/3368, AN. "Commentaires sur la presse arménienne," 11 September 1946, f/1a/3364, AN.

62　Direction générale de la sûreté nationale, "Le Propagande anti-française dans la colonie arménienne," 14 September 1946, f/1a/3364, AN. "A.S. de la propagande effectués par la presse arménienne au cours de la semaine du 5 au 13 octobre 1946, notamment par le quotidien 'joghovourt' en vue de décider les arméniens à rejoindre l'Arménie soviétique," 14 October 1946, f/1a/3368, AN.

63　Mouradian and Ferro, "L'Arménie soviétique," p. 543.

64　Direction générale de la sûreté nationale, "La Colonie arménienne de la Loire devant la question de retour dans la mère patrie," 9 September 1946, f/1a/3364, AN. Another report suggested that the most enthusiastic partisans of the repatriation were, in fact, those who had benefited financially from the occupation and who had joined the Front national arménien after liberation out of fear of reprisals. Not wanting to leave France themselves, they hoped to win the confidence of the directors of the FNA. Direction générale de la sûreté nationale, "Réactions provoqués par le rapatriement en URSS des réfugiés d'origine arménienne," 2 December 1946, f/1a/3368, AN.

65 "A.S. de la propagande effectués par la presse arménienne au cours de la semaine du 5 au 13 octobre 1946, notamment par le quotidien 'joghovourt' en vue de décider les arméniens à rejoindre l'Arménie soviétique," 14 October 1946, f/1a/3368, AN. "Commentaires de la presse arménienne," 21 October 1946, f/1a/3368, AN. "Commentaires de la presse arménienne," 6 November 1946, f/1a/3364, AN.

66 "Au sujet de menaces dont ferait l'objet de le directeur de l'Institut arménien de France," 10 September 1946, f/1a/3368, AN. "Reconnaissance officielle du Front national arménien," 23 November 1946, f/1a/3364, AN.

67 "Activité du nommé Marmarian, président du Front national arménien," 7 December 1946 and "Sur l'Office des réfugiés arméniens," 12 December 1946, f/1a/3364, AN. Direction générale de la sûreté nationale, "Crise au sein de l'Union générale arménienne," 12 October 1946, f/1a/3364, AN.

68 Direction générale de la sûreté nationale, "Arrivé en France de Mgr. Sumeian, Représentant du chef de l'église Gregorienne arménienne d'Erivan," 28 August 1946, f/1a/3368, AN. Direction générale de la sûreté nationale, "Séjour en France de Mgr. Sumeian, Nonce de l'église gregorienne arménienne," 19 November 1946, and "Élection de la chambre de la prélature de l'église gregorienne d'Arménie," 17 December 1946, f/1a/3368, AN.

69 Khédérian cited in Sernin, L'Homme de Tokat, pp. 109–10. Ter Minassian, "Les Arméniens de Paris depuis 1945," p. 209.

70 Dikran Iranyan, Je ne retournerai pas en U.R.S.S. (Paris: Éditions Sogedo, 1959), p. 13.

71 Parvanian, Au-delà de l'espérance, pp. 8–12, 18.

72 Ibid., pp. 22–23; Iranyan, Je ne retournerai pas, pp. 13–14.

73 Le Tallec, La Communauté arménienne de France, p. 196.

74 Fransahay mshakut'ayin miut'iwn, pp. 87–88; Basmadjian, Les Arméniens, pp. 144–48.

75 Basmadjian, Les Arméniens, pp. 144–48; Hovanessian, Le Lien communautaire, pp. 124–28.

76 Hovanessian, Le Lien communautaire, pp. 114, 124–28; Basmadjian, Les Arméniens, p. 144.

77 Ter Minassian, "La diaspora arménienne," p. 29.

Conclusion

1 Bernard Wasserstein, Vanishing Diaspora: Jews in Europe since 1945 (Cambridge, Mass.: Harvard University Press, 1996), p. 290.

Bibliography

Archival Material

Alliance Israélite Universelle, Paris

American Joint Distribution Committee (AJDC), New York

Anglo-British Association and Federation of Jewish Relief Organizations of Great Britain, Parkes Library, Hartley Library, Southampton, England

Archives de la Préfecture de la Police, Paris

Archives départementales des Bouches-du-Rhône, Marseille

Archives du Ministère de Finance, Paris

Archives Nationales (AN), Paris

Board of Deputies of British Jewish Deputies and Office of the Chief Rabbi, Greater London Records Office (GLRO), London

Consistoire de Paris, Paris

Documents on French Jewish Communities, Jewish Theological Seminary (JTS), New York

Papers of the Délégation nationale, Société France-Arménie, and the Légion d'Orient, Bibliothèque Nubar, Paris

Published Sources

Abitol, Michel. *Les Deux terres promises: Les Juifs de France et le Sionisme, 1897–1945.* Paris: O. Orban, 1989.

Activité des organisations juives en France sous l'occupation. Études et Monographies. Paris: Centre de documentation juive contemporaine, 1947.

Adler, Jacques. *The Jews of Paris and the Final Solution: Communal Response and Internal Conflicts, 1940–1944.* Oxford: Oxford University Press, 1985.

"Affirmation de l'Arménie chrétienne." In *Histoire des Arméniens*, edited by Gérard Dédéyan, 141–84. Toulouse: Éditions Privat, 1982.

Aghkʿadtakhnamě ĕnkerutʿiwn Pʿarizi hayotsʿ: Hogelianakan hishatanaranj: 1890–1930. Paris: Société de bienfaisance des Armeniens de Paris, 1932.

Albert, Phyllis Cohen. *The Modernization of French Jewry: Consistory and Community in the Nineteenth Century.* Hanover, N.H.: Brandeis University Press, 1977.

———. "Ethnicity and Jewish Solidarity in Nineteenth-century France." In *Mystics, Philosophers, and Politicians: Essays in Jewish Intellectual History in Honor of Alexander Altman*, edited by Jehuda Reinharz and Daniel Swetschinski, 249–74. Durham, N.C.: Duke University Press, 1982.

———. "L'Intégration et la persistence de l'ethnicité chez les juifs dans la France moderne." In *Histoire politique des Juifs en France*, edited by Pierre Birnbaum, pp. 221–43. Paris: Presses de la Fondation nationale des sciences politiques, 1990.

———. "The Right to Be Different: Interpretations of the French Revolution's Promises to the Jews." *Modern Judaism*, no. 12 (1992): 243–57.

Alderman, Geoffrey. *Modern British Jewry.* Oxford: Clarendon Press, 1992.

Alverez, Alex. *Governments, Citizens and Genocide: A Comparative and Interdisciplinary Approach.* Bloomington: Indiana University Press, 2001.

American Jewish Committee. *Aspects of French Jewry.* London: Vallentine Mitchell, 1969.

Amouroux, Henri. *La Grande histoire des Français après l'Occupation.* Vol. 9, *Les Règlements de comptes, septembre 1944–janvier 1945.* Paris: Robert Laffont, 1976–93.

Ancel, Robert. *Napoléon et les Juifs.* Paris: Presses Universitaires de France, 1928.

Andesian, S., and M. Hovanessian. "L'Arménien: Langue rescapée d'un génocide." In *Vingt-cinq communautés linguistiques de la France*, edited by Geneviève Vermès. Paris: L'Harmattan, 1988.

Andonian, Aram. "Gabriel Noradounghian: Extraits des memoires." *Revue d'histoire arménienne contemporaine* 1 (1995): 199–245.

L'Arménie et le peuple arménien. Paris: Imprimerie H. Turabian, 1941.

Aron, Robert. *Histoire de l'épuration.* Paris: Fayard, 1969.

Atanassian, A. *Témoignages sur l'origine des Arméniens.* Paris: Imp. Turabian, 1945.

Attard-Maraninchi, Marie-Françoise, and Emile Temime. *Histoire des migrations à Marseille*, Vol. 3: *Le Cosmopolitisme de l'entre-deux-guerres (1919–1945).* Marseille: Edisud, 1990.

Azimi, Vida. "L'étranger sous la révolution." In *La Révolution et l'ordre juridique privé: Rationalité ou scandale?* Paris: Presses Universitaires de France, 1988.

Badia, Gilbert, ed. *Les Bannis de Hitler: Acceuil et luttes des exilés allemands en France (1933–1945).* Paris: Études et documentation internationales, Vincennes: Presses Universitaires de Vincennes, 1984.

Badinter, Robert. *Libres et égaux . . . L'émancipation des Juifs sous la Révolution française (1789–1791).* Paris: Fayard, 1989.

Bakalian, Anny. *Armenian-Americans: From Being to Feeling Armenian.* New Brunswick, N.J.: Transaction Publishers, 1993.

Barcellini, Serge, and Annette Wieviorka. *Passant, souviens-toi! Les lieux du souvenir de la Seconde Guerre mondiale en France*. Paris: Plon, 1995.

Basch, Linda, Nina Glick Schiller, and Christina Blanc Szanton. "Transnationalism: A New Analytic Framework for Understanding Migration." In *Towards a Transnational Perspective on Migration: Race, Class, Ethnicity, and Nationalism Reconsidered*, edited by Linda Basch, Nina Glick Schiller, and Christina Blanc Szanton, 1–24. New York: New York Academy of Sciences, 1992.

Basmadjian, Varvara. *Les Arméniens: Réveil ou fin*. Paris: Édition Entente, 1979.

Bastide, Roger. "Les Arméniens de Valence." *Revue internationale de sociologie* 39, nos. 9–10 (1931): 17–42.

Bâtir de nouvelles communautés. Paris: Association consistoriale israélite de Paris, 1966.

Bauer, Yehuda. *My Brother's Keeper*. Philadelphia: Jewish Publication Society of America, 1974.

———. *American Jewry and the Holocaust: The American Jewish Joint Distribution Committee, 1928–1939*. Jerusalem: Institute of Contemporary Jewry, Hebrew University; Detroit: Wayne State University Press, 1981.

———. *Out of the Ashes: The Impact of American Jews on Post-Holocaust European Jewry*. Oxford: Pergamon Press, 1989.

———. "The Place of the Holocaust in Contemporary History." In *Holocaust: Religious and Philosophical Implications*, edited by John K. Roth and Michael Berenbaum, 16–42. New York: Paragon House, 1989.

———. *Rethinking the Holocaust*. New Haven: Yale University Press, 2001.

Benayoun, Chantal. *Les Juifs et la politique*. Paris: Centre national de recherche scientifique, 1984.

Benguigui, Georges, Josiane R. Bijaoui, and Georges Levitte. *Aspects of French Jewry*. London: Vallentine Mitchell, 1969.

Bensimon, Doris. *Les Juifs de France et leurs realtions avec Israel, 1945–1988*. Paris: Éditions L'Harmattan, 1989.

Bensimon, Doris, and Sergio Della Pergola. *La Population juive de France: Socio-démographie et identité*. Jerusalem: Institute of Contemporary Jewry, 1984.

Bensimon, Doris, and Benjamin Pinkus, eds. *Les Juifs de France, le Sionisme et l'état d'Israel*. Paris: Publications Langues'O, 1989.

Bensimon-Donath, Doris. *L'intégration des Juifs nord-africains en France*. Paris: Mouton, 1971.

———. *Socio-démographie des Juifs de France et d'Algérie: 1867–1907*. Paris: Publications Orientalistes de France, 1976.

Bérard, Victor. *Le Sultan et l'Europe*. Paris: Calmann-Lévy, 1896.

Berg, Roger. "La Communauté juive de Paris en 1957." *Bi-tefutsot ha-golah (Dispersion et Unité)* 1 (1960): 38–52.

———. "La pratique du Judaïsme en France." *Yod* 21 (1985): 81–87.

Berkovitz, Jay R. *The Shaping of Jewish Identity in Nineteenth-century France*. Detroit: Wayne State University Press, 1989.

——. "The French Revolution and the Jews: Assessing the Cultural Impact." *AJS Review* 20, no. 1 (1995): 25–86.

Bernard, Jean-Jacques. "Réflexions d'un français juif." *Revue juive de Genève* (October 1934): 23–27.

——. *Le Camp de la mort lente (Compiègne 1941–42).* Paris: Éditions Albin Michel, 1944.

——. *Mon Père: Tristan Bernard.* Paris: Éditions Albin Michel, 1955.

Bernard, Philippe, and Henri Dubief. *The Decline of the Third Republic, 1914–1938.* Translated by Anthony Forester. Cambridge, England: Cambridge University Press; Paris: Éditions de la Maison des sciences de l'homme, 1988.

Billig, Joseph. *Le Commissariat Général aux questions juives, 1941–44.* 3 vols. Paris: Éditions du Centre, 1954–60.

Birnbaum, Pierre. *Un Mythe politique: "La République juive." De Léon Blum à Pierre Mendès France.* Paris: Fayard, 1988.

——. *Les Fous de la République: Histoire politique des Juifs d'état, de Gambetta à Vichy.* Paris: Fayard, 1992.

——, ed. *Histoire politique des Juifs de France: Entre universalisme et particularisme.* Paris: Presses de la Fondation nationale des sciences politiques, 1990.

——. *Jewish Destinies: Citizenship, State, and Community in Modern France.* Translated by Arthur Goldhammer. New York: Hill and Wang, 1999.

Black, Eugene C. *The Social Politics of Anglo-Jewry, 1880–1920.* Oxford: Basil Blackwell, 1988.

Bolchover, Richard. *British Jewry and the Holocaust.* Cambridge, England: Cambridge University Press, 1993.

Bonnet, J.-Ch. *Les Pouvoirs publics français et l'immigration dans l'entre-deux-guerres.* Lyon: Centre Pierre-Léon d'Histoire économique et sociale, 1976.

Boudjikanian-Keuroghlian, Aïda. *Les Arméniens dans la région Rhône-Alpes: Essai géographique sur les rapports d'une minorité ethnique avec son milieu d'accueil.* Lyon: Association des Amis de la Revue de géographie de Lyon, 1978.

——. "Un peuple en exil: La Nouvelle diaspora (XIXe–XXe siecles)." In *Histoire des Arméniens,* edited by Gérard Dédéyan, 601–68. Toulouse: Éditions Privat, 1982.

Boulard, Fernand, Gérard Cholvy, and Hilaire Yves-Marie, eds. *Matériaux pour l'histoire religieuse du peuple français, XIXe–XXe.* 3 vols. Paris: Ed. du CNRS, EHCSS, FNSP, 1982–92.

Bourdrel, Phillippe. *L'Epuration sauvage, 1944–5.* 2 vols. Paris: Perrin, 1988–91.

Bourgade, Frédéric. *Les Arméniens de Valence: Histoire d'une integration réussie.* Valence: Éditions "Les Bonnes Feuilles," 1991.

Boyarin, Jonathan. *Polish Jews in Paris: The Ethnography of Memory.* Bloomington: Indiana University Press, 1991.

——. *Storm from Paradise: The Politics of Jewish Memory.* Minneapolis: University of Minnesota Press, 1992.

Brah, Avtar. *Cartographies of Diaspora: Contesting Identities.* New York: Routledge, 1996.

Brendin, André. *The Affair: The Case of Alfred Dreyfus.* New York: George Braziller, 1986.

Brenner, Michael. *The Renaissance of Jewish Culture in Weimar Germany.* New Haven: Yale University Press, 1996.

———. *After the Holocaust: Rebuilding Jewish Lives in Postwar Germany.* Translated by Barbara Harshav. Princeton: Princeton University Press, 1997.

Brubaker, Rogers. *Citizenship and Nationhood in France and Germany.* Cambridge, Mass.: Harvard University Press, 1992.

———. *Nationalism Reframed: Nationhood and the National Question in the New Europe.* Cambridge, England: Cambridge University Press, 1996.

———. "The Return of Assimilation? Changing Perspectives on Immigration and Its Sequels in France, Germany, and the United States." *Ethnic and Racial Studies* 24, no. 4 (2001): 531–48.

Bruneau, Michel. "Espaces et territoires de diasporas." In *Diasporas,* edited by Michel Bruneau, 5–23. Montpellier: Reclus, 1995.

Buton, Philippe, and Jean-Marie Guillon. *Les Pouvoirs en France à la Liberation.* Paris: Éditions Belin, 1994.

Caron, Vicki. *Between France and Germany: The Jews of Alsace-Lorraine 1871–1918.* Stanford: Stanford University Press, 1988.

———. "Loyalties in Conflict: French Jewry and the Refugee Crisis, 1933–1935." *Leo Baeck Institute Yearbook* 36 (1991): 305–38.

———. "The Missed Opportunity: French Refugee Policy in Wartime, 1939–40." *Historical Reflections/Réflexions historiques* 22, no. 1 (1996): 117–57.

———. "The Antisemitic Revival of the 1930's: The Socieconomic Dimension Reconsidered." *Journal of Modern History* 70 (1998): 22–73.

———. *Uneasy Asylum: France and the Jewish Refugee Crisis, 1933–1942.* Stanford: Stanford University Press, 1999.

Charmetant, Le P. *Martyrologe arménien.* Paris: Oeuvre d'Orient, 1896.

Cholvy, Gérard. *La Religion en France de la fin du XVIIIe à nos jours.* Paris: Hachette, 1991.

Cholvy, Gérard, et al., eds. *Histoire religieuse de la France contemporaine.* Vol. 3. Paris: Bibliothèque Historique Private, 1988.

Ch'ormisean, Levon. *Fransahayeru patmut'iwně* Vol. 1: *Hay sp'iwṛk'ě.* Beirut: Imprimerie G. Doniguian & fils, 1975.

Cohen, Asher. *Persécutions et sauvetages: Juifs et Français sous l'occupation et sous Vichy.* Paris: Éditions du Cerf, 1993.

Cohen, Erik H. *L'étude et l'éducation juive en France ou L'avenir d'une communauté.* Paris: Les Éditions du Cerf, 1991.

Cohen, Richard. *The Burden of Conscience: French Jewish Leadership during the Holocaust.* Bloomington: Indiana University Press, 1987.

Conan, Eric, and Henry Rousso. *Vichy and Ever-Present Past.* Translated by Nathan Bracher. Hannover, N.H.: University Press of New England, 1998.

Connor, Walker. "The Impact of Homelands upon Diasporas." In *Modern Diasporas in International Politics,* edited by Gabriel Sheffer, 16–46. New York: St. Martin's Press, 1986.

Cross, Gary S. *Immigrant Workers in Industrial France*. Philadelphia: Temple University Press, 1983.

Curiel, André Weil, and Raymond Castro. *Spoliation et restitution: Commentaire théorique et pratique de la législation relative aux spoliations*. Paris: Éditions R. G., 1945.

Dadrian, Vahakn N. "Genocide as a Problem of National and International Law: The World War I Armenian Case and Its Contemporary Ramifications." *Yale Journal of International Law* 14, no. 2 (1989): 221–334.

——. "Towards a Theory of Genocide Incorporating the Instance of Holocaust: Comments, Criticisms and Suggestions." *Holocaust and Genocide Studies* 5, no. 2 (1990): 129–43.

——. *The History of the Armenian Genocide: Ethnic Conflict from the Balkans to Anatolia to the Caucasus*. Providence, R.I.: Berghahn Books, 1995.

——. "The Tripartite Edifice of the Holocaust and the Imagery of Uniqueness." *International Network on Holocaust and Genocide* 1, no. 2 (1996): 13–21.

Davidson, A. A. "A Citizen of France." *Commentary* 15 (1953): 90–91.

De Rothschild, Guy. "Pour un judaïsme ouvert." In *Assemblée générale du Xe anniversaire du Fonds social juif unifié*. Paris: Fonds social juif unifié, 1960.

——. *The Whims of Fortune: The Memoirs of Guy de Rothschild*. New York: Random House, 1985.

Dédéyan, Gérard, ed. *Histoire des Arméniens*, Toulouse: Éditions Privat, 1982.

Der Sarkissian, Jean, and Lucie Der Sarkissian. *Les Pommes rouges d'Arménie*. Paris: Flammarion, 1987.

Downs, Laura Lee. *Manufacturing Inequality: Gender Division in the French and British Metalworking Industries, 1914–1939*. Ithaca, N.Y.: Cornell University Press, 1995.

Dramp'yan, T. S. *Fransahay komunistnerě gimagrut'yan tarinerin 1941–44*. Yerevan: "MITK'" Hratarakch'ut'yun, 1967.

Efron, John M. *Defenders of the Race: Jewish Doctors and Race Science in Fin-de-siècle Europe*. New Haven: Yale University Press, 1994.

Elazar, Daniel J. *Community and Polity: The Organizational Dynamics of American Jewry*. Revised and updated ed. Philadelphia: Jewish Publication Society, 1995.

Endelman, Todd. "Native Jews and Foreign Jews in London, 1870–1914." In *The Legacy of Jewish Migration: 1881 and Its Impact*, edited by David Berger, 109–21. New York: Columbia University Press, 1983.

——. "Continuities and Discontinuities in Constructions of Jewishness in Europe, 1789–1945." In *The Construction of Minorities: Cases for Comparison across Time and around the World*, edited by Raymond Grew and André Burgière. Ann Arbor: University of Michigan Press, 2000.

——, ed. *Comparing Jewish Societies*. Ann Arbor: University of Michigan Press, 1997.

Etmekjian, James. *The French Influence on the Western Armenian Renaissance, 1843–1915*. New York: Twayne Publishers, 1964.

European Jewry Ten Years after the War: An Account of the Development and Present Status of the Deci-

mated Jewish Communities of Europe. New York: Institute of Jewish Affairs of the World Jewish Congress, 1956.

Farmer, Sarah. "Out of the Picture: Foreign Labor in Wartime France." In France at War: Vichy and the Historians, edited by Sarah Fishman et al. Oxford: Berg, 2000.

Feuerwerker, David. L'Émancipation des Juifs en France, de l'Ancien Régime à la fin du Second Empire. Paris: A Michel, 1976.

Finkielkraut, Alain. The Imaginary Jew. Translated by Kevin O'Neill. Lincoln: University of Nebraska Press, 1994.

Forbes, Jill, and Michael Kelly. French Cultural Studies. New York: Oxford University Press, 1995.

Fransahay mshakutʿayin miutʿiwn: 30 Tari i tsaṛayutʿiwn fransahay hamaynkʿin. Paris: Union culturelle française de France, 1980.

Friedlander, Judith. Vilna on the Seine: Jewish Intellectuals in France since 1968. New Haven: Yale University Press, 1990.

Friedlander, Saul. When Memory Comes. Translated by Helen R. Lane. New York: Noonday Press, 1991.

———. Memory, History, and the Extermination of the Jews of Europe. Bloomington: Indiana University Press, 1993.

———, ed. Probing the Limits of Representation: Nazism and the "Final Solution." Cambridge, Mass.: Harvard University Press, 1992.

Gilman, Sander L. Jewish Self-Hatred: Anti-Semitism and the Hidden Language of the Jews. Baltimore: Johns Hopkins University Press, 1986.

Goldin, Liliana R., ed. Identities on the Move: Transnational Processes in North America and the Caribbean Basin. Albany, N.Y.: Institute for Mesoamerican Studies, 1999.

Goldsztejn, Isabelle. "Le Role de l'American Joint dans la reconstruction de la communauté." Archives juives: Revue d'histoire des Juifs de France 28, no. 1 (1995): 23–37.

Gottlieb, Amy Zahl. Men of Vision: Anglo-Jewry's Aid to Victims of the Nazi Regime, 1933–1945. London: Widenfeld & Nicolson, 1998.

Gourfinkel, Nina. Aux Prises avec mon temps: L'Autre patrie. Paris: Éditions du Seuil, 1953.

Graetz, Michael. Les Juifs en France au XIXieme siècle: De la Révolution française à l'Alliance israélite universelle. Translated by Salomon Malka. 2d ed. Paris: Éditions du Seuil, 1989.

Green, Nancy. The Pletzl of Paris: Jewish Immigrant Workers in the Belle Epoque. New York: Holmes and Meier, 1985.

———. "L'Histoire comparative et le champ des études migratoires." Annales ESC 6, no. 6 (1990): 1335–50.

———. "To Give and to Receive: Philanthropy and Collective Responsibility among Jews in Paris, 1880–1914." In The Uses of Charity: The Poor on Relief in the Nineteenth-Century Metropolis, edited by Peter Mandler, 199–226. Philadelphia: University of Pennsylvania Press, 1990.

———. "The Comparative Method and Poststructural Structuralism: New Perspectives for Migration Studies." Journal of American Ethnic History 13, no. 4 (1994): 3–20.

———. *Ready to Wear, Ready to Work*. Durham, N.C.: Duke University Press, 1997.

Le Guide des étrangers. Paris: A-DER, 1937.

Hagopian, Gayané. "The Immigration of Armenians to the United States." *Armenian Review* 41, no. 2–162 (1988): 17–25.

Harari, Aby. *Situation de l'apatride et du réfugié dans la législation française actuelle*. Paris: Librairie du Recueil Sirey, 1940.

Hargreaves, Alec G., and Mark McKinney. *Post Colonial Cultures in France*. New York: Routledge, 1997.

Harp, Stephen. *Learning to Be Loyal: Primary Schooling as Nation Building in Alsace and Lorraine, 1850–1940*. DeKalb: Northern Illinois University Press, 1998.

Harris, André, and Sédouy Alain. *Juifs et Français*. Paris: Éditions Grasset & Fasquelle, 1979.

Helmreich, William. *Against All Odds: Holocaust Survivors and the Successful Lives They Made in America*. New York: Simon and Schuster, 1992.

Hertz, Henri. *Tragédies des temps volages: Contes et poèmes, 1906–1954*. Paris: Seghers, 1955.

Hertzberg, Arthur. *The French Enlightenment and the Jews: The Origins of Modern Anti-Semitism*. New York: Columbia University Press, 1968.

Holborn, Louise. "The League of Nations and the Refugee Problem." *Annals of the American Academy of Political and Social Science* 203 (1939).

Hommage à l'Arménie: Compte-Rendu de la manifestation qui eut lieu le 9 avril 1919 dans la grand amphithéâtre de la Sorbonne. Paris: Éditions Ernest Leroux, 1919.

Hovanessian, Martine. "Soixante ans de présence arménienne en région parisienne (Le Cas d'Issy-les-Moulineaux)." *Revue européenne des migrations internationales* 4, no. 3 (1988): 73–90.

———. *Le Lien communautaire: Trois générations d'Arméniens*. Paris: Armand Colin, 1992.

———. *Les Arméniens et leurs territoires*. Paris: Les Éditions Autrement, 1995.

Hovannisian, Richard G. *Armenia on the Road to Independence*. Berkeley: University of California Press, 1967.

———. *The Republic of Armenia*. 4 vols. Berkeley, Los Angeles, London: University of California Press, 1971–1996.

———, ed. *The Armenian Genocide in Perspective*. New Brunswick, N.J.: Transaction Publishers, 1986.

———, ed. *History, Politics, Ethics*. New York: St. Martin's Press, 1992.

Hyman, Paula. *From Dreyfus to Vichy: The Remaking of French Jewry, 1906–1939*. New York: Columbia University Press, 1979.

———. *The Emancipation of the Jews of Alsace: Acculturation and Tradition in the Nineteenth Century*. New Haven: Yale University Press, 1991.

———. *The Jews of Modern France*. Berkeley: University of California Press, 1998.

Iranyan, Dikran. *Je ne retournerai pas en U.R.S.S.* Paris: Éditions Sogedo, 1959.

Ireland, Patrick R. *The Policy Challenge of Ethnic Diversity: Immigrant Politics in France and Switzerland*. Cambridge, Mass.: Harvard University Press, 1994.

Johnston, Robert H. *"New Mecca, New Babylon": Paris and the Russian Exiles, 1920–1945*. Montreal: McGill-Queen's University Press, 1988.

Josephs, Jeremy. *Swastika over Paris: The Fate of French Jews*. London: Bloomsbury, 1989.

Kapel, Samuel René. *Au Lendemain de la Shoa: Témoignage sur la naissance du Judaïsme de France et d'Afrique du Nord, 1945–1954*. Jerusalem: Diffusion, R. Mass, 1991.

Kaplan, Jacob. "La Renaissance du Judaïsme français." In *Reconstruction of European Jewish Life and the Conference of European Rabbis*, edited by Maurice Rose. London: Conference of European Rabbis, Standing Committee, 1967.

Karp, Abraham J. *To Give Life: The UJA in the Shaping of the American Jewish Community*. New York: Schocken, 1981.

—— "Overview: The Synagogue in America—A Historical Typology." In *The American Synagogue: A Sanctuary Transformed*, edited by Jack Wertheimer. Cambridge, England: Cambridge University Press, 1987.

Kaspi, André. "L'Affaire des enfants Finaly." *L'Histoire* 76 (1985): 40–53.

——. *Les Juifs pendant l'Occupation*. Paris: Seuil, 1991.

Kaspi, André, Anne Grynberg, Catherine Nicault, Ralph Schor, and Annette Wieviorka. *La Libération de la France: Juin 1944–Janvier 1946*. Paris: Perrin, 1995.

Kaspi, André, and Antoine Maris, eds. *Le Paris des étrangers: Depuis un siècle*. Paris: Imprimerie nationale, 1989.

Katz, Steven. *The Holocaust in Historical Context*. Vol. 1. New York: Oxford University Press, 1994.

Kaufman, David. *Shul with a Pool: The "Synagoguge Center" in American Jewish History*. Hanover, N.H.: University Press of New England, 1999.

Kelly, Michael, Elizabeth Fallaize, and Anna Ridehalgh. "Crisis of Modernization." In *French Cultural Studies*, edited by Jill Forbes and Michael Kelly, pp. 17–28. New York: Oxford University Press, 1995.

Khayadjian, Edmond. "La communauté arménienne de Marseille." *Marseille, Revue municipale trimestrielle* 118 (1979): 32–39.

——. *Archag Tchobanian et le mouvement armenophile en France*. Marseille: Centre national de documentation pédagogique, 1986.

Kherumian, R. *Les Arméniens, Race, Origines ethno-raciales*. Paris: Vigot, 1941.

Kieval, Hillel. *The Making of Czech Jewry: National Conflict and Jewish Society in Bohemia, 1870–1918*. New York: Oxford University Press, 1988.

Kivisto, Peter. "Theorizing Transnational Immigration: A Critical Review of Current Efforts." *Ethnic and Racial Studies* 24, no. 4 (2001): 549–77.

Klarsfeld, Serge. *Vichy-Auschwitz: Le Rôle de Vichy dans la solution finale de la question juive en France, 1943–1944*. Paris: Fayard, 1983.

Klarsfeld, Serge, André Delahaye, and Diane Afoumado. *La Spoliation dans les camps de Province*. Paris: Mission d'étude sur la spoliation des Juifs de France, 2000.

Korcaz, Sylive. *Les Juifs de France et l'état d'Israël*. Paris: Éditions Denoël, 1969.

Koreman, Megan. *The Expectation of Justice: France 1944–1946.* Durham, N.C.: Duke University Press, 1999.

Kossovitch, Nicholas. *Relations entre les groupes sanguines des Arméniens et les autres caractéristiques anthropométriques de cette race.* Institut international d'anthropologie, IIIe session, Amsterdam, 20–29 September 1927. Paris: Librairie E. Nourry, 1928.

Kouymjian, Dickran. "The Destruction of Armenian Historical Monuments as a Continuation of the Turkish Policy of Genocide." In *A Crime of Silence: The Armenian Genocide—The Permanent People's Tribunal,* edited by Gerard Libaridian, 173–83. Cambridge, Mass.: Zoryan Institute, 1985.

Kritzman, Lawrence D., ed. *Auschwitz and After: Race, Culture, and "the Jewish Question" in France.* New York: Routledge, 1995.

Kuisel, Richard F. *Seducing the French: The Dilemma of Americanization.* Berkeley: University of California Press, 1993.

Kushner, Tony. *The Holocaust and the Liberal Imagination: A Social and Cultural History.* Cambridge, Mass.: Blackwell, 1994.

Landau, Philippe. "Les Juifs de France et la Grande Guerre 1914–1941: Un Patriotisme républicain." Ph.D. diss., Université Paris 7, 1991.

Laskier, Michael M. *The Alliance Israélite Universelle and the Jewish Communities of Morocco, 1862–1962.* Albany: State University of New York Press, 1983.

Lasry, Jean-Claude, and Claude Tapia, eds. *Les Juifs du Maghreb: Diasporas contemporaines.* Paris: Éditions Harmattan, 1989.

Lazare, Lucien. *La Resistance juive en France.* Paris: Stock, 1987.

le Bras, Hervé, and Emmanuel Todd. *L'Invention de la France: Atlas anthropologique et politique.* Paris: Livre de Poche, 1981.

le Tallec, Cyril. *La Communauté arménienne de France, 1920–1950.* Paris: L'Harmattan, 2001.

Lebovics, Herman. *True France: The Wars over Cultural Identity, 1900–1945.* Ithaca, N.Y.: Cornell University Press, 1992.

Leonian, René, ed. *Les Arméniens de France sont-ils intégrés ou assimilés.* Issy-les-Moulineaux: Imprimerie IMEAF, 1986.

Lequin, Yves, ed. *Histoire des étrangers et de l'immigration en France.* Paris: Larousse, 1992.

Leveyre, Maurice. *La Vérité sur les massacre d'Arménie: Documents nouveux ou peu connus—Rapports de témoins oculaires, correspondances particulières, extraits de journaux.* Paris: P. V. Stock, Éditeur, 1986.

Lottman, Herbert R. *L'Épuration, 1943–1953.* Paris: Fayard, 1986.

Lowell, Pierre. "Les Foyards." *Évidences* 27 (1952).

MacColl, Malcolm. *L'Arménie devant l'Europe: Le Gourvernement turc est une théocratie.* Paris: Typographie A. Davy, 1897.

Maga, Timothy P. *America, France, and the European Refugee Problem, 1933–1947.* New York: Garland, 1985.

Malino, Frances. *The Sephardic Jews of Bordeaux: Assimilation and Emancipation in Revolutionary and Napoleonic France.* Tuscaloosa: University of Alabama Press, 1978.

Malino, Frances, and Bernard Wasserstein, eds. *The Jews in Modern France*. Hanover, N.H.: University Press of New England, 1985.

Malinovich, Nadia. " 'Orientalism' and the Construction of Jewish Identity in France, 1915–1932." Paper presented at the Association for Jewish Studies, Boston, 21–23 December 1997.

———. "Le Réveil d'Israel: Jewish Identity and Culture in France, 1900–1932." Ph.D. diss., University of Michigan, 2000.

Mandel, Arnold. "French Jewry in a Time of Decision." *Commentary* 18, no. 6 (1954): 533–42.

Mandel, Maud S. "In the Aftermath of Genocide: Armenians and Jews in Twentieth-Century France." Ph.D. diss., University of Michigan, 1998.

———. "Faith, Religious Practices, and Genocide: Armenians and Jews in France following World War I and II." In *In God's Name: Genocide and Religion in the Twentieth Century*, edited by Omer Bartov and Phyllis Mack. New York: Berghahn Books, 2001.

———. "Philanthropy or Cultural Imperialism? The Impact of American Jewish Aid in post-Holocaust France." *Jewish Social Studies* 9, no. 1 (2002): 53–94.

Manouchian, Mélinée. *Manouchian*. Paris: France Loisirs, 1974.

Marrus, Michael. *The Politics of Assimilation: A Study of the French Jewish Community at the Time of the Dreyfus Affair*. New York: Oxford University Press, 1982.

———. *The Unwanted: European Refugees in the Twentieth Century*. New York: Oxford University Press, 1985.

Marrus, Michael, and Robert Paxton. *Vichy France and the Jews*. New York: Basic Books, 1981.

Les Massacres d'Arménie: Témoignage des victimes. Paris: Mercure de France, 1986.

Mathorez, J. "Les Arméniens en France de 1789 à nos jours." *Revue des études arméniennes* 2, no. 2 (1922): 293–314.

Mauco, Georges. *Les Étrangers en France: Leur rôle dans l'activité économique*. Paris: Librairie Armand Colin, 1932.

Mazian, Florence. *Why Genocide: The Armenian and Jewish Experiences in Perspective*. Ames: Iowa State University Press, 1990.

Melson, Robert. *Revolution and Genocide: On the Origins of the Armenian Genocide and the Holocaust*. Chicago: University of Chicago Press, 1992.

———. "The Armenian Genocide as Precursor and Prototype of Twentieth Century Genocide." Paper presented at the The Armenian Genocide, An Eighty Year Perspective, 1915–1995, UCLA, 7–8 April 1995.

Mesnil-Amar, Jacqueline. *Ceux qui ne dormaient pas: 1944–46, Fragments de journal*. Paris: Éditions de Minuit, 1957.

Michel, Alain. *Les Éclaireurs israélites de France pendant la seconde guerre mondiale: Septembre 1944, action et évolution*. Paris: Édition de EIF, 1984.

Michel, Henri. *Bibliothèque critique de la résistance: Bibliography*. Paris: Institut pédagogique nationale, 1964.

Millman, Richard. *La Question juive entre les deux guerres: Ligues de droite et antisémitisme en France*. Paris: Armand Colin, 1992.

Milton, Sybil. *In Fitting Memory: The Art and Politics of Holocaust Memorials.* Detroit: Wayne State University Press, 1991.

Mirak, Robert. *Torn between Two Lands: Armenians in America, 1890 to World War I.* Cambridge, Mass.: Harvard University Press, 1983.

Mission d'étude sur la spoliation des Juifs de France. "Rapport d'étape." Paris, 1997.

———. "Dossier d'information sur les travaux en cours." Paris, 1998.

———. "Rapport générale." Paris, 2000.

Moore, Deborah Dash. *At Home in America: Second Generation New York Jews.* New York: Columbia University Press, 1981.

Mouradian, Claire. "L'Arménie soviétique depuis la mort de Staline." Ph.D. diss., École des hautes études en sciences sociales, 1982.

Mouradian, Claire and Marc Ferro. "L'Arménie soviétique (1920–1980)." In *Histoire des Arméniens,* edited by Gérard Dédéyan. Toulouse: Éditions Privat, 1982.

Mutafian, Claude. "La France en Cilicie: Histoire d'un échec, 1919–1939." *Les Temps modernes,* nos. 504–6 (1988): 90–108.

Nalbandian, Louise. *The Armenian Revolutionary Movement: The Development of Armenian Political Parties through the 19th Century.* Berkeley: University of California Press, 1967.

Nicault, Catherine. *La France et le Sionisme, 1897–1945: Une rencontre manquée.* Paris: Calmann Lévy, 1992.

Noiriel, Gérard. "Russians and Armenians in France." In *Cambridge Survey of World Migration,* edited by Robin Cohen, 145–47. Cambridge, England: Cambridge University Press, 1995.

———. *The French Melting Pot: Immigration, Citizenship, and National Identity.* Translated by Geoffroy de Laforcade. Minneapolis: University of Minnesota Press, 1996. Originally published as *Le Creuset français: Histoire de l'immigration XIXe–XXe siècle* (Paris: Le Seuil, 1988).

———. *Réfugiés et sans-papiers: La République face au droit d'asile.* Paris: Hachette Littératures, 1998.

Novick, Peter. *The Resistance versus Vichy.* New York: Chatto and Windus, 1968.

———. *The Holocaust in American Life.* Boston: Houghton Mifflin, 1999.

Ohanian, Marig. *Un Arménien parmi les autres.* Paris: Back, 1988.

Oshagan, Vahé. "The Impact of the Genocide on West Armenian Letters." In *The Armenian Genocide in Perspective,* edited by Richard Hovannisian. New Brunswick, N.J.: Transaction Books, 1986.

Pʻarizi hay tiknantsʻ miutʻiwně: Ir Keankʻn u gortsě-hngewtasnamean hobeleanin artʻiw, 1913–1929. Paris, 1929.

Parvanian, Jacques. *Au-delà de l'espérance.* Vol. 1, *La Foi.* Paris: La Pensée Universelle, 1979.

Pattie, Susan Paul. *Faith in History: Armenians Rebuilding Community.* Washington, D.C.: Smithsonian Institution Press, 1997.

Paxton, Robert O. *Vichy France: Old Guard and New Order, 1940–1944.* New York: Columbia University Press, 1972.

Penslar, Derek. *Shylock's Children: Economics and Jewish Identity in Modern Europe*. Berkeley: University of California Press, 2001.

Peroomian, Rubina. *Literary Responses to Catastrophe: A Comparison of the Armenian and Jewish Experience*. Atlanta, Ga.: Scholars Press, 1993.

Philippe, Béatrice. *Être juif dans la société française du moyen-âge à nos jours*. Paris: Éditions Montalba, 1979.

Phillips, Jenny. "Symbol, Myth, and Rhetoric: The Politics of Culture in an Armenian-American Population." Ph.D. diss., Boston University, 1978.

Piette, Christine. *Les Juifs de Paris (1808–1840): La Marche vers l'assimilation*. Quebec: Presses de l'Université Laval, 1983.

Pisani, P. *Les Affaires d'Arménie: Extrait du correspondant*. Paris: De Soye et Fils, 1985.

Plottel, Jeanine Parisier. "Jewish Identity in Raymond Aron, Emmanuel Berl, and Claude Lévi-Strauss." In *Auschwitz and After: Race, Culture, and "the Jewish Question" in France*, edited by Lawrence D. Kritzman, pp. 98–118. New York: Routledge, 1995.

Poirier, Véronique. *Ashkénazes et Séfarades: Une Étude comparée de leurs relations en France et en Israel (années 1959–1990)*. Paris: Cerf, 1998.

Poznanski, Renée. "L'Héritage de la guerre: Le Sionisme en France dans les années 1944–1947." In *Les Juifs de France, le Sionisme et l'État d'Israel*, edited by Doris Bensimon and Benjamin Pinkus. Paris: Publications Langues'O, 1989.

———. "Le Sionisme en France pendant la deuxième guerre mondiale: Développements institutionnels et impact idéologique." In *Les Juifs de France, le Sionisme et l'État d'Israel*, edited by Doris Bensimon and Benjamin Pinkus. Paris: Publications Langues'O, 1989.

———. *Être juif en France pendant la Seconde Guerre mondiale*. Paris: Hachette, 1994.

Prat-Flottes, Eugène. *Ce qu'il est utile de connaître a fin de pouvoir mener une lutte active contre la Tuberculose dans les milieux Arméniens*. Toulon: Imprimerie G. Rougeolle, 1929.

Le Problème des revendications matérielles juives à l'égarde l'Allemagne. Paris: Fédération des sociétés juives de France, 1952.

Quillard, Pierre, and Louis Margery. *La Question d'Orient et la politique personnelle de M. Hanotaux*. Paris: P. V. Stock, Éditeur, 1897.

Rabi, W. *L'Affaire Finaly: Des fonts, des affaires, des dates*. Marseille: Éditions du Cercle intellectuel pour le rayonnement de la pensée et de la culture juive, 1953.

———. *Anatomie du judaisme français*. Paris: Les Éditions de Minuit, 1962.

Rabinovitch, Jacques, and Raymond Sarraute. *Examen succinct de la situation actuelle juridique des Juifs*. Paris: Centre de documentation des déportés et spoliés juifs, 1945.

Raphael, Marc Lee. *A History of the United Jewish Appeal*. Chico, Calif.: Scholars Press, 1982.

Rayski, Adam. *Les Choix des Juifs sous Vichy: Entre soumission et résistance*. Paris: Éditions de la Decouverte, 1992.

Rebérioux, Madeleine. "Jean Jaurès and the Armenians." *Armenian Review* 44, no. 2–174 (1991): 1–11.

Rioux, Jean-Pierre. *The Fourth Republic, 1944–1958*. Translated by Godfrey Rogers. Cambridge, England: Cambridge University Press, 1987.

Robben, Antonius C. G. M., and Marcelo M. Suàrez-Orozco, eds. *Cultures under Siege: Collective Violence and Trauma.* Cambridge, England: Cambridge University Press, 2000.

Roblin, Michel. *Les Juifs de Paris: Démographie–Économie–Culture.* Paris: Éditions A. et J. Picard & Cie., 1952.

Rodrigue, Aron. *De l'Instruction à l'émancipation: Les Enseignants de l'Alliance Israélite Universelle et les Juifs d'Orient, 1860–1939.* Paris: Calmann-Lévy, 1989.

——. *French Jews, Turkish Jews: The Alliance Israélite Universelle and the Politics of Jewish Schooling in Turkey 1860–1925.* Bloomington: Indiana University Press, 1990.

——. "Rearticulations of French Jewish Identities after the Dreyfus Affair." *Jewish Social Studies* 2, no. 3 (1996): 1–24.

Rose, Maurice, ed. *Reconstruction of European Jewish Life and the Conference of European Rabbis.* London: Conference of European Rabbis, Standing Committee, 1967.

Rosenbaum, Alan S. *Is the Holocaust Unique?* Boulder, Colo.: Westview Press, 1996.

Rosenfeld, Alvin, ed. *Thinking about the Holocaust: After Half a Century.* Bloomington: Indiana University Press, 1997.

Rosenfeld, Gav. "The Politics of Uniqueness: Reflections on the Polemical Turn in Holocaust and Genocide Scholarship." *Holocaust and Genocide Studies* 13, no. 1 (1999): 28–61.

Ross, Kristen. *Fast Cars, Clean Bodies: Decolonization and the Reordering of French Culture.* Cambridge, Mass.: MIT Press, 1995.

Rouquet, François. *L'Épuration dans l'administration française: Agents de l'État et collaboration ordinaire.* Paris: Éditions du CNRS, 1993.

Rousso, Henry. *The Vichy Syndrome.* Translated by Arthur Goldhammer. Cambridge, Mass.: Harvard University Press, 1991. Originally published as *Le syndrome de Vichy: De 1944 à nos jours,* 2d ed. (Paris: Seuil, 1990).

——. "L'Épuration en France: Une histoire inachevée." *Vingtième siècle revue d'histoire* 33 (1992): 78–105.

Rozenblit, Marsha. *Reconstructing a National Identity: The Jews of Habsburg Austria during World War I.* New York: Oxford University Press, 2001.

Ryan, Donna. *The Holocaust and the Jews of Marseille: The Enforcement of Anti-Semitic Policies in Vichy France.* Urbana: University of Illinois Press, 1996.

Safran, William. "France and Her Jews: From 'Culte Israelite' to 'Lobby Juif.'" *Tocqueville Review* 5, no. 1 (1983): 101–35.

——. "Diasporas in Modern Societies: Myths of Homeland." *Diaspora* 1, no. 1 (1991): 83–99.

Sahlins, Peter. *Boundaries: The Making of France and Spain in the Pyrenees.* Berkeley: University of California Press, 1989.

Samuel, Julien. "Rapport moral: Regard sur 10 années d'activité du Fonds social juif unifié." In *Assemblée générale du Xe anniversaire du Fonds social juif unifié.* Paris: Fonds social juif unifié, 1960.

Sarafian, Ara. "The Absorption of Armenian Women and Children into Muslim Households as a Structural Component of the Armenian Genocide." In *In God's Name: Genocide and Religion in the Twentieth Century,* edited by Omer Bartov and Phyllis Mack, 209–21. New York: Berghahn Books, 2001.

Sartre, Jean-Paul. *Anti-Semite and Jew.* Translated by George J. Becker. New York: Schocken Books, 1948, 1976.

Sassoun et les atrocités hamidiennes: Interpellation des atrocités, rapport officiel. Genève: L'Union des étudiants arméniens de l'Europe, 1904.

Schangaldian, Nikola. "The Political Integration of an Immigrant Community into a Composite Society: The Armenians in Lebanon, 1920–1974." Ph.D. diss., Columbia University, 1979.

Schnapper, Dominique. *Jewish Identities in France: An Analysis of Contemporary French Jewry.* Translated by Arthur Goldhammer. Chicago: University of Chicago Press, 1983.

——. *L'Europe des immigrés.* Paris: Éditions François Bourin, 1992.

——. *La France de l'intégration: Sociologie de la nation en 1990.* Paris: Éditions Gallimard, 1994.

Schneider, William H. *Quality and Quantity: The Quest for Biological Regeneration in Twentieth-Century France.* Cambridge, England: Cambridge University Press, 1990.

Schor, Ralph. *L'Opinion française et les étrangers, 1919–1939.* Paris: Publications de la Sorbonne, 1985.

——. *L'Antisémitisme en France pendant les années trente: Prélude à Vichy.* Brussels: Ed. Complexes, 1992.

——. *Histoire de l'immigration en France de la fin du XIXe siècle à nos jours.* Paris: Armand Colin, 1996.

Schuker, Stephen A. "Origins of the 'Jewish Problem' in the Later Third Republic." In *The Jews in Modern France,* edited by Frances Malino and Bernard Wasserstein, pp. 135–80. Hanover, N.H.: University Press of New England, 1985.

Schwarzfuchs, Simon. "Un Aspect démographique de la communauté parisienne." *Journal des communautés* (22 January 1954).

——. *Napoleon, the Jews and the Sanhedrin.* London: Routledge and Kegan Paul, 1979.

Segev, Tom. *The Seventh Million: The Israelis and the Holocaust.* Translated by Haim Watzman. New York: Hill and Wang, 1993.

Sernin, André. *L'Homme de Tokat.* Paris: Éditions France-Empire, 1987.

Sewell, William. "Marc Bloch and the Logic of Comparative History." *History and Theory* 1 (1967): 208–18.

Shapiro, Edward S. *A Time for Healing: American Jewry since World War II.* Baltimore: Johns Hopkins University Press, 1992.

Sheffer, Gabriel. "Ethnic Diasporas: A Threat to Their Hosts?" In *International Migration and Security,* edited by Myron Weiner, 263–85. Boulder, Colo.: Westview Press, 1993.

Shennan, Andrew. *Rethinking France: Plans for Renewal, 1940–1946.* Oxford: Clarendon Press, 1989.

Sibelman, Simon. "Le Renouvellement juif: French Jewry on the Eve of the Centenary of the Affaire Dreyfus." *French Cultural Studies* 3 (1992): 263–76.

Silverman, Maxim. *Deconstructing the Nation: Immigration, Racism, and Citizenship in Modern France.* New York: Routledge, 1992.

Simpson, John Hope. *The Refugee Problem: Report of a Survey.* London: Oxford University Press, 1939.

Simpson, Christopher. *The Splendid Blond Beast: Money, Law, and Genocide in the Twentieth Century.* New York: Grove Press, 1993.

Smith, Anthony D. *Myths and Memories of the Nation.* Oxford: Oxford University Press, 1999.

Société de bienfaisance. *Comptes rendus de la 37ème année: Société de bienfaisance des Arméniens de Paris.* Paris: Société de bienfaisance, 1928.

Sommer, Robert. "La Doctrine politique et l'action religieuse du Grand-Rabbin Maurice Liber." *Revue des études juives* 125 (1966): 9–20.

Soucy, Robert. *French Fascism: The Second Wave, 1933–1939.* New Haven: Yale University Press, 1995.

Spira, Edgard. "Compte rendu financier." *Journal des communautés* (24 June 1960).

Spire, André. *Souvenirs à bâtons rompus.* Paris: Éditions Albin Michel, 1962.

Stern, Frank. *The White Washing of the Yellow Badge: Anti-semitism and Philosemitism in Post-War Germany.* Translated by William Templer. New York: Vidal Sasoon International Center for the Study of Antisemitism, Hebrew University of Jerusalem, 1992.

Sternhell, Zeev. "The Roots of Popular Antisemitism in the Third Republic." In *The Jews in Modern France,* edited by Frances Malino and Bernard Wasserstein, pp. 135–80. Hanover, N.H.: University Press of New England, 1985.

Strudel, Sylvie. *Votes juifs.* Paris: Presses de la Fondation nationale des sciences politiques, 1996.

Suny, Ronald Grigor. *Looking toward Ararat: Armenia in Modern History.* Bloomington: Indiana University Press, 1993.

———. "Empire and Nation: Armenians, Turks, and the End of the Ottoman Empire." *Armenian Forum* 1, no. 2 (1998): 17–51.

Sur le chemin de la libération, 1940–44: Réseau Liban. Paris: Imprimerie de Bresnik, 1952.

Szajkowski, Zosa. *Analytical Franco-Jewish Gazetteer: 1939–1945.* New York: American Academy for Jewish Research, Lucius N. Littauer Foundation, Gustav Wurzweiller Foundation, 1966.

———. *Jewish Education in France, 1789–1939.* Edited by Tobey B. Gitelle. Jewish Social Studies Monograph Series 2. New York: Conference on Jewish Social Studies, 1980.

Tapia, Claude. *Les Juifs sépharades en France (1965–1985): Études psychosociologiques et historiques.* Paris: Éditions L'Harmattan, 1986.

———. "Religion et politique: Interférence dans le judaïsme français après l'immigration judéo-maghrébine." In *Les Juifs du Maghreb: Diasporas contemporaines,* edited by Jean-Claude Lasry and Claude Tapia. Paris: Éditions Harmattan, 1989.

Tarzian, Mary Mangigian. *The Armenian Minority Problem, 1914–1934: A Nation's Struggle for Security.* Atlanta, Ga.: Scholars Press, 1992.

Tchakarian, Arsène. *Les Fusillés du Mont Valérine*. Paris: L'Écritoire pour le Comité National du Souvenir des Fusillés du Mont Valérine, 1991.

Tchobanian, Archag. *L'Arménie sous le joug Turc*. Paris: Plon-Nourrit, 1916.

Temime, Emile. "Les Arméniens de la deuxième génération à Marseille et dans les Bouches-du-Rhône." *Greco 13, Recherches sur les Migrations Internationales* 4, no. 5 (1982).

——, ed. *Histoire des migrations à Marseille*. 4 vols. Aix-en-Provence: La Calade, 1989.

Ter Minassian, Anahide. *La Questionne arménienne*. Roquevaire: Éditions Parenthèses, 1983.

——. *Nationalism and Socialism in the Armenian Revolutionary Movement, 1887–1912*. Translated by A. M. Berrett. Cambridge, Mass.: Zoryan Institute, 1984.

——. "Les Arméniens de France." *Les Temps modernes* 43, no. 504–506 (1988): 189–234.

——. "Les Arméniens et le Paris des libertés." In *Le Paris des étrangers depuis un siècle*, edited by André Kaspi and Antoine Marès. Paris: Imprimerie nationale, 1989.

——. "Arméniens de France, Arméniens d'Union Soviétique: Exil et enracinement." *Les Nouveaux Cahiers* 108 (1992): 33–40.

——. "Les Arméniens de Paris depuis 1945." In *Le Paris des étrangers depuis 1945*, edited by Antoine Marès and Pierre Milza, 205–39. Paris: Publications de la Sorbonne, 1994.

——. "La Diaspora arménienne." In *Diasporas*, edited by Michel Bruneau, pp. 24–41. Montpellier: Reclus, 1995.

Ternon, Yves. "Le Génocide de Turquie et la guerre (1914–1923)." In *Histoire des Arméniens*, edited by Gérard Dédéyan, 483–523. Toulouse: Éditions Privat, 1982.

——. *La Cause arménienne*. Paris: Éditions du Seuil, 1983.

Terzian, Aram. "Growth of the Armenian Community in Paris during the Interwar Years 1919–1939." *Armenian Review* 27, no. 3–107 (1974): 260–77.

Tölölyan, Khachig. "The Role of the Armenian Apostolic Church in the Diaspora." *Armenian Review* 41, no. 1–161 (1988): 55–68.

——. "The Nation-State and Its Others: In Lieu of a Preface." *Diaspora* 1, no. 1 (1991).

——. "Rethinking Diaspora(s): Stateless Power in the Transnational Moment." *Diaspora* 5, no. 1 (1996): 3–36.

Trigano, Shmuel. "The French Revolution and the Jews." *Modern Judaism* 10, no. 2 (1990): 171–90.

Turabian, Aram. *L'Éternelle victime de la diplomatie européenne*. Paris: Sous le patronage des anciens volontaires arméniens des armées alliés, 1929.

——. *Trente ans en France: Ma vie*. Marseille: Imp. Nouvelle, 1928.

——. *La France, Les Arméniens, et les Juifs*. Paris, 1938.

Varzhapetean, Hovh. *Ughetsʿoytsʿ Marsēyli: Patkeradzard ev kʿartisawor B. Tpagrutʿiwn/Guide de Marseille en langue arménienne*. Marseille: Tpagrutʿiwn "ALIS," 1930.

——. *Guide de Marseille/Ughetsʿoytsʿ Marsēyli*. Marseille: Imprimerie Daron, 1939.

Vegh, Claudine. *I Didn't Say Goodbye*. Translated by Ros Schwartz. New York: Dutton, 1984.

La Vérité sur les massacres d'Arménie: Documents nouveaux ou peu connus—Rapports de témoins oculaires, correspondances particulières, extraits de journaux. Paris: P. V. Stock, Éditeur, 1896.

Verneuil, Henri. *Mayrig*. Paris: Robert Laffont, 1985.

Vidal-Naquet, Pierre. "The Holocaust's Challenge to History." In *Auschwitz and After: Race, Culture, and "the Jewish Question" in France*, edited by Lawrence D. Kritzman, pp. 25–34. New York: Routledge, 1995.

Vormeier, Barbara. "La Situation administrative des exilés allemandes en France (1933–1945): Accueil-répression-internement-déportation." *Revue d'Allemagne* 18, no. 2 (1986): 185–94.

Walker, Christopher J. *Armenia: The Survival of a Nation*. 2d ed. New York: St. Martin's Press, 1980.

Wasserstein, Bernard. *Britain and the Jews of Europe, 1939–1945*. New York: Clarendon Press, 1979.

———. *Vanishing Diaspora: The Jews in Europe since 1945*. Cambridge, Mass.: Harvard University Press, 1996.

Weber, Eugene. *Peasants into Frenchmen: The Modernization of Rural France, 1870–1914*. Stanford: Stanford University Press, 1976.

———. *The Hollow Years: France in the 1930s*. New York: Norton, 1994.

Weil, Patrick. *La France et ses étrangers: L'Aventure d'une politique de l'immigration de 1938 à nos jours*. Paris: Gallimard, 1994.

Weinberg, David. *A Community on Trial: The Jews of Paris in the 1930s*. Chicago: University of Chicago Press, 1974.

———. "The Reconstruction of the French Jewish Community after World War II." In *She'erit hapletah, 1944–1948: Rehabilitation and Political Struggle: Proceedings of the Sixth Yad Vashem International Historical Conference, Jerusalem 1985*. Jerusalem: Yad Vashem, 1990.

———. "France." In *The World Reacts to the Holocaust*, edited by David S. Wyman. Baltimore: Johns Hopkins University Press, 1996.

Weinberg, Henry. *The Myth of the Jew in France, 1967–1982*. Oakville, N.Y.: Mosaic Press, 1987.

Weisberg, Richard H. *Vichy Law and the Holocaust in France*. New York: New York University Press, 1996.

Wenden, Catherine Wihtol de. *Les Immigrés et la politique: Cent cinquante ans d'évolution*. Paris: Presses de la fondation nationale des science politiques avec le concours du Centre nationale de la recherche scientifique, 1988.

Wenger, Beth S. *New York Jews and the Great Depression: Uncertain Promise*. New Haven: Yale University Press, 1996.

Wertheimer, Jack. *Unwelcome Strangers: East European Jews in Imperial Germany*. New York: Oxford University Press, 1987.

———, ed. *The American Synagogue: A Sanctuary Transformed*. Cambridge, England: Cambridge University Press, 1987.

Wiedmer, Caroline. *The Claims of Memory: Representations of the Holocaust in Contemporary Germany and France*. Ithaca, N.Y.: Cornell University Press, 1999.

Wiesel, Elie. *Memoirs: All Rivers Run to the Sea*. New York: Schocken Books, 1995.

Wieviorka, Annette. *Déportation et génocide: Entre la mémoire et l'oubli*. Paris: Plon, 1992.

———. "Les Juifs en France au lendemain de la guerre: État des lieux." *Archives Juives: Revue d'histoire des Juifs de France* 28, no. 1 (1995): 4–22.

———. *Les Biens des internés des camps de Drancy, Pithiviers et Beaune-La-Rolande.* Paris: Mission d'étude sur la spoliation des Juifs de France, 2000.

———. "Despoliation, Reparation, Compensation: The Case of the Jews in France." In *Starting the Twenty-First Century: Sociological Reflections and Challenges,* edited by Ernest Krausz and Gitta Tulea, 201–19. New Brunswick, N.J.: Transaction Publishers, 2002.

Wilson, Stephen. *Antisemitism in France at the Time of the Dreyfus Affair.* Rutherford, N.J.: Farleigh Dickinson Press, 1982.

Wolitz, Seth L. "Imagining the Jew in France from 1945 to the Present." *Yale French Studies* 85: *Discourses of Jewish Identity in Twentieth-Century France* (1994): 119–34.

Woocher, Jonathan. *Sacred Survival: The Civil Religion of American Jews.* Bloomington: Indiana University Press, 1986.

Wormser, Georges. "Le Leçon des évènements." Introduction to *La Communauté de Paris après la libération.* Paris: Consistoire israélite de Paris, 1946.

———. *Français Israélites: Une Doctrine, une tradition, une époque.* Paris: Les Éditions de Minuit, 1963.

Wright, Gordon. *France in Modern Times: From Enlightenment to the Present.* 4th ed. New York: Norton, 1987.

Yablonka, Hanna. *Survivors of the Holocaust: Israel after the War.* Translated by Ora Cummings. New York: New York University Press, 1999.

Yerushalmi, Yosef Haim. *Zakhor: Jewish History and Jewish Memory.* Seattle: University of Washington Press, 1982.

Young, James E. *The Texture of Memory.* New Haven: Yale University Press, 1993.

———. *At Memory's Edge.* New Haven: Yale University Press, 2000.

Zeitoun, Sabine. *L'Œuvre de secours aux enfants (OSE) sous l'occupation en France.* Paris: L'Harmattan, 1990.

Zeldin, Theodore. *France 1848–1945.* 2 vols. Oxford: Clarendon Press, 1973–77.

Zertal, Idith. *From Catastrophe to Power: Holocaust Survivors and the Emergence of Israel.* Berkeley: University of California Press, 1998.

Zuccotti, Susan. *The Holocaust, the French, and the Jews.* New York: Basic Books, 1993.

Index

Consistoire de Paris: on assimilation, 109–10; Conseil représentatif israélite de France (CRIF), 136–37, 167, 267 n.65; Fonds social juif unifié (FSJU) and, 171–72, 281 nn.75, 76; on Jewish loyalty to France, 142–43, 257 n.96; post–World War II membership, 163–64; refugee support of, 278 n.57; State of Israel, support for, 139–44

Cross, Gary S., 211 n.10, 219 n.5, 286 n.29

Curiel, André Weil, 237 n.51

Dadrian, Vahakn, 211 nn.9, 12, 218 n.50

De Gaulle, Charles, 53, 56, 57, 187, 234 n.12

Delahaye, André, 240 n.66

Della Pergola, Sergio, 211 n.10, 213 n.29

Delmas, C., 222 n.29

Der Sarkissian, Jean, 88

Destel, Roland, 230 n.94

Diaspora, 15–16, 119, 201, 217 n.47, 218 n.51

Downs, Laura Lee, 6, 212 n.17

Dreyfus Affair, 50, 104–5, 254 n.75, 266 n.60, 276 n.48

Efron, John, 231 n.104, 238 n.13

Elazar, Daniel J., 279 n.62

Endelman, Todd, 6, 212 n.15, 254 n.65

Fallaize, Elizabeth, 234 n.13

Feuerwerker, David, 215 n.37

Fisher, Joseph, 144

Fonds social juif unifié (FSJU), 165, 167–72, 175, 281 nn.75, 76

France: expulsion policies in, 38–40, 42–43, 227 n.73, 228 nn.74, 75, 76, 77, 79, 229 nn.81, 82; integrationist policies of, 11–14, 29, 36–38, 51, 216 n.42, 217 nn.43, 46; League of Nations' Convention (October 28, 1933), 43; naturalization policies in, 29, 186–87, 286 nn.29, 30; secularism in, 163, 276 n.44. See also Armenians; Jews; Political activism, Armenian; Relief services; Restitution; Vichy government

France, Pierre Mendes, 233 n.7

Francs-Tireurs et Partisans français, 184

Friedlander, Judith, 213 n.29

Gamzon, Robert, 94, 111

Germany: Armenian resistance to, 182–84, 188–89, 285 nn.18, 24, 25; forced labor, 181, 284 n.6; restitution of, 172–73, 282 n.80; Soviet Union, 182

Gilman, Sander, 50, 232 n.110

Goldhammer, Arthur, 213 n.29

Goldin, Liliana R., 218 n.48

Goldsztejn, Isabelle, 278 n.59

Gottlieb, Amy Zahl, 278 n.59

Gourfinkel, Nina, 58

Graetz, Michael, 215 n.39

Great Britain, 144–46, 269 nn.91, 92, 93, 278 n.59

Green, Nancy, 6–7, 212 n.16, 254 n.65, 280 n.68

Guerdan, L. G., 222 n.29

Hargreaves, Alec G., 216 n.40

Harp, Stephen L., 217 n.43

Harris, André, 213 n.29

Harshav, Barbara, 209 n.2

Hatchikian, Takvor, 153–54, 271 n.5

Helmreich, William, 209 n.2

Hertz, Henri, 11, 109, 110, 256 n.92, 257 n.93

Hertzberg, Arthur, 215 n.37

Holocaust: demographic consequences of, 202–3; deportations, 91–92, 250 n.22; displaced persons after, 94–96, 251 nn.30, 32, 33; impact on French Jewish life, 10, 214 n.30; Jewish identity and, 10, 107–10, 202–3, 212 n.19, 213 n.29, 214 n.30, 256 n.88; silence about, 7–8, 53, 108–9, 112, 212 n.19, 213 n.23, 236 n.53. See also Germany; Jews; State of Israel; Vichy government

Homeland. See Soviet Armenia; State of Israel

Hovanessian, Martine, 152, 192, 211 n.11, 284 n.3

Hovannisian, Richard G., 220 n.14, 261 n.10

Hyman, Paula, 104, 210 n.6, 215 n.39

Maud S. Mandel is Dorot Assistant Professor of Judaic
Studies and Assistant Professor of History at Brown
University.

Library of Congress Cataloging-in-Publication Data
Mandel, Maud S.
In the aftermath of genocide : Armenians and Jews in
twentieth-century France / by Maud S. Mandel.
Includes bibliographical references and index.
ISBN 0-8223-3134-9 (cloth : alk. paper) —
ISBN 0-8223-3121-7 (pbk. : alk. paper)
1. Holocaust survivors—France—Social conditions—
20th century.   2. Armenian massacres survivors—
France—Social conditions—20th century.   3. Jews—
Cultural assimilation—France.   4. Armenians—Cultural
assimilation—France.   5. Social integration—France.
6. France—Ethnic relations.   7. Holocaust, Jewish
(1939–1945)—Influence.   8. Armenian massacres,
1915–1923—Influence.   I. Title.
DS135.F83M364 2003   305.891'992044'0904—DC21   2003000437